THE
Management
BOOK

THE

Management

BOOK

EVERYTHING YOU NEED TO KNOW TO BE AN EFFECTIVE MANAGER

Moi Ali, Stephen Brookson, Andy Bruce,
Robert Heller, Tim Hindle, Ken Langdon

LONDON, NEW YORK,
MUNICH, MELBOURNE, DELHI

Editor Sarah Goulding
Senior Editorial Co-ordinator Camilla Hallinan
Senior Designer Adrienne Hutchinson
Senior Design Co-ordinator Sophia M Tampakopoulos Turner
Category Publisher Sue Grabham
Production Controller Julian Deeming
With thanks to the original teams:
Claire Ellerton, David Tombesi-Walton, Tracy Miles,
Ellen Woodward, Adèle Hayward, and Nigel Duffield

Cover design by WHSmith

Published in Great Britain in 2002
for WHSmith by Dorling Kindersley Limited,
80 Strand, London WC2R 0RL
A Penguin Company

ABOUT THIS BOOK

The Management Book is a comprehensive guide to the most important areas of business life, covering interpersonal and professional skills vital to those who hold, or seek to hold, management positions in any organization, large or small.

THIS BOOK WILL HELP YOU TO BUILD AS wide a range of key management skills as possible, whether you are a first-time or a more experienced manager. Instantly accessible, reliably authoritative and indispensably comprehensive, *The Management Book* shows you how to analyse and improve your professional performance, so that you achieve all-round excellence at every level, in every action.

The Management Book is organized in seven clearly defined sections, each covering a major aspect of your role. To enable you to access specific information as quickly as possible, each section is divided into concise, well signposted subsections.

Every page highlights vital information in a range of at-a-glance panels: Points to Remember and Do's and Don'ts that summarize key advice; Questions to Ask yourself and others; Case Studies on

real-life management problems; and Cultural Differences in business practices around the world.

Throughout each section, 101 quick tips cover every situation you are likely to face, and serve as handy memory aids. A Self-Assessment exercise at the end of each section helps you to analyse your performance in that particular area.

Fully illustrated with annotated photographs, charts and flow diagrams, *The Management Book* is written in jargon-free English by leading professionals in management and training. It is packed with commonsense advice to help you solve even the most challenging management predicaments.

Above all, *The Management Book* allows good managers to become outstanding ones, making it an invaluable source of day-to-day reference in any office or organization.

CONTENTS

MANAGING PEOPLE

INTRODUCTION

Today's fast-moving business environment demands that the effective manager be both a well-organized administrator and highly adept in understanding people's basic needs and behaviour in the workplace. Gaining commitment, nurturing talent, and ensuring that people are motivated and productive requires open communication and trust between managers and staff. Managing People will help you to master the fundamentals of successful management techniques that will enable you to get the best out of the people who work for you. It also demonstrates how, by identifying and avoiding common problems, managers can turn potential failure into success for their organization. A wealth of practical advice is supplemented by 101 useful tips and a comprehensive self-assessment exercise.

DEVELOPING BASIC PEOPLE SKILLS

Knowing why people behave as they do is the key to gaining their commitment. Aim to understand people's needs in order to motivate them and thus meet the demands of the organization.

UNDERSTANDING BEHAVIOUR

Natural, instinctive behaviour is not always appropriate in the workplace. Make an effort to produce behavioural patterns that lead to productive and effective teamwork in your employees.

BEHAVING NATURALLY

People at work naturally tend to adopt instinctive modes of behaviour that are self-protective rather than open and collaborative. This explains why emotion is a strong force in the workplace and why management often reacts fiercely to criticism and usually seeks to control rather than take risks. People also tend to leap to conclusions and fragment into small, often warring, groups. Companies exhibiting "natural" behaviour like this are highly political and emphasize status and hierarchy. They are less pleasant to work for and generally at odds with the needs of people and the marketplace.

▲ **ENCOURAGING CONSTRUCTIVENESS**
You can encourage constructive attitudes in people most effectively by example and reward, and by always approving of their good conduct and positive contributions.

BEHAVING APPROPRIATELY

Natural behaviour is based on subjective responses that can often lead not only to negative feelings (such as insecurity), but also to mistaken perceptions concerning the intentions of other staff members. More constructive behavioural attributes will encourage co-operation, openness, and self-confidence. Some readily recognizable traits of people with appropriate behavioural skills include a proven facility to communicate positively and confidently with colleagues at all levels; the swift and generous recognition of the achievements of others; the ability to learn from mistakes and failures; and a general approach that is based on collaboration with fellow workers rather than competition.

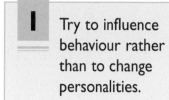

1 Try to influence behaviour rather than to change personalities.

2 Encourage and reward constructive behaviour.

REPLACING NEGATIVE CHARACTERISTICS

NATURAL BEHAVIOUR

- Reacting emotionally when information is received.
- Avoiding risks through fear or insecurity.
- Fighting fiercely and defensively when under threat.
- Making snap judgments about people and events.
- Spreading gossip throughout the organization.
- Competing for status and its symbols.
- Dwelling on past successes.
- Feeling more comfortable in small factions.
- Always seeking hierarchical superiority.

APPROPRIATE BEHAVIOUR

- Establishing the facts using a pragmatic approach.
- Taking risks in an entrepreneurial fashion.
- Forming collegiate, collaborative, non-combative relationships.
- Insisting on detailed analysis before judgment.
- Practising totally open communication.
- Recognizing achievement, not status.
- Learning from mistakes.
- Choosing to work in co-operative groups.
- Operating within flat, non-hierarchical structures.

UNDERSTANDING PEOPLE'S NEEDS

People's needs go far beyond basics, such as good working conditions and fair pay. But you cannot meet people's higher needs, such as pride in work and sharing in the corporate goals, without addressing the basics.

> **3** Take care that people's lower-level needs are met.

▼ PRIORITIZING NEEDS

The psychologist Abraham Maslow has identified a five-stage "hierarchy of needs", starting with basic needs for food and shelter, and culminating in higher-level "self-actualization", or self-fulfilment, needs.

MEETING NEEDS

People have various kinds of needs. Examples of lower-level needs are salary, job security, and working conditions. You have to meet these basic needs, but doing so will not by itself give satisfaction. Failures with the basic needs nearly always explain dissatisfaction among staff. Satisfaction, on the other hand, springs from meeting higher-level needs, such as responsibility, progress, and personal growth.

3) Social needs are fulfilled by friendly interaction with other people

2) Secondary needs are for personal security

1) Basic needs are for food, shelter, and warmth

4) Higher-level esteem needs are met by recognition of achievements

5) Self-actualization needs are realized by achieving total individual potential

ENCOURAGING PRIDE

People need to feel that their contribution is valued and unique. Pride in work has two forms: individual and collective. If you work on an assembly line, for example, you are pleased with your own performance at, say, installing a car door. But you are also proud of the whole car to which you have contributed. As a manager, seek to exploit this pride in others, and be proud of your own ability to handle staff with positive results. Both management and staff should feel proud to belong to an admired company.

4 Say thank you to people whenever it is merited.

5 Add public praise to private words to raise pride.

IDENTIFYING SOURCES OF SATISFACTION

LOWER-LEVEL NEEDS	HIGHER-LEVEL NEEDS
CONDITIONS Reasonable hours, a pleasant environment, and adequate equipment: "I approve of the physical working conditions".	**JOB INTEREST** Satisfaction derived from the actual job content and its execution: "I like the kind of work that I do".
SUPERVISION Empowerment and encouragement given by immediate managers: "I like the way I am treated by those who supervise me".	**ACHIEVEMENT** Motivation to hit targets and to perform tasks at high levels of effectiveness: "My work gives me a sense of accomplishment".
SECURITY Confidence in the organization's outlook and a feeling of belonging: "I feel good about the future of the organization".	**COMMITMENT** Pleasure through belonging to the organization and identifying with it: "I am proud to say I work for the organization".
MANAGEMENT An understanding of management methods: "I think the organization is making the changes necessary to be competitive".	**RESPONSIBILITY** Work requirements that stretch the individual, but are fair and rewarding: "I welcome the amount of work I am expected to do".
COMMUNICATION Full awareness of the organization's plans and involvement in the planning: "I understand and identify with the organization's strategy".	**IDENTIFICATION** People understand how they fit into the overall plan: "I see how my work connects with the organization's strategies".

LEARNING THE BASICS

To understand people's attitudes, you need to be open to all the ways in which they communicate. Learn to listen to what they say – and do not say – and look out for other signals, such as body language.

> **6** Ask open questions that encourage total honesty.

LISTENING CAREFULLY

In many areas of a manager's job, from meetings and appraisals to telephone calls, listening plays a key role. Listening benefits both you and your staff: you gain a greater insight into people and potentially receive useful ideas about how your organization can be improved, while staff feel their views are being heard and will therefore respond more openly. Consider how you listen: do you interrupt frequently or cut people short to make your point? If so, practise remaining quiet and concentrating on the speaker; if necessary ask brief questions to ensure you have understood what they are saying. If you are easily distracted, practise focusing on the speaker's words, repeating key phrases silently to fix them in your mind. As well as actually hearing what a person says, you need to look and behave as if you are listening, for example, by appearing relaxed and open and nodding frequently.

> **7** Give people ample opportunity to express their true feelings.

Employee expresses true feelings

DISCUSSING ▶ OPENLY
Make an effort to understand people's attitudes by careful listening and questioning and by giving them the opportunity to express themselves.

INTERPRETING CORRECTLY

Listen to what a person says, and then mentally review their words to check you have understood their meaning. If you have not, ask them to clarify what they have said. You can also rephrase what they have said and repeat it back to them, giving them a chance to agree with or correct your statement. Look at the whole meaning of what a person is saying rather than selecting the parts you want to hear. Always take what you are told on trust, unless you have good reason not to. If the person is contradicting themselves or being evasive, they may not be telling the whole story, so continue questioning until you are satisfied.

8 Keep asking questions until you understand what someone means.

9 Practise reading people's body language.

READING BODY LANGUAGE

Body language is the term for the unconscious physical movements we all make that communicate thoughts and feelings. Interpreting body language correctly is a complex art, but you can easily learn to read broad messages. An open, relaxed posture and good eye contact are indications that a person is comfortable with themselves and what they are saying or hearing. A tense posture, perhaps with arms crossed and little eye contact, may indicate evasiveness, suppressed anger, or disagreement. Leaning forwards when seated may indicate interest or agreement, while leaning back indicates lack of interest or resistance. Be aware of these signals in yourself as well as in others.

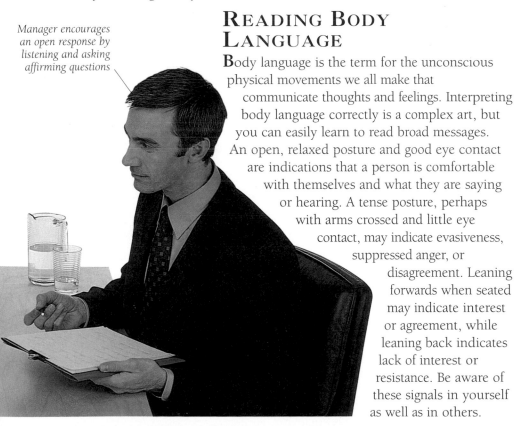

Manager encourages an open response by listening and asking affirming questions

BUILDING CONFIDENCE

Most people suffer from insecurity at some time. The many kinds of anxiety that affect people in organizations can feed such insecurity. Your antidote is to build confidence by giving recognition, high-level tasks, and full information.

10 Go to the rescue at once if people show that a task is beyond them.

REDUCING INSECURITY

Some people conceal their insecurity better than others, but do not be deceived. Everybody needs to be told that they are performing well and that they are respected, both for what they are and for what they have done and are doing. Praise is a very effective (and very economical) way of improving confidence, but be sure that it is deserved. Then suit the method of praise to the circumstances.

▼ **WELCOMING INPUT**
Bolster the confidence of all individuals, especially more reticent types, by allowing everyone at a meeting to speak in turn.

Committee leader invites input from all

Unconfident member is encouraged to speak

11 Avoid giving false reassurances – be frank if the news is not good.

ENCOURAGING ABILITY

Lack of confidence often holds people back from seeking out (or sometimes accepting) new challenges at work. Even very confident people operate at a small percentage of their maximum capacity or potential. Encourage staff to believe in their own abilities by giving them additional tasks – for instance, asking them to serve on committees tackling key issues. Do not accept the response "I'm no good at that". This is often merely an unconscious excuse for inaction.

ELIMINATING FEAR

People suffer from many kinds of fear: fear of personal failure; fear that the organization will fail or be taken over; fear that jobs will disappear through reorganization; or fear of the possible adverse consequences of change. None of these anxieties is irrational. They are only eased, though never completely eliminated, by full, frank, and open communication – with individuals and groups. The anxieties can be exacerbated by secretive management that uses fear as a way to control people. Drive out fear and you will find that trust, optimism, and kindness are much more effective.

Open, upright posture shows confidence

Withdrawn appearance shows lack of self-belief

▲ READING BODY LANGUAGE

The outward appearance of a person often gives insight into their feelings. An employee exhibiting defensive body language and a negative attitude may be feeling insecure.

12	Insist on people working together and communicating freely and openly.

ENABLING PARTICIPATION

Confidence in the workplace stems from true participation in the work. This can only happen when employees – singly or in groups – share information and therefore have a real influence over what actually happens. The advantages are democratic, motivational, and practical. Research shows that productivity is lower when jobs are closely prescribed, compared with situations in which people are allowed to contribute in their own ways to meeting goals.

POINTS TO REMEMBER

- Stepping back and letting others take the lead helps both you and your staff to be confident.
- Letting your own insecurity show will infect your team.
- Uncertainty always breeds low morale.
- It is important to inform people of company developments quickly and honestly.

COMMUNICATING CLEARLY

Sometimes highly organized, sometimes haphazard, communication happens all the time. Improve its quality by being open, honest, and accessible to everybody. You can never communicate too much, whether informally or formally.

13 Go out of your way to chat to staff on an informal basis.

THINGS TO DO

1. Keep appointments with all members of staff, regardless of their status.
2. Make sure you talk to or acknowledge people as often as you can.
3. On outside visits, talk to everybody, not just the boss.
4. If you want to speak with a staff member, make the effort to meet them in person rather than using the telephone.

OPEN PLANNING ▶
Open-plan offices encourage open communication and team spirit as well as making managers more accessible to staff.

14 Split large working units into several smaller ones with close links.

ENCOURAGING CONTACT

Many managers like to hide away behind closed office doors, keeping contact to a minimum. That makes it easy to be an administrator, but very hard to be a leader. It is far better to keep your office door open (as a general rule) and to encourage people to visit you when the door is open. Contact is made easier by open-plan work spaces, which is why some multi-millionaire managers in Silicon Valley, USA, have abandoned their executive suites for desks in an open-plan office. If you have not talked to a particular member of staff for a while, make sure you do so. The more people who know you and can see you, the better working relationships are likely to be.

CUTTING BUREAUCRACY

If left unchecked, bureaucracy can severely impede communications, rendering attempts to improve productivity and morale ineffective. Although there is a need for some bureaucracy, it is important that you keep strict control over forms, reports, and other such documents. Avoid wasting time waiting for a proposal to be "rubber-stamped" when a decision can be taken in a quick but effective, informal meeting.

 15 Clear out manuals and forms and replace only those that are missed.

CONSIDERING HOW ORGANIZATIONS COMMUNICATE

TYPE OF ORGANIZATION	EFFECTS ON COMMUNICATION
BUREAUCRATIC Dominated by hierarchies of power.	A domineering, "who reports to whom?" structure leads to rigid control, abundant manuals, systems, reports, and paperwork.
MATRIX Divided by product, geography, and function.	This type of organization is supposedly co-ordinated, but the leadership is divided and the bureaucracy is strong.
DECENTRALIZED Divided into separate operating units.	The individual units function separately or independently, so communication is difficult – the organization is primarily driven by budgets.
MARKET-ORIENTATED Organized by product and/or geography.	A strong sales culture is dominated by commands from head office, so communication with outside staff is limited.
ENTREPRENEURIAL Flat structure with risk-taking philosophy.	The tendency to "hire-and-fire" people can lead to a culture of fear. Decisions are usually dependent on one or two key people.
PEOPLE-BASED Employees own shares and enjoy responsibility.	Staff are motivated by ownership in the company. People participate in and have responsibility for the company's management.

One-to-One Meetings

Instead of relying on memos and other written communications, consider the immediacy of the one-to-one meeting as the most efficient way to deal with issues or problems that arise. Instant feedback and endorsements can be given at these personal meetings, and enthusiasm and commitment to new proposals or fresh ideas can be conveyed much more effectively and unambiguously than through written responses. Ensure that you have enough time available to give your full attention to matters under discussion, and that the meeting will not be unnecessarily interrupted or cut short.

16 Ask customers for both suggestions and complaints.

Using Different Media

One channel of communication is never enough – the more there are, the better. Your objective is to pass on information as quickly as possible, and to learn, just as speedily, about reactions to your messages. Noticeboards, newsletters, and magazines all have their place, as do suggestion boxes. But electronic media are more immediate and powerful. You can use digital noticeboards, Web sites, in-company television, video, and e-mail. The same rules apply to all media: work to professional standards, match content to employees' needs, encourage feedback, and be prepared to change the format if the presentation is ill-received. Analyze the response to ensure that your message has been fully understood and has had the effect that you intended.

Company Web site

◀ **USING NEW MEDIA**
The wealth of new technology available to organizations means that company communications can be made more immediately and with greater impact than ever before.

USING THE "GRAPEVINE"

People at work form social networks and interact in the same way as all human groups. They value informal contacts, such as personal greetings and chats over tea and coffee. They also gossip. Some managers distrust the grapevine and worry that inaccurate, premature, and alarming information will spread. The grapevine, though, can be fed by management with accurate "rumours". Disarm its disruptive potential with swift information on matters that concern people. Often the best way to learn what is on people's minds is through informal meetings, so make sure that you participate fully in them.

▼ REMAINING INFORMAL
Informal chats are a useful way of finding out how your staff feel and of discouraging rumours and gossip.

Employee discusses team problems

Manager eases concern at source

17 Act swiftly to deny rumours if they are inaccurate.

18 Ensure that all those at meetings need to be there.

USING TEAM MEETINGS

In most organizations meetings occur more often than is necessary. Ensure that every meeting has a purpose, and that all attendees are directly concerned with that purpose. Regular team and management meetings are an important method of keeping people informed and answering their questions. Treat these meetings seriously. Unarranged meetings are also valuable, with any number of attendees from two upwards. They require less formality but should be brief. Keep written notes of what has been decided or what needs to be done, and circulate the notes so that staff feel that they are fully involved.

GAINING TRUST AND COMMITMENT

A committed employee is extraordinarily valuable. You can gain staff commitment by meeting people's key needs; paying attention to people at all levels; trusting and being trusted; tolerating individuality; and creating a blame-free, "can-do" culture.

19 Give staff the opportunity to show that you can trust them.

QUESTIONS TO ASK YOURSELF

Q Do you trust others enough so you can delegate effectively?

Q Will you leave the delegate, after briefing, to complete the job without interference?

Q Do you show people that you trust them not to let you down?

Q Do you rely on rules and regulations to judge other people's work?

Q Do you instil trust in others by always being truthful and keeping your promises?

NURTURING TRUST

The quality and style of leadership are major factors in gaining employees' trust and commitment. Clear decision-making should be coupled with a collaborative, collegiate approach. This entails taking people into your confidence and explicitly and openly valuing their contributions. You should also make yourself as visible as possible, and show yourself to be approachable and willing to listen to others. People respond well to a collective ambition with which they can identify. Remember that to earn trust, you must first learn to trust those who work for you.

WINNING ▶ TRUST
These are the key managerial qualities that inspire trust and commitment in employees. Work on developing such qualities in yourself to help create a fully committed workforce.

Willingness to work long hours

Holding personal values consistent with the organization's

Creating a strong sense of team spirit

Pride in telling others about the organization

Feeling personally involved in work

Sense of ownership in the organization

Commitment to the organization

20 Make sure you address people's intellectual and emotional needs.

21 Listen to unhappy employees – they may reveal serious problems.

WINNING MINDS, SPIRITS, AND HEARTS

The full commitment of staff cannot be realized unless you address people's psychological needs. Research has shown that most management activities are directed towards intellectual needs, some attention is paid to the expression of individuality, but even less attention is paid to emotional needs. By giving equal weight to all three areas, you are more likely to win the minds, spirits, and hearts of your employees. The means to achieve this include: allowing people some autonomy in creating their work environment; making them feel valued by openly recognizing their achievements; and empowering them by handing over as much control as possible in their areas of responsibility.

Remains loyal, despite unvoiced complaints

Loyal and enthusiastic

CHAMPION　　WALKING WOUNDED

Highly critical of the company

Disenchanted and unproductive

DETRACTOR　　MISSING IN ACTION

◀ **DEGREES OF COMMITMENT**
You must understand your staff in order to develop true commitment. One marketing classification of four customer types also applies to employees. Aim to build communication policies that reach those "missing in action", and identify the "walking wounded" and the "detractors". Then devise programmes that will take them into the "champion" ranks.

22 Endeavour to transform all employees into "champions".

KEEPING STAFF COMMITTED

One of the most effective ways of keeping employees committed and raising retention, is to enrich their jobs and increase motivation. This can be achieved by a number of means, including raising interest levels, ensuring that each employee has a stimulating variety of tasks to perform, and providing the resources and training through which new skills can be developed. A multi-skilled employee will be able to perform a range of interesting tasks, while a person with limited skills may be prone to boredom through repetition. Continually encouraging your staff to make suggestions for efficiency improvements will further motivate them, as well as give them a sense of involvement in a task or project and commitment to its success.

23 Investigate fully whenever figures for employee retention start to drop significantly.

▼ **DIFFERING PERCEPTIONS**
A survey conducted in several different organizations revealed that managers, in contrast to employees, have greater confidence in the personal-development factors their organization provides.

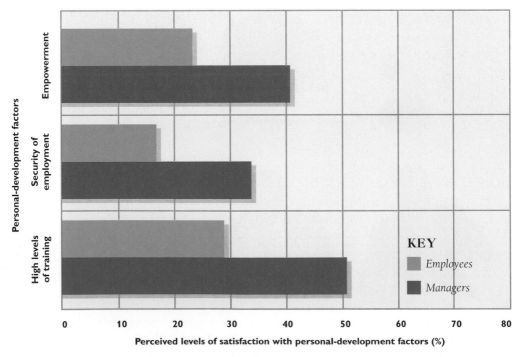

Personal-development factors

Empowerment

Security of employment

High levels of training

KEY
Employees
Managers

0   10   20   30   40   50   60   70   80

Perceived levels of satisfaction with personal-development factors (%)

REWARDING EXCELLENCE

Acknowledging excellence is vital in maintaining an employee's commitment and job satisfaction. Consider rewarding exceptional performance and high productivity with financial incentives. These could include one-off salary rises, bonus payments, or, if appropriate, share options. If an employee has substantially reduced the organization's costs, this could also be financially rewarded. For more modest levels of achievement, other benefits – such as inclusion on senior staff training weekends – are highly motivating. Above all, never underestimate the value of a simple "thank you".

QUESTIONS TO ASK YOURSELF

Q Have I devised financial reward schemes for excellence?

Q Have I considered non-monetary rewards?

Q Do I always say "thank you" when a job is done well?

Q Am I creating "heroes" that other staff can admire?

24 Ensure you involve everybody in a personal project.

PROJECT ▶ "HERO"
Recognition of a popular leader encourages others to show commitment.

Success is publicly celebrated

Employee's self-belief is bolstered

STAYING POSITIVE

To create a positive environment within your organization, it is important to create a "can-do" atmosphere. This should be built on mutual trust, in which people, whatever their self-doubts, are sure that the organization can achieve whatever it is asked to do. Actual achievement is essential to foster this confidence. Start group projects at every opportunity, choosing tasks that have a clear purpose and a positive, measurable outcome. Also, seek to create "heroes" – well-respected and productive employees (including project leaders) that other staff members admire. Be sure to celebrate each hero's successes: this not only bolsters the hero's self-belief, but also encourages others to trust in the can-do culture and to commit to the organization's goals.

ADJUSTING YOUR APPROACH

How you manage people has a deep impact on their behaviour. It is useful to alter and direct your management methods to suit different people and different situations. Your aim is always to encourage people to motivate and manage themselves.

25 Apply discipline, but combine it with empowerment and trust.

COMBINING MANAGEMENT STYLES

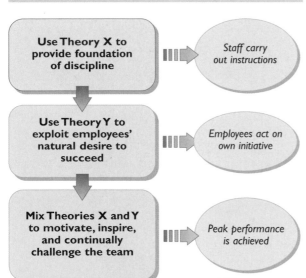

Use Theory X to provide foundation of discipline → Staff carry out instructions

Use Theory Y to exploit employees' natural desire to succeed → Employees act on own initiative

Mix Theories X and Y to motivate, inspire, and continually challenge the team → Peak performance is achieved

26 People who enjoy their work will produce the best results.

THEORY X MANAGEMENT

The traditional "order and obey" approach to managing people can be an effective way of motivating them. Tell staff what to do and how to do it, and they either perform as ordered or pay the penalty, with dismissal as the last resort (sometimes the first). Researcher Douglas McGregor named this style Theory X management. You need a bedrock of Theory X discipline in any organization.

THEORY Y MANAGEMENT

In contrast to the Theory X approach, Theory Y states that self-discipline springs from enjoying responsibility. The better educated and skilled your workforce, the more you can rely on these natural drives. Theory Y works well only when people have strong objectives. Combine Theories X and Y to achieve the most effective management.

TRADITIONAL APPROACH

Job completed

RETHINKING METHODS

A traditional approach to allocating work is to split tasks into components that are given to a number of different workers. Although this gives you a high degree of control, it can be monotonous for staff. Also, because the task "waits" in a new queue at every desk, this method tends to be inefficient. A better idea is to entrust all or most of a task to one person. This is quicker and more motivating, as the individual feels "ownership" of the task, even though that means more responsibility.

Single worker completes task in one day

MULTI-TASKING

▲ OWNING THE PROJECT
Allocating a task to a single employee not only reduces the time needed to complete it, but also promotes job satisfaction.

27 Most people prefer responsibility to too little work.

28 Cut down layers after reforming processes.

CONSULTING PEOPLE

Aim to be flexible in your approach to people, but avoid following one system one day and another the next. Regularly ask your staff what they would like from you. They may like more responsibility or, conversely, more guidance – try to comply with their wishes as far as you can, while serving the best interests of the team.

DEVELOPING PEOPLE

Helping individuals to achieve their potential is in the best interests of the person and the organization. Aim to train, encourage, and provide opportunities for willing people.

PROVIDING TRAINING

Developing the abilities of staff at all levels is so important that some organizations have their own education facilities, and many engage outside trainers and advisers. Top-quality training and development are vital to all organizations.

29 Make training the last thing you cut back, never the first.

30 Ask people about their long-term goals and aspirations, and assist in their realization.

ARRANGING TRAINING

Try to allocate a percentage of revenues to training (1.5 per cent at least), or to lay down minimum training hours – five days per year is a reasonable target. If such policies are sacrificed under short-term financial pressure, your organization loses the benefit of better-trained employees, and it is implied that training is not essential. Provide training that is *specific*, to improve current performance; *general*, to provide wider skills; and *in advance*, to prepare for promotion and change.

EVALUATING FORMS OF STAFF DEVELOPMENT

TYPE OF TRAINING	BENEFITS AND REINFORCEMENTS
TECHNICAL Training in the specifics of a particular job – usually provided in-house and during working hours by specialist instructors or supervisors.	● Enables high-quality performance of tasks. ● Must be repeated at regular intervals to maintain newly enhanced skills. ● Best coupled with an exam that gives a qualification.
QUALITY Training in the principles of total quality, together with the technical tools required for improvement – needs specialist instruction.	● Provides both "quick fixes" for immediate problems and longer-term, organization-wide benefits. ● Instils a philosophy of continuous practical improvement. ● Must be sustained indefinitely to become a way of life.
SKILLS Financial accounting, creative thinking, speaking, IT, writing, presentation, chairing, languages, interviewing, selling, etc. – in-house or external.	● All employees benefit from a general, multi-skill grounding. ● Nervousness about using skills in public is cured. ● Opportunities for practice are needed to build and maintain effectiveness.
PROFESSIONAL Education to obtain qualifications, for example, in accountancy, law, banking, engineering – external and either full-time or part-time.	● Provides portable skills, which are valuable to the individual as well as to the employer. ● Specialization leads to a more select choice of future appointments in the organization. ● Requires effort over a considerable period.
FUNCTIONAL Education in marketing, planning, sales management, purchasing, human resources management, etc. – external, but not usually full-time.	● Functional training almost always leads to better performance and improved career paths. ● Must be linked with appointment to functional role. ● Area is often wrongly ignored by companies who simply "hope for the best".
ACTIVITY "Outward Bound"-type courses, in which people learn leadership and teamwork by engaging in physical tasks, such as rock-climbing.	● Provides an effective means of team bonding and re-energizing the workforce. ● Must be supplemented by and co-ordinated with more direct management training.
MANAGERIAL Providing expertise and knowledge in fields such as strategy and change management – business school focus, either internal or external.	● Managers identify, work on, and solve real corporate problems. ● Invaluable grounding if learning is applied to the job. ● Both sides benefit if student remains committed.

IMPROVING SKILLS

Aim to train your staff in as many specific skills as possible. Mental abilities matter greatly in modern organizations, as do the skills needed to master computers. Training in thought processes will improve the execution of practical tasks.

31 Teach people to think analytically – this will benefit the whole organization.

THINKING CLEARLY

Like any other skill, thinking can be taught and improved on. The ability to analyze is basic to this, revolving around the question "Why?" – "Why do we need to cut our price?" or "Why have profits fallen?". Encourage your staff to analyze their work and to ask questions constantly. Analysis requires a high degree of mental organization, which can improve with practice if analysis is part of the corporate way of life.

USING MULTISKILLING

The more skills in which a person is trained, the more valuable they are as an employee and the greater their personal potential. In "manufacturing cells" within factories, employees are given responsibility for an entire product – from initial research to sourcing materials, manufacture, and marketing. The people are interchangeable, which makes them flexible and provides them with a useful knowledge of each other's work. Office work can follow the same ideas on a project basis. Widening people's skills cuts down on cost and time, provides greater flexibility, and greatly encourages team spirit and collaboration.

WORKING IN "CELLS" ▼
Provide people with opportunities to operate in working cells or groups. They will learn the skills of other members of the group, which will increase their effectiveness and improve morale.

32 Get staff into the habit of constantly improving their range of skills.

▼ USING NEW TECHNOLOGY

Make sure that everybody who possibly can be is computer-literate. Both the individual and the organization will suffer in the long term if new technology is not mastered.

33 Invest heavily in training for key computer skills: this will improve the performance of your company.

A trained employee benefits the company

On-line course gives practical experience

Study aids help develop new skills

MASTERING COMPUTERS

The use of electronics in business is growing so fast that you should regard technology such as computers as something that everybody must know how to use. If your organization does not have an Intranet (internal computer system) or some way of connecting people and files, you must press hard for the installation of such a set-up. If portable computers can improve operations (for instance, those of service engineers), try to provide them. There will be problems to resolve, ranging from security and privacy to the over-use of e-mail. But all these obstacles can be overcome. More difficulties will be created unless everybody who can usefully become computer-literate is given the necessary training and equipment.

QUESTIONS TO ASK YOURSELF

Q Have my staff been sufficiently trained in computer skills?

Q Is their training both up-to-date and updated regularly?

Q Do people have opportunities to practise their new skills in order to master them?

Q Have I listened to other people's suggestions regarding new technology?

Q Does the organization have sufficient technical support?

Q Is the company using all the computer programs available to improve performance?

GUIDING OTHERS

All managers coach. They tell people what they are doing right or wrong on the job, train them, assess them, and counsel them. The mentor's role overlaps with those of the coach and the counsellor, but the three roles have separate purposes.

34 If mistakes are made, ask yourself if you played any part in them.

BEING A COACH

Giving clear instructions about what you expect is the first step of coaching. This stage often produces a drop in motivation as reality challenges the employee's ability. At this point you become a helper, coaching the employee to recognize his or her strengths and to form ambitions. Finally, the person is in control of him- or herself and the job. You then step aside and assume the role of adviser, to be consulted when needed.

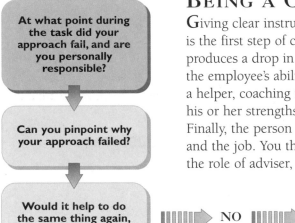

At what point during the task did your approach fail, and are you personally responsible?

Can you pinpoint why your approach failed?

Would it help to do the same thing again, with improvements?

NO

YES

By analyzing what went wrong, and when and how the problems occurred, you can and should devise a series of improvement measures to ensure that failure does not occur on a similar task or project.

COACHING QUESTIONS

If someone you are coaching has experienced failure in his or her work, ask the person these questions in sequence. It may be that his or her work efforts can be improved with simple adjustments to current working methods. Alternatively, the person's basic approach to tasks may need reassessing.

Did you plan the task and, if so, how?

What wrong decisions were made?

What must you do differently next time?

Design a programme to correct defects.

Use your years of work experience and your knowledge of the organization to steer junior employees along the most appropriate career paths.

BEING A MENTOR

A mentor is a senior manager who establishes a special relationship with a particular junior. As a mentor, you should never be in a line relationship with the mentored (a "line" being the route along which orders pass from the top of the organization to the bottom), otherwise you cannot guarantee a disinterested, objective viewpoint. Do not consider mentoring only in times of trouble. Instead, take a continuous interest in the progress of the junior. He or she will expect to discuss work difficulties with you, and you can intervene with line managers if the situation demands it.

Experienced manager coaches an employee, helping his development

Employee receives valuable guidance and encouragement

BEING A COUNSELLOR

As a counsellor you are called upon to deal with personal problems. These may be problems at work or home. Either way, the junior employee needs to tell a sympathetic listener about his or her troubles. You should ideally help the person to find his or her own solution, though it may be necessary to make strong suggestions. Usually, the employee will turn to an immediate superior, especially since the problem may demand time off. Never turn away from a counselling need, and call in others (possibly outside experts) if the problem is beyond your powers.

35 Find every junior a wise mentor who gives good advice.

36 Encourage employees to suggest ways to solve problems.

TEACHING BY EXAMPLE

As the boss of a group you are likely to be a prime role model – the person who sets the tone of the unit. You must also create the right atmosphere for successful teamwork and use example purposefully to teach and encourage good practice.

37 Use opportunities to lead from the front and set a good example.

38 Teach by showing how, not by giving people your orders.

ACTING AS A ROLE MODEL

Employees expect their manager to set a positive example. It is therefore very important that you neither fall below the high standards that you set yourself nor behave disparagingly to members of staff who do fall short of them. Above all, you should behave consistently at all times.

COMPETENCE

SUPPORTIVENESS

CHARISMA

FAIR-MINDEDNESS

HONESTY

INSPIRING PEOPLE
According to research, there are ten personal qualities that are the most admired characteristics of respected organizational leaders. These qualities are less to do with making the right or wrong decisions and more to do with integrity and straightforward behaviour.

VISION

INTELLIGENCE

COURAGE

BROAD-MINDEDNESS

DIRECTNESS

SHARING SKILLS

Team members often make very effective teachers, either by tutoring less experienced members or by sharing different sets of skills. You should consider an organized, on-the-job programme of development with one team member sitting by another to learn about their job. This will help both parties reach a deeper understanding of the work of the team, as well as transferring new skills. You can achieve a similar effect by forming a mini-team or taskforce to tackle a particular issue, not necessarily related to the team's main objective. Adopting a strategy like this ensures that team members learn how to develop solutions and turn them into action.

CULTURAL DIFFERENCES

The emphasis placed on teaching varies from country to country, but the Japanese in particular place great importance on action learning. Germans tend to be more formal, expecting people to follow instructions. Americans are more likely to have been taught about managing and will often adopt new "empowering" methods, which may later be neglected. English managers are likely to improvise and regard skills as natural, untaught assets.

39 Bring in outside trainers as often as possible.

Colleague is able to learn by practising skills

Senior employee explains job to colleague

◀ **LEARNING ON THE JOB**
Action learning is more effective than sedentary learning involving books and lectures. Encourage more experienced staff members to take the lead.

NURTURING TALENT

Identifying and using individual talent is one of the most satisfying and productive aspects of a manager's work. Finding good people is only part of the task – talented people can be difficult to manage, but the effort is well worthwhile.

40 Regard staff losses as opportunities to introduce new strengths.

QUESTIONS TO ASK ABOUT OTHERS

Q Do they have, or could they develop, a special expertise?

Q Can they combine talents such as research and management?

Q Do they show signs of organizational ability?

Q Are they successful at bringing in new business?

Q Have they shown the ability to lead others?

FINDING TALENT

Individual talents within organizations, especially large ones, are often underemployed or even unnoticed. Look out for signs of abilities that are not being fully used (or used at all) and find ways in which the individuals concerned can contribute more. People who engage in non-work activities, like running a company social club or event, may be sources of untapped talent. Bringing talent to the foreground not only relaunches the individual's career, but also strengthens the organization's success potential.

PLANNING SUCCESSION

The more successful subordinates are, the more likely they are to leave your company for "better" things. You should welcome this, as you are the friend and supporter who has helped them to develop and display their talents. However, their promotion will leave gaps. You should always have an answer to the question "What will I do if Jean or John leaves?". This may create an opportunity to reorganize work so that a replacement is not needed. More likely, you will be able to reward someone with promotion, thereby creating another vacancy. Maintain a succession folder, regularly update it, and pencil in potential successors for every key job.

41 Promote talented individuals, even if they excel in their current job.

42 Speak out if you believe someone is being moved to the wrong job.

Personal qualities of drive and perseverance	**Ability to form relationships and to communicate**	**Ability to identify and to recognize individual talent**	**Target-setting, appraising, coaching, and giving feedback**

THE INDIVIDUAL'S CONTRIBUTION   THE ORGANIZATION'S CONTRIBUTION

Energy and strong needs, drives, and motives	**Continual willingness to learn and develop**	**Giving rewards, incentives, and recognition**	**Investment in personnel training and development**

DEVELOPING ▲ TALENT

The development of talent depends equally on input from both the organization and the individual.

MAXIMUM DEVELOPMENT OF INDIVIDUAL TALENT

FOCUSING ON CONTRIBUTION

What is your attitude towards people who are "difficult, demanding, disagreeable, disobedient, dislikable, disorganized, disputing, disrespectful, and discordant"? An obvious answer is that you do not want them around. But the "9D" characteristics, according to American consultant Michael J. Kami, are those of the "talented gorillas", who may be the most productive employees you have. Above all, concentrate on people's contributions, not their personalities.

UNCONVENTIONAL EMPLOYEE ▶
Nonconformist staff members may be difficult to manage, but are sometimes the most productive.

Unorthodox appearance may accompany willingness and talent

ENCOURAGING MANAGEMENT POTENTIAL

Avoid typecasting people and being typecast. Your staff may have abilities that go well beyond their present roles, and that will take them upwards in the organization – perhaps into management.

43 Seek to promote from within in the first instance.

44 Encourage staff to apply for any internal openings.

POINTS TO REMEMBER

- People's abilities are more likely to be underestimated than rated too highly.
- Classroom learning is an essential element of management development.
- Lack of ability can usually be improved with training.

SPOTTING ABILITIES

The fact that somebody has mastered a particular job gives grounds for supposing that he or she could advance to higher levels. When vacancies or opportunities occur, always look first to see whether someone already employed in the organization could fill the post. Remember that technical deficiencies can generally be made good by training. Look for personal characteristics (such as energy and perseverance), good interpersonal behaviour, strong motivation, the ability and willingness to learn, excellent organizational skills, and flexibility. Task forces and other ad hoc groups provide a relatively risk-free way of testing whether a person has the ability to rise.

RECOGNIZING ▶
MANAGEMENT
QUALITIES
More people have management ability than is commonly supposed. Look out for employees with these key qualities, and earmark them for future promotion to management posts.

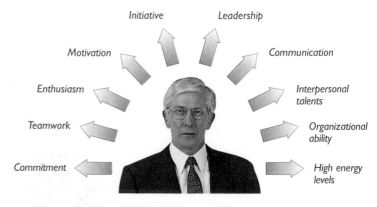

Initiative Leadership
Motivation Communication
Enthusiasm Interpersonal talents
Teamwork Organizational ability
Commitment High energy levels

MAKING MANAGERS

In your search for management potential, remember that management is not a rarefied activity requiring a high degree of education. Although managers are supposed to spend their time in intellectual activities – such as planning, organizing, and co-ordinating – in reality their days are very fragmented and dominated by practical matters. They may have only half an hour of uninterrupted work every two days. You need to ask yourself if the person you are considering for promotion is capable of working effectively in these conditions. If your potential manager prefers to work on only one task at a time, then elevation to management may not be appropriate.

45 Allow people to show that they can manage.

▼ **COPING WITH PRESSURE**
Aspiring managers should be practical and able to handle several tasks at once. Give people the chance to demonstrate their ability and they may well prove to be candidates for promotion.

Employee is able to cope with interruptions

Several duties are managed simultaneously

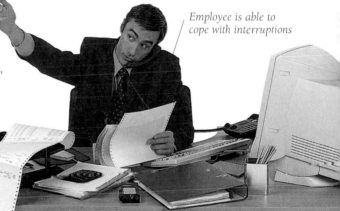

46 Train staff for higher duties as early as you can.

47 Make a list of good co-workers and keep it for future reference.

FACILITATING PROMOTION

You may be tempted to keep people where they are – doing a good job – rather than move them onwards and upwards. Not promoting people is bad for their career development and for the organization, which is not using talent to the full. Some organizations even refuse to train adequately because they are frightened of losing the trained employee to someone else: this condemns them to having an undertrained labour force. Reconcile yourself to the fact that people are likely to move on from time to time. If you think the move is good for them, encourage and congratulate them.

MOTIVATING PEOPLE

Receiving orders is far less motivating than taking part in planning and decision-making. Enable your staff to achieve their ambitions and to manage themselves in order to achieve the desired results.

48 Use the strategic thinking of all employees.

MOTIVATING FACTORS

FACTOR	ACTION
SELF-FULFILMENT	Enable employees to take on challenges.
RECOGNITION	Tell employees how well they are doing.
PEER RESPECT	Celebrate the individual's success publicly.
EXPERTISE	Encourage development of special knowledge.
COMPETENCE	Provide training to develop key skills.
ACHIEVEMENT	Agree on targets that are achievable.
AUTONOMY	Allow employees to plan and design own work.
SELF-CONFIDENCE	Make sure that allocated tasks can be done well.
SELF-RESPECT	Increase the individual's regard for self.
MEMBERSHIP	Ensure employees enter "club" of co-workers.

SHARING THE STRATEGY

It is very important to inform people about strategic plans and their own part in achieving the strategies. Take trouble to improve their understanding and to win their approval, as this will have a highly positive influence on performance. Never forget that employees invest their lives and financial security in the company.

Manager explains how task relates to overall strategy

▲ **ENRICHING A JOB**
Give people jobs that enable them to feel good about the organization and its management.

49 Allow others to take decisions that they can make just as well as you.

DELEGATING DECISIONS

Pushing the power of decision-making downwards reduces pressure on senior management. It motivates people on the lower levels because it gives them a vote of confidence. Also, because the decision is taken nearer to the point of action, it is more likely to be correct. The main reasons for hoarding decisions that could be taken lower down are bad ones: you want to keep the decision power all to yourself, or you do not trust those in positions below to get things right (which calls into question the appropriateness of your appointments). You should certainly take all the decisions that only you as a manager can make, but even then you can draw on all the valuable input available from colleagues and subordinates.

HANDING DOWN POWER

MANAGEMENT DECISIONS
The manager sets out the agenda for a particular task, decides on the powers she must keep for herself, and selects the people who she thinks will best carry out the delegated duties.

DELEGATED DECISIONS
The delegates each have a clearly defined role that they have helped establish. They choose their own working methods, make decisions as necessary, and are responsible for meeting the agreed aim.

INTRODUCING SELF-MANAGEMENT

The standard approach to establishing self-management among staff is to define individual job requirements so that employees can carry out the processes effectively. This is contradictory because somebody other than the self-manager is managing the tasks, and probably explaining how to do the tasks as well. Motivational empowerment only comes about if you can answer "Yes" to four key questions (right). If any answers are "No", reassess your approach to self-management.

QUESTIONS TO ASK YOURSELF

Q Do individuals define their own tasks?

Q Do they define the behaviour that is required to perform their tasks?

Q Do managers and the managed jointly define performance goals that are challenging for the individual?

Q Do individuals define the importance of the goal?

IMPROVING PERFORMANCE

All improvement programmes run out of steam unless you make conscious efforts to renew people's support. Improvement stems from repetition, but greater gains come from focused planning and training.

50 Aim to improve the quality of all company processes.

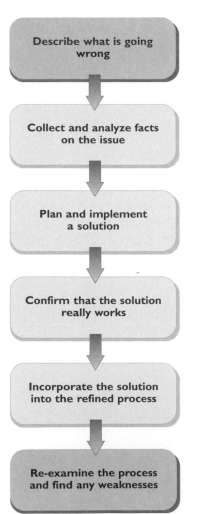

Describe what is going wrong

Collect and analyze facts on the issue

Plan and implement a solution

Confirm that the solution really works

Incorporate the solution into the refined process

Re-examine the process and find any weaknesses

◀ **SIX STEPS TO BETTER QUALITY**
These six steps can be applied by individuals or teams. Encourage staff at all levels to use them to examine and improve processes and systems.

MANAGING QUALITY

Total Quality Management (TQM) is built around the idea that individuals can always improve their work by learning new techniques and applying them. In TQM workshops people master techniques, such as how to use the "six management and planning tools" required to resolve issues. This may sound complicated, but using such tools speeds up processes, eliminates task stages, and reduces costs quickly. The objective is to cut out waste and to increase customer satisfaction by improving product or service quality, employee performance, and value for money. This approach satisfies people's natural urge to do a better job and to see improvements.

51 Focus quality work on producing real customer benefits.

52 Use training in quality skills to increase people's general ability.

LEARNING BY EXPERIENCE

As people gain experience in a job, they see ways of doing it better, cutting costs, and saving time. Encourage staff to come forwards with such ideas – this will improve performance and raise morale. Consider holding regular ideas meetings where people can make constructive suggestions. Such meetings often provide the inspiration for others to develop the ideas further. Always act on these proposals where possible – it is especially motivating if the person who brought forwards the original idea is the one to implement it.

53 Listen to staff and ask for their improvement ideas.

54 Expect people to continue achieving better results.

◀ **LEARNING CURVE**
As people gain experience of their work, their performance will naturally improve. The pattern of a learning curve shows how a period of intensive development is followed by a "levelling-off" stage.

Skills learnt

Time period

55 Concentrate on one initiative at a time to avoid confusion.

MAINTAINING MOMENTUM

A common mistake is to abandon an improvement initiative before it has a real chance to pay off, and to replace it with another, which then suffers the same fate. This "flavour of the month" policy breeds cynicism and lethargy. A far better policy is to stick to one basic programme (such as TQM), but to revise and improve it all the time. At the same time, select new themes for the initiative (say, every year) to refocus and renew the forwards drive. In a large team or department you could involve different groups in developing the new themes, and in this way everyone will feel more committed to the programme. The focus one year could be on responding to customers, the next target could be streamlining in-house systems, and the next could be boosting quality – but all of them would be aiming to deliver what the customer wants more quickly and cost-effectively.

MAKING PROGRESS

The more responsibility you give to people, the greater their interest and productivity are likely to be. The same principle applies to their knowledge of the organization and how they contribute to its success – the more knowledge, the better.

56 Make "right first time" a key aim for everybody in your team.

QUESTIONS TO ASK YOURSELF

Q Do I enable people to take pride in the quality of their own work?

Q Do I constantly look for ways to increase group morale?

Q Have I considered setting up specialist groups within my organization?

Q Am I making best use of a deployment policy and annual review?

Q Am I setting objectives that will motivate people?

GETTING IT RIGHT FIRST TIME

Make people responsible for the quality of their own work and it will usually inspire them to do better. Quality used to be maintained by trained inspectors who would check the work and send back anything imperfect – an expensive and wasteful method. Instead, increase training and assistance to help people produce only perfect work in the first place. Use supervisors as "enablers" who help groups and individuals whenever needed. This will keep work that needs redoing to a minimum, and should allow you to greatly reduce the numbers of supervisors.

RAISING GROUP MORALE

High group morale can enrich individual motivation and performance remarkably. In difficult situations, when companies are in crisis and can only be saved by major effort, group morale often rises to far higher levels than before. Individual objections and objectives are bypassed in the collective drive to do what must be done. But you need not wait until crisis strikes to instil this attitude in your staff. This does not mean you have to create an artificial emergency: build urgency by setting important objectives to which everyone subscribes and has a clear, agreed plan for reaching.

57 Expect people to supervise their own performance.

58 Encourage acceptance of and desire for change at all times.

Using Policy Deployment

Policy deployment may sound daunting, but it is based on simple principles. Firstly, a vision of the company's future is developed with the help of all its staff. "Improvement themes" are selected, again with people's help, that will produce better results. The themes, such as "Getting it Right First Time" or "Increasing Competitive Advantage", generate objectives for every unit and everyone in every unit. Detailed plans are made for the theme's implementation, and progress is reviewed every month. An annual review is also necessary to modify the vision and associated themes when necessary. The goal is to align individual and team ambitions with those of the organization. Everyone, from the chief executive downwards, shares in the vision and the strategy for realizing it, and knows their own part in achieving it.

ENRICHING JOBS ▶
USING DEPLOYMENT
By involving everyone in the organization with a new corporate vision and plans to realize that vision, you can enrich jobs and greatly increase people's motivation levels.

59 Ask questions to see if every person is aware of the team's strategy.

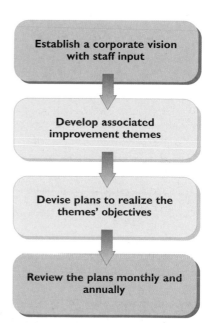

Establish a corporate vision with staff input

Develop associated improvement themes

Devise plans to realize the themes' objectives

Review the plans monthly and annually

Outsourcing to Increase Profitability

Many companies have "outsourced" jobs by establishing their employees as independent suppliers of products or services. Sometimes these moves are driven by negative cost-cutting motives, which often backfire. Used positively, the approach enables the company to retain the services of highly skilled experts, whose full-time employment is not justified (for example). In return, the employees gain the freedom to work profitably on their own terms. The flexibility that outsourcing offers can enrich people's working lives greatly. You can, however, enrich jobs in this way without cutting the employee loose from the organization by creating a "firm within the firm" – an expert, in-house group with specific responsibilities.

FINDING SOLUTIONS

Sensitive interpersonal skills are essential for creating a comfortable and productive working environment. Use your skills to resolve individual difficulties and to deal with conflicts.

BUILDING ENVIRONMENTS

Creating an atmosphere in which people feel appreciated and an essential part of a team is a challenge for every manager. A successful effort in this direction, however, will reduce the likelihood of problems.

 60 If a group grows too large, divide it into smaller parts.

▲ **TEAM SPIRIT**
Encourage the workforce to consider themselves as an elite, closely knit team. A good analogy is the united football team.

ENSURING COHESION

An employee who feels neglected and who is excluded from a cohesive working group is more likely to be unmotivated and prone to dissatisfaction than the person who has support and recognition from colleagues and managers. Encourage people to react positively and make effective contributions. This can be done by creating structures in which each staff member identifies with a group in which the responsibilities are clearly understood by all. An unselfish interest in the success of other group members is generated in a team that is closely bound together by common goals.

CONTROLLING OFFICE POLITICS

Strong feelings are aroused by the subject of office politics – anyone who has worked in an office will have experienced its effects. The negative side of office politics surfaces when it is used by individuals to increase personal power at the expense of colleagues and/or the organization. Strive to create a working environment in which status and hierarchy have as little importance as possible and the politics will stop.

61 Celebrate the achievements of your organization.

62 Whenever you can, involve people in specific tasks with clear aims.

CASE STUDY

Jan, a shopfloor worker, noticed that every so often her department had to write off stocks of components that had become obsolete. This was obviously expensive, and she wondered why the stock control was so ineffective. She found that the excess was held as "buffer stock" in case supplies became short. She reasoned that the cost of holding the stock must be so high that putting in a better system for ordering and locating needed parts would pay for itself many times over. Jan received full support from management and her colleagues to begin an improvement project, which she led from start to finish. She enlisted the help of other colleagues in completing her project. The stocks held in the department were halved, and the obsolete and obsolescent items reduced by 90 per cent.

◀ **ENCOURAGING INITIATIVE**
Jan was encouraged by her superiors to embark on what could be termed a one-person "Quality Improvement Project" (QIP). Such projects involve detailed studies of significant areas where money is being wasted. They are only possible in working environments that support and nurture the initiative of the individual.

USING POSITIVE EMOTIONS

An openness and responsiveness to people's spontaneity and originality will generate a positive atmosphere in which creative ideas can flourish and demotivating boredom is reduced. Informality, and a reasonably tolerant acceptance of your staff's inevitable mistakes, will also generate an environment in which recognition for success, rather than blame for failure, is the dominant culture. Take every opportunity to generate excitement over what the company and individuals have achieved and what challenges must be met for the future of the organization.

OPENING CLOSED MINDS

People are often reluctant to accept ideas *from outside sources. The "Not Invented Here" (NIH) syndrome occurs when individuals ignore ideas from other parts of the organization or other companies. Discourage this syndrome among your staff.*

> **63** Clearly emphasize that new ideas will not be rejected as a matter of course.

ACCEPTING IDEAS

The consequences of NIH are often expensive and sometimes disastrous. Antidotes must come from the organization's management. Welcome all ideas, accept those that are good, and explain the reasons for any rejections. This will ensure a flow of ideas, and people will be encouraged to see plans as opportunities, rather than threats, and to welcome them. Also, encourage people to act as "spies", reporting on any good ideas they have spotted in other organizations, businesses, or countries.

Manager listens to idea and suggests changes

Employee's confidence is boosted

WELCOMING INPUT ▲
Always give new ideas careful thought and consideration. If you dismiss them, the flow of ideas will soon start to dry up.

> **64** Make creative contributions a part of all meetings.

ENCOURAGING CREATIVITY

Creativity involves exploring and adopting new ideas that may produce better results. Many people believe that they are uncreative: in fact, everybody has potential and can be taught resourceful techniques. Stage workshops in which people can apply their skills to real-life issues. People are often reluctant because they fear that the new approach may fail. Explain that not taking risks can lead to rivals seizing the best opportunities.

CHANGING MINDSETS

Remember that people have a logical basis for rejecting a creative plan. Saying "No" means that no further action need be taken; saying "Yes" may well mean extra work, as well as extra risk. People who start new projects and fail often suffer as a result, whereas managers are seldom sacked for the opportunities they missed. This helps to develop negative mindsets, which mean that people spot the reasons for doing nothing and so miss the benefits from taking new action. You can change negative mindsets into positive ones by starting special projects that require creativity and by providing incentives for those involved. Regularly monitor such new initiatives, and ensure that senior management are aware of any progress or success and of who has contributed effectively.

CREATING POSITIVE MINDSETS ▶

Provide incentives for creativity. Encourage managers to include in their monthly reports any creative initiatives that were taken in the period, who was involved, and what is planned for the future.

Establish a special creative project to encourage initiative

⬇

Include non-managerial staff who will work effectively in a team

⬇

Insist that such new initiatives are recognized throughout the company

⬇

Openly celebrate the positive results of the creative projects

65 Always insist that opportunities are seized after the risks are assessed.

66 Stress that not taking risks is usually due to lack of self-confidence.

TAKING RISKS

Since you want people to be active and to show initiative, you must make it clear that risk-taking is encouraged. Otherwise, the normal human tendency to prefer the known to the unknown will inhibit progress both inside the company and in the marketplace. Risk can be defined as "incurring the chance of unfortunate consequences by doing something". You should not let the threat of unfortunate consequences prevent action. Reward successful risk-taking, and do not penalize failure except in two circumstances:

● The person has not carefully analyzed and understood the risks before acting;
● The person has repeated past mistakes.

DEALING WITH CONFLICT

Conflict is unavoidable when people interact at work. If faced with conflict or an angry person, adopt a positive and rational approach to defuse any heightened emotions, then look for a resolution based on pragmatism and compromise.

67 Remember that you are concerned with behaviour, not with character.

QUESTIONS TO ASK YOURSELF

Q Where is the problem and what is it exactly?

Q What are the potential solutions?

Q Which solution out of all the alternatives is the best?

Q How is the solution best implemented?

FACING PROBLEMS

Dealing with conflicts between employees is an inevitable part of managerial life. Once you are aware of conflict, take immediate action and invite the disagreeing parties to voice their points of view in a meeting. The key is to minimize the emotive element and to substitute it with a rational pragmatism. Even if you believe one position to be correct, be prepared to consider the other point of view; if it is valid, then try to reach a compromise.

▼ **FINDING A SOLUTION**
Provide an environment where disagreeing employees can openly voice their problems and then work towards effecting a resolution.

Employee freely airs his point of view

Manager acts as arbiter

Plans for a solution to the conflict are noted

Employee voices her opinion

DEFUSING NEGATIVE EMOTIONS

Guilt, anxiety, and anger are common negative emotions that must be managed carefully. Try to impress upon your employees that guilt will not repair whatever action has caused the upset, that anxiety will not prevent a future event that causes fear, and that anger is not an appropriate or helpful response to any situation. A person usually reacts angrily because others have not acted as he or she wants. You can defuse this anger by presenting a more reasonable point of view.

68 Carefully analyze problems as they arise.

69 Ask a close colleague to help defuse your anger.

DEALING WITH ANGER

Discussing the negative effects of anger with a disgruntled employee may help to resolve a situation of conflict. Beset by emotions that will probably have been growing in intensity over a period of time, the person will benefit from your rational observations of their inappropriate and misdirected behaviour and your suggestions for dealing with these feelings.

SIGNS OF ANGER

- Projecting bad feelings on to others, and resorting to sarcasm and ridicule.
- Avoiding the need for rational, unemotional responses.
- Concealing the loss of an argument, and making excuses for failure.
- Making excuses for intimidating and manipulating others.

ANTIDOTES TO OFFER

- Analyze the reasons behind angry feelings.
- Remember that it is possible to disapprove without being angry.
- Turn to a trusted, uninvolved friend before venting your anger.
- Ask whether expectations of others are reasonable.
- Expect to be disagreed with and displeased sometimes.
- Apologize to the objects of anger.

◀ REGAINING COMPOSURE
By addressing some of the reasons and emotions behind a person's anger, you may be able to help them regain their composure.

WORKING COLLECTIVELY

*I*f *general conflicts arise, resolutions may be found through a frank and open airing of grievances, or by rethinking current working methods. Unions can play a vital part in the proceedings as intermediaries between an organization and its employees.*

70 Encourage your workers to recognize your management skills.

71 Avoid demonizing a union or any one person, but treat issues on merit.

▼ **BEING POSITIVE**
When negotiating, restructuring, or resolving disputes, always seek a firm conclusion, and use a working method that strengthens people's natural instincts to be full members of a winning team.

RESOLVING CONFLICT

If conflict occurs within teams, you must work quickly to identify its causes and to implement workable, mutually agreed solutions. Consider whether a disruptive conflict is growing between two or more members that is affecting the rest of the team, or if the group as a whole is expressing general dissatisfaction with an issue. Conflicts between individuals should be resolved through firm but even-handed intervention. You may need to change the membership of the team to resolve the issue finally.

HANDLING UNIONS

Employers tend to regard unions as the enemy, vice versa, but an orderly, sympathetic union can be helpful to a well-run organization. Employees like to have representatives who can look after their interests more effectively than they can as individuals. Do not, however, make the mistake of identifying the union as the workforce: your contract is with each employee. Reserve for the union only those matters that belong to the union (representing individuals in dismissals, for example), and treat union officials with the same respect you would show any associate.

72 Never give in to demands that are unreasonable, but seek compromise.

STANDING FIRM ▶

Alan's new working methods gave the workers much more say in their work, which improved quality and reduced costs. This enabled Alan to raise pay while still making large savings.

CASE STUDY

Alan was appointed to run the maintenance operation for a large vehicle fleet. It depended on skilled, unionized workers who had a long history of trouble-making. A strike broke out shortly after Alan took charge. The workers, testing the new boss, demanded pay rises that the operation could not afford. They would not make any concessions. Alan also stood firm, and the staff walked out. Calling his managers together, Alan offered a package that addressed some of the employees' grievances. His proposal was eventually accepted, the strike ended, and the staff resumed work. Alan had successfully asserted management's right to manage, but he felt that more needed to be done. He went on to devise new methods of working that would help prevent future conflict.

QUESTIONS TO ASK YOURSELF

Q Is the dispute caused by a deep-seated grievance?

Q How widespread is the dispute?

Q Will a financial reward resolve the problem?

Q Have I taken all factors into consideration?

Q Will the proposed solution be effective in the long term?

CONFRONTING TROUBLE

When major disputes arise, do not stop at analyzing the apparent difficulties. It is essential to look for the underlying causes of the problem. Once the root causes have been identified, you can produce plans for finding effective and long-term tactical solutions – whether they be strategic, financial, or otherwise. If you leave the causes untouched, however, the difficulties will only recur. Your object is not only to cure the present troubles, but to ensure that they are permanently eliminated – with beneficial results for everybody.

DEALING WITH PERSONAL DIFFICULTIES

All managers are ultimately personnel officers. From time to time, you may have to deal with difficult personal matters that your staff bring to you. Take fast action, because such issues rarely improve with time.

73 Encourage people to bring their complaints and problems to you.

Manager asks that grievances be discussed separately.

MEETING NEEDS

Performance at work can be affected by anything from illness and bereavement to marital break-up and financial woes. Whether or not performance suffers, the person concerned requires attention and sympathy. This can take the form of allowing time off, or insisting that it be taken. Often practical assistance is required, perhaps involving money or helping to find legal advice, for example.

◀ **UNEARTHING PROBLEMS**
Aggressive behaviour in the workplace may disguise personal difficulties – avoid leaping to conclusions and be prepared to listen.

ENCOURAGING OPENNESS

Develop a personal rapport with your staff – this will help you to recognize any changes in their behaviour. If an employee displays unusual irritability, tension, or other negative behaviour, do not hesitate to approach them. Do not reprimand them for their work performance, but encourage them to talk openly about their problem. Listen sympathetically. Your availability will contribute to a caring environment in which people feel they can share their concerns.

74 Never take sides in a quarrel – be clearly impartial.

75 Handle personal problems as a friend, not a boss.

CULTURAL DIFFERENCES

British managers tend to be sympathetic to people with difficulties, while Americans and Germans are generally less understanding. The Japanese expect people to work, even in times of personal crisis.

PROVIDING SUPPORT

A manager dealing with a troubled employee must be supportive without getting too involved. Some specific problems – such as alcoholism and other types of compulsive behaviour – can require professional help. Display a positive attitude towards therapy and encourage the employee to choose this option. In the workplace, make the employee feel that their services are still needed and valued. This will boost their confidence as well as maintain a level of normality.

Employee explains why her work is suffering

Manager listens and offers advice

◀ **OFFERING SYMPATHY**
It may be that an attentive ear will be enough to meet a need. Sometimes, however, you may have to refer a member of staff to a counsellor.

76 Make time to talk to any employee who comes to you with problems.

DEALING WITH GENDER ISSUES

The issue of gender in the workplace goes far beyond harassment, sexual or otherwise. Harassing women is both offensive and an offence and must not be tolerated. There is no acceptable alternative to both practising and preaching true equality: make sure that all employees are judged by what they contribute to the organization, not by their gender. If one of your employees is being subjected to patronizing behaviour, act swiftly. But do not expect to change intolerance overnight. Make the change a key objective, however, and be prepared to take any action necessary to create an atmosphere in which both men and women feel comfortable, and in which any family needs, such as child care, are understood and accommodated.

MANAGING CHANGE

Managers often focus on the mechanics of change, concentrating on ensuring that their plan is followed. If their staff are not satisfied, however, the plan is likely to fail. If you listen to people's needs, they will respond positively to change.

77 Treat resistance to change as a problem that can always be solved.

78 Motivate your staff by acting positively on their creative ideas for change.

79 Use measured, continuous change to stimulate staff and avoid staleness.

BALANCING NEEDS

Some managers fall into the trap of putting production needs ahead of other organizational needs; others put concern for people above that for production. Both styles are erroneous, though the latter is popular with employees. Change, both large and small, is managed effectively only by showing equal concern for both needs. Attention to employees as people, coupled with strong interest in their welfare, wellbeing, and wishes, pays off in terms of better acceptance of changes and better performance. Change management that pays inadequate attention to people threatens productivity and is likely to misfire.

INVOLVING PEOPLE

When employees feel excluded from the decisions that will determine the way they do their work, demotivation and resentment can be the negative results. Ensure, therefore, that staff are given the opportunity to contribute and involve themselves at many levels of the decision-making process before any changes have to be made. This could range from having a say in how the office is furnished, for example, to the all-important task of setting long-term objectives. Consulting people before major changes take place will also reinforce their commitment and trust.

THINGS TO DO

1. Consider all staff input, no matter how small.
2. Identify "change agents" and encourage them to meet.
3. Form clear plans for change and share your intentions.
4. Tackle resistance to change as early as possible.

IDENTIFYING A "CHANGE AGENT"

Is capable of thinking laterally

+

Is driven to improve and transform

+

Is strong and emotionally in control

+

Thinks forcefully and independently

+

Creates new frames of reference

81 Involve many people in producing plans for change.

80 Show people how they will gain personally from the changes that you consider are necessary.

MANAGING RESISTANCE

You are likely to encounter varying degrees of resistance from staff when initiating change or revising existing procedures. Do not dismiss or ignore these objections. Some may arise from fear of what lies ahead, so listen to people's objections and, when possible, focus carefully on unwarranted fears in order to reassure staff. Others may arise from reasonable concerns of which you may have been unaware; offer staff the opportunity to explain their worries to you, then clarify how the proposed changes will affect them. Once they feel fully informed, their fears should recede.

QUALITIES FOR CHANGE AGENTS

Organizational change can be blocked by having the wrong people in key roles. Identify members of staff who are open to change – "change agents" – and put them where their enthusiasm for change becomes infectious and allays the fears of other employees. Use them in meetings, allowing them to take a leading role in facilitating the acceptance of change. Place these agents at any level of the organization: they will help you gather feedback on staff morale and reactions to change.

ASSESSING AND REWARDING

People are employed to get good results for the company. Their rates of success are intrinsically linked to how they are directed, reviewed, rewarded, and trusted by management.

EVALUATING PERFORMANCE

When choosing methods of assessing your staff's performance, always make sure that the end result has a positive effect on motivation and increases people's sense of self-worth. Realistic targets, positive feedback, and listening are key factors.

82 Begin an appraisal by concentrating on what a person has done well.

CULTURAL DIFFERENCES

The British have formal appraisal systems, but are often lax in administering them. The French and Germans set high standards and expect compliance. In Asia, group performance is rated above individual action, whereas Americans are motivated to achieve personal targets.

APPRAISING TO MOTIVATE

Regular, one-to-one assessments with your staff provide an efficient two-way forum in which to set and review realistic achievement targets, provide feedback on performance, and listen to and consider any problems employees may have. For example, a sales executive may feel that he or she is underperforming, when in fact sales targets have been set too high. During the appraisal, these targets could be reviewed and set at more realistic levels. Remember that your chosen methods of assessment must have a positive effect on people's performance levels and motivation.

JUDGING FAIRLY

An appraisal should leave staff feeling motivated and happy about their work, so make a point of recognizing employees' achievements and unique skills, and offer guidance on ways in which they could improve their performance. Try to avoid using these meetings negatively to criticize and dwell on faults, although do not avoid giving constructive criticism as necessary.

83 If people fail, ask what you can do to help them.

▼ **QUALITIES TO APPRAISE**
Understand what personal attributes go with successful work behaviour, and your judgments and suggestions at appraisals will contribute more effectively to success.

APPRAISING PERSONAL ATTRIBUTES

POSITIVE	NEGATIVE
● Enjoys uncertainty	● Expects certainty
● Asks questions	● Accepts what he or she is told
● Tolerates ambiguity	● Dislikes ambiguity
● Looks for alternatives	● Ignores conflicting evidence
● Is self-critical	● Is impulsive
● Seeks and weighs evidence	● Values "gut feelings"
● Reflects on matters	● Uses "either/or" thinking
● Communicates effectively	● Is unresponsive
● Is willing	● Is reluctant to take on new tasks
● Gets on well with other staff	● Is unpopular
● Uses initiative	● Is not proactive
● Can work unsupervised	● Requires constant supervision
● Is flexible	● Is not adaptable

DEALING WITH UNDERACHIEVEMENT

If objectives are not achieved, ask three key questions (right), and avoid accepting excuses for the answers. You want to find out exactly why the person failed to meet the objectives to prevent it happening again. People regret underachieving, so agree objectives with them that are fair but reasonably stretching. Remember that what seems daunting often proves to be surprisingly easy.

QUESTIONS TO ASK YOURSELF

Q Was the situation understood but the objective too difficult?

Q Was the situation misunderstood or was the objective inappropriate?

Q Was the failure to meet the objective entirely due to causes within the person's control?

PROMOTING STAFF

Giving people new or better jobs shows that you recognize their achievements and encourages them to achieve further success. Rewarding exceptional performance also inspires colleagues to improve their contribution in the workplace.

84 Encourage people to set their own high targets for performance.

▲ WILL DO – CAN DO
The employee who shows the standard of behaviour that you should always expect is a perfect candidate for promotion.

▲ WILL DO – CAN'T DO
The willing employee who experiences difficulties should respond positively to training and encouragement.

▲ WON'T DO – CAN DO
The unmotivated person is in danger of losing her job unless motivation can be raised.

▲ WON'T DO – CAN'T DO
The incompetent employee who is unwilling to improve should obviously not be retained.

CHOOSING STAFF FOR PROMOTION

A simple, effective way to promote people focuses on two main aspects. Are they able to do the work required? Are they willing to do the work? There are four possible combinations of staff attitude and ability. The willing and able person is the only one you should consider for promotion. At the other extreme, somebody who is neither able nor willing has no place in the organization, let alone on the promotion ladder. The people in-between, who are lacking in either motivation or ability, pose the real challenge to their managers. Motivating an unmotivated person is far more difficult than training a willing individual to perform better. The prospect of promotion, however, may push the unwilling person into trying harder.

THINGS TO DO

1. Prepare a clear and accurate job description.
2. Promote the person who best fits the job description, regardless of age.
3. Seek to promote an employee with a "will do – can do" attitude.
4. If there were other candidates, let them know why they were unsuccessful.
5. Ensure other staff members know the reasons why an employee was promoted.

PROMOTING THE RIGHT PEOPLE

In a traditional, hierarchical system, age comes before ability when people are selected for promotion. However, the diversity of skills in the modern workplace, and people's different aptitudes for them, means that this system is no longer appropriate. Avoid making promotions just because a person was successful in one job· they may not be suited to another. Others whose skills are more suited to the job may feel aggrieved, and the person being promoted will feel insecure. To get the best-qualified person for the job, start with an accurate job specification, and then match the skills and characteristics of the person to the job requirements. Let others know why you have chosen that particular person.

HANDLING DISMISSALS

Job losses are always traumatic and need to be handled sensitively. Whether dismissals are due to redundancies or individual performance problems, once you have made the decision to dismiss someone, implement it quickly. Delaying bad news is always counterproductive: rumours circulate and create anxiety. Set out the facts clearly in all cases of demotion or job loss, so that those affected can understand why the decisions need to be taken. Prepare yourself by considering objections, so that you can deal with them calmly. Be tactful and sympathetic, and as generous as possible with redundancy payment. In some cases you might consider counselling for those affected. You want those leaving to feel that they have been treated as fairly as possible, and you want to sustain the highest possible morale among your remaining staff.

85 Dismiss only as a last resort, and never fire just to set an example.

86 Be as generous as possible with all severance payments.

TURNING FAILURE INTO SUCCESS

When somebody fails on a project, always consider whether the failure can be turned into a success. Satisfy yourself that you will not be wasting time and money. Then, if there is a reasonable chance of saving the project and the person, take it.

87 Think before you give up on people or plans – giving up is irreversible.

ASSESSING FAILURE

Sometimes an employee does not complete a project successfully. Analyze these failures carefully. Perhaps you or the employee did not have all the necessary information or made false assumptions. Alternatively, if the assumptions were correct, they may have been invalidated by bad execution in which case, identify the mistakes and find out why they were made. The key question is whether, given the results of your research, you would assign another, similar project to the same person. Your answer will determine how best to deal with the employee so as to prevent future failures.

88 Consider cutting your losses rather than carrying on in vague hope.

▼ DISCUSSING PROBLEMS AT SOURCE
If an employee has failed on a particular project, you need to discuss the failure with them in detail. If the failure was due to a misunderstanding, for example, the project may be resurrected.

IMPROVING PERFORMANCE

To improve the productivity of an employee who is not performing to the required standard, first consider the factors responsible for this failure. If the person is lacking skills, arrange appropriate training immediately. For minor reasons, such as time-wasting, a verbal warning should be enough. If the reasons are more complex, such as chronic demotivation, consider a plan of action to measure improvement in their performance over a given period. Reassess the situation at the end of this time, and discuss the progress made.

89 There is usually a good reason why an employee is not performing well.

DEALING WITH POOR PERFORMANCE

FAILURE FACTORS	REMEDIAL ACTION
DEMOTIVATION Lacks motivation and energy to improve.	● Tackle the problem immediately. ● Find out possible reasons for drop in motivation. ● Base the improvement plan on a schedule of achievement.
LACK OF SKILLS Cannot cope with the technical demands of the job.	● Find out exactly which skills the employee is lacking. ● Arrange training sessions as soon as possible. ● Assign a person with more appropriate skills to the task.
PROCRASTINATION Finds excuses for not getting on with work.	● Break down the job into more manageable stages. ● Do not let the procrastinator overestimate the time required. ● If necessary, provide hands-on help to get the job started.
ABSENTEEISM Avoids work and dodges responsibility.	● Sternly emphasize the negative effects of absenteeism. ● Ensure that the employee feels an important part of a team. ● Consider if more flexible hours would reduce the problem.
HABITUAL LATENESS Is invariably late and always has an excuse.	● Let it be known that you are not interested in excuses. ● Try a counselling approach before disciplining the employee. ● See if peer pressure from other team members helps.
PERSONAL PROBLEMS Lets personal worries affect work.	● Concentrate on a person's performance, not their problems. ● Consider giving sick leave or reassigning duties. ● If necessary, advise the employee to seek professional help.

REMUNERATING EFFECTIVELY

The way you pay people forms an essential foundation for effective people management. Money is by no means the only motivator of people, but too little money demotivates powerfully, and financial reward remains a strong incentive.

90 Keep basic pay below top rates – use bonuses to give top incomes.

PAYING THE BASICS

The key question for pricing goods – "How much is the market prepared to pay?" – applies just as strongly to remuneration. Ask yourself what level of basic wages and salaries will attract, retain, and motivate people of the calibre that you require. Large companies take pains to discover competitive levels for basic pay, so that they can aim towards the upper limits for their industry. But you should not be concerned only with comparability. You want exceptional results, not comparable performance. Exceptional productivity will more than cover the extra pay. People want to feel fairly rewarded – but they naturally prefer to be rewarded very well.

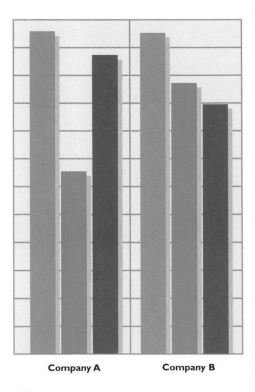

Company A   Company B

▶ INCREASING PAY WITH BETTER PRODUCTIVITY
Higher levels of efficiency allow you to pay your staff more. Even with fewer labour hours, company A managed to achieve the same level of productivity as company B, making higher rates of pay possible. Company A reached its productivity target thanks to the commitment and motivation of its staff.

KEY
▇ Productivity
▇ Labour hours
▇ Rates of pay

Paying by Results

The simplest form of payment by results (PBR) is piecework – the employee gets a fixed sum for each unit produced. In theory, this gives the employee the best incentive to maximize output. In fact, employees tend to put a ceiling on their earnings and thus on their effort, so this system has largely disappeared (especially now that more workers are in the information or service industries where piecework cannot be applied). The same principle – more pay for more production – still exists, however, in many forms. In sales, for example, commission can make up a very large proportion of total pay. In many cases, though, the PBR share of remuneration may be less than is necessary to add any real incentive – perhaps as low as five per cent. Constantly revise any kind of PBR system that you are involved with to ensure that you are not overpaying for output or getting less output than you require.

Test Your Payment Knowledge

Answer True or False to the following propositions:
1. Wages and associated expenses determine the cost of labour.
2. The cost of labour determines how competitive your business is.
3. The main way to motivate people is to give financial incentives.
4. The primary incentive for most people at work is money.

(None of these propositions is true.)

91 Always involve employees in pay scheme revisions.

92 Make it clear that extra pay is for special achievement.

93 Let team members decide how the team's bonus payment is divided.

Giving Bonuses

Regard bonus payments as ways for the employee to share in the company's success – not as incentives. Avoid giving all employees an automatic 13 months' pay: they will come to take the annual bonus for granted as part of their basic income. Bonus schemes can operate at any or all of three levels: company, team, and individual. Ideally, if the company does well, the individual gets a percentage addition to pay, and the same principle applies if his or her team (maybe a whole division) exceeds its targets. A bonus element tied to individual achievement alone must be reasonably large to be valued. Note the phrase "exceeds its targets": do not pay extra for what has been accepted as a sensible objective.

USING INCENTIVES

Non-cash incentives and fringe benefits can have a powerful influence on attitudes, which should in turn improve results. You can give employees the greatest incentive, however, by imparting a sense of ownership in the organization.

94 Use share schemes to reward people for contributing to team success.

95 Surprise people with gifts they do not expect.

96 Remember: giving people incentives of any kind sends a very positive signal.

SHARING THE SHARES

An employee who sees his or her efforts rewarded in company shares will, in theory, identify with the company, be committed to its success, and perform more effectively. In reality, it may be hard to tell whether the company's success is due to employees owning shares, or whether the success itself has led the company to issue shares. It is also difficult to know whether employees would have performed less effectively if no shares had changed hands. However, by giving people a stake in the company, you are making a highly positive statement about them, which encourages them to feel positive in return.

GIVING GIFTS

Expected remuneration has less impact than the unexpected. Even generous pay rises are taken for granted after a while, as salary aspirations increase accordingly. A far smaller "payment" – in the form of a gift – has a disproportionate worth in the eyes of the recipient. An employee could use a cash award to buy a gift (perhaps a weekend trip), but that provides less satisfaction than a payment in kind from you as reward for work well done. Presents are also a cost-effective method of motivating staff when cash is short or when competition does not allow an increase in pay.

QUESTIONS TO ASK YOURSELF

Q Have I ensured that rewards I have given are what people really want?

Q Am I acting to align the staff's interests with the goals and needs of the organization?

Q Do I always reward achievement and ability in preference to seniority?

Q Have I examined all possible ways of rewarding my staff?

OPTIMIZING BENEFITS

Fringe benefits have become much less effective financially in many countries because of tax changes. Good pension schemes, however, have become more attractive wherever state-funded provision has fallen. The same applies to medical insurance – the knowledge that the company cares for its people in sickness, health, and old age is a basic yet very powerful factor. Other benefits, such as company cars, paternity leave, education, and sabbaticals, improve the quality of people's lives. Electronic devices, from mobile telephones to computers, directly benefit the company, but the individual also gains personally from their availability. Ultimately, loyal and happy employees tend to work harder, leading to increased overall productivity.

▼ BENEFIT PACKAGES
Non-cash incentives, such as holidays, personal gifts, company cars, private medical insurance, help with children's education and care, and other benefits can greatly improve the way employees view and relate to the organization.

97 Make all welfare provisions as generous as possible.

98 Abolish status symbols that act in a divisive, "them and us" way.

ENDOWING STATUS

The modern company, with its flat structure, horizontal management, and open style, avoids status symbols that are divisive and counter-productive. Reserved parking places and separate dining rooms are rightly shunned. However, important-sounding job titles are an easy and economical way of providing recognition and psychological satisfaction. Moreover, outsiders like to deal with important people (although there is an obvious limit to the number of directors and vice-presidents you can appoint). Management can also confer status on those chosen to represent the company at prestigious events, such as conferences and key negotiations.

CREATING PARTNERSHIPS

When people feel that their own success and that of the company are linked, they will be motivated to give their personal best for the good of all. Value the opinions of staff as partners in the company, and treat them with the care you give clients.

99 Encourage people to work together as partners who help each other.

WORKERS AS PARTNERS

If a partnership is to work, you must treat employees like partners. Wherever possible, involve your staff in processes like decision-making and problem-solving to foster feelings of involvement and equality. Build a sense of community by providing opportunities to see how other departments within the organization operate. This will help everyone to relate to the company as a whole, and to understand the impact of their own contribution to its success. A shared vision is the strongest factor in the employee and organization partnership.

101 Make sure you let people know all the key facts about the business.

DO'S AND DON'TS

✔ Do enable your staff to understand the business.

✔ Do involve staff in decision-making.

✔ Do encourage staff to find partners to work with closely.

✘ Don't keep secrets that can safely be shared among staff.

✘ Don't leave staff in any doubt about future organization plans.

✘ Don't treat people as "cogs in a machine".

100 Value all your employees – they deserve the same treatment and respect as your customers.

WORKERS AS CUSTOMERS

Employees are valuable customers, and should be treated as such. They are customers in two senses. Firstly, they rely on management for their livelihoods, and secondly, they might be potential or actual buyers of the company's goods or services. Look after your own people as carefully as you would your best customers. Happy people who feel valued will outperform those who do not.

CASE STUDY

One of the major problems at Pro-Act Ltd, as with many firms, was that customer requests and enquiries were not passed on from department to department. The management felt that valuable feedback from the sales engineers' customer visits was being wasted, but was unsure how to resolve the matter. As part of a quality improvement exercise the issue was passed over to the engineers themselves for study and resolution. The engineers came up with the idea of a toll-free telephone line. If a customer asked them about a product other than the one they were selling, they could dial the free number, and a central desk would see that the enquiry reached the right place and monitor response. Sales increased, management was delighted, and the engineers were proud of their role.

◀ **PROCESSING FEEDBACK**

The case of Pro-Act highlights the significance of employee suggestions and the importance of acting on them. The toll-free telephone line scheme was adopted permanently and proved to be a major success. By adopting an employee-driven improvement scheme, Pro-Act both increased sales (and therefore profits for the company) and raised the morale and sense of partnership and belonging felt by the engineers.

ACTING ON SUGGESTIONS

THANKING PEOPLE ▼
Suggestion schemes provide just one way of making your employees feel that they are in partnership with you and the company. Failure to acknowledge or act on suggestions, however, will have a detrimental effect.

Formal suggestion schemes are an easy way for you to make your staff feel involved in the company. Employees are usually deeply knowledgeable about the business, and will have valuable ideas about ways in which it could improve operations. Process suggestions and ideas rapidly, and let people know the fate of their suggestion – preferably by a note signed by their most senior manager. The acceptance of ideas is often accompanied by a small bonus. However, it is healthier if people regard improving the business as part of their normal activity, and expect and get warm recognition for their ideas and contribution to the company's success, rather than financial rewards.

Senior manager gives warm thanks for a helpful suggestion

Employee feels part of a winning team

ASSESSING YOUR ABILITY

Your ability to manage people should improve with experience, but many of the basic requirements can be mastered from the beginning of your career. The following questionnaire covers the key elements in getting people to work with you and for you to your mutual satisfaction – and to the benefit of the organization. If your answer is "never", mark Option 1; if it is "always", mark Option 4, and so on. Use your answers to identify the areas that need most improvement.

OPTIONS
1 Never
2 Occasionally
3 Frequently
4 Always

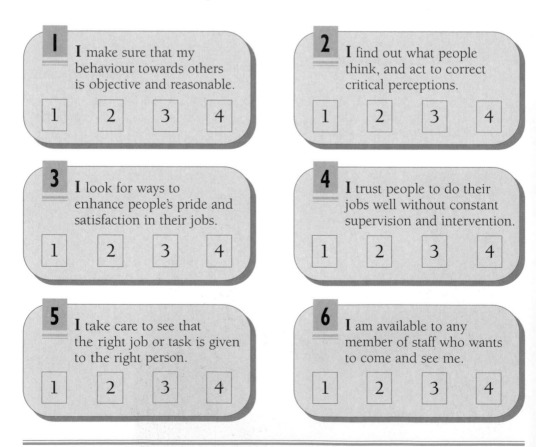

1 I make sure that my behaviour towards others is objective and reasonable.

1　2　3　4

2 I find out what people think, and act to correct critical perceptions.

1　2　3　4

3 I look for ways to enhance people's pride and satisfaction in their jobs.

1　2　3　4

4 I trust people to do their jobs well without constant supervision and intervention.

1　2　3　4

5 I take care to see that the right job or task is given to the right person.

1　2　3　4

6 I am available to any member of staff who wants to come and see me.

1　2　3　4

7 I prepare carefully for any meeting with individuals or with groups.

| 1 | 2 | 3 | 4 |

8 I involve people fully in plans for change and its implementation.

| 1 | 2 | 3 | 4 |

9 I rely on people's natural wish to do their work well, without orders.

| 1 | 2 | 3 | 4 |

10 I check to see that everybody is getting enough good-quality training.

| 1 | 2 | 3 | 4 |

11 I make a conscious effort to "talent-spot" among present and potential staff.

| 1 | 2 | 3 | 4 |

12 I discuss important issues with my people and ask for their opinions.

| 1 | 2 | 3 | 4 |

13 I motivate people with encouragement and example, rather than commands.

| 1 | 2 | 3 | 4 |

14 I welcome people's ideas for improvement, and implement good ones.

| 1 | 2 | 3 | 4 |

15 I ask for feedback on my performance from subordinates and peers.

| 1 | 2 | 3 | 4 |

16 I take opportunities to coach my people in ways to improve performance.

| 1 | 2 | 3 | 4 |

17 I give people the chance to demonstrate their management abilities.

1   2   3   4

18 I set high standards and insist that those standards are met.

1   2   3   4

19 I give people clear responsibility for a task that they can "own".

1   2   3   4

20 I form small groups or teams to tackle specific projects or needs.

1   2   3   4

21 I ask everybody in the team to come to a discussion with one or two new ideas.

1   2   3   4

22 I deal with people's personal problems swiftly and sympathetically.

1   2   3   4

23 I am prepared to listen to others and change my mind on issues.

1   2   3   4

24 I keep anger and other negative emotions out of my decisions and actions.

1   2   3   4

25 I try to understand the opposing point of view in cases of conflict.

1   2   3   4

26 I resolve interpersonal disputes quickly and without prejudice.

1   2   3   4

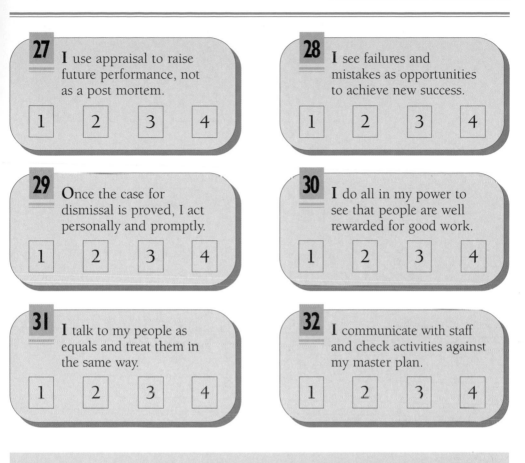

27 I use appraisal to raise future performance, not as a post mortem.

1 2 3 4

28 I see failures and mistakes as opportunities to achieve new success.

1 2 3 4

29 Once the case for dismissal is proved, I act personally and promptly.

1 2 3 4

30 I do all in my power to see that people are well rewarded for good work.

1 2 3 4

31 I talk to my people as equals and treat them in the same way.

1 2 3 4

32 I communicate with staff and check activities against my master plan.

1 2 3 4

ANALYSIS

Now that you have completed the self-assessment, add up the scores and check your performance by referring to the corresponding evaluations:

32–63: You are clearly having difficulties in dealing with people. The problems must be having a noticeable and unwelcome effect on your performance as well as your working environment. It is important to take action at once, probably with help from others, to begin badly needed improvement.

64–95: You are reasonably good with people but, in human relations at work, good is not enough. Use the questionnaire to identify your weaker areas, and work on them to get better results from yourself and others.

96–128: You should be pleased with your success with people, but remember that dealing with them is an on-going process that can always be improved on.

EFFECTIVE LEADERSHIP

INTRODUCTION

The key to truly effective leadership lies in mastering a wide range of skills, from implementing and administrating processes to inspiring others to achieve excellence. Effective Leadership shows you how to make the most of opportunities to learn to lead, whether by observing others, through formal training, or through careful evaluation of practical experience. It provides a thorough grounding in the essential techniques, and shows you how to put them into action in a variety of situations. With invaluable information on the key leadership skills, including communication, coaching, using authority, learning to delegate, and developing individuals and teams, as well as 101 practical tips, this book helps you to become an inspirational and confident leader, capable of heading an effective team. Two self-assessment exercises allow you to assess and improve your leadership ability.

LEARNING TO LEAD

Excellent leaders are made as well as born. To be the best, learn the essential skills of leadership through formal training courses and on-the-job experience.

FOCUSING ON QUALITY

The aim of leadership is to help others to achieve their personal best. This involves setting high but realistic performance goals for yourself and your staff, finding ways to improve operations and procedures, and striving for total quality in all areas.

> **1** Always strive to preach quality and practise improvement.

APPLYING STANDARDS ▼

Work closely with subordinates to set measurable quality standards that they can seek to achieve or exceed.

Leader discusses possible areas for improvement in standards of work

SETTING STANDARDS

Before you or your staff can achieve quality goals you need to be very clear about your own expectations regarding how things should be done and the standards of performance that must be reached. Once you have defined these expectations you can communicate them clearly to staff, emphasizing your own commitment and the fact that achieving excellence is everyone's responsibility.

RAISING STANDARDS

Maintaining and exceeding standards is an on-going process involving everyone. Encourage staff to analyze problem areas and to work together to find solutions. Involve them in looking for ways to improve products, processes, and performance, and, if extra skills are needed, arrange the necessary training. This approach not only generates ideas and innovation, but creates an atmosphere of participation and increased motivation, which in turn results in raised quality standards.

> **2** Ensure that you involve all staff members in quality-improving schemes.

IMPROVING STANDARDS OF QUALITY

TARGET STANDARDS	HOW TO ACHIEVE QUALITY
LEADERSHIP Lead your team towards total quality by constantly improving every process and product.	● Ensure that all staff drive towards continuous improvement in all aspects of performance. ● Recognize and appreciate individuals and teams for the success of their efforts.
STRATEGY Seek to uphold and develop the organization's vision, mission, values, and direction.	● Determine all objectives with the aim of reaching the highest quality standards. ● Communicate strategic aims clearly to everybody, and review and update them regularly.
PEOPLE Ensure that staff are motivated, well managed, and empowered to improve continuously.	● Train all staff in the skills and capabilities they need to meet their quality targets. ● Practise two-way communication, top-down and bottom-up, through all available media.
RESOURCES Aim to use financial and other resources efficiently to achieve the organization's objectives.	● Ensure money is managed efficiently and everyone understands what is happening financially and why. ● Use the best technology available and consistently update it to state-of-the-art levels.
PROCESSES Ensure that all vital processes, including management, are consistently highly effective.	● Develop performance measures and feedback to maintain the improvement momentum. ● Stimulate people to formulate innovative and creative ideas for improving processes.

LEARNING FROM OTHERS

*E**very successful singer has a singing coach, and top singers often give master-classes. The principle is just the same for leaders. You learn better leadership skills by being coached, and you develop those skills further by coaching others.***

IMPROVING SKILLS

Leaders must continually assess their performance and look for ways to improve and extend their skills. A great deal can be learned by simply observing others whose behaviour appears to get results. A mentor will provide informal guidance where needed, or you may choose a more formal avenue of learning, such as a training programme.

3 Always be on the look-out for chances to learn valuable lessons.

4 Take a refresher course if you feel you need to brush up on rusty skills.

Personnel director explains new trends

USING FORMAL TRAINING

Even leaders with years of on-the-job experience can benefit from some formal training from time to time. Outside training gives you an opportunity to get away from day-to-day activities, and provides a fresh perspective. Use training to keep abreast of current trends and to brush up on or acquire specific skills. Do not wait to be asked – assess your strengths and weaknesses and put yourself forward for courses that match your needs.

Leader gains an insight into how trends may affect the organization

◀ WIDENING KNOWLEDGE
Take advantage of colleagues' expertise in specific areas to broaden your own skills. You can learn a great deal from people with an in-depth knowledge of their field.

COACHING OTHERS

Training others provides a valuable source of education in the skills needed to become an effective leader, such as communicating clearly, giving instructions, getting feedback, delegating, motivating, and developing people. Always ask for feedback from those you are coaching – they can provide useful insights into your own performance. Share your experience and expertise with other people to help you to clarify your own attitudes, beliefs, and priorities, and to analyze your own performance. Use any time spent coaching your staff to discover their needs, what motivates them, and how they respond to your leadership style. Develop skills in other people to enable you to delegate some of your tasks, leaving more time available for you to spend on activities that will improve your own skills as a leader.

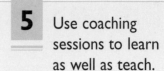

5 Use coaching sessions to learn as well as teach.

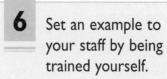

6 Set an example to your staff by being trained yourself.

▼ **RAISING STANDARDS**

Learn new skills, develop existing ones, and use your knowledge and experience to benefit colleagues. In this way, you will improve performance all-round.

Learn ➤ Coach ➤ Raise performance

BEING A ▶ GOOD COACH

Taking over the task that he had assigned to Jean seemed the easy option to Gordon. But he learned from this experience that he had avoided the important issue. He was looking at the problem in the short term, rather than focusing on helping Jean to improve her skills and perform better in future. He realized that training people was far more productive than doing everything himself.

CASE STUDY

Gordon asked Jean, one of his second-level managers, to produce a report that involved a degree of financial knowledge. He took it for granted that she understood the basics of management accounting, and was unpleasantly surprised to find that Jean had made many errors through ignorance. Since time was pressing, and since this was work that came easily to him, Gordon rewrote the report and passed it on. Jean asked for an interview. She was angry, and Gordon assumed that this was because he had taken over writing the report. But Jean was cross for a different reason. As she said, "How do you expect me to learn if you don't tell me what I've done wrong?". Gordon realized that he had failed Jean. He set aside time to coach her in management accounting, and also sent her on a course in finance.

GAINING EXPERIENCE

P romotion to leadership positions used to depend on rising up the company hierarchy. Now, vital work is increasingly carried out by temporary teams working on specific projects, which provide ideal opportunities for learning leadership skills.

> **7** Use projects as a way of learning more about other disciplines.

JOINING PROJECT TEAMS

Widen your knowledge and learn new skills by joining a project team. These are usually set up to work on new projects within an existing organization. Such teams can become permanent if the project takes off, and are independent of the vertical hierarchy. The longer the project lasts, the more likely it is that team membership and roles will change during the project's life. This means you can join a project in a subordinate position, but with the hope of finding a leadership role later. The larger the team, and the wider its remit, the greater the chance to change roles or be promoted within the team. Gaining experience on projects led by other people is also an invaluable education in how to lead your own project.

Subordinate is promoted to lead own team

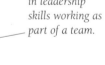

Subordinate gains experience in leadership skills working as part of a team.

◀ **LEARNING SKILLS ON PROJECT TEAMS**
Working on a project team can provide you with all the necessary experience to run your own team. Show your initiative and make the most of any opportunities that arise.

LEARNING FLEXIBILITY

The leadership of a project is often passed to different people at different stages. For example, it could move from the design department to the production staff to the marketing people, each passing on the baton in turn. This gives you the opportunity to learn crucial lessons in how to organize and collaborate with different functions and departments, from finance to sales, engineering to purchasing. Although the baton changes hands, everyone still works as part of a harmonious team at all times. The abilities to be flexible and to understand how other departments work are essential in leadership.

> **8** Make friends with people in different departments, and get to know how they operate.

BROADENING KNOWLEDGE

Use your experience in multidisciplinary project teams to broaden your general business skills. It is too easy to become and stay a specialist. The Japanese, for instance, believe that every manager should be a proper businessman or woman, able to lead any part of the business successfully. So a personnel head can move easily into sales, or a finance expert into marketing. Get to understand the principles of business and what part each component skill plays in achieving sales and profits. Broaden your knowledge by reading, and by establishing and nurturing contacts in different departments – such efforts will pay great dividends in future.

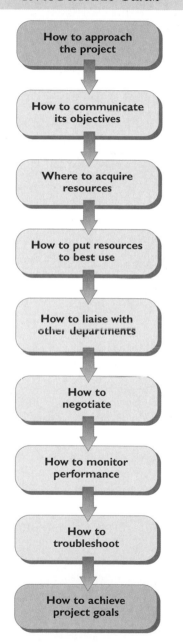

SKILLS TO BE LEARNED ON A PROJECT TEAM

How to approach the project

How to communicate its objectives

Where to acquire resources

How to put resources to best use

How to liaise with other departments

How to negotiate

How to monitor performance

How to troubleshoot

How to achieve project goals

MASTERING ROLES

Leadership is a multi-dimensional function, requiring knowledge and understanding of many organizational needs. As a leader, you must master the various roles that are required to handle different people and circumstances with skill and efficiency.

9 Think carefully about the best way to behave in every situation.

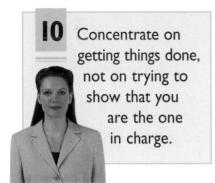

10 Concentrate on getting things done, not on trying to show that you are the one in charge.

TAKING THE OVERVIEW

A leader's role differs materially from that of a manager. While a manager must focus on implementing specific tasks, the leader must act as a grandmaster, a strategist, directing the game as a whole, and organizing the players. All leaders have different talents, and may be stronger in some skills than in others. To be successful you must be able to fill a number of roles, using a range of skills and leadership styles according to the task, the situation, and the people involved.

BEING AN ADMINISTRATOR

Administration is a key role of the leader, and nowadays there is much more to the role than simply "running a tight ship" on a predetermined course. The modern administrator is expected to be creative, devising processes and streamlining activities, not only to ensure the smooth running of procedures, but also to increase efficiency. To get the best from your team, set aside time to organize systems that will minimize time-wasting and improve productivity. Look for ways to reduce paperwork – direct communication is usually more effective. Liaise with other departments to ensure that everyone knows what is expected of them, and keep an open team diary for instant checks on current tasks and deadlines.

QUESTIONS TO ASK YOURSELF

Q Do I communicate directly with my team and also with other departments?

Q Am I sure that every member of the team understands his or her role fully?

Q Am I setting sufficiently ambitious goals?

Q Do I have procedures in place that allow me to check on team progress instantly?

Q Am I constantly looking for new ways to improve efficiency and productivity?

COMPARING LEADERS AND MANAGERS

LEADERS	MANAGERS
Administer	Implement
Originate	Copy
Develop	Maintain
Inspire trust	Control
Think long term	Think short term
Ask what and why	Ask how and when
Watch the horizon	Watch bottom line
Challenge status quo	Accept status quo
Are their own people	Are good soldiers
Do the right thing	Do things right

BECOMING A STRATEGIST

As a leader you need to focus on the wider issues that may affect your team's effectiveness, as well as the day-to-day business of getting things done. With your team, plan what you want to achieve in a given time, and break this down into attainable goals and objectives, ensuring that everyone is aware of their responsibilities. Unexpected problems may require adjustments to elements of the plan, so always leave plenty of room for revision.

11 Keep a checklist of key leadership duties and ensure that you do them.

Promoter of change

Administrator

Communicator

Expert

Strategist

12 Always look beyond the detail and consider the bigger picture.

◀ **FULFILLING KEY ROLES**
A leader must be a good communicator who cares for staff; an expert who is knowledgeable in his or her field; a strategist who looks to the future; an administrator who gets things done; and a proponent of change.

PROMOTING CHANGE

Change is vital for success in the future. By seeking to lead change, you are helping your organization to remain competitive and grow, and creating opportunities for individuals to enrich their careers and personal lives. Dare to be different – if everyone in your industry is stuck in the same pattern, search for changes that will be welcomed by customers and that will enable you to stand out. Encourage staff to generate ideas for change, and involve your team in the planning and implementation of change programmes.

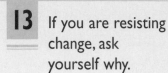

13 If you are resisting change, ask yourself why.

▼ **INSTIGATING CHANGE**
To ensure minimum disruption, communicate every aspect of a change to those concerned as soon as possible. Stress the positive aspects of the change, and gain commitment from others through your own dedication to the project.

| Communicate | Reassure | Stand firm |

FOCUSING ON PEOPLE

Leader suggests a training course to help team members improve skills

The effective management of others is paramount to success. As a leader you must be, and be seen to be, a people person who has the best interests of staff, as well as the organization, at heart. Seek to develop a climate of openness in which people are not afraid to express their opinions and share their ideas with you. Constantly encourage them to adopt the values and behaviour that help the team and the organization to reach its goals. Above all, ensure that your people get the training they need to achieve their maximum potential.

◄ **BEING AN EXPERT**
As leader, you should possess an in-depth knowledge of your chosen field. Ensure that your staff have all the technical skills needed to enable them to perform effectively.

EVALUATING KEY LEADERSHIP ROLES

KEY ROLES	HOW TO FULFIL THEM
EXPERT Has in-depth understanding of his/her field.	● Strive for the best possible performance, and increase your knowledge in your specific field. ● Use your expertise to improve technical performance and technological strength in key areas.
ADMINISTRATOR Ensures the smooth running of operations.	● Cut down on paperwork, and devise progressive systems to increase efficiency. ● Set rules, systems, boundaries, and values in order to ensure effective control.
PEOPLE PERSON Makes staff and their training a top priority.	● Believe and act on the principle that success flows from the effective management of others. ● Seek to develop a climate of openness, and work with, and for, everybody equally.
STRATEGIST Thinks long term and looks to the future.	● Always ensure that you plan ahead, devising strategies and goals for future success. ● Concentrate systematically on where the organization needs to go and how it will get there.
CHANGE AGENT Uses change as a key to progress and advancement.	● Be adventurous, and endeavour to focus on enterprise and initiative rather than control. ● Seek to lead change, and actively encourage the generation of new ideas in others.

USING DIFFERENT STYLES

There are many different leadership styles, and to be truly effective in any given situation, you should not only be aware of them all, but able to use elements of each simultaneously. For example, while managing and developing people, you still need to keep your eye on the strategic future at all times. If you are implementing a major change programme, do not neglect your administrative duties or you run the risk of being unable to implement the changes effectively.

14 The greater your expertise, the more authority you will have.

DEVELOPING STRENGTHS

All the attributes that you will require as a leader can be developed, even drive and energy. Self-confidence and self-determination, combined with an ability to manage people and money, will make you a strong leader able to attain your targets.

15 Always work on and build upon your own strengths.

SETTING HIGH GOALS

You cannot hope to achieve without the self-confidence to take risks, which should be carefully calculated, on paper, to ensure that they are acceptable. This will enhance your ability to form high but realistic and achievable goals. Evaluation on paper helps put you in control of your own destiny, and will aid long-term vision of your own future and that of the business.

16 Put all your ambitions down on paper to help you realize them.

17 Understand what you are doing in order to achieve your aims.

ELIMINATING WEAKNESSES

Facing up to your own mistakes and weaknesses is the first step towards eliminating them and raising your leadership ability. You may need help from a mentor, as well as feedback from your people. List aspects of your people management that are unsatisfactory, and work out how to improve them. Ultimate success means getting others to work with you and for you productively.

MASTERING FIGURES

Some leaders are uncomfortable with money. If this applies to you, make sure you take a course. No sensible employer will refuse to pay for this education. There is no substitute, though, for sitting down and working out the figures of a real business, and seeing in real life how reality is reflected and portrayed by the numbers.

18 Never accept any weakness as one that you cannot correct and cure.

BUILDING PERSONAL STRENGTHS

STRENGTHS	HOW TO DEVELOP THEM
DRIVE AND ENERGY The ability to put maximum mental and physical effort behind reaching objectives and to keep going until the aims are achieved.	● Keep physically fit. Join a gym or take up a competitive sport. ● Constantly work through lists of tasks and ensure their completion.
SELF-CONFIDENCE A belief in your ability to carry out self-appointed and other tasks to your satisfaction and that of colleagues.	● Learn to calculate and accept moderate risks. ● Review your work at frequent intervals, comparing plans with outcomes.
MONEY MANAGEMENT Knowing how to read balance sheets, draw up budgets and management accounts, and track paths to higher profits.	● Acquire good training in financial basics – attend a course if necessary. ● Always work out financial consequences of plans and decisions in detail.
MANAGING PEOPLE Understanding how to get the best from your staff, and encouraging them to use their initiative to achieve better results.	● Ask regularly for feedback from your superiors, peers, and subordinates. ● Learn to look at situations through other people's eyes.
GOAL-SETTING Knowing how to set targets that are high enough to stimulate exceptional effort, but are still within achievement range.	● "Benchmark" organizations in your own and other industries to see where and what improvements can be made. ● List your goals and keep reassessing them.
SELF-DETERMINATION The belief that your destiny and that of the business are in your hands, not subject to others or outside forces.	● Form long-range aims for yourself and the organization. ● Put your aims down on paper, complete with plans for implementation.
SELF-EVALUATION The ability to recognize and learn from mistakes and failures, while also analyzing the lessons of success.	● Conduct regular, honest examinations of recent decisions and actions. ● If you discover any weaknesses, draw up plans for rectifying them.
COMPETITIVENESS The will to win, and to take defeat as a challenge, not a disaster, coupled with the pursuit of high personal standards.	● Take every opportunity to study winners, corporate and individual. ● Adopt, adapt, and apply the techniques or qualities that make winners successful.

ASSESSING YOUR LEADERSHIP POTENTIAL

*E*valuate how well you measure up as a prospective leader by responding to the following statements, and mark the options closest to your experience. If your answer is "never", mark Option 1; if it is "always", mark Option 4; and so on. Add your scores together, and refer to the Analysis to see how well you fared. Use your answers to identify the areas that most need improvement.

OPTIONS
1 Never
2 Occasionally
3 Frequently
4 Always

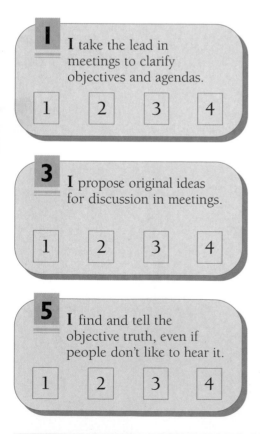

1 I take the lead in meetings to clarify objectives and agendas.

1   2   3   4

2 I focus strongly on achieving results from the tasks I undertake.

1   2   3   4

3 I propose original ideas for discussion in meetings.

1   2   3   4

4 I make friends easily and have many useful outside contacts.

1   2   3   4

5 I find and tell the objective truth, even if people don't like to hear it.

1   2   3   4

6 I maintain friendly relations with everyone on the team.

1   2   3   4

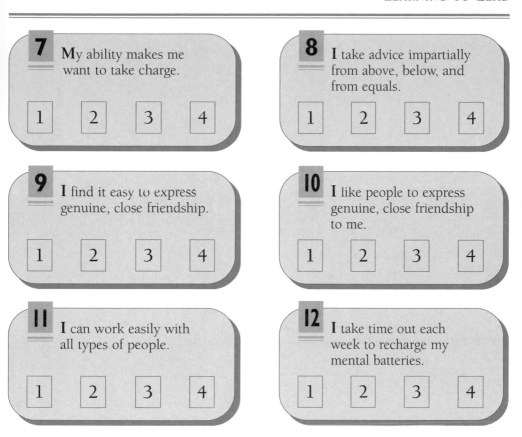

7 My ability makes me want to take charge.

1   2   3   4

8 I take advice impartially from above, below, and from equals.

1   2   3   4

9 I find it easy to express genuine, close friendship.

1   2   3   4

10 I like people to express genuine, close friendship to me.

1   2   3   4

11 I can work easily with all types of people.

1   2   3   4

12 I take time out each week to recharge my mental batteries.

1   2   3   4

ANALYSIS

Now that you have completed the self-assessment, add up your total score, and check your ability by reading the corresponding evaluation. However great your potential as a leader may be, remember that there is always room for improvement. Identify your weakest areas, and refer to the relevant sections in this book, where you will find practical advice and tips to help you understand what it takes to lead others and improve your leadership skills.

12–24: You are potentially competent, but you need to do a lot of work before you can excel in a leadership role.

25–36: Although you have the makings of a good leader, some areas still need to be improved. Identify and work on them.

37–48: Your leadership promise is high, but do not become complacent. Strive to realize it.

LEADING OTHERS

How well you lead others is the prime factor in your team's success. To be an effective leader, you must facilitate, inspire, and implement, rather than control.

PREPARING TO LEAD

Leading others is a stimulating challenge for any leader. Get to know the people who are working for you, establish a framework in which everyone can operate comfortably, and set challenging goals that will motivate and inspire.

19 Take time to get your bearings in a new job – but do not take too long.

QUESTIONS TO ASK YOURSELF

Q What are we trying to achieve?

Q In what ways are we trying to achieve it?

Q What major issues do we face?

Q What do others think of the organization – good and bad?

Q Are we properly organized to achieve what we want in the way we want?

GATHERING INFORMATION

Your first priority as a leader, especially if you happen to be taking over a new situation, is to find out what you have, in terms of people, policies, problems, and opportunities. An excellent approach is to go round either all the people, or (in a larger organization) the key ones, and find out their views by asking questions. Discover what they think about the organization and what they are trying to achieve. Not only will you learn a great deal about your new responsibility, but the response to your questions will also teach you a great deal about the people concerned.

ESTABLISHING A FRAMEWORK

Every leader must think about the framework in which the leader and the led can operate effectively and comfortably, both as individuals and as part of a team. Ensure that there are systems in place that enable good, open communication between you and your staff. Be clear about the roles of each team member, and make sure that everyone is aware of their responsibilities.

DO'S AND DON'TS

☑ Do use all means to communicate with your staff.

☑ Do strive to regard your associates as competent people.

☑ Do try to create a positive atmosphere, free from rigidity.

☑ Do show your staff loyalty and support.

☑ Do set challenging, ambitious goals.

☒ Don't ask people to do things that you wouldn't do yourself.

☒ Don't forget that trust is a two-way process that can take time and effort to establish.

☒ Don't take sides or show any favouritism.

☒ Don't dissuade staff from speaking out.

☒ Don't be vague about team members' roles.

---

20 Actively seek the views of your team members.

ESTABLISHING OBJECTIVES

A leader must always be aware of the ultimate goals of the organization, and know how their own objectives fit in with them. Once these goals have been established, you must ensure that your team understands the direction in which they are heading and why, and the purpose of their own activities within the overall plan. The ultimate objective should be broken down into attainable, yet challenging goals that ideally will be inspiring and motivating for the whole team. Aims should also relate directly to the specific skills of each individual within the team. Working together towards a shared goal gives people a sense of ownership and responsibility, and builds an atmosphere of team spirit.

Leader meets with colleague personally to obtain feedback

◄ **TALKING TO STAFF**
The leader should talk to colleagues personally in order to discover their views. This results in useful feedback that will help the team to work more effectively.

FORMING A TEAM

*E*stablishing a team or appointing new team members is the responsibility of the leader. Find the best candidates to form a balanced and dynamic team, either through internal promotion or external recruitment, and help them to feel part of the team.

21 Avoid appointing a candidate simply because you are short-staffed.

22 When recruiting team members, look for their growth potential.

FINDING CANDIDATES

Cast the widest possible net, and spend as much time as needed on the selection process. Draw up a list of criteria, essential characteristics, and skills that the appointee must have. Make sure that the criteria are relevant. A common mistake is to insist on "industry experience", when research shows that it bears little relationship to success in the job. Candidates who fulfil all your criteria will be rare, so be prepared to be flexible at the selection stage.

▼ **RECRUITING STAFF**
There are many channels for recruiting people, and all of them should be explored. However, personal contacts are most likely to succeed.

Advertise in relevant press for applicants

Recruit from within your organization

Approach local colleges for new recruits

Ask friends and colleagues for suggestions

Recruit from government training schemes

Commission an agency to find best candidates

PROMOTING INSIDERS

Internal promotion is not only cheaper, but tells everybody that they have the opportunity to rise, which is the most satisfying form of reward. Leaders should constantly be on the look-out for abilities that can be exploited in higher-level teams. When recruiting internally, give consideration to the morale of other staff, who may feel that they have been passed over. Explain clearly to all concerned why the person that you selected is right for this assignment, and emphasize that there will be other opportunities. Then allow your candidate to prove you right.

BALANCING SKILLS

For any team to function effectively, there must be a balance of technical, problem-solving, decision-making, and interpersonal skills among its members. The ideal group will be creative yet disciplined, able to generate new ideas and find solutions to difficulties, and, at the same time, organized enough to plan and implement a task within a given timescale.

23 Take into account the feelings of staff when promoting internally.

Leader announces that staff member has been promoted

Newly promoted member of team seeks colleague's support

Employee congratulates colleague on appointment

MAKING AN INTERNAL ▶ APPOINTMENT
Announce the appointment to staff and ensure that they understand your reasons for selecting the candidate.

24 When a referee has reservations, always probe more deeply.

25 Ask candidates what they did really well in their previous jobs.

26 Ensure there are no interruptions during interviews.

CONDUCTING INTERVIEWS

Allow 45 minutes for an interview, preferably with one colleague, or at most, two, joining in. Keep your own talking to a minimum. You want the candidate to say as much as possible about their understanding of the job, your company, their past performance. What did they do best? You are interested in their strengths first, weaknesses second. Observe them carefully, taking into account body language and appearance.

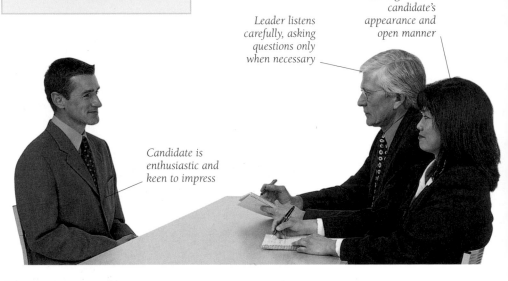

Colleague notes candidate's appearance and open manner

Leader listens carefully, asking questions only when necessary

Candidate is enthusiastic and keen to impress

JUDGING SUITABILITY

Psychometric tests and handwriting analysis (graphology) are sometimes used to evaluate candidates' suitability. But these methods are no substitute for personal judgment, reinforced by the person's track record and references, and by any appropriate skill tests. Conflicts and rivalry within groups are counterproductive, so avoid candidates who display a degree of personal assertiveness that may fracture the team spirit.

▲ ASSESSING A CANDIDATE

Observe the candidate carefully. Keep your checklist of attributes and skills in front of you, and make sure that you address them all. Above all, do not ignore your intuition or your personal reaction – it is very important that you actually like the candidate. Ask yourself whether the candidate seems "nice" and if he or she will fit in.

LEARNING FROM RECRUITS

A leader can learn a great deal from new recruits by exploiting their knowledge of other organizations, methods, or ideas. They have the advantage of an outsider's eye, before being assimilated into your company's ways. Make time for conversations with recruits, asking them for their first impressions. Acting on their suggestions is an important way of promoting their confidence.

27 See that new recruits are welcomed and fully supported.

"Nursemaid" colleague sits in on meeting

Leader asks recruit for her impressions of the company

EASING IN ▶ RECRUITS
Help new employees to learn about their new environment and master the work by appointing a suitable colleague to act as "nursemaid" while they settle in.

QUESTIONS TO ASK YOURSELF

Q What did I do wrong – did I recruit poorly?

Q Did the person lack the necessary support?

Q Have circumstances changed so that the person no longer fits the original job?

Q Is there another job in which they could succeed?

HANDLING MISFITS

Recruitment failures will inevitably occur, however much trouble has been taken. Whenever you contemplate dismissing somebody, always ask yourself "why has this happened?". Learn from your analysis, and if the person can be "saved" by making changes, make them. If not, do not allow the person to stay after you have, consciously or subconsciously, decided against it. Explain your reasons fully to the individual, and be as generous as possible in negotiating severance. Also, ensure that co-workers know what has happened and why.

EXERCISING AUTHORITY

The role of a leader is to ensure that everyone understands instructions and carries them out effectively. Since it is rare for everything to go according to plan, put into place reporting systems that enable you to deal with any deviations swiftly.

28 Make sure that any instructions you give are clear and concise.

29 Encourage people to approach you if things go wrong.

30 Act quickly when you learn of any real problems.

GIVING INSTRUCTIONS

The method of giving instructions matters far less than the quality of their content. If a decision has been reached in concert with the team, the leader has no need to win acceptance. But having to say "This is an order" is a sign of malfunction on one side or the other. Before you issue instructions, be absolutely clear in your own mind what your requirements are. This will be reflected in your tone of voice and body language and will reinforce your message. Ask people if they have any reservations about what you have asked of them, so that problems can be cleared up at the outset.

MANAGING BY EXCEPTION

Leaders often spend too much time double-checking everything to ensure conformance with instructions and procedures. The better approach is to manage by exception, which involves concentrating on what is going awry rather than what is not. You should not expect to hear about actions that proceed as planned, but staff or delegates should inform you immediately if there is a serious deviation from the plan. For example, if a sales executive is asked to handle key accounts, and sales targets or profit margins are being missed, he or she must report the problem to you at once.

Marketing director reports that the month's sales of an important product have fallen substantially

BEING CONSISTENT

Since leadership is about getting other people to do what you want, it is essential to maintain the co-operation and respect of your staff. Be consistent in the way you exercise authority, so that people can trust you and know that you mean what you say. This avoids ambiguity, and the danger of ill-feeling or resentment developing is reduced. Being consistent does not mean being overindulgent towards staff – as long as you are always honest, direct, and fair in your dealings with other people, they will respond positively to your authority, even under difficult or stressful circumstances.

31 Insist that staff tell you all the news, good or bad.

32 Use crises as an opportunity to develop people.

Leader asks production boss to report capacity bottlenecks in future

A plan is devised to divert unused capacity for another product, and to raise output to meet the unsatisfied demand

Leader is told that shortfall is caused by lack of capacity

Leader discovers that production is down. He calls in production boss

▲ **ORGANIZING CONTROLS**
By putting into place a new reporting system, the leader ensures that, in future, he will be aware of any production problems before they affect sales.

DELEGATING TASKS

As leader, you should concentrate your time on activities that nobody else can do. Delegation is a form of time management. It is a way of exercising control and meeting your own responsibilities more effectively, while developing the skills of your staff.

33 Remember that delegation boosts morale and builds confidence.

34 Never keep work simply because you do it better.

35 Set high targets in agreement with your delegates.

INCREASING YOUR TIME

Managers often claim that the demands of operational and routine duties leave them little time to concentrate on important, long-term matters, such as strategic planning and training. To create more time for yourself, it is essential to hand down more routine tasks by delegation. Even if you, the leader, are better and faster at a task than anybody else in the team, the golden rule is that you should not, and cannot, do everything yourself. Leadership involves handing over the task to others, and then helping them to match or exceed your standards.

BRIEFING DELEGATES

Give the delegate a clear, written brief, developed in consultation, that sets out the objectives, the resources available, the constraints, and the time schedule, if relevant. Supplement the written brief with an interview to ensure mutual understanding. If the circumstances change, alter the brief to suit – do not stick to it slavishly.

Delegate seeks clarification on unclear points

Leader asks delegate to summarize key points of brief

EXPLAINING THE BRIEF ▶
Make sure that the delegate fully understands the assignment by asking relevant questions at a face-to-face meeting. Invite the delegate to do the same.

SUPERVISING EFFECTIVELY

Allow the delegate to develop and execute his or her plans, subject only to keeping you fully informed. Constant interference, countermanding decisions and actions taken by the delegate, and checking up continually all add up to poor leadership. By intervening heavily, you will also frustrate the delegate and deny him or her the chance to learn new skills and gain experience. Monitor the progress of the work with a system of written reports and face-to-face meetings with the delegate, and by observing performance.

36 If time pressure increases, ask if you are delegating enough to others.

37 Check regularly and informally on progress of delegated tasks.

REINFORCING A DELEGATE'S ROLE ▼

Always introduce a new delegate to existing team members, as this will help him or her to feel part of the team. It is also important to inform any customers or suppliers who need to know what specific responsibilities the new delegate will have.

New delegate made to feel welcome

Leader introduces new delegate and clearly states her responsibilities

Team member understands new delegate's role within team

RETAINING TASKS

There are some responsibilities that a leader cannot delegate. These include key areas, such as controlling overall performance, meeting strategic objectives, and confidential human resources matters – how people are rewarded, appraised, promoted, informed, disciplined, coached, and counselled. You may also need to supervise dealings with important customers if delegating ultimate responsibility for these contacts would endanger the relationship.

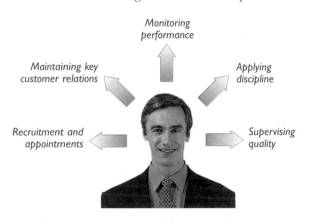

Monitoring performance

Maintaining key customer relations

Applying discipline

Recruitment and appointments

Supervising quality

◀ **KEEPING KEY TASKS**
As a leader, you must keep charge of sensitive matters, such as applying discipline and making appointments, and retain control of important areas, including finance and strategy.

38 Keep an open door for all your delegates.

39 Intervene fast when the delegate cannot cope.

PROVIDING SUPPORT

An open-door policy aids effective delegation. The delegate should be able to approach the delegator at any time for advice, information, or revision. The delegator should also be able to approach the delegate, whenever necessary, for an informal, encouraging discussion on how the task is going. If the delegator visits too often, either this is bad delegation, or the delegation is going badly. If delegates come through the door too often, they are either insecure or inadequate. If you are confident in their ability, give them a clear message: "I am confident that you can manage."

CHECKING PROGRESS WITH DELEGATES

When discussing progress with delegates, use positive questions, such as those below, that will encourage delegates to suggest their own solutions to problems. Avoid questions that may discourage or demoralize the delegate.

" Is there anything you want to bring to my notice? "

" We failed to meet that target. Any suggestions as to how that might have happened? "

" I see that costs are over-running. What steps are you taking to bring them back in line? "

" How do you think we can avoid making this mistake again? "

DEVELOPING DELEGATES

Look out for signs that the delegate is taking too much on his or her own shoulders, and not allowing people who work for them to show initiative and tackle their own tasks without interference. "Getting out of the way" is the key to getting the best from others, and applies to the delegate too. Encourage delegates to think issues through and come up with answers to problems before bringing them to you. The most important lesson for the delegate is that of being accountable for results, with no opportunity for excuses.

40 Make sure that everybody knows what must always be left to you.

◀ ENCOURAGING SOLUTIONS

Being a good delegator, the leader in this case did not want his people to become dependent on him and his decisions. So he forced them to make up their own minds. The boss was still prepared to discuss the issue, but his insistence helped this subordinate to be a real leader.

CASE HISTORY

John was working for a new boss in a new company and a new country. He was given the task of organizing a new project team, complete with an excellent brief. But problems arose. With existing resources, there was no hope of meeting the production targets from internal supply, as ordered. He went back to his American boss, Chuck, with the problem – and was disconcerted by the response.

"I don't want people bringing me problems without solutions", said Chuck. "I want two solutions every time, with your recommendation on which one to take. If you ever bust in here without the two solutions, you'll leave the office a damn sight faster than you came in". John went away and returned with two solutions: sub-contract some of the work, or ask for more finance and people. He preferred the first, and so did Chuck.

COMMUNICATING CLEARLY

The ability to communicate with staff is essential in leadership. To ensure that messages are received and understood all the way down, flatten the hierarchy of your team structure. To keep communication two-way, invite feedback from your staff.

41 Talk honestly with your staff and you will get honest answers in return.

42 Take steps to get accurate reports of team opinions.

COMMUNICATING DIRECTLY

The leader at the apex of the pyramid hierarchy passes down information and instructions, level by level, throughout the team. The trouble with this top-down management style is that you cannot always be sure that your message has got through, or how it has been received, since there is little feedback from the lower levels. Wherever possible, deliver your message in person to ensure that it has been clearly understood by the recipient.

▼ **FLATTENING THE HIERARCHY**
You need only three levels of hierarchy and four types of staff. Leaders work in concert with managers, while staff take charge of their own output. All three levels are assisted by experts, such as information technology specialists.

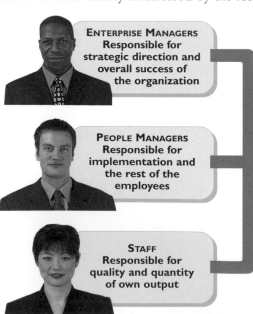

ENTERPRISE MANAGERS
Responsible for strategic direction and overall success of the organization

PEOPLE MANAGERS
Responsible for implementation and the rest of the employees

STAFF
Responsible for quality and quantity of own output

EXPERTS
Responsible for specific areas, such as finance and technologies, etc.

COMMUNICATING ON ALL LEVELS

To ensure that the right message has been received and the right action taken, the top-down process needs to be checked by bottom-up communication. Spend as much time as possible with all levels of staff, and make it clear that you appreciate feedback and are willing to listen and respond. Remember that excellent ideas can come from anywhere, and are not just confined to leaders. Make use of the fact that other people know their own area of work, and can make an invaluable contribution to related issues.

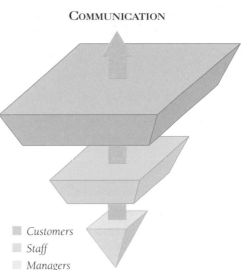

- Customers
- Staff
- Managers

43 If all feedback is positive, you may not have been told the whole truth.

44 Be prepared for misunderstanding of what you are trying to achieve.

▲ INVERTING THE PYRAMID

Some leaders mentally balance the pyramid on its point to reverse the direction of the flow of information. Customers and their needs are put on top, followed by the employees, then the managers.

LISTENING TO STAFF

Encourage people to be open and honest with you by showing that you value their opinions and are willing to listen to them. The best way to do this is through informal conversations, either one-to-one or with groups of staff. Make it clear that even negative feedback is viewed as a positive opportunity for improvement. You must ensure that staff are not intimidated by fear of any repercussions when they express criticisms. Do not always wait for staff to come to you – solicit feedback from them by asking for their comments on issues that affect them. If you want to gain a broad picture of staff attitudes, you will have to use a more formal approach. Many techniques are available, such as surveys, sample polling, suggestion boxes, or focus groups.

DYNAMIZING GROUPS

To dynamize a group, you must give it strong purpose, strong membership, and strong leadership. Use "hot groups" for special operations, choosing the ablest and most motivated candidates for the group. Encourage innovation and creativity.

45 Encourage groups to achieve by setting high but realistic targets.

IMPARTING PURPOSE

A group of people striving towards a common goal should be highly motivated, with a strong sense of excitement and anticipation. The way that you, as leader, convey the purpose of the task to your group can help to instil this positive attitude. Emphasize the fact that the group has been put together for a specific purpose, and that the particular skills of each individual member are fundamental to the success of the project. This helps people to identify with the organization's goals, and empowers them to use their creativity.

ROUSING THE TROOPS

Talking to a group as a unit provides an essential test of leadership quality. Be positive and enthusiastic – your energy will inspire confidence and encourage your group to follow your example. While it is important to put across your personality, policies, and objectives, you should also reinforce group identity by providing plenty of opportunities for discussion and debate. Be firm about your expectations, but remember that enjoyment is a key motivator.

Team member provides update on progress and invites comment

Team member reminds team of what is still to be done

STAYING FOCUSED ▶
Hold regular meetings to inform everyone of what has been achieved and how much more needs to be done. Use these times to reinforce motivation and purpose.

FORMING HOT GROUPS

Nothing is more exciting in management than leading a "hot group", a team assembled for a special operation, such as a new product launch. Success requires finding the ablest people and placing them under highly motivated, effective leadership (which encourages sub-leadership). The group continues to recruit talent as a key activity, concentrating on people who are right for each job and can share a powerful vision. It helps to detach the group from all other operations, and to focus change on a chosen rival: "the enemy".

Team member suggests ways of completing tasks

Leader keeps group focused on main task

BRIEFING HOT GROUPS
Introduce the subject (and yourself, if appropriate)
↓
Announce the objective
↓
Express confidence in the people present
↓
Emphasize group/team working
↓
Look forwards, not backwards
↓
Put across your authority
↓
Express confidence in the group's ability
↓
Banish doubt and doubters
↓
Emphasize that efforts will be fully supported

COLLEGIATE LEADERSHIP

*A*re you a *"man on horseback" or a first*
among equals? The first kind of leader is
the military model; the second is the collegiate
model. The collegiate style is increasingly
winning out, since it promotes a sense of unity
and motivation within a company.

46 Always be ready
to allow others
to take the lead
when appropriate.

47 Remember that
everyone in a
team thinks in a
different way.

LEADING AS AN EQUAL

The first-among-equals model is formalized in
German business, where the chief executive is
called the "spokesman" of the management board.
The reason why this approach is spreading is
because many minds are more powerful than one.
Create a pool of shared talent and an environment
of total communication, and consult all team
members before an important decision is made.
Even in small firms, the range of expertise
required has expanded greatly, probably beyond
the reach of one individual. At particular stages,
moreover, one of your experts should have the
decisive voice by virtue of his or her expertise.

MEETING AS EQUALS ▼
Working with genuine colleagues
demands the same behaviour whether or
not you are the leader. Respect goes to
expertise, not to rank or seniority.
Do not engage in internal politics but
focus on what will achieve the group's
objectives, in the knowledge that
everybody benefits from a job well done.

Expert gives technical
assessment of issue

Colleague evaluates
specialist information

Leader invites expert
to give her opinion

Team member checks anger and lowers his voice

Leader calms down both parties

Colleague begins to feel less distressed

HANDLING ▶
DISPUTES
When colleagues seriously disagree, you should intervene to discover what is at issue. No matter what the provocation, never lose your temper. Anger is a bad adviser.

RESOLVING DIFFICULTIES

Even successful partnerships can develop disagreements. When resolving an issue, whether involving yourself or between colleagues, try to analyze the situation calmly. Start with the team's objective. Is it shared by the combatants? If so, what factual points are at issue? If they can be resolved, what are the emotional problems that are preventing agreement? You may conclude that one of the parties, or perhaps both, is intransigent and has lost sight of the aims. If you cannot persuade them to alter their attitude, they will have to leave the team.

48 Seek to defuse emotion before tackling issues.

49 Treating everyone equally will avoid causing resentment.

SEEKING THE ▶
BEST OUTCOME
The leader in this case faced a real conflict between valued members of staff. It was important not to take sides, and to see that the best solution for the company was found. Involving another member of the team got to the real issue, and the leader was able to bring this out into the open and make a clear decision.

CASE STUDY
Roger, in charge of distribution, and Ann, customer services manager, put forward two rival plans for reorganizing the marketing department. Neither would accept the other's arguments. Their boss, Barry, asked Norman, manager of new product development and an excellent analyst, to examine the two plans. The report came down strongly in favour of Ann's scheme. Confronted with the choice, Roger still refused to agree: the reorganization would mean that he reported to Ann, and he did not want to work for a woman. Barry confronted him with this blockage and gave him a choice: accept or leave. Roger argued that his plan had been unfairly treated. Barry brought Norman into the meeting and asked him to give his reasons. Reluctantly, Roger accepted the logic and stayed.

IMPROVING YOUR EFFECTIVENESS

There are many different ways of leading. But for the greatest success and impact, you need to work on upgrading and extending your basic skills.

MAKING DECISIONS

All decisions involve a series of other decisions, notably when to settle the issue, who else to involve in the decision-making process, and what alternatives to consider. Get these decisions right and you will be able to make the correct move.

> **50** If decisions can safely be taken quickly, always do so at once.

TIMING DECISIONS

What kind of decision do you face? Time is the starting point. Does your decision have to be made immediately; by a later deadline; at your discretion; or never? Taking no decision is a decision in itself, and possibly a fateful one. If you take no action, the time may come when an urgent decision is demanded, but it may be too late to undo the damage caused by inaction. Usually, the sooner a decision is taken, the better. Even if you do not know what to do, always avoid procrastination. Seek guidance from a trusted colleague, or superior, then decide on the best course of action.

Colleague expresses his opinions freely

CONSIDERING ALL OPTIONS

Some decisions make themselves. Other decisions have either/or choices. Others have multiple options. For decisions with two or more alternatives, be systematic in your approach. Take time to list all the available options and assess their validity and likely consequences – if necessary involve others to generate ideas and gather relevant information. Only when you have fully researched all the options are you in a good position to select a course of action.

51 If you ask for advice from any co-worker, expect to act on it.

SEEKING CONSENSUS

Involving others in the decision-making process requires method. The normal Western system is to debate the issue and to argue about the pros and cons of the alternatives. The Eastern approach is for each participant to state his or her opinion in turn, without discussion. Either way, encourage those you consult to speak their mind. You then summarize, seek whatever degree of consensus is possible – and, above all, finally decide yourself.

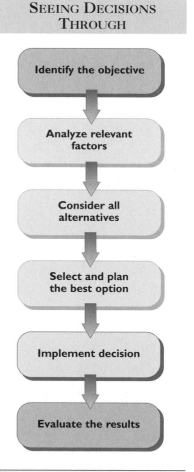

SEEING DECISIONS THROUGH

Identify the objective

Analyze relevant factors

Consider all alternatives

Select and plan the best option

Implement decision

Evaluate the results

▼ **SHARING DECISIONS**
Discussing a problem with colleagues and analyzing alternatives together is often the best way to move towards a decision. Encourage those you consult to speak their minds.

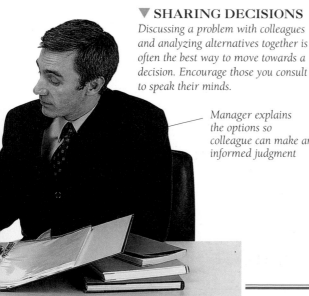

Manager explains the options so colleague can make an informed judgment

SETTING GOALS

Goals are the essence of planning, whether for the long, medium, or short terms. They should be ambitious but achievable. Set stretching, hard-headed, but feasible sub-goals to help your team attain their ultimate goal.

> **52** Seek to turn the impossible into a target that you can achieve.

TESTING CRITERIA FOR GOALS

- Are they clear, hard, and measurable?
- Are they approved by the implementers?
- Can they realistically be achieved?
- Do they have a clear, sensible time-frame?
- Have they been translated into full plans?
- Will they be revised as events dictate?
- Will reaching them advance our strategy?
- Will they generate rewards for people?
- Do they translate into individual goals?

BEING AMBITIOUS

The degree of ambition in setting goals is important because people respond to the promise of high achievement, in sports and business alike. A leader who thinks big can prove that what seemed unrealistic and impossible to achieve is actually within everyone's grasp. Set goals whose accomplishment will fill team members with pride and observers with admiration.

AIMING HIGH ▶
Without dynamic leadership and a highly motivated team, space exploration would have remained a dream. Seemingly unattainable goals can be achieved with the correct attitude and determination.

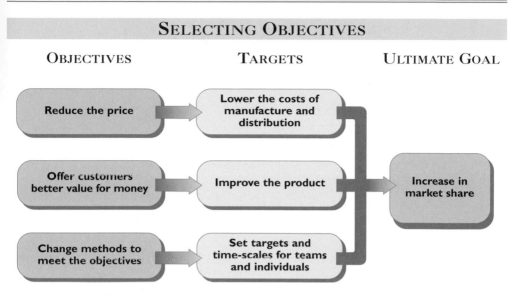

SELECTING OBJECTIVES

OBJECTIVES	TARGETS	ULTIMATE GOAL

Reduce the price → Lower the costs of manufacture and distribution

Offer customers better value for money → Improve the product

Change methods to meet the objectives → Set targets and time-scales for teams and individuals

→ Increase in market share

SETTING OBJECTIVES

Goals are seldom met without having to overcome unexpected difficulties, disappointments, and even disasters. Achieving your aims despite such setbacks is a crucial test of leadership. First, do not panic or blame. Neither will help to get the plan back on track, if that still remains feasible. You should take immediate action to deal swiftly and surely with the negative event and its consequences. Remember that a positive state of mind is crucial in reaching goals, so try to instil this in your team.

REVISING GOALS

If you suffer a setback, reassess the viability of the goal as soon as possible. Does it need serious revision? Must more time and/or money be allowed? You may have to abandon the goal – but take this step only if dispassionate analysis shows it to be the only practicable alternative. Try to use the upset as a trigger to stimulate renewed effort by being positive and decisive yourself.

▲ ACHIEVING END-GOALS
By selecting your objectives, individuals and teams can be given targets and time-scales that, if achieved, will slot together to meet the ultimate goal.

53 Expect setbacks, and always have contingency plans fully prepared.

54 Cut your losses fast if failure is truly inevitable.

DEVELOPING TEAMWORK

For a team to work well, several roles must be played – not independently, but collectively. The leader's role is to develop a team that thinks and acts together, with individual and team interests aligned.

55 Ensure that team members share the same goals.

ASSIGNING ROLES

The efficient team consists of people who can play several key roles (including co-ordinator, critic, ideas person, implementer, external contact, inspector, and team builder) in addition to the skills they bring to the basic tasks of the team. As leader, ensure that all these roles are played, sometimes with people combining roles. When organizing the team, fit the roles to the talents available, and provide training if necessary.

DEVELOPING TEAM LEADERSHIP SKILLS

To be an effective team leader, you must:
- Ensure that everyone on the team is working towards agreed, shared objectives;
- Criticize constructively, and make sure that you praise good work as well as find fault;
- Monitor the team members' activities continuously by obtaining effective feedback;
- Constantly encourage and organize the generation of new ideas within the team;
- Always insist on the highest standards of execution from team members;
- Develop the individual and collective skills of the team, and seek to strengthen them by training and recruitment.

KEY TEAM ROLES

CO-ORDINATOR
Pulls together the work of the team as a whole.

CRITIC
Guardian and analyst of the team's effectiveness.

IDEAS PERSON
Encourages the team's innovative vitality.

IMPLEMENTER
Ensures smooth running of the team's actions.

EXTERNAL CONTACT
Looks after the team's external contacts.

INSPECTOR
Ensures that high standards are maintained.

TEAM BUILDER
Develops the teamworking spirit.

MULTISKILLING

Teams can function well in a situation where each member has a specific task and does nothing else. But in many cases you need more flexibility, which is when multiskilling becomes important. Teams function better when people understand each other's jobs. Allocate time for your team members to work with others on the team. For example, encourage a production worker to accompany a salesperson to see a customer, or sit a marketing person next to an engineer. This broadens perceptions as well as skills, and promotes co-operation.

▲ BUILDING A STRONGER TEAM

Provide the training that enables people to master more than one task, and then your multiskilled team members can be used as understudies and as co-workers when help is needed.

56 Encourage competition between ideas, not individuals.

POINTS TO REMEMBER

● Roles should be matched to personality rather than the personality fitted into the role.

● If a team has only a few members, roles can be doubled or trebled up to ensure that the team's needs are covered.

● Once roles have been allocated, consult the team members to get their agreement on what needs to be done and how.

● Specific tasks should be allocated to each team member, complete with timescales and reporting responsibilities.

● Performance must be monitored at team meetings.

● It is important to concentrate on collective achievement.

● Individual contributions should be dealt with in a team context.

57 Boost a team's effectiveness by training members in new skills.

EMPOWERING TEAMS

Empower team members by giving them whole tasks and allowing them to find the best way of performing them, but make any suggestions you feel necessary for improvement. In this way you are enabling them to use their talents more fully. Let everybody exercise the right to think and contribute their intelligence to the team.

▲ TAKING A BACK SEAT

As leader, step back and let team members take the lead when appropriate. You do not have to chair every meeting or make every decision. The more you encourage the team to develop and use leadership skills, the stronger your own leadership will be.

58 Ask people if they have enough responsibility.

59 Do not accept the opinions of others on team abilities.

INHERITED TEAMS

If you inherit a team, or have its membership decided for you, do not jump to conclusions about the members until you have got to know them reasonably well and have understood their present capabilities. Set aside time to talk to each team member, one-to-one, about their individual tasks, their ideas, and their views of their own performance. This will give you a clear insight into their characters and abilities. You can then decide what roles and tasks are appropriate, and whether any training is needed.

UNDERSTANDING REWARDS

Rewards for good performance can take several forms, including pay rises, bonuses, profit-sharing schemes, share ownership, and recognition such as holidays or prizes. The object of a reward scheme is to motivate teams and individuals to perform even better. Good leadership also recognizes that team members deserve to share financially in the success that they have created. The best idea is to let employees help to decide how bonus payments should be made.

60 Allow new people and teams to prove how good they are.

61 Reward real merit openly, but never appear to have any favourites.

REWARDING INDIVIDUALS

There is a conflict between the interests of the team and those of the individual. For example, if an individual asks for a pay rise and you meet their demand, you must expect the team to learn what has happened. If they feel the rise is unfair, that might disrupt team-working. You cannot be unfair to an individual because of the perceptions of other team members. Be frank, explain your decision fully, and stand by it.

CHOOSING A REWARD SYSTEM

REWARD	IMPLEMENTATION	ADVANTAGES
SALARY INCREASES Increases in basic rate of pay, not directly related to performance.	Requires management to decide on overall salary scale and placing of particular jobs within the scale.	● Individuals know exactly where they stand financially. ● Can reduce element of competition within teams.
BONUSES One-off payments linked to performance or financial targets.	Can take several forms, such as sharing financial savings, but payments must be based on meaningful measures.	● Increases motivation and job satisfaction. ● Gives staff incentive for cost-cutting and quality drives.
PROFIT-SHARING An allocated share of the profits is split between employees.	Management must find a fair method of profit distribution, either on a corporate or divisional basis.	● Is an excellent motivator of individuals. ● Gives teams a sense of working towards common aim.
SHARE OWNERSHIP Gift of shares or chance to buy them on preferential terms.	Any rewards are directly linked to corporate success, and are moving down from top levels in many corporations.	● Encourages long-term loyalty and a sense of involvement. ● Helps staff identify with overall group results.
RECOGNITION REWARDS Many options, including prizes, holidays, parties.	Care should be taken to avoid implying that performing to the highest standards is the exception rather than the rule.	● Can reward teams or individuals. ● Staff are highly motivated by recognition, even if only verbal.
COMPOSITE REWARDS Rewards allocated for individual, team, and company results.	Allows management to combine individual with company-wide rewards, with elements tied to teamwork.	● Varying the reward packages keeps interest fresh. ● Recognition of teamwork elements boosts team spirit.

LEADING DISCUSSIONS

Whether they are formal or casual, involve groups of people, or are conducted on a one-to-one basis, discussions allow people to share ideas or concerns freely. By playing a leading role, you can keep discussions productive and purposeful.

TALKING TO YOUR TEAM

As a leader, you should call your team together on a regular basis to collect feedback, generate ideas, and make decisions. Even when holding small, informal discussions it is important to keep the purpose and a time limit in mind. Give people time to prepare, and make sure that everyone involved is given an opportunity to air their views. Encourage open conversation but discourage digressions and keep the subject matter moving forwards towards an action agenda.

62 Give people a time for meetings and always keep the appointment.

QUESTIONS TO ASK YOURSELF

Q Am I seeking to give people information or instructions, or am I merely making an announcement?

Q Am I holding a discussion with the aim of making a decision or decisions?

Q Is the purpose to obtain feedback on progress?

Q Is it a negotiation or a disciplinary meeting?

Q Do I want to discuss long-term strategy?

Q Am I dealing with a short-term matter, perhaps a crisis?

Q Am I only trying to find the facts?

Member feels free to speak openly

▲ **MEETING INFORMALLY**

Informal one-to-one meetings provide opportunities to discuss issues frankly and reach decisions quickly. They also enable leaders to forge stronger relationships with individual members of staff.

63 Keep discussions informal whenever possible to ease staff relationships.

ENCOURAGING DISCUSSION

Facilitate personal contacts by organizing office space to give staff the chance to meet and exchange information. Extra-wide corridors encourage casual discussions, as does sitting staff at round tables in open-plan offices. One company has lifts that stop at only one floor so that people must meet in them. Intranets and other networks achieve the same result electronically. This type of office contact is vital for sharing ideas and information, and for developing friendships.

▲ GETTING TOGETHER SOCIALLY

Events such as lunches, celebrations, and parties are important to foster easy exchanges of information and ideas. Socializing outside the office also helps to strike up friendships and smooth working relations between team members. As leader, you should be at the centre of these circles, participating in them fully.

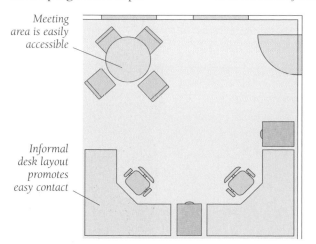

Meeting area is easily accessible

Informal desk layout promotes easy contact

CULTURAL DIFFERENCES

In order to facilitate discussion, some top bosses in the United States have abandoned executive suites for open-plan floors. The same can happen in Japan. Although individual offices hinder the flow of information, Germans and Britons still prefer them for prestige reasons.

▲ FOSTERING COMMUNICATION

An open-plan office is far more conducive to good communication than an enclosed, square-table office. In a more relaxed and informal setting, round tables are set aside for meetings in quieter areas away from desks. The important factor is to strike a balance between easy contact and efficiency.

64 Never hide behind the closed doors of private offices.

USING MEETINGS

Organizations breed meetings, but often they lack any clear purpose. Ensure that meetings have valid goals – there is no point in bringing people together to rubber-stamp decisions that have already been made – and that they are time-effective.

65 Use meetings to take decisions as fast as possible, not to delay them.

66 Ask only relevant people to meetings to keep the numbers down.

67 Allow staff to stay away if they feel they have nothing to contribute.

MINIMIZING MEETINGS

Most leaders feel pressured by the amount of time that they are expected to spend in meetings. But how many meetings really serve a useful purpose? As leader, always consider the validity of a meeting before arranging it. Is it worth your own and others' time? For example, if you hold a weekly team meeting, does it serve a purpose or are you doing it purely out of habit?

QUESTIONING MEETINGS

To help you decide whether to call a meeting, assume that it is unnecessary unless it can pass the following triple test. Does the meeting have:
● A clearly defined purpose?
● Measurable outcomes?
● An entirely functional membership?
Used unwisely, meetings can reduce the opportunity for leadership because, instead of taking decisions, meetings postpone them and dilute responsibility. Never use a meeting when individuals could do the same work.

RUNNING MEETINGS

Go into every meeting with a plan for what you want accomplished, while accepting that this may mean changing your own ideas. Except in emergencies, ensure that all documentation is distributed well before the meeting. In taking the chair, your role is to run an orderly discussion and to ensure that everybody who has something to say says it. End the meeting with a summary that includes an action plan, with deadlines and personal responsibilities for every action.

68 If you are in the chair, do not use the position to be dictatorial.

Leader keeps team standing to ensure meeting is brief

AVOIDING DELAYS

It is important that fixed meetings do not gum up the works. Learn from the example of a store chain that allows one manager to make decisions on a supplier's proposed price change off his own bat. A rival sends all these decisions to a pricing committee that meets every Monday. The result can be a seven-day delay, which could result in serious competitive loss. Leave similar authorizations to individuals wherever possible.

◀ **STANDING MEETINGS**
Follow the principle used by General Gus Pagonis, supply chief in the Gulf War. His morning meetings were literally standing. Since nobody was allowed to sit down, meetings were brief and to the point.

69 Keep meetings to the shortest time needed to cover a brief agenda.

ANALYZING PROBLEMS

The word problem means "something that is difficult to solve", "a puzzle", "something perplexing". By being positive and using analysis of the issue, you can overcome any obstacles and replace the problem with a solution.

70 Keep it simple and look first for the easy solution.

71 Regard problems as opportunities for team learning.

72 Consider an issue from every possible angle.

THINKING POSITIVELY

One leader found the word "problem" so negative that he banned its use. Instead of problems, managers were told to talk about opportunities. His attitude was right. The word problem really describes the need to choose between alternatives. If you are baffled, that is usually because you are unclear about what you want to accomplish, or because you are unwilling to accept the right alternative, even when analysis makes the best choice obvious. Recognizing the emotional blockage often helps the problem disappear.

EXAMINING THE FACTS

The issue could be a one-off, such as whether to build a Web site. Or it may be recurrent, like how to control expenditure. In all cases, ask: What questions do I wish to answer? Why is there an issue? In pursuing the control issue, for example, you will want to know answers to the following questions: How much are the present controls costing? What benefits will result from change? What systems do others use? Who will supervise and who devise the controls? What are the difficulties? What are the alternatives? Keep on until the questions run dry. The answers will provide the essential facts, without which you cannot hope to generate the best solution.

73 Look for the positive side of any negative situation.

74 Ensure you have all the facts before taking action.

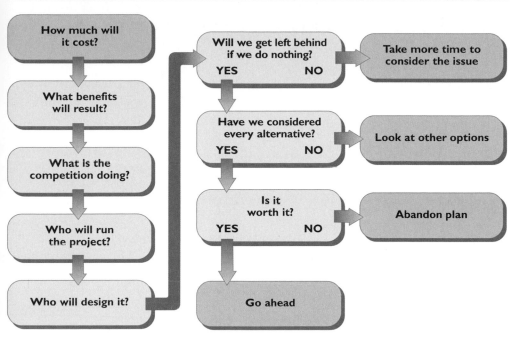

OVERCOMING OBSTACLES

Many issues tend to revolve around gaps. This means that there is a distance between where you are and where you want to be. The question is how to get from A to B. There may be a number of obstacles in your path, such as a shortage of resources (people or money, for example), powerful competitors, planning regulations, or many other snags. You can either explore ways of removing the obstacles or compromise on the objective. However, it is important that you do devise a plan for reaching your goal: only weak leaders, having identified the gap, take no action to close it.

▲ **ASKING QUESTIONS**
When attempting to resolve a problem, it is essential to ask yourself all the relevant questions. Once you have the answers available, the solution will follow.

▼ **TAKING ACTION**
Management writer Peter Drucker defines management as: "Knowing what to do; knowing how to do it, and doing it." The first two steps (Analysis and Planning) are useless without the third (Action).

Analyze → **Plan** → **Act**

GIVING SUPPORT

Trust can be difficult to build, but it is easy to lose. This is partly because people start with a distrustful mindset. As a leader, you need to work hard at earning trust, fostering that trust by showing loyalty, and supporting your team fully.

75 Find ways of showing people that you trust them to act effectively.

POINTS TO REMEMBER

● If promises are made, they should always be kept.

● Going behind people's backs is not permissible.

● People should be kept fully informed of anything that might directly affect them.

● Performance should be judged and rewarded fairly.

BUILDING TRUST

Leaders have to prove themselves trustworthy by word and deed, and then prove themselves all over again. Even then, a few people will continue to believe that you have a hidden agenda, however many assurances and reassurances they have received. Start from the assumption that you are trustworthy and will be trusted. Then, if you are honest, keep your promises, and play fair with people, trust will generally follow.

LOOKING AFTER PEOPLE

Taking care of people is your prime duty as their leader. In the workplace, that involves seeing that working conditions are as pleasant as possible and that sensible requests for changes or improvements are dealt with sensitively. With individuals, it often means working as chief welfare officer. Be prepared to make exceptions to help people in trouble, and do not hesitate if you suspect problems. It is important not to allow situations to worsen. Ask if something is wrong and, if it is, act.

76 Never refuse a request without careful thought.

◄ SHOWING SYMPATHY
People bring their personal difficulties to a good leader. Whether or not the problems are affecting their work, a prompt and sympathetic response is required.

IMPARTING CONFIDENCE

Achievement builds confidence. People may doubt their ability to achieve a difficult target. When the target is met or surpassed, their feelings about themselves will improve. Reinforce these feelings by celebrating individual and team contributions, using presentations or other media. If mistakes occur, point them out, but do not undermine the person. Conscientious workers will be hard enough on themselves.

77 Reward success with praise as well as material recognition.

78 Always be loyal to your people in any public situation.

79 If you have to criticize someone, do so in private.

PROVIDING BACK-UP

The most important support is psychological and costs nothing: loyalty. If you expect loyalty, give it. In confrontations with outsiders, support your colleagues so far as the facts will allow. Any reprimand or disciplinary action takes place in private, between leader and staff member, and not in front of third parties. Material back-up is also vital. Giving people the equipment and other resources they need to perform an excellent job is no less than they deserve. Being seen to fight for resources on their behalf, moreover, will strengthen trust and loyalty.

CASE STUDY
Harry managed an important unit in which errors had reached unacceptable levels and staff morale was low. The relationship between Harry and his immediate superior, Lynn, had deteriorated to the point of non-communication. When a new functional director, George, was appointed, Lynn said that his first job was to fire Harry. But George insisted on making his own decision. He arranged a meeting at which Lynn and Harry aired their differences. They hinged around minor grievances that Lynn had failed to handle, because she took them as symptoms of Harry's general unworthiness. George dealt with the grievances, insisted that Harry and Lynn should meet only in his presence, and gave Harry his confidence. The unit's performance was transformed as Harry proved himself an excellent leader.

◀ INSTILLING FAITH
In this case, an important unit was performing very badly. Its leader had lost his confidence, since his immediate superior seemed to have no faith in his ability. Once the leader's confidence was restored, and his feelings about himself improved, morale and performance within his unit were quickly transformed.

ASSESSING YOUR LEADERSHIP SKILLS

Gauge your ability as an effective leader by responding to the following statements, and mark the options closest to your experience. Be as honest as you can: if your answer is "never", mark Option 1; if it is "always", mark Option 4; and so on. Add your scores together, and refer to the Analysis to see how you scored. Use your answers to identify the areas that need improving.

OPTIONS
1 Never
2 Occasionally
3 Frequently
4 Always

1 I ignore employees' small mistakes and focus on more important matters.

| 1 | 2 | 3 | 4 |

2 I am able to accept criticism and always react to it well.

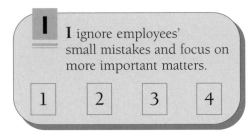

| 1 | 2 | 3 | 4 |

3 I am relaxed at work and keep calm when dealing with others.

| 1 | 2 | 3 | 4 |

4 I am extremely secure and confident in what I undertake.

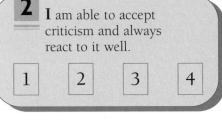

| 1 | 2 | 3 | 4 |

5 I keep professional and personal relationships separate.

| 1 | 2 | 3 | 4 |

6 I give credit to the team as a whole when high levels of productivity are achieved.

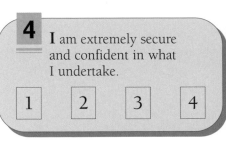

| 1 | 2 | 3 | 4 |

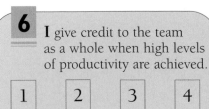

7 I am seen as a fair and just person who never takes sides.

1   2   3   4

8 I convey feelings of security and tranquillity to my team.

1   2   3   4

9 I convey a sense of friendliness and concern for the problems of others.

1   2   3   4

10 I treat people in inferior positions with respect when dealing with them.

1   2   3   4

11 I treat my subordinates in exactly the same way as my superiors.

1   2   3   4

12 I avoid making a point of being the boss, and treat others as equals.

1   2   3   4

13 I show that I am an excellent communicator and can motivate my team.

1   2   3   4

14 I participate with vigour to help my team achieve a specific goal.

1   2   3   4

15 I feel that I am well-respected and held in good opinion by my team.

1   2   3   4

16 I show impartiality in respect of colour, religion, nationality, or gender.

1   2   3   4

17 I accept the opinions of others, even when they differ from my own.

1   2   3   4

18 I am just and impartial when awarding prizes and promotions.

1   2   3   4

19 I endeavour to help the group stick together during a crisis.

1   2   3   4

20 I choose between speed and perfection, depending on the situation.

1   2   3   4

21 I involve myself in situations only when my intervention is required.

1   2   3   4

22 I demonstrate deep knowledge of my area of expertise.

1   2   3   4

23 I perform better than my staff if I have to replace someone temporarily.

1   2   3   4

24 I clearly distinguish between what is urgent and what is important.

1   2   3   4

25 I concentrate less on small details and give more time to important matters.

1   2   3   4

26 I show that I am a creative person who is always change-orientated.

1   2   3   4

27 I promote creativity and innovation so that people feel free to suggest ideas.

1 2 3 4

28 I choose the right people as far as my team is concerned.

1 2 3 4

29 I make excellent use of the financial resources at my disposal.

1 2 3 4

30 I make sure that training and related matters are properly done.

1 2 3 4

31 I perform my tasks well and prove myself to be trustworthy.

1 2 3 4

32 I represent the company well, encouraging other people to trust it.

1 2 3 4

ANALYSIS

Now that you have completed the self-assessment, add up your total score, and check your performance by reading the corresponding evaluation. Whatever level of success you have achieved in leading people, it is important to remember that there is always room for improvement. Identify your weakest areas and refer to the relevant chapters to find practical advice to help you develop and refine your leadership skills.

32–64: You may be losing the authority to lead. Use this opportunity to learn from your mistakes and improve your performance, using this book to help you.
65–95: Your leadership skills are generally sound but could improve. Develop those areas where you scored poorly.
96–128: You are a fine leader. Now work to improve further.

INSPIRING EXCELLENCE

The difference between leadership and management lies in the leader's ability to inspire the will to excel. Spur people on to achieve their best through motivation and example.

MOTIVATING OTHERS

People are capable of remarkable achievement if they are given the right motivational leadership. To mobilize a team's inner drive, enthusiasm, and vigour effectively, you need to be a credible leader who sets an inspiring example.

80 Never seek to get results by bullying people beneath you.

81 Use discipline sparingly, but make it swift and effective.

82 Keep the "carrot" visible but the "stick" in hiding.

SHARING A PURPOSE

The key to motivation is to communicate a strong sense of shared purpose. That can only be developed, of course, by sharing the purpose, involving everybody in plans, reviews, and getting results. Organize regular meetings to ensure that staff are up to date on the progress of the company. This knowledge makes team members more aware of their roles. As a result, they feel that their efforts make a difference to achieving common goals. Create the desire to succeed, not only for personal gratification, but also out of a sense of identification with the team objective.

SETTING AN EXAMPLE

A decisive leader who welcomes change and shows personal drive develops similar qualities in others. People will excel themselves for a leader in whose strength and wisdom they truly believe. Your self-set standards are therefore crucial. On top of that foundation, a high level of energy and purposeful activity is vital.

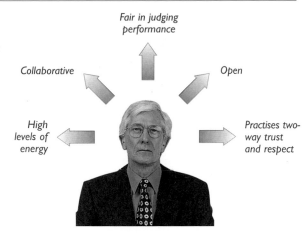

Fair in judging performance

Collaborative

Open

High levels of energy

Practises two-way trust and respect

▲ EVALUATING THE INSPIRATIONAL LEADER

A leader must be fair, open, trustworthy, and wise to inspire others. He or she also needs boundless energy and enthusiasm. Without these qualities, the basis for credibility will not exist.

TESTING YOUR CREDIBILITY

If you can agree with the statements below, you are a credible leader who is able to inspire others.

- I perform to the highest level of competence.
- I take initiatives and risks.
- I adapt to change.
- I make decisions promptly.
- I work co-operatively as a team member.
- I am open, especially with information and knowledge.
- I trust and am trustworthy.
- I respect others and myself.
- I answer for my actions and accept responsibility.
- I judge and am judged, reward and am rewarded, on the basis of performance.

KEEPING MOTIVATION HIGH

When problems or failures occur, a good leader confronts them squarely and seeks to understand their causes before using them as springboards for success. After a careful analysis of the reasons behind failure, be prepared to take responsibility for your own errors. Making honest mistakes once is common and is forgivable in a motivating, no-blame culture. But to keep motivation high, you cannot allow mistakes to be repeated time and again. Discuss with your staff what can be learned from these expensive lessons, and ensure that they are equipped to do better next time.

83 Share responsibility for mistakes and failures, and analyze errors so you can prevent them next time.

ESTABLISHING A VISION

Human beings find it easier to look back rather than forwards. But effective and inspirational leadership begins with the long view. Establish a vision of where you want to be in the long term, and your visionary zeal will inspire others to look to the future.

> **84** Write down your ambitions, and revise them periodically.

DEVELOPING A VISION

A vision is an aim for the future – at any level, from team, to department, to organization. To develop a vision, define what you are aiming to achieve in the future, and compare it with where you are now. Map out what you will need to bridge the gap, from extra staff or training to purchasing new technology. As leader, you must consider all the necessary steps to achieve the vision.

> **85** If your vision seems unattainable, simply intensify your efforts.

EVALUATING ATTITUDES

VISIONARY
Can see the benefits of change, and has the courage to carry out change despite obstacles.

PRAGMATIST
Will accept innovation, but only after it has been proved to work by somebody else.

CONSERVATIVE
Resists change and is creative only in inventing excuses for rejecting the new.

CREATING VISIONARIES

Any organization can be broken down into visionaries, pragmatists, and conservatives. The last group leads the opposition to change, while pragmatists are followers rather than leaders. You need the pragmatist's interest in proof, facts, and figures and the conservative's attachment to abiding values and accumulated experience. But both need to be animated by the visionary's strong leadership. Involving pragmatists and conservatives in plans for change may, over time, make them more inclined to share visions.

EXPRESSING A VISION

Visions need to be expressed as statements to communicate a clear understanding of the long-term aim and the principles underlying it. When creating such a statement, ask yourself if anybody reading it would be able to extract a practical understanding of the business you are in, where your leadership is going, and how it is getting there. That requires a triple focus: on the customers, on the people who serve the customers, and on the constantly improved performance that makes that service excellent. Ensure that you apply that focus in ways that are different to and better than the competition. That is unlikely to be the case if your statement reads much like everybody else's. Become the strongest critic of your own vision.

86 Keep vision and mission wording brief, clear, and prescriptive.

87 Give statements to others to check before you finalize them.

STRENGTHENING VISION STATEMENTS

WEAK STATEMENTS	QUESTIONS RAISED	STRONG STATEMENTS
"We have a strong people orientation and demonstrate care for every employee in the company."	● What does "people orientation" mean in practice? ● What kind of "care"?	"We will lead local suppliers in share, product/service quality, value, customer satisfaction, and good conduct by being different and measurably better."
"We sustain a strong results orientation coupled with a prudent approach to business."	● What does "results orientation" mean in practice? ● What is "prudence" about?	"Strategies, policies, and implementation are designed for and by our people, who ally with suppliers to achieve high customer ratings."
"Our aim is to be the biggest and best in our market."	● What do "biggest and best" actually mean? ● On what criteria are they applied?	"We invest and innovate to double real revenues every three years, while raising operating profits, cash flow, giving added value, and sharing the rewards."

GENERATING IDEAS

The leader does not have to be the most inventive person on the team. But as leader, you need to release the potential for generating ideas that exists in all individuals and teams. This will help in both achieving a vision and resolving day-to-day issues.

88 Make people see that it is everyone's job to generate ideas.

PROMOTING CREATIVITY

Actively promote creativity by example, encouragement, rewards, training, procedures, budgeting processes, and promotion. Lower any creative barriers by tolerating failure and eccentricity, flattening organizational structures and removing blockages, and refusing to tolerate conceptions such as "Not invented here", "It will never work", "If it was any good somebody else would have done it", and their equivalents. Also, recognize that consensus can be the enemy of creativity, and do not allow the pursuit of agreement to kill creative initiatives. If a creative idea is proposed to you, always consider it.

89 Try to implement suggestions, as long as they will cause no harm.

STIMULATING IDEAS

If you wait for ideas to come, they probably will not. A few rare people spout ideas all the time. But most of those attending an ideas meeting will be relatively dumb participants. To stop that happening, insist on two rules. First, everybody must come to the meeting with two or three genuinely new ideas, which can be as far-fetched as they like. Second, nobody is allowed to "shoot ideas down in flames" – rubbishing proposals without discussion. The important needs are to get ideas on the table and to encourage everybody to believe in their own powers of idea generation.

Challenger visualizes an idea

Dreamer conceptualizes the idea

BRAINSTORMING

Getting people together to generate ideas, or brainstorming, has sent many groups down the wrong path to creativity. Badly practised, it encourages the belief that throwing ideas into the pot is itself creative. Organized creativity is far more effective. A simple procedure is to start by analyzing the situation and to end with a shortlist of strong ideas. At each stage of this process there should be a challenging session, in which people can challenge assumptions. Often what is taken for granted should not be.

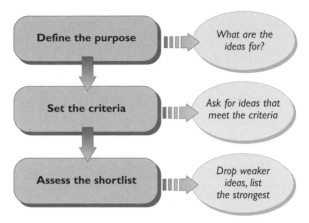

Define the purpose	▷	What are the ideas for?
Set the criteria	▷	Ask for ideas that meet the criteria
Assess the shortlist	▷	Drop weaker ideas, list the strongest

▲ **IDENTIFYING THE BEST IDEAS**
Organized creativity can be extremely productive.
A brainstorming meeting should be divided into three main stages, enabling the group to agree on a shortlist of strong ideas.

Explorer analyzes the idea

Map-maker mobilizes troops and resources

Path-cutter realizes the idea and makes it happen

90 Make sure ideas are challenged with respect and not with contempt.

◀ **UNDERSTANDING INNOVATION**
A good creative team comprises individuals who can take an idea from conception to fruition. The first stage is to come up with a concept. Next, the team must assess whether the concept will work, evaluate the practical implications, and decide how the idea will be implemented. Finally, the plan has to be followed through. Each stage fits and needs different personalities.

137

MANAGING OPENLY

Sharing information has a positive effect on performance. Withholding it has the opposite effect. By trusting your staff with information and by being open and honest with them, you will help and inspire them to perform better.

91 If unsure about whether or not you should pass on information, do so.

COMMUNICATING FULLY

As the leader of a multinational company said, "However much you communicate, it is never enough." Information is the lifeblood of an organization, and communication its main artery. Make sure that the channels of communication are always open in all directions. Keeping staff up-to-date with the latest developments generates goodwill towards the company. Use every means available to ensure that whatever you know, your staff know, and as soon as possible.

Leader openly discusses facts and figures with team member

SECRETIVE MANAGEMENT

Employee acts deceptively to gain information

AVOIDING SECRECY ▲

Unnecessary secrecy demoralizes people and diminishes their potential. Conversely, their performance is enhanced, often greatly, by fuller knowledge. Financial information, for instance, is often on the secret list. But if people are given figures that reflect the performance of their part of the company, they will understand the financial results of their actions.

OPEN MANAGEMENT

CHOOSING COMMUNICATION TOOLS

E-MAIL
This prime means of communication is fast, effective, and user-friendly.

MEETINGS
Face-to-face meetings build relationships and trust, and promote instant feedback.

JOURNALISM
In-house newsletters and magazines are a good way of keeping people informed.

INTERNAL MARKETING
Colourful marketing is a good way of "selling" change using consumer techniques.

NOTICEBOARDS
Bulletin boards are a basic means of giving information that can also be used by staff.

TELEPHONE
The telephone is vital for one-to-one communication, but not for lengthy talks.

92 Ensure that your messages reach all members of staff.

93 Make sure that you encourage staff to participate in decision-making.

SHARING INFORMATION

Open management involves regular exchanges of information between leaders and team members. Problems and tactics are discussed openly, and everybody is invited to make suggestions. Open management favours the creation of a positive, motivational atmosphere in the workplace: staff feel that they are part of the decision process and that their opinions are valued. Leaders also benefit: they can keep a finger on the pulse and learn of potential problems at an early stage. Make sure that you are visible and approachable: staying behind closed doors makes you remote and inaccessible. Be available for discussion, and, if you can, facilitate collaboration among team members by having open-plan layouts.

BOOSTING ACHIEVEMENT

A *good leader insists on positive outcomes for both short-term goals and for the long-term vision. Make sure that team members know what your desired result is, and monitor their performance as individuals and as a team in terms of output.*

94 Always keep your mind firmly on the outcome that you are seeking.

95 Encourage people to seek clarification if they are unsure about any of their objectives.

MONITORING PROGRESS

It is essential to keep an eye on how plans are progressing so that you can spot problems early on. If all is going well, you may want to raise targets to exploit the opportunity. The key is to make progress measurable. For example, build in key dates and quality targets, and compare budgets with actual expenditure. Regular checks should help you and your staff to adjust targets, budgets and so on, while keeping teams on course to achieve the desired outcome. As a leader, you are in a good position to see the overall picture – if several aspects are going awry, drastic action may be needed.

CHOOSING A MONITORING SYSTEM

SYSTEM	RESULT
WRITTEN REPORTS Staff provide written summary of actions, results, and figures.	Encourages staff to organize their thoughts and review their actions clearly.
PERSONAL REPORTS Regular meetings are held with each team member to assess progress.	Allows for informal updates and facilitates early airings of potential problems.
OPEN-DOOR POLICY Individuals are encouraged to discuss day-to-day problems at any time.	Shows strong support, but may prevent team members from using their initiative.
APPRAISAL Formal interviews are held to assess performance and set improvement targets.	Appraisal produces improved results if practised continuously and informally.

96 Make the outcome measurable if at all possible.

JUDGING OUTPUT

Are your staff contributing enough towards the overall desired outcome? If the answer is "Yes", your leadership has passed the first and most important test. If the reply is "No", you have two options. Either tell subordinates precisely what you want from them and how you want it achieved, or be clear about the outcome but leave the choice of route and methods to them.

97 Get staff fully involved in achieving the ultimate objective.

98 Let your staff know exactly what you expect from them.

99 Use appraisals to develop your staff, not as ends in themselves.

RAISING OUTPUT

Annual appraisals provide an opportunity for a leader to discuss performance and output with staff and to set targets for improvement. However, you will find the process far easier if you practise continuous appraisal, talking to everyone about their jobs. This informal contact helps to keep people focused on desired outcomes, as well as keeping you up to date with their progress. Provide feedback to ensure that staff feel a sense of direction and achievement; ask for and act on their input; and provide support and training readily when necessary. Continuous involvement should help to boost morale and thus raise output.

HELPING PEOPLE TO IMPROVE OUTPUT

It is important to talk to people regularly about their jobs and how you and they think performance could be improved. Remember to include your own role in the discussion. Always use positive questions, such as the following:

66 *Is there anything you think could be done better?* 99

66 *What am I doing that is stopping you from performing your job better?* 99

66 *Can I do something that would help you to excel?* 99

66 *Is there any way in which we could change the project to achieve better results?* 99

BEING COMPETITIVE

Entrepreneurs, people who spot and take a new business opportunity, are inspirational leaders who know that it is vital to accept the risk of failure to achieve anything worthwhile. Emulate such people by seeing risks and threats as opportunities.

> **100** Do not gamble, but back your own best judgment in going for results.

IDENTIFYING OPPORTUNITIES

Taking charge of a project may not in itself be entrepreneurial, but you still need to identify and express the objective, form and activate an effective team, and realize the ultimate goal by executing an excellent plan. The more you behave like an entrepreneur, the more successful your leadership is likely to be. What opportunities exist – not only in the marketplace, but internally – that could bring higher profits and greater customer satisfaction? What new, higher ambitions will transform the unit's prospects?

TAKING RISKS

Leaders realize that every opportunity involves two risks: first, that the perceived opportunity may not exist; second, if it does, that poor execution may lose you the perceived chance. Either way, the resulting failure can cause loss and humiliation. But the key to risk-taking is certainty: you must have complete confidence in your ability to win. You should also take every care (using analytical and intuitive skills) to ensure that you do not lose. Do this by listing the possible consequences of the risk, and assess how likely each is to occur. Be clear-sighted, and seek to minimize negative consequences and maximize positive ones.

The chance of making gains is small

The risk of large losses is great

▲ WEIGHING UP THE RISK

It makes no sense to risk large losses (the downside) in order to make small gains (the upside). Always compare the downside risk with the upside potential to make sure that the risk is really worthwhile. If not, you need to look at ways of substantially reducing the risk or increasing the gains.

TACKLING COMPETITION

All leaders want to outdo the competition. As well as a spirit of determination, this takes careful thought and forward planning. Do not base your actions or reactions on the belief that a rival business is bound to fail or does not know what it is doing. Instead, assume that the competition will succeed unless you mount a vigorous response. Never ignore signs that customers prefer other, competitive offerings. The true competitor must outperform rivals on every aspect that matters to the customer.

POINTS TO REMEMBER

- Reports and rumours of errors by opponents should never lead you to lower your guard.
- Reports of opponents' successes should not be discounted either.
- All angles and alternatives should be considered before reacting.
- Respond to a threat with a better strategy that turns the tables on the competition.

101 Keep up to date on the progress of competitors.

COVERING EVERY ANGLE

Leaders must always be on the look-out for potential threats. The main questions to ask are:

COMPETITION AND THE MARKET
- Could newcomers create damaging competition?
- Is there an existing powerful force in the market that could muscle into your territory?
- Does a competitor have a stronger hold on your biggest customers?
- Is the market developing in ways that favour competitors more than you?
- Is there a growing market segment where you are being left behind?

CUSTOMERS
- Are you aware of the latest customer feedback?
- Could your customers take away major sources of revenue?

OUTSIDE THREATS
- Is there a rival technology or other differentiator that could generate a major development?
- Could an unsuspected challenge arrive from outside the existing industry?

PLAYING TO WIN

Running scared is much healthier than being overly complacent. To avoid complacency, always analyze your strengths, weaknesses, opportunities, and threats, and those of the competition. Keep abreast of changes and developments in your field, and spend time analyzing trends. Some threats can be predicted, but unpredictable threats increasingly arise. With a flexible attitude, you will be ready to treat each one on its merits.

NEGOTIATING SKILLS

INTRODUCTION

N egotiation involves two or more parties, who each have something the other wants, reaching an agreement through a process of bargaining. This section explains the principles of this exchange and gives you the confidence and skills to conduct negotiations and achieve a mutually acceptable outcome. Designed for easy access to relevant information, and including 101 practical tips, the section covers the whole process of negotiation, from preparation to closing a deal, and is suitable for novices and seasoned negotiators alike. It includes essential advice on devising a strategy, how to make concessions, what to do when negotiations break down, and how to make use of third parties to resolve deadlock and conflict.

PREPARING FOR A NEGOTIATION

To negotiate successfully you need a game plan – your ultimate aim and a strategy for achieving it. Prepare thoroughly before a negotiation to facilitate the success of your game plan.

DEFINING NEGOTIATION

Negotiation occurs when someone else has what you want and you are prepared to bargain for it – and vice versa. Negotiations take place every day between family members, with shopkeepers, and – almost continuously – in the workplace.

1 To become a good negotiator, learn to "read" the other party's needs.

2 Bear in mind that it is almost impossible for a negotiator to do too much preparation.

UNDERSTANDING THE PRINCIPLES

Successful negotiating – an attempt by two people to achieve a mutually acceptable solution – should not result in a winner and a loser. It is a process that ends either with a satisfying conclusion for both sides (win/win), or with failure – for both sides (lose/lose). The art of negotiation is based on attempting to reconcile what constitutes a good result for you with what constitutes a good result for the other party. To achieve a situation where both sides win something for themselves, you need to be well prepared, alert, and flexible.

RECOGNIZING THE SKILLS

Negotiation is a skill that anyone can learn, and there are plenty of opportunities to practise it once learned. The core skills required for successful negotiations include:

- The ability to define a range of objectives, yet be flexible about some of them;
- The ability to explore the possibilities of a wide range of options;
- The ability to prepare well;
- Interactive competence, that is, being able to listen to and question other parties;
- The ability to prioritize clearly.

These proficiencies are useful in everyday life as well as in negotiations. By taking the time to learn them, you will be able to enhance more than just your bargaining abilities.

3 Start by visualizing possible gains, not losses.

4 Practise negotiating to improve upon your skills.

▼ **STUDYING NEGOTIATION**
At the start of a commercial negotiation, two teams face each other around a table. Note how each team member's body language is supportive of their partner.

TEAM A

Head is tilted towards partner

Body leans towards partner

Eye contact is maintained with partner

TEAM B

CATEGORIZING TYPES

Different negotiation types require different skills. In business and commerce, each instance of negotiation displays certain characteristics. It may be formal or informal, ongoing or a one-off, depending on who is negotiating for what. The parties involved in a business – such as employees, shareholders, trade unions, management, suppliers, customers, and the government – all have different interests and individual points of view. Whichever group you belong to, you need to reconcile such differences through negotiation: for example, shareholders negotiate with boards of directors over company strategy, unions negotiate with employers over pay and conditions, and governments negotiate with accountants over taxation.

 5 Be prepared to compromise when you negotiate.

 6 Determine your strategy according to the type of negotiation.

TYPES OF NEGOTIATION IN ORGANIZATIONS

TYPES	EXAMPLES	PARTIES INVOLVED
DAY-TO-DAY/ MANAGERIAL Such negotiations concern internal problems and the working relationship between groups of employees.	● Arranging pay, terms, and working conditions. ● Defining job roles and areas of responsibility. ● Increasing output via, say, more overtime.	● Management ● Subordinates ● Colleagues ● Trade unions ● Legal advisers
COMMERCIAL The driving factor in these negotiations, which take place between an organization and an external party, is usually financial gain.	● Winning a contract to supply customers. ● Scheduling the delivery of goods and services. ● Agreeing on the quality and price of products.	● Management ● Suppliers ● Customers ● Government ● Trade unions ● Legal advisers
LEGAL These negotiations are usually formal and legally binding. Disputes over precedents can become as significant as the main issues.	● Complying with local authority and national planning laws. ● Communicating with regulators (such as anti-trust authorities).	● Local government ● National government ● Regulators ● Management

APPOINTING AGENTS

John F. Kennedy, US President, once said, "Let us never negotiate out of fear; but let us never fear to negotiate". In reality, of course, you may be reluctant to negotiate because you are afraid of an unfamiliar process. If this is the case, you can find someone to negotiate for you. Such people are known as "agents", and they can be assigned as much or as little responsibility as you, the "principal" who employs them, wish to give them in a given negotiation. However, you should always clearly lay out the full extent of that responsibility in advance of the negotiation.

Some common examples of agents include trade union members, who negotiate as agents on behalf of employees, and lawyers, who often negotiate as agents on behalf of all types of stakeholder in an organization, including management, shareholders, and customers.

7 Define an agent's responsibilites very clearly.

POINTS TO REMEMBER

- When negotiating, you need to know where you are prepared to give ground – or not.
- A matter under negotiation may be intangible, and therefore must be defined before negotiation can proceed.
- Negotiation implies that you are willing to compromise on the issue under discussion.
- Anything that applies to you as a negotiator applies to the person with whom you are negotiating.

NEGOTIATING INFORMALLY IN DAILY LIFE

Domestic situations often involve negotiation. For example, you may agree to take your neighbour's children to school every Monday and Thursday if they take yours on Tuesday and Friday, and you each do alternate Wednesdays. On occasion, negotiated terms may need to be renegotiated. For example, you may have negotiated a price for one vase in a bazaar, but if you buy more than one vase, you should be in a position to renegotiate for a lower price on the first vase. When putting in an offer on a house, you may have to raise your offer and renegotiate terms if someone else is interested.

▲ NEGOTIATING WITH AN AGENT
If you are considering buying a house, you will need to discuss terms and conditions of the purchase with an agent, who represents the needs of the vendor.

UNDERSTANDING THE PRINCIPLE OF EXCHANGE

W*ith a proper understanding of all the processes involved (preparation, proposal, debate, bargaining, and closing), negotiating can create a successful outcome for all parties. Central to this is the principle of exchange: you must give in order to receive.*

8 Clarify your priorities: be ready to concede less important points.

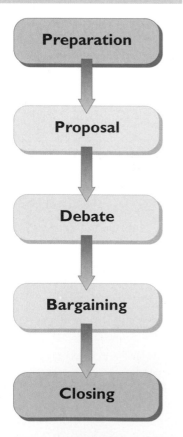

STAGES OF NEGOTIATION

- Preparation
- Proposal
- Debate
- Bargaining
- Closing

WINNING ON EACH SIDE

The key to negotiation is to realize that all parties need to gain something of value in exchange for any concessions they make. Only then can they all come away feeling successful. Try to achieve this by understanding that what is valued by your party may not be valued by the other. Whereas in a competitive sport victory is valued by both parties – so if one side wins, the other loses – negotiations, in contrast, can end in a win/win conclusion. When trade unions negotiate with a company's management, they may gain more pay for their members, while the management may gain assurances about increased productivity.

CULTURAL DIFFERENCES

Different cultures approach negotiations in very different ways. For example, Europeans and Americans often find the Japanese reluctance to engage in outright confrontation confusing or ambiguous. On the other hand, the Japanese find apparently unequivocal statements or viewpoints unsubtle and difficult to work into a compromise.

BEING FLEXIBLE

Flexibility is a vital characteristic around any negotiating table. The balance of power between the parties fluctuates as negotiations progress. For example, if you are bargaining in a market over a souvenir, you may become less enthusiastic when you discover that the vendor is not able to deliver to your home – anything you buy, you are going to have to take away with you. The vendor should be alert to any such loss of interest, and, in this case, you can expect them to lower their price in order to compensate and to keep you interested.

9 Be flexible – it is a sign of strength, not of weakness.

10 If you agree in haste, you may repent at leisure.

CASE STUDY

Freelance architect John was short of work when Bill, a property developer, asked him to draw up some plans for a warehouse that he was developing on a valuable site.

John agreed, and Bill, seeing John was keen to work, offered him half his normal rate of pay. John objected, but eventually agreed to do the work for about 60% of his usual rate. It was dull, boring work and involved long journeys. Both parties thought Bill had won and John had lost. After a few weeks, John got a big new contract and began to resent Bill's job. He would do the work in a hurry at the end of the day when he was tired.

When finished, the warehouse had an awkward leak, perhaps the result of John's half-hearted effort. Bill tried unsuccessfully to mend it cheaply. Customers were few, and Bill closed the warehouse after three years.

◀ EXCHANGING UNSUCCESSFULLY

In this situation, negotiations led, at the beginning, to an apparent winner and an apparent loser. However, over time, these positions become reversed as John, the supposed loser, ends up ahead, while Bill, the apparent winner, realizes that he has made an expensive mistake by trying to save money at the outset.

NEGOTIATING A ▶ FAIR EXCHANGE

Both parties in this case can be said to have won. Juan was aware that no more hard cash would be offered by the software company, so they joined in an alliance. Both parties achieved their common aim, which was to minimize their loss if the venture failed, and to maximize their profits if it succeeded.

CASE STUDY

Juan was a computer software designer with an idea for a new computer game that he believed would be hugely successful. However, it would take a long time to program it, and he needed to earn a living in the meantime.

He went to see his friend Maria, an executive at a large computer company. Maria and her colleagues liked the idea, but offered Juan only $10,000. Juan said it would take him nine months to develop the game, and while $10,000 would enable him to survive, it was not sufficient reward.

He suggested that the $10,000 should act as an advance on future profits, and that he and the company share the profits in the ratio 25:75. Eventually, a 20:80 split was agreed upon. The game was launched with a big marketing campaign and was a huge success, making both parties a lot of money.

IDENTIFYING OBJECTIVES

The first step in planning any form of negotiation is to identify all your objectives. What do you want to get out of the negotiation? Only when you know that can you begin to formulate a game plan that will enable you to achieve these goals.

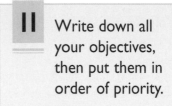

11 Write down all your objectives, then put them in order of priority.

12 Identify issues that are open to compromise and those that are not.

13 Express each objective in a single sentence.

CLARIFYING OBJECTIVES

There is rarely just one objective to a negotiation. You may be buying a chess set in a foreign country, but you also want to take it back to your home country without paying duty, and you want to pay by credit card. Therefore buying the chess set is not your sole objective. Similarly, when unions are negotiating for a pay rise for their members, they may also be looking to reduce anti-social working hours or to improve the rate that members will be paid for working at weekends.

Before entering a negotiation, make a list of all your objectives, then put them in your order of priority and identify those that you can live without. When it comes to compromise, you will be aware of which objectives to yield first.

ASSIGNING DIFFERENT PRIORITIES		
FOR COMPANY	PRIORITY	FOR SUPPLIER
Price	First	Quality
Time	Second	Price
Quality	Third	Time
Quantity	Fourth	Quantity

CLASSIFYING PRIORITIES

Divide your priorities into three groups:
- Those that are your ideal;
- Those that represent a realistic target;
- Those that are the minimum you must fulfil to feel that the negotiation has not been a failure.

Assign each of them a value. For example, if buying a chess set is your prime objective, give it a value of ten. Paying by credit card may be something that you can yield on, so give it a lower value of two. Finding the chess set in marble may not be crucial but still have a value of, say, seven. Prioritizing in this way ensures that you do not end up compromising on the wrong issues.

14 Abandon any totally unrealistic objectives before you negotiate.

◀ **ASSESSING PRIORITIES**

In Anil's case, a decent pension was more important than the other assets of the job; on GUT's side, the expense and trouble of changing the pension fund outstripped the benefits of gaining a talented recruit.

CASE STUDY

Anil was about to accept a new job with Great Universal Technology, who offered him an increased salary and relocation. The only drawback was that GUT, without explanation, said that it was not prepared to include him in its company pension plan, but would pay a comparable sum into a new pension plan that he took out on his own. He talked to an accountant and discovered that he would lose out by starting a new fund in this way. Thinking that GUT would be accommodating, he insisted that it sign him on to its own scheme.

GUT withdrew its job offer, saying that to accommodate him would have involved changing the pension scheme of everybody else in the company, and that it was not prepared to do this. The negotiation broke down because GUT had not explained the problem in full.

DISTINGUISHING BETWEEN WANTS AND NEEDS

A useful distinction that can help in assigning values to different objectives is that between "wants" and "needs". On the one hand, you may decide that you would like to replace your basic telephone with a sophisticated new telephone with lots of automatic functions. On the other hand, when your computer hard drive breaks down irretrievably, you need that replaced as soon as possible to be able to function properly in the office. So, while you *want* a new phone, you do not need one. What you *need* is a computer hard drive. Understanding the subtlety of this difference is vital to recognizing your opponent's wants and needs around the negotiating table.

PREPARING YOURSELF

Preparing yourself for serious negotiation involves thorough research. You will need to seek out useful information to support your objectives – once you have identified them – and find information that will help you to undermine the other party's case.

15 Be sure to gather all key information relevant to a negotiation.

USING PREPARATION TIME

Allowing for preparation time before you start negotiating is vital, as is the constructive use of that time. Allow yourself enough time to complete your research satisfactorily. You may need time to find statistics and case studies to support your arguments and thumbnail sketches of the personalities with whom you will be negotiating. Absorb this information, and use it tactically. For example, if you plan to use complex statistics, prepare an explanation to show how they support your case, rather than undermine the other party by exposing their ignorance of your material.

ASSEMBLING DATA

One valuable use of your preparation time is to acquire in-depth information about the people with whom you will be dealing and their business. This will be available from both electronic and paper-based sources. Visit a library; search the Internet; talk to others who know the people with whom you are about to negotiate. Look at the company's annual reports, at market research, and at old press cuttings. A careful trawl of such sources can help you to come up with telling arguments to support your case. But be absolutely certain of the accuracy of the information you have gleaned.

▲ ASSEMBLING DOCUMENTS
Arrange your data so it is easily accessible. Photocopy key pages of text; use coloured pens to highlight points. Time spent checking data is not wasted.

DEVELOPING LOGIC

Having compiled plenty of data, begin to develop a logical argument. You will need to follow through your logic in one of two basic ways:

- Deductively – a conclusion follows from a set of premises. For example, "I am a shareholder in Great Universal Technology. GUT will pay a dividend this quarter of 0.7 pence per share. Therefore I shall receive a dividend of 0.7 pence per share this quarter."
- Inductively – a conclusion is drawn from examples based on experience. For example, "Every time someone in GUT has become vice-president, they have received a pay rise. I am being made vice-president, therefore I will receive a pay rise." If the expected pay rise fails to follow promotion on just one occasion, it undermines the logic.

16 Sit in as an observer on other people's negotiations.

17 Learn tactics from the biographies of famous negotiators.

ANTICIPATING POSSIBLE DIRECTIONS OF A NEGOTIATION

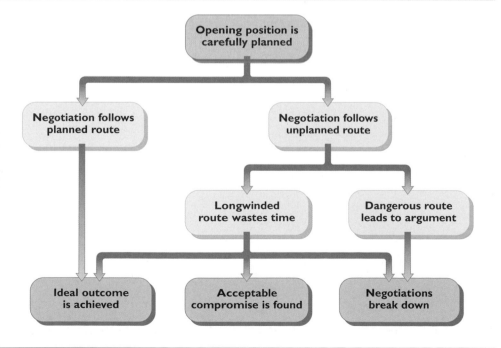

157

ASSESSING THE OPPOSITION

*W*hen *preparing your case, it is to your advantage to study the likely strengths and weaknesses of the opposition's negotiating position, and to research the background of the individuals who are doing the negotiating. Find out about their negotiating histories.*

18 Talk to people who know the other party in the negotiations.

QUESTIONS TO ASK YOURSELF

Q Are the opposition experienced negotiators?

Q Are there any differences in opinion among the opposition?

Q Do the opposition have the knowledge and facts necessary to achieve their aims?

Q Do the opposition have the power and authority to achieve their aims?

Q Are the opposition under pressure to settle quickly?

LOOKING AT THEIR CASE

Study the opposition's case in the round – that is, look at all aspects of their case. It will have strengths and weaknesses. Aim to expose its major weaknesses in order to undermine its strengths.

Although the logical argument in favour of the opposition's case may be strong, you may be able to counter a logical proposition with, say, a moral objection. For example, if a fish farm wants to use a new type of feed that makes the fish grow 15 per cent more rapidly, look for any repercussions of such a fast weight gain. Research may show that the feed makes the bones of the fish so weak that they can hardly swim.

ASSESSING STRENGTHS

Since negotiation involves a process of gradual convergence towards agreement or compromise, you need to assess the opposition's starting point and their strengths. Do they have a strong case? Is it logical? Is it morally acceptable? Do they have a strong leader with good negotiating skills? Once you have an idea of the opposition's strong points, assess in what direction they might go once you begin to bargain. How much room do they have to negotiate? Would an adjournment work in their favour, for example, should they want to consult with a higher authority?

19 Be aware that the opposition might have a hidden agenda.

IDENTIFYING OBJECTIVES

Try to identify the opposition's objectives – just as you have identified your own. Make a list of their supposed objectives, and prioritize them. Categorize them according to whether you think they are top, middle, or low priority. But remember that these judgments can only be guesswork, and that they need to be tested by observation as the negotiations proceed.

GUESSING AT THE OPPOSITION'S OBJECTIVES

TOP PRIORITY
These are the objectives that you think the opposition considers as vital to achieve.

MIDDLE PRIORITY
These are the objectives that you think the opposition would like to achieve.

LOW PRIORITY
These are the objectives that you think the opposition would regard as bonuses if achieved.

ANALYZING THEIR WEAKNESSES

Just as you need to understand the opposition's strengths, you also must be aware of their weaknesses – both of their case and of their individual skills. For instance, if the opposition comprises a group of people, analyze whether there is any scope to divide and rule – say, by yielding one point that you know will please some of them but displease others. Research weaknesses in their arguments in advance by looking for morally or politically problematic areas in their case that you could fully exploit. For example, a motion by the sales director of an electrical goods wholesaler to sell off at a high discount some damaged electrical goods raises various ethical and legal problems that could be exploited.

20 Keep testing your own assessment of the opposition against the way they behave during the negotiations.

USING FORMAL SOURCES OF INFORMATION

Carefully examine all formal written information about your opponents. For example, analyze articles printed in trade journals and other allied publications that detail what they have done. They may include invaluable background information about your opponent's present state, history, and current strategic objectives. You can also examine all of the publicly available documentation held by government agencies about an opponent's legal history and financial circumstances.

LEARNING FROM EARLIER ENCOUNTERS

Negotiations often take place between people who have already dealt with each other over similar issues, such as suppliers renegotiating an annually renewed contract, or employees negotiating changes in their terms of employment. If you are negotiating with a known party, analyze the way previous negotiations were handled. Re-examine old minutes or notes, and consult with any of your colleagues who were present. Reshape your tactics accordingly, but remember that as you become more familiar with the opposition's modus operandi, so they will be formulating objectives in line with their knowledge of your previous strategies.

POINTS TO REMEMBER

● The balance of power in earlier negotiations may not be the same as it is in the current round.

● The opposing negotiator may have a new job with more authority and more power.

● An opposing negotiator's new job may expose new weaknesses along with strengths.

● The time pressures for both teams may be different.

● The amount of preparation done by each party may be different in any round of a negotiation.

21 If possible, always consult with any members of a previous negotiating team.

22 Research in advance who will be representing the opposition.

FINDING COMMON GROUND

Negotiation involves mapping out ways of finding common ground for agreement or compromise. This goal may be achieved more readily by parties who have previously negotiated and are more likely to understand the concessions that the other side may be willing to make.

For example, if an employee approaches a manager wanting to negotiate a salary increase, he or she may find that the manager's budgetary constraints or a general company ruling prohibit any direct salary increases that year. However, instead of a direct monthly increase, the employee and the manager could discuss and agree on alternative ways of fixing on a financial reward which would circumvent these constraints. Both parties could agree on an extra week of annual leave, for example, as an alternative to a pay rise. Such a flexible attitude being shown by both parties, as well as the willingness to seek out common ground, can result in an appropriate compromise being made.

NEGOTIATING WITH MORE THAN ONE GROUP

When the opposition consists of more than one interest group, as well as assessing each group and individual as you would normally, you should assess whether there are any conflicts between these parties. Additionally, identify who has the power to make important decisions on behalf of the various groups. If, for example, you are the bidder in a corporate takeover, start by negotiating with the shareholders. In situations where a government body is involved, use a different strategy: address the wider effects of a takeover and use a team that includes lawyers to negotiate and examine all the implications.

CULTURAL DIFFERENCES

Cultural differences exist between races, age groups, and sexes, and you may be able to use these to your advantage. If your opponent is a middle-aged Russian, for example, you may imply that he or she lacks experience of commercial markets. Similarly, a well-educated but young American might be accused of lack of relevant work experience.

USING INFORMAL SOURCES OF INFORMATION

To be proficient at gathering information you must train yourself to think like a detective. Use informal social occasions, business networks, casual encounters, or timely phone calls to the appropriate people to find out how your opponents operate on a day-to-day basis. You can also send someone to their offices to see how they treat their staff and their customers, or invite one of their long-standing customers to lunch and ask a few discreet questions. Disenchanted ex-employees can also prove to be a mine of useful information, but beware in case they are unwittingly passing on to you disinformation with little basis in reality.

COLLECTING ▶
INFORMATION
Use an informal social occasion with someone who has connections with both parties in the negotiations to acquire as much information about your opponents and their strategies as possible.

CHOOSING A STRATEGY

Once you are clear about your objectives and have analyzed your opponents' probable objectives, you should be ready to formulate a strategy for achieving your ends. Use the strengths of the personalities in your team to devise your strategy.

23 Always keep your negotiating strategy simple and flexible.

QUESTIONS TO ASK YOURSELF

Q How will you decide on a strategy and tactics?

Q How many people do you need in your negotiating team?

Q How long will it take you to formulate a strategy?

Q Do all team members need to attend all the negotiations?

Q When can you rehearse your roles and tactics?

CONSIDERING OBJECTIVES

A strategy is an overall policy designed to achieve a number of specified objectives. It is not to be confused with tactics, which are the detailed methods used to carry out a strategy.

Your strategy will depend on several factors including personality, circumstance, and the issue under negotiation. Look carefully at the dynamics of the members of your team in relation to the reasons for and subject of the negotiation, and choose players whose combined strengths and skills can best achieve the team's objectives.

UNDERSTANDING ROLES

Just as every soccer team needs a goalkeeper, so every negotiating team requires certain "classic" roles to be filled in order to conclude negotiations successfully. These roles include the Leader, Good Guy, Bad Guy, Hard Liner, and Sweeper. Other roles can also be adopted to suit the circumstances of each particular negotiation you are involved in.

The ideal negotiating team should have between three and five members, and all the key roles should be represented. It is not essential, however, for every role to be filled by a single person – it is common for individual team members to adopt a number of roles that complement each other, and that reflect their own character traits.

24 Hide short tempers and frustration when negotiating, and never walk out in a rage.

DEFINING ROLES WITHIN TEAMS

ROLES

RESPONSIBILITIES

LEADER
Any negotiating team needs a leader. This may be the person with the most expertise, not necessarily the most senior member of the team.

- Conducting the negotiation, calling on others occasionally when needed.
- Ruling on matters of expertise – for example, deciding if there is enough money available to finance a takeover bid.
- Orchestrating the other members of the team.

GOOD GUY
This is the person with whom most members of the opposing team will identify. They may wish that the Good Guy was their only opponent.

- Expressing sympathy and understanding for the opposition's point of view.
- Appearing to backtrack on a position previously held by their own team.
- Lulling the members of the opposing team into a false sense of security, allowing them to relax.

BAD GUY
The opposite of the Good Guy, this person's role is to make the opposition feel that agreement could be more easily reached without him or her.

- Stopping the negotiations from proceeding, if and when needed.
- Undermining any argument or point of view the opposition puts forward.
- Intimidating the opposition and trying to expose their weaknesses.

HARD LINER
This member takes a tough line on everything. He or she presents the opposition with complications, and is often deferred to by team members.

- Delaying progress by using stalling tactics.
- Allowing others to retreat from soft offers that they might have made.
- Observing and recording the progress of the negotiations.
- Keeping the team focused on the objectives of the negotiations.

SWEEPER
This person picks up and brings together all the points of view expressed, and then puts them forward as a single, cogent case.

- Suggesting ways or tactics to get out of a deadlocked negotiation.
- Preventing the discussion from straying too far from the main issues.
- Pointing out any inconsistencies in the opposition's argument.

ASSIGNING ROLES

In negotiation, good strategy involves the appropriate deployment of personnel. You must decide on the roles and responsibilities that you want your team members to assume. Are they better at observing and listening than talking? Have they met any of the opposition before? Are they extroverted? An extroverted member of your team could, for example, play the role of the Good Guy. Allocate roles carefully, since your team must be able to tackle any moves made by the opposition.

> **25** Draw up a written schedule of times for briefings and rehearsing tactics.

▼ REHEARSING ROLES

When you have selected your team, gather them together for a rehearsal, each member playing out their role. Resolve any gaps or duplication of roles in the team.

Practise using visual aids

Encourage note-taking for reference during the real negotiations

THE IMPORTANCE OF APPEARANCE

Carefully consider your appearance in advance – first impressions count for a lot. Think about the type of negotiation you are entering, and dress accordingly. Power dressing can influence the way that people perceive you and your authority, but it can carry negative connotations of aggression. Encourage your team to dress in the same way, and if you want to appear formal, wear a jacket when you arrive. If in doubt, dress conservatively.

26 Wear clothes that you find comfortable but which are smart and fairly conservative.

BRIEFING YOUR TEAM

In order for members of your negotiating team to play particular roles successfully, you must brief them thoroughly. Avoid sending out contradictory messages during negotiations by keeping absent members up to date. For example, if the Leader claims early on that he or she has full authority to agree on a price, make sure that the Hard Liner does not come into the meeting later and, in an attempt to stall for time, assert that head office will have to be consulted for approval on the price. Such an inconsistency can seriously undermine the credibility of your team.

As well as encouraging individual preparation, make sure that the complete team is present for at least one dress rehearsal that uses actual data and visual material where possible. Take notes that can be used afterwards to analyze how the team can improve their strategies and tactics.

27 Practise being silent around a negotiating table.

CASE STUDY

Beth and Kurt were sent to Hong Kong by their employer, an electronics company, to persuade a manufacturer to buy some of its microchips.

Before they left, they rehearsed a number of good arguments, and decided that Beth was to make the case. In Hong Kong, the factory managers approved of the proposal, and seemed happy. However, while Beth was talking, Kurt overheard someone say that "Westerners never accept the first price offered". So when the Chinese put forward their price, expecting it to be rejected, Kurt interrupted.

Beth was taken aback, since she thought that the offer price was perfectly reasonable. However, she was pleased to have been interrupted when the Chinese agreed to a price 10% higher than their original offer. Both sides departed happy with the deal.

◀ WORKING TOGETHER

In this example of teamwork, Beth was acting as the Leader and Kurt fulfilled the other roles. It would have been much more difficult for a single negotiator, working on his or her own, to have picked up sufficient information to clinch this deal as successfully.

USING AN AGENDA

*I*n *certain types of negotiation, it is helpful to draw up an agenda – a written list of issues to be debated. Use an agenda to gain agreement from all the participants, before the negotiating begins, on the areas that are to be discussed or left out altogether.*

28 Try to set the agenda – it will influence the rest of the meeting.

POINTS TO REMEMBER

● Items should be allocated a fixed period of time on an agenda.

● A draft agenda should be sent to all parties in advance.

● Typed agendas should have wide margins for making notes.

● Supplementary papers should be distributed with an agenda.

● Agendas can be so important that sometimes their content needs to be negotiated.

DRAFTING AN AGENDA

The items to be discussed on an agenda can become a central part of negotiating strategy, through both the order in which they are to be considered and the time that is given to each. It is therefore sometimes necessary to hold extensive discussions in order to draft an agenda before negotiations begin. Bear in mind when drafting an agenda that it should:

● Formally define what the discussion is about;

● Informally influence the substance of the discussion by prioritizing issues.

◀ WRITING AN AGENDA
An agenda helps to focus a negotiation on its aims and objectives. As negotiation is not about airing grievances but achieving solutions, headings should use unchallenging and non-specific language.

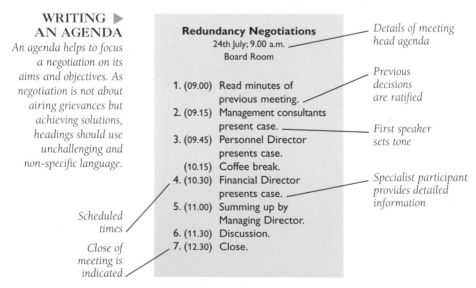

Redundancy Negotiations
24th July; 9.00 a.m.
Board Room

1. (09.00) Read minutes of previous meeting.
2. (09.15) Management consultants present case.
3. (09.45) Personnel Director presents case.
  (10.15) Coffee break.
4. (10.30) Financial Director presents case.
5. (11.00) Summing up by Managing Director.
6. (11.30) Discussion.
7. (12.30) Close.

Details of meeting head agenda

Previous decisions are ratified

First speaker sets tone

Specialist participant provides detailed information

Scheduled times

Close of meeting is indicated

AGREEING AN AGENDA

If you receive an agenda from the other party, analyze it and adjust your strategy accordingly. The party that sets the agenda is the party with the greatest interest in the meeting, and will usually claim the first speaking slot. Thus, you may wish to re-arrange the order of speakers to your advantage. If an agenda is relayed to you by phone, ensure you are not wrong-footed by the informality. Absorb all the information and consult the opposition about changes you wish to make.

29 Arrive a little early for meetings so you will look efficient and relaxed.

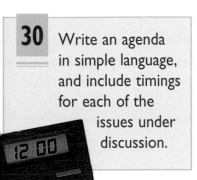

30 Write an agenda in simple language, and include timings for each of the issues under discussion.

SCHEDULING AGENDAS

In some negotiations, a time limit is imposed due to the busy schedules of the people involved. Other negotiations require the parties involved to sit around a table for as long as it takes to reach agreement (in the case of peace treaties, for instance, or of juries in courts of law). Always set a target time for the meeting to end, and schedule the discussion to fit within that time constraint. Remember that most people will become irritable if a meeting overruns its schedule.

RECORDING INFORMATION

Negotiation inevitably involves making concessions that a negotiating team might regret (or at least have second thoughts about). Thus, many people like to record the proceedings on audio cassette. This can be problematic, however, for a number of reasons: it can be difficult to position a tape recorder or dictaphone to pick up all the dialogue; vital parts of the discussion may also be lost if batteries have to be changed; cassettes rarely last the duration of a negotiation. If you want to record the meeting in this way, obtain the agreement of the other party in advance. In addition to tape recordings, experienced negotiators always ensure that detailed written minutes of the proceedings are taken.

TAKING NOTES ▶
Use a dictaphone to record comments or notes quickly and easily.

CREATING THE RIGHT ATMOSPHERE

The outcome of a negotiating session can be influenced by the environment in which it is held. Create a positive atmosphere for opposing teams from the outset of the proceedings by ensuring the venue is suitable for the size and formality of the occasion.

31 Do not run a negotiation longer than two hours without a break.

32 Keep a clock on the wall so that everybody can see what time it is.

DECIDING ON LOCATION

There are many considerations to take into account when selecting a location, including convenience, neutrality, and facilities. Do you require audio-visual aids or flip-charts? Do you need to hire them, and where from? How long are the facilities booked for? Can you stay overnight nearby if agreement is not reached within one day? Choose a venue that fulfils as many of your requirements as possible.

TYPES OF LOCATION FOR NEGOTIATIONS

LOCATION	FACTORS TO CONSIDER
HOME GROUND An office or room in your company building is considered home territory.	● It is easy for you to organize strategic interruptions. ● It is difficult to avoid unplanned interruptions. ● It is easy to call on your own in-house experts for relevant contributions to the negotiations.
NEUTRAL GROUND The office of a third party, or a hired public room, is considered neutral ground.	● Neither party gains the upper hand because of their familiarity with the location. ● Both sides have to "ship in" their experts and any background material they might need.
AWAY GROUND Away ground is an office or room belonging to the other negotiating party.	● Lack of familiarity with the surroundings can be disturbing. ● You have no control of the logistics. ● You can procrastinate by saying that you have to refer the matter back to someone in your office.

ATTENDING TO DETAILS

When hosting a negotiation, take complete control of the situation: manipulate the atmosphere, timing, and the nature of the breaks to increase your advantage. Supply paper and pens for taking notes during the proceedings. Check the bathroom facilities, and make sure that the lighting in the negotiating room is adequate, especially if audio-visual aids are being used. Physical comfort can also be a decisive factor; lower the temperature of the negotiating room by a few degrees, or delay the refreshments, to encourage a quicker decision from your opponents. If proceedings extend over a break, serve refreshments away from the meeting table, and avoid alcoholic drinks.

33 Do not reveal all your tactics at once when negotiating.

◀ **PROVIDING REFRESHMENTS**
Although your team members may lose their appetites during protracted negotiations, they will not lose their thirst. The combination of tension, unfamiliar surroundings, and pressure makes throats dry, so always provide water.

34 If needed, ensure that all parties have access to private phone lines.

35 Take a laptop computer if you need to access company data.

TAKING CONTROL OF AN AWAY-GROUND NEGOTIATION

Some negotiators prefer to visit the opposition on their home territory. Use this ploy to imply a willingness to make an effort and give a positive start to the proceedings. One advantage you may gain by this approach is that you will be able to dictate the time of the meeting to exert maximum pressure on your hosts. If there is no fixed agenda in advance of the negotiation, on your arrival ask your hosts if they mind you setting one. The opposition may be willing to make this concession since you are on their home ground. If you do set the agenda in this way, you must take full advantage of the opportunity – ensure that you build into it the details that you want, and you will start to tip the scales in your favour.

Using Seating Plans

*T*he way in which negotiators are seated around a table – whether facing each other in a confrontational manner or seated collaboratively at a round table – can have a marked effect on the tone and even the outcome of a negotiating session.

36 Make sure that the Leader can make eye contact with all the key players.

▼ **SEATING YOUR TEAM**

For anything other than extremely formal negotiations, a team of five is the accepted maximum. The "across the table" approach, in which teams sit facing each other, is usual, and is favoured when negotiators want to emphasize their separate identities. Sit each member of the team where their skills will be of most use, and in a way that presents a united front.

SEATING SMALL TEAMS

For negotiations between small teams, the parties often face each other across a rectangular table. This is the most formal and confrontational arrangement. To undermine the opposition, try to seat your team leader at the head of the table to create the impression that they control the proceedings.

To help soften any hardline attitudes that are hindering negotiations, make the seating as informal as possible, preferably using a round table.

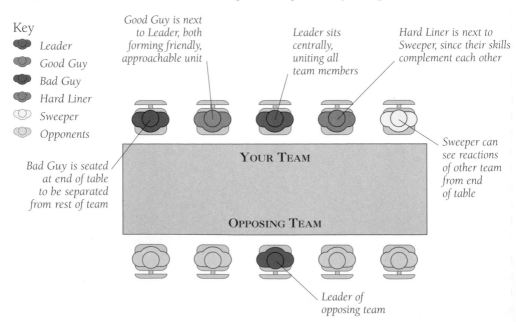

Key
- Leader
- Good Guy
- Bad Guy
- Hard Liner
- Sweeper
- Opponents

Good Guy is next to Leader, both forming friendly, approachable unit

Leader sits centrally, uniting all team members

Hard Liner is next to Sweeper, since their skills complement each other

Bad Guy is seated at end of table to be separated from rest of team

YOUR TEAM

OPPOSING TEAM

Sweeper can see reactions of other team from end of table

Leader of opposing team

USING SEATING TACTICALLY

When seating any size of team for negotiations, find the most comfortable chairs possible. As an alternative to the traditional or informal seating plan around a table, make it difficult for a visiting team to present a cohesive opposition by seating them among your own team. If possible, seat the most vocal or aggressive member of the visitors' team right next to the leader of your team.

However the teams are seated, eye contact is very important. It helps negotiators read the mood of the opposition, and also enables team leaders to get feedback from their own team. The absence of eye contact is disorientating; you may wish to exploit this factor when seating your opponents.

37 Seat your Hard Liner away from your opponent's Hard Liner.

38 Position chairs at an equal distance from each other.

SEATING LARGE TEAMS

If negotiations are between many parties, with only a few representatives of each present (such as at the United Nations or the International Monetary Fund), seat the participants in a large circle, and arrange for individuals to speak from a podium to make their case. If negotiations are between a few parties, each of which has a large number of representatives, divide the seating into groups, facing each other if possible. This is the way in which national parliaments are often seated, and is an arrangement that can be used at either trade union or staff committee negotiations.

INFLUENCING SEATING PLANS

When you arrive at a negotiation hosted by others, ascertain whether there is a prearranged seating plan. If there is no plan, try to seat your team first at the negotiating table so that you can tactically select your positions. Your choice of seats will depend on the dynamics of your team – whether you want to present a united front by sitting together, prefer to divide your opponents by sitting among them, or want to take control at the head of the table.

If you have been allocated seats, try to determine whether there is any logic behind the arrangements. The plan may give clues about the other parties and their views, or your perceived status. Seating may suggest that the talks are expected to be informal, confrontational, or dominated by your hosts. Once you gauge the tone, you can alter your approach accordingly. If you are not happy with the seating arrangements, ask if they can be changed.

CONDUCTING A NEGOTIATION

Plan your opening negotiating moves carefully to establish a positive tone. Then stay alert and be flexible to create and make use of all your opportunities in the course of a negotiation.

JUDGING THE MOOD

Negotiating is as much about listening and observing as it is about talking. You need to be very alert to the mood of the negotiations, since this can change quickly. Being alert involves using all your senses to pick up signals given off by others.

39 Begin any negotiations with uncontroversial, general points.

40 Stress the need for agreement from the outset.

▼ **STUDYING REACTIONS**
Throughout a negotiation, examine the other party's reactions and messages, trying to spot any inconsistencies.

ANTICIPATING THE TONE

Your preparation should help you to anticipate how the opposition will approach the negotiation. Once in the negotiation, try to judge whether you anticipated correctly by noticing non-verbal signals, such as gestures. If you are expecting an aggressive start, try to confirm this by reading signals from the other team – if they appear tense, your suspicions may be correct.

| Listen to what the other party say | Listen to how they say it | Observe non-verbal signals |

READING NON-VERBAL SIGNALS

Non-verbal signals include body language, gestures, facial expressions, and eye movements. Learning to read body language among the opposition team will help you to compile a true picture of their case – their signals may reinforce or contradict what they are saying. Clear-cut body language includes crossing of arms and legs, which betrays defensiveness, and leaning back on a chair, which expresses boredom. Small gestures and movements, such as hesitating or fidgeting, may indicate lack of conviction; raised eyebrows are a clear sign of surprise. Eye contact is another good source of information: team members may glance at each other when an important point in the negotiation has been reached.

41 Listen to a person's tone of voice as well as their words.

POINTS TO REMEMBER

- Speaking slowly and deliberately indicates that a person feels confident and at ease.
- Smiling unnecessarily and speaking quickly indicates nervousness.
- People who want to leave tend to look and turn their lower bodies towards the exit.

CULTURAL DIFFERENCES

Shaking hands may mean "Goodbye" to one party and "We've struck a deal" to the other. Make sure you understand the cultural rules before offering a handshake. In many Asian cultures, physical contact between the opposite sexes is discouraged. Women should therefore consider carefully whether to shake hands with men, or vice versa.

Direct eye contact is used

Handshake is firm, but not over-hearty

SETTING THE MOOD ▶
Shaking hands gives clues about the opposition. A confident handshake shows respect and openness; a forceful one indicates dominance; a limp one, passivity.

MAKING A PROPOSAL

Making a proposal is fundamental to all negotiation. It is vital to decide early on in the planning process whether you wish to speak first, or to respond to the proposal from the opposition. This decision is a crucial part of negotiating strategy.

42 Put forward a proposal with as little emotion as possible.

43 Do not start speaking until you have something relevant to say.

KEEPING OPTIONS OPEN

Leave yourself plenty of room for manoeuvre when presenting your case. Do not make brash statements that suggest that your position is immovable – make your proposals hypothetical to leave scope for both sides to make concessions at any time. Likewise, do not try to pin down the other party to a fixed position too soon – they need room for manoeuvre, too. Avoid forcing them into a corner or into making promises at an early stage of the proceedings, since this reduces their options when you come to make concessions later.

DO'S AND DON'TS

✔ Do listen carefully to the other party.

✔ Do leave enough room for manoeuvre in your proposals.

✔ Do feel free to reject the first offer received.

✔ Do make conditional offers, such as "If you do this, we'll do that".

✔ Do probe the attitudes of the opposition: "What would be your feelings if...?"

✘ Don't make too many concessions at an early stage.

✘ Don't make your opening offer so extreme that you lose face if you have to climb down.

✘ Don't ever say "never".

✘ Don't answer questions directly with a simple "yes" or "no".

✘ Don't make the opposition look foolish.

44 Pay close attention to the proposal of the other party.

45 Use humour when appropriate, but do not try to be too clever.

TIMING A PROPOSAL

The outcome of all negotiations depends on the presenting and discussing of proposals made by all parties concerned. These will be expanded and compromised upon until an agreement is reached. There are advantages in letting the other party make the opening proposal since you may find that there is less distance between their demands and yours than you suspected. If this is the case, adjust your own strategy accordingly. If you decide to make the opening proposal, it will be generally regarded as unrealistic, so make your initial demands greater than you expect to receive, and offer less than you expect to give. If you open with an offer that you think is genuinely fair, there is a danger that the other party will interpret it as being very different from your actual requirements.

THINGS TO DO

1. Listen carefully to your opposition – their wishes may be closer to yours than you expect.

2. Be willing to adjust your strategy if you can see a compromise early on in the proceedings.

3. Make your initial offer unrealistic, and compromise from that point onwards.

4. Take notes of all the offers made, trying to record them verbatim.

PHRASING A PROPOSAL

It is important that you present your initial proposal fluently and with confidence so you are taken seriously by your opponents. While speaking, emphasize the need to reach agreement, saying, for example: "I know that everybody here today is eager to see this project move forward as quickly as possible". When making your proposal, explain the conditions attached before making your initial offer. Summarize your offer briefly, and then keep quiet to show that you have finished, and to allow the other party time to digest your words.

Posture is open and confident

Direct eye contact is made with other party

MAKING A PROPOSAL ▶

Sit upright in your chair, and lean forward slightly. Using positive body language such as this encourages the other party to take both you and your proposal seriously.

RESPONDING TO A PROPOSAL

Try to avoid showing any immediate reaction, favourable or otherwise, when responding to a proposal. Do not be afraid to remain silent while assessing the offer, but be aware that your opposition will be studying you to gauge your reaction.

46 Look for any similarities in your negotiating positions.

47 Wait for the other party to finish before responding.

SEEKING CLARIFICATION

When you have heard the other party's offer, do not feel obliged to respond immediately with a counter-offer. Remain as inscrutable as possible while summarizing the proposal as you have understood it. This gives you more time to think about what has been said, and also provides an opportunity to confirm that you have understood it correctly. This is the time to focus on any issues that you feel unsure of, and challenge the other party to correct you. For example, "If I grasp what you are saying, we cannot expect to see any goods until next December", or "Can we clarify that you have taken into account the length of time it takes to clear cheques in Singapore?" It is crucial that you understand the other party's position completely.

◀ **MAKING YOUR RESPONSE**
Use open body language – making eye contact, sitting upright, with hands loosely crossed in front of you – to indicate that you have understood and accepted what has been offered to you. However, do not give away too much – keep the other party guessing as to your reactions.

STALLING FOR TIME

Use stalling tactics only if you do not want to respond to your opponent's offer immediately, and then use them sparingly. These are the tactics that you can use without seriously jeopardizing the outcome of your negotiations:

- Interrupt the other party's proposal – but only if you can disguise this as seeking clarification of a point or refocusing the discussion;
- Answer a question with a question, or ask lots of questions – after all, it does no harm to have extra information at your disposal;
- Break off the negotiations for consultation with your colleagues, especially if you have already established that there is an external authority from whom you need to seek feedback.

48 Always use stalling tactics subtly and sparingly, if at all.

49 Indicate that every concession you make is a major loss to you.

POINTS TO REMEMBER

- Your position may be damaged if you respond to the other party's proposal too quickly.
- Information should be exchanged as part of a compromise, and not merely given away.
- Questions can be asked constantly. The more information you have, the more you can control the negotiations.
- It is a good idea to summarize the other party's proposal.
- Hidden agendas on either side slow down the proceedings and should be guarded against.

50 Ask for a break to consider any new proposals.

PROPOSING ALTERNATIVES

If you decide to make a counter-offer, try to do so immediately after you have completed your summing up of the other team's offer – sometimes it is appropriate to strike while the iron is hot. To become a successful negotiator, learn to recognize that there are alternatives to every situation. Decide what you can offer as a counter-proposal by working out which issues are priorities to your opposition. From these, identify the priorities that are least important to you, and incorporate them into your counter-offer. In this way you will appear willing to compromise, but will not in fact give away anything of great value to your team.

In a classic example, two brothers are arguing about how to divide the last piece of pie. Each wants a larger slice. Their father suggests that one son cuts the pie any way he wants, and that the other then chooses which piece he wants. Such a piece of lateral thinking can bring a negotiation to a speedy and satisfactory conclusion.

RESPONDING TO PLOYS

Good negotiators need to be able to recognize – and counter – the ploys and tactics that are commonly used by people during negotiation. Identify and resist manipulative tactics as they occur to avoid costly mistakes when negotiating.

51 If you are foiled by a successful ploy, think before you respond.

52 Practise your response to a variety of tactics that are often used in negotiation.

UNDERSTANDING PLOYS

It is common during negotiations to encounter tactics employed to enable one party to benefit while conceding as little as possible. These ploys work by creating the perception that your power to get what you want is inferior to that of the other party, thus lowering your resistance to giving the other party its own way.

While you may not choose to use these ploys, it is important that you are able to recognize and counter them so that you remain focused on your objectives and avoid wasting time on distractions.

IDENTIFYING PLOYS

Recognizing the tactics that other parties use to influence negotiations takes practice. To learn how to identify and deal with such ploys without risking expensive mistakes, observe the other parties very carefully and bear in mind that manipulative tactics usually have three main aims:

● To distract your team, allowing the opposition to dominate the discussions;

● To shift the emphasis of the negotiation in order to shape the deal on terms that are purely to the benefit of the opposition;

● To manipulate your team into closing negotiations before you are entirely satisfied with the terms being offered.

COUNTERING TYPICAL TACTICS

TACTICS	COUNTER-TACTICS
MAKING THREATS Warning of unwelcome repercussions if you fail to agree to the terms on offer; emphasizing that penalties will be incurred by your side.	Tell the other party that you cannot negotiate under duress, and that concessions will be made only if they can prove the merits of the case. Review other options available to you.
OFFERING INSULTS Questioning the performance of your company or your professional competence; criticizing the quality of your product or service.	Stay calm; do not lose your temper or offer insults in return. Restate your position firmly, and warn that you will break off negotiations unless the other party is more constructive.
BLUFFING Threatening punitive action without being too specific; making dubious assertions, such as suggesting that competitors can undercut prices.	Call their bluff: refuse to agree to the other party's terms, and wait for a reaction. Question all statements, and ask for evidence to support any claims that appear dubious.
USING INTIMIDATION Keeping you waiting; making you sit in an awkward or uncomfortable place; receiving phone calls or visitors during negotiations.	Recognize that these are ploys to make you feel less confident. Do not drop your original terms unless you have gained concessions in return, and do not be coerced into settling.
DIVIDING AND RULING Exploiting potential disagreements among members of your team by appealing to the person most sympathetic to their case.	Brief team members in advance, and decide on a position that is acceptable to everyone. Call an adjournment if differences of opinion arise within your team during the meeting.
USING LEADING QUESTIONS Asking you a series of questions, which lead you to declare a weakness in your negotiating position; forcing concessions from your side.	Avoid answering questions when you do not understand the intention behind them. Check any claims made by the other party. Attach conditions to any concessions you make.
MAKING EMOTIONAL APPEALS Accusing you of acting unfairly in not agreeing terms; stressing their sacrifices; claiming to be offended by your lack of trust.	Affirm your commitment to achieving a fair settlement on business terms. Ask questions to test the validity of manipulative claims. Lead the conversation back to discussing the issues.
TESTING THE BOUNDARIES Gaining additional concessions through minor infringements of the terms agreed, resulting in substantial gain over a long period.	Be clear on exactly what you are agreeing to when you reach a settlement. Draw up a clearly worded statement of terms agreed, and hold the other party to these at all times.

DEALING WITH UNHELPFUL BEHAVIOUR

Emotional outbursts from attendees can suddenly change the mood of a negotiation. These outbursts may declare indecision, confusion, or aggression, but the most common type is a team member losing their temper. Unhelpful behaviour works well as a ploy because it shifts attention from the issue under negotiation to one individual. When this occurs, decide whether it is a ploy or is unintentional, and steer the discussion back on course as quickly as possible. You cannot make a decision if you are not negotiating. Handle these situations well, and people will be less likely to try such ploys again.

53 Adjourn when an unknown element is introduced into a negotiation.

54 Engage only in arguments that are constructive.

HANDLING PLOYS AND UNHELPFUL BEHAVIOUR

PROBLEMS	POSSIBLE SOLUTIONS
CONFUSED NEGOTIATOR	● Use visual aids to clarify complex issues that are causing confusion. ● Put complex proposals in writing, using short, clear sentences. ● Follow a concise step-by-step agenda to prevent further confusion. ● Be prepared to involve a third party to review the issues with a fresh eye.
INDECISIVE NEGOTIATOR	● Proceed slowly and methodically, and be prepared to reiterate points. ● Promise a review of the issues under discussion after a set period of time. ● Adjourn to allow an indecisive negotiator to consult others in their team. ● Try to present the issues in a fresh and original way.
AGGRESSIVE NEGOTIATOR	● Reiterate all the facts, keeping calm and avoiding emotional language. ● Refuse to be drawn into a battle of words, and stay calm at all times. ● State firmly that intimidation, bullying, and threats are unacceptable. ● Suggest an adjournment in the negotiations until tempers cool.
EMOTIONAL NEGOTIATOR	● Do not challenge the motives or integrity of the negotiator. ● Do not interrupt outbursts; wait patiently to make your response. ● Respond to any emotional outburst with rational questioning. ● Adjourn to allow the emotional negotiator to calm down.

ADJOURNING A NEGOTIATION

The natural way to cope with ploys such as emotional outbursts is through an adjournment. But an adjournment may itself be used as a stalling ploy, either by you or your opponent. If an adjournment is called for by one party, the other side must either accept or call off the negotiations.

Adjourn negotiations to allow the opposition to calm down and realize that losing their temper is unlikely to help them achieve their objectives. Alternatively, use an adjournment to review your position and tactics if new issues are introduced unexpectedly. However, be aware that adjournments can delay an agreement and become a disadvantage. If you call for an adjournment, summarize and record the discussion so far before breaking.

55 Call for an adjournment when a completely new issue is introduced.

56 When you agree to talk "off the record", always keep your word.

ADJOURNING FOR INFORMAL DISCUSSION

If formal negotiations have reached a stalemate, it may be helpful to continue the discussion on a different footing. Suggest that you talk "off the record", without recording your conversation as part of the official minutes of the meeting and without either party being held to anything discussed. Encourage the other party to talk informally and in confidence about their reservations over making concessions. Move to another room nearby, if one is available, since a different environment may be more conducive to relaxed discussion. If experts disagree on a specific technical matter, suggest that they ask another expert for an independent opinion.

CHATTING IN CONFIDENCE ▶

An informal chat away from the formal table across which parties usually face each other can smooth out negotiations. Use such an opportunity to show an opponent that you are reasonable and approachable.

UNDERSTANDING BODY LANGUAGE

A lot can be learned about the attitude of the other side in a negotiation from their body language. Watch the eyes, which are the most expressive part of the body, but also pay attention to the rest of the face and the postures of members of the other team.

57 Assign one of your team to detect signals given off by the opposition.

READING BASIC SIGNS

Eye contact with another person indicates a desire to transmit and receive information. When talking, most people make eye contact with each other that lasts for a few seconds at regular intervals. Recognise that eye contact is one of the most important aspects of body language, but also take into account what your opponents are thinking by "reading" the signs given off by their gestures and their overall postures.

UNDERSTANDING SIGNS ▶

You need only a few seconds to obtain significant feedback about your opponents' initial reactions to what you are saying. Recognize and understand their expressions and use this knowledge to your advantage. Pinpoint their most receptive listeners and address your remarks to them.

58 Be alert. Key signals may last for only a second.

Open expression shows interest in proceedings

Leaning back implies hostility

Posture suggests attentiveness

Crossed arms indicate disbelief

EXPRESSING OPPOSITION

SHOWING INTEREST

DEALING WITH DUPLICITY

Skilled negotiators can use body language to mislead the other party in a debate. Do not take all body language at face value – it is easy to add a smile to an expression that is otherwise hostile. A person who fulfils the criteria for showing interest may in fact be preparing for a scathing attack. Therefore, always look at an individual's body language in conjunction with that of the members of the other party to get an average reading of the group's mood. It is essential to stay alert, even if you think that the negotiations are proceeding smoothly.

> **59** Learn to trust your instincts about other people's body language.

Direct eye contact implies positive thoughts

Hand on chin shows thoughtfulness

Inattentive gaze means lack of concentration

Wide eyes and warm expression indicate willingness to be persuaded

Open arms imply indecision

Fiddling with a pen confirms thoughts are elsewhere

MAKING DECISIONS

LACKING INTEREST

REMAINING NEUTRAL

ESTABLISHING POSITIONS

The negotiating process can begin in earnest once each team has explored their own position after hearing the other side's proposal. Start to move towards a mutually acceptable agreement once both parties have reassessed their positions.

60 Ask a lot of "how" questions to imply a willingness to compromise.

61 Watch for changes in body language, and adjust your tactics accordingly.

REINFORCING POSITIONS

After you have heard the other team's proposal, your team may need to reassess its strategy or tactics in order to retain a strong bargaining position. Look for any mutual points of interest between the two sides, and consider the points on which you are prepared to give or concede. Decide whether there are any major differences between the two cases that will require you to prepare a counter-proposal in response to the opposition's proposal, or whether you need to make a few minor adjustments to reinforce your current position before beginning the debating stage.

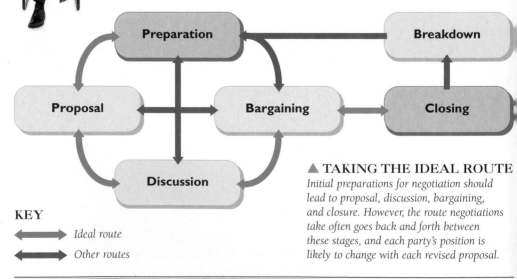

Preparation — Breakdown

Proposal — Bargaining — Closing

Discussion

KEY
⬅➡ *Ideal route*
⬅➡ *Other routes*

▲ **TAKING THE IDEAL ROUTE**
Initial preparations for negotiation should lead to proposal, discussion, bargaining, and closure. However, the route negotiations take often goes back and forth between these stages, and each party's position is likely to change with each revised proposal.

READING FACIAL EXPRESSIONS

Most people involuntarily show their emotions in their facial expressions, so watch carefully for a triumphant twitch of the lips or a suppressed yawn. Such signals are particularly valuable at the debating stage, when parties are exploring their positions.

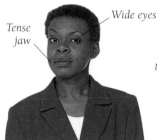

Tense jaw

Wide eyes

Head tilted to side

Steely gaze

Hand touches ear

Averted gaze

▲ EXASPERATION
The wide-eyed expression and raised eyebrows convey irritation tinged with frustration. Often, exasperation is experienced when progress is slow.

▲ BOREDOM
The tilted head, raised eyebrows, averted gaze, and set mouth all convey boredom. Use a lack of interest to your advantage to move the proceedings forwards.

▲ DISBELIEF
The unconscious touching of the ear and evasive eye movements suggest that the listener is not convinced by what the other party is telling her.

POINTS TO REMEMBER

● Once you have established your position, use tactics to maintain it.

● Proposals should be revised to accommodate new information from the other party's proposal.

● All possible routes should be explored: "But if we were to do that, then would you…?"

● A mutually beneficial outcome should always be aimed for.

62 Summarize the assessment of your positions regularly.

DEBATING THE ISSUES

Once both parties have outlined their basic positions, there may be extensive discussion about the underlying assumptions and facts. This debating time is a crucial stage in the negotiating procedure. Use it to search for some common ground and strengthen your case.

Debate can easily become emotional and heated if accusations and counter-accusations are made. Keep every debate calm. If you are frustrated or angry, try not to let it show. Do not score points off the opposition; instead, work to form a bond with them. If they make a mistake, be aware that it strengthens your case, but allow them to retreat without loss of credibility. It may help if you start the discussion on points of mutual agreement before moving on to issues on which you disagree.

STRENGTHENING YOUR POSITION

Gaining the upper hand in negotiations reinforces an argument immediately. Introduce as many relevant points as possible to strengthen your position, so that the opposing party is overwhelmed by the strength and thoroughness of your case.

> **63** Use repetition and positive body language to stress your key points.

KEEPING THE ADVANTAGE

Strength is about power – the power that you can wield to influence the outcome of a negotiation. When you have made a powerful point, maintain a strong position by reminding the other party of all the disadvantages of rejecting your proposal. Try to make it as easy as possible for the other side to change their position. This will help to strengthen relationships and avoid deadlock.

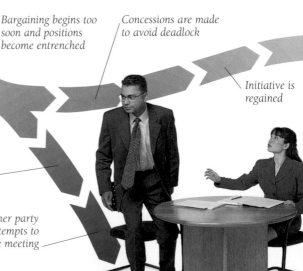

Negotiation starts positively

Bargaining begins too soon and positions become entrenched

Concessions are made to avoid deadlock

Initiative is regained

Negotiations break down as stalemate is reached

Other party attempts to leave meeting

64 Refer matters to a third party if you need an arbitrator to mediate.

65 Never undermine the dignity of the opposing party.

STAYING IN CONTROL

Negotiating can be a stressful process. Anxiety over the outcome may be heightened by worries about peer pressure and showing yourself in a favourable light. The negotiations may focus on an emotive issue, or you may feel threatened by the opposition's tactics. Never take things personally, otherwise you may lose control of the situation. Concentrate on the issues, and restate your position firmly if necessary. Avoid criticizing an antagonist, and never be tempted to resort to personal insults over the negotiating table.

If you are forced to make concessions to prevent negotiations from breaking down, attach your own conditions. This way, you will not have to give ground without receiving something in return. Take the long-term view, and remember that compromise can be a constructive tactic to help you reach an agreement.

Agreement is reached

Final points of deal are discussed

▲ CLINCHING A DEAL

This illustration shows two of the possible routes a negotiation can take. Despite a very positive start, the proceedings can be followed by deterioration to the point of breakdown. In this scenario, the negotiators avoid deadlock in their meeting by making concessions and compromising on minor issues in order to reach a mutually satisfactory outcome.

POINTS TO REMEMBER

● Your points should be reiterated in a loud but calm voice – assertively but not aggressively.

● Emphasizing the positive hides the negative; for example, "We may not have made a profit last year, but look at this year's figures."

● Any mistakes should be acknowledged immediately, so you can carry on with confidence.

● Appearing arrogant may hinder your chances of reaching an agreement with the other party.

● A deal is made, not won. Opponents should be persuaded that the deal will benefit everyone.

● Your original aims should be firmly fixed in your mind.

WEAKENING THE OTHER PARTY'S POSITION

To achieve a successful outcome in negotiations, strengthen your own position and look for ways to weaken the opposition at the same time. Use one or more of a range of tactics to diminish your opponent's influence in negotiations.

66 Press home your advantage when the opposition loses momentum.

67 Avoid negotiating on major issues at the end of the day, when your energy levels are low.

UNDERMINING OPPONENTS

When negotiating, undermine the other party's confidence, and even their credibility, but only by casting doubt on the validity of their information. Continually test the validity of your opponent's case; look for weakness such as errors of logic, misuse of statistics, omissions of fact, and hidden agendas. Avoid the temptation to try to weaken the other party's position by attacking individual personalities. You may face a backlash if the opposition responds in similar vein. Unprovoked attacks are also unlikely to gain you sympathy with a third party if one is called in to mediate or arbitrate.

USING EMOTION

A show of emotion at the negotiating table may convince others of your feelings and the honesty of your argument, and help weaken the other party's position. Use this tactic sparingly, however; repeated displays will be increasingly ineffectual. Emotional outbursts can also backfire unless handled carefully; instead of swaying the opposition, they may inflame tempers and lead to a breakdown in the negotiations.

68 Continually test for weaknesses in the other party's position.

RECOGNIZING ERRORS

An effective way to weaken your opponent's position is to find errors of fact or logic in their proposals. Look out for the selective use of statistics: if you are presented with details that seem too good to be true, ask about the things that are not being talked about. They may be hiding the bad news. If you find flaws, bring them immediately to everybody's attention.

POINTS TO REMEMBER

- Threats may not weaken the opponent – and they may backfire.

- If one party contains employees on strike, they will enter into negotiations having already made an impact on their opposition.

- Teamwork can help to maintain pressure on your opponents.

USING TACTICS TO WEAKEN THE OPPOSITION

TYPES OF TACTIC	EXAMPLES OF HOW TO USE TACTICS
FINANCIAL Imposing costs on one or both parties if agreement is not reached.	- Inform the other parties that costs will be incurred if, for example, goods are held in a warehouse until it is possible to resolve a dispute over their ownership. - Point out to the opposition that opportunity costs will occur if the negotiation is prolonged.
LEGAL Using santions or injunctions to prevent one party from taking action or to cause delays to proceedings.	- Threaten to pursue a course of legal action, if you have a solid case, and emphasize the cost, both in time and money, to the other party if they lose. - Cause lengthy legal wrangles to effect delays in production and consequently loss of finance to achieve an agreement.
SOCIAL Imposing restrictions by disapproving of a proposed course of action on moral grounds.	- Tell your opponents that their proposals are an insult to the people they are likely to affect. - Demonstrate how unfair suggested proposals are when compared to the treatment that other people receive in similar situations.
HUMILIATION Publicly humiliating one party or individual in the eyes of their peers.	- Humiliate an opposing party in order to damage their image or reputation. This can cause some long-term damage to their credibility but is unlikely to have any drastic effect on the party's business. Be aware that they may seek revenge for the humiliation in the future.
EMOTIONAL Making opponents feel guilty if they do not make any concessions.	- Emotionally blackmail your opponent if they are not giving you enough ground. Note that this tactic can be uneven in its effectiveness. Sometimes, people who feel they have been emotionally manipulated may be even more unwilling to make concessions in future.

CLOSING A NEGOTIATION

A negotiation can be brought to a successful conclusion only when both parties have made concessions that are mutually acceptable in order to reach agreement.

TRADING POSITIONS

Trading positions is a delicate process of bargaining whereby each party makes concessions to reach an agreement. However, if you are the weaker party, or your main aim is to minimize your losses, bargaining can be stressful and costly.

69 Offer the smallest concessions first – you may not need to go any further.

70 Make steady eye contact to emphasize that each concession is a serious loss for you.

MAKING CONCESSIONS

When you are forced to make concessions, it is important that you take a long-term view. Try to retain some control of the situation by:

- Judging how much ground you need to yield – put a value on what you are prepared to give so that it can be matched with concessions from the other side;
- Compromising without losing face. For example, if you have to backtrack on a point you had established as your final position, you can say, "Since you have changed your position on…, we may be able to change ours on…".

MAKING HYPOTHETICAL PROPOSALS

Test how flexible your opponents may be by making hypothetical proposals before giving concessions. "If" is the important word in the questions below, which do not commit you to anything, yet may help you to identify the issues important to the other party.

❝ *If we come up with another million, will you give us the Rome operation and the cargo boat?* ❞

❝ *If I reduce the price by 20 per cent, will you give me firm orders in advance?* ❞

❝ *If I give you 90 days credit instead of 60, will you give me the interest that you would have paid?* ❞

DISCUSSING TERMS

As you near the end of a negotiation, you need to discuss the terms of your agreement. Use your hypothetical proposals to help you work out a basic deal. The terms of the deal will involve the method of payment, the timescale of payment, how long the agreement should stand before being revised, and what to do if any problems arise over implementation of the deal – whether, for example, arbitration should be sought.

71 Do not concede ground unless you receive something in return.

◀ TRADING SUCCESSFULLY

Here is an example of a successful negotiation. The dealer establishes how much his customer wants to pay, and the customer gets what she wants at a price she can afford.

CASE STUDY

Jane wanted a red carpet she had seen in a shop window. She walked into the shop and asked how much it was. The dealer did not tell her but knew it cost him $150, and offered Jane a cup of tea. Jane began to get defensive and said she really wanted something with more brown in it. "I have lovely brown carpets", said the dealer, offering to show her some. Backtracking again, Jane said she wanted a denser pile, and again the dealer said that he had such a carpet.

So Jane decided to negotiate to get the red carpet. She asked the price again. He told her it was $700. "That is too much", said Jane, starting to walk away. She offered $300. "You can have it for $650", said the dealer. "No, thank you", Jane said, walking towards the door. Believing he would lose a sale, the dealer let Jane buy it for $300, doubling his outlay. Both were happy with the deal.

NEGOTIATING A PACKAGE

As you move towards closing a negotiation and start to discuss terms, try to draw together the various items under negotiation. Group related items together, rather than negotiating for each individually. This gives you scope to make painless concessions: you can yield ground on issues of lesser importance within the package to gain extra leverage for your main objective. For example, do not concentrate only on a new pay deal. Link pay with demands for longer holidays, higher pension contributions, and more generous health benefits. Be prepared to concede on pension and holiday demands to gain your main objective of shorter working hours. Negotiating a package is also a good way of finding out the true priorities of the opposition. Thus, you may be dealing with another party that has to fill a half-empty cargo ship, and so is not too concerned about the price per item of the consignment of goods.

72 Make concessions on a minor issue to lessen intransigence on a major one.

73 Remind the other party of areas of agreement to help break a deadlock.

CONCENTRATING ON ▶ ELEMENTS OF A PACKAGE

This pie chart shows an example of the proportions of time spent in a negotiation between employers and staff on various aspects of a pay and benefits package. The most time was spent on salaries – the top priority for the staff. They were prepared to concede to their employer's demands about holidays and pensions to spend more time on their principal aim.

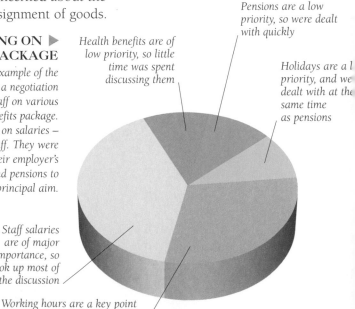

Pensions are a low priority, so were dealt with quickly

Health benefits are of low priority, so little time was spent discussing them

Holidays are a l priority, and we dealt with at the same time as pensions

Key
- Health benefits
- Pensions
- Holidays
- Working hours
- Salaries

Staff salaries are of major importance, so took up most of the discussion

Working hours are a key point for the employees, so took up considerable negotiation time

AVOIDING REJECTION

The benefit of packaging proposals together is that the least important elements can be rejected without either party losing face, while using hypothetical proposals enables you to refine your negotiations until a compromise is reached. In both cases, you can gain valuable insight into what your opposition is prepared to accept – as well as what they might relinquish – based on their reactions to your bargaining.

Avoid situations in which your final offer will be rejected. This undermines your negotiating position and may make it hard to restore a favourable balance of power in the negotiations. For example, if the other party says, "Your final offer of $400 is totally unacceptable," a response of, "What if we raise it to $500?" signals a serious loss of credibility on your part. Prevent outright rejection by refining your package as you edge closer to an agreement.

RECORDING A DEAL

Once you have successfully completed your negotiations, summarize your agreement in writing, and obtain everyone's approval of the summary. This avoids confusion and possible hostility later on. Remember that the summary must clearly record who gets what, how, and when, and the action to be taken. Both parties must sign the agreement. Clarify any ambiguous terminology, such as "adequate", "fair", or "significant", at this stage. If there is not enough time to obtain everybody's written agreement immediately, record the conclusion of the negotiations (either on an electronic notepad, a tape recorder, or in note form),

and have a detailed set of minutes drawn up immediately after the meeting. Send a copy to the other party, and ask for their written confirmation that the minutes represent a true and fair view of the result of the negotiations. Speed in circulating the minutes is essential, because if there is confusion or disagreement over what has been agreed you can reopen negotiations and resolve the problem quickly.

**MAKING ▶
RECORDS**
Take notes or use electronic organizers to record agreements during a negotiation.

Choosing How to Close

As you draw near to an agreement, check that all parties share the same understanding of the issues and confirm what has been agreed. Then you can close the negotiation. There are various ways of closing, so select the one that suits your team.

74 Record fully all agreements finalized at a negotiation's close.

Focusing on Issues

Before moving towards closure of a negotiation, it is important to ensure you are clearly focused on the relevant issues, and that you have not allowed personal feelings about the other side's negotiating tactics to colour your judgment and decisions. Are you holding out for a higher price because you need to make a profit, or just so the other party does not feel they have beaten you down?

75 Read over any notes covering the early part of your negotiations.

Confirming Terms

At this stage in a negotiation, it is important to be sure that all parties are talking about the same thing. Examine the terminology you are intending to use in your final agreement. If you are drawing up a commercial contract, define any key terms, or use easily understood vocabulary. It is vital that your terms are recorded clearly and accurately, since both parties agree to abide by these conditions in the event of a dispute. Reviewing both teams' understanding of the agreement in this way can also highlight previously unnoticed misunderstandings. The close of the negotiations must include ironing out these problems, which may give you or the other party room to negotiate new concessions: for example, "If I'd realized that you meant delivery in New York, I would never have agreed to such high freight costs – let's look at it again."

76 Discuss and define any words that might be ambiguous in a written format.

77 Make sure you do not ignore issues in order to speed up negotiations.

METHODS OF CLOSING A NEGOTIATION

METHODS OF CLOSURE	FACTORS TO CONSIDER
MAKING CONCESSIONS THAT ARE ACCEPTABLE TO ALL PARTIES Proposing and accepting concessions that help to clinch the deal without jeopardizing your party's position.	● This continuation of the process of trading can break a deadlock. ● The other party may be tempted to try to gain even more concessions. ● Making concessions late in the negotiations may undermine your credibility.
SPLITTING THE DIFFERENCE BETWEEN ALL PARTIES Agreeing between all sides involved in the negotiations to move towards the middle ground in order to reach a deal.	● It may be difficult to judge what is a fair split of the difference. ● This is an indication that you are still prepared to make some concessions. ● Neither party will feel that they have won or lost at the end of the negotiations.
GIVING ONE PARTY A CHOICE OF TWO ACCEPTABLE ALTERNATIVES Encouraging the other party to move forward by offering them two different options from which to choose.	● This suggests that any "final" offer you have already made was not really your last call. ● Finding two options that are equally acceptable to you may not be easy. ● There is no guarantee that the other party will agree to either of the proposals.
INTRODUCING NEW INCENTIVES OR SANCTIONS Bringing pressure to bear on the other party by introducing new incentives or sanctions.	● The threat of sanctions may increase the opposition's feelings that you are being hostile. ● Introducing new incentives can completely alter the balance of a negotiation. ● This can provide the push necessary to bring the other party to agreement.
INTRODUCING NEW IDEAS OR FACTS AT A LATE STAGE Bringing new ideas to the meeting table provides an incentive for new discussion and may lead to an agreement.	● This gives the other party room to see new concessions that they could make. ● This may undermine your credibility – you should have introduced the new ideas earlier. ● This may undermine the basis of the negotiation and take you back to square one.
SUGGESTING AN ADJOURNMENT WHEN STALEMATE OCCURS Adjourning allows each side in the negotiations time to consider what will happen if there is no agreement.	● This gives each party an opportunity to consult with outside advisers. ● Circumstances may change the position of the parties during the adjournment. ● It may prove to be too difficult to reconvene a further meeting at another time.

MOVING TO A CLOSE

Having chosen your method of closing, you can now move to execute it – but be aware of any shifts of mood in the other party. Timing your final offer to coincide with an upbeat phase in the talks can make the difference between success and failure.

TIMING YOUR OFFER

An offer presented at the wrong moment may be rejected, while exactly the same offer – presented at a different moment – is accepted. Make your final offer when the other party is receptive; using all your skills to produce the right atmosphere:

- Praise the other party – "That was an excellent point. I think that in view of that I can offer…";
- Be self-deprecating – "I'm afraid that I've been unable to come up with any bright ideas, but I think we could agree to…";
- Emphasize how far you have come together – "I think we've made really good progress today, and I feel able to offer…".

78 Be assertive but not aggressive when you are closing a deal.

79 Make sure your opponent has full authority to close the deal.

▼ CLOSING A DEAL
When a team of negotiators is about to make a closing move, they will look to their leader to take the first step.

Team leader summarizes and makes final offer

Body language is supportive

Team member backs up leader with data

LEADING UP TO AN OFFER

As you near conclusion, beware of "crying wolf". Earlier in the process, you may have felt a need to imply that certain offers were "final". This tactic is often used, but be careful not to say in so many words that a proposal is final when you know it is not, since this may prevent the other party from believing your "final final offer". Think in advance how to indicate this "final final offer". Make it clear that you would prefer not to strike any deal than to compromise any further on the proposed terms.

80 Look at the other party when making your final offer.

81 If you are not satisfied with a deal, do not sign it.

MAKING A FINAL OFFER

Indicate to the other party that you are making your "final final offer" by choosing the right words, tone of voice, and body language. Create an atmosphere of decisiveness: gather up your papers, stand up, walk about, and generally look as if you intend to leave (in contrast to previous offers, when you may have been leisurely leaning back in your chair, implying that you expected the negotiations to continue). Increase the urgency and firmness of your tone of voice, but do not rush to close the negotiations.

REINFORCING A FINAL OFFER

A carefully selected phrase can indicate that you are about to make your final offer. Use firm, unequivocal language when making your final offer, and reinforce the impact of your words by using a calm, authoritative tone of voice and maintaining steady eye contact.

I have no authority from head office to make another offer.

I have already gone much further than I intended to go.

This is my "final final offer". I have no room whatsoever to move further than this.

I am running out of time. Agree to my proposal, or I shall have to leave for another meeting.

ENCOURAGING CLOSURE

When you have made your final offer, the other party may simply accept it as it stands. If they do not, you may be able to nudge them towards making a final offer acceptable to you. Look for points that have not occurred to them – even apparently trivial ones – that could help you to reach an agreement. Try to put yourself in the other party's shoes, and to understand what might be preventing them reaching an agreement.

82 Emphasize the common ground you have found during a debate.

HELPING THE OTHER PARTY TO MOVE TO A CLOSE

METHODS	RESULTS
EMPHASIZING BENEFITS Concentrate on explaining to the other party how the proposed deal will be of benefit to them. However, you should avoid mentioning how the same deal will benefit your own side.	● Helps the other party to see advantages in agreeing to a deal that they may not previously have considered. ● Creates the perception of a win/win situation rather than a win/lose situation.
ENCOURAGING AND APPLAUDING Welcome any constructive proposal by the other party, no matter how long it takes to emerge. If you do not want to agree to it, you can still reject it later on in the negotiations.	● Creates a positive mood in which to move negotiations towards a close. ● Allows you to avoid criticism of your own counter-proposals. ● Avoids antagonizing the other party at what may be a critical point in the debate.
AVOIDING A WIN/LOSE SITUATION Point out that you are looking for an outcome that is equally acceptable to both parties. Do not push through an acceptance that your opponents will later feel has been forced upon them.	● Avoids confrontation, which is likely to result in increasing hostility and deadlock. ● Fosters a relaxed atmosphere in which constructive discussion can take place. ● Allows counter-proposals to be made.
SAVING FACE Give the other party an escape route by asking hypothetical questions or making hypothetical proposals, such as, "How would you feel about...?" or "What if we...?"	● Increases the likelihood of your proposals being given proper consideration by the other party. ● Means the other party feels under less pressure to accept or reject your proposals, but may come to a decision sooner.

WORKING TOWARDS COMPROMISE

At every stage of a negotiation, try to create a culture of compromise. By the time you are near closing, the other party should know that you are flexible, and are not dogmatic about any issues. If the debate has followed a proper course, an atmosphere of compromise should have developed naturally. Each party will have realized that the other's argument has points in its favour, and that each side must compromise at certain points. Even towards the end of the process, try to hold on to a few bargaining chips (minor issues that can be conceded easily) to trade if necessary. Do not respond too hastily to the other party's offers. They may continue to suggest new approaches that you had not considered before.

83 Try to understand the other party's hesitancy.

84 Agree on a date to review concessions made to break a deadlock.

POINTS TO REMEMBER

● A little ambiguity may enhance a proposal. There is an old saying: "The wheels of diplomacy turn on the grease of ambiguity".

● A sudden leap forwards can make the opposition nervous. It is best to move slowly.

● There is a saying: "It is better to sell the wool than the sheep." Main objectives should not be conceded, but small points can be.

● Phrases that seem to lay down the law, such as "I insist on...", should be avoided.

85 Be polite but persistent. This will gain you respect.

OVERCOMING LAST-MINUTE HESITATION

There is always extra sensitivity on both sides of a negotiating table when a deal looks near to conclusion. The time between reaching a verbal agreement and signing on the dotted line is particularly delicate. Negotiators often get nervous and may try to back out at this stage.

If the other party is hesitant, sympathize with them. Remind them that the deal means changes for you, too, and that you are also nervous about it. If the other party persists in trying to back out, point out to them that this dishonourable behaviour will tarnish their reputation, leaving them with an image of unreliability that may affect future negotiations. If you are in a position that allows you to force the deal through despite the objections of the opposition, remember this may well affect future negotiations with the same party.

HANDLING BREAKDOWN

*W*hen negotiations break down,
immediate action is vital to prevent
the situation becoming irretrievable. The
longer an acrimonious breakdown is left to
fester, the more bitter it becomes, and the
harder it is to restore a balanced attitude.

86 Avoid the
temptation to
respond with "an
eye for an eye".

▼ LEAVING IN ANGER

*Breakdowns often occur when one
party stands up in anger and leaves
the meeting. If this happens, the other
negotiators need to think carefully
about how to restore the discussion.*

LIMITING DAMAGE

To limit the damage from a breakdown in
negotiations, the two parties should re-establish
communication as quickly as possible. The best
way to do this is in a face-to-face meeting. However,
if a breakdown has been very acrimonious, it
may be more appropriate to make overtures of
reconciliation in writing. E-mails are perfect for
this because they are private and fast.

*Angry negotiator
unwilling to
continue discussion*

*Opposition team
member rises to
retrieve situation*

*Team member
explaining
colleague's action*

*Opposition leader
responds angrily
to walkout*

HEALING A RIFT

Try to retrieve a breakdown without appealing to outside help. If one member of a team has walked out of a meeting, persuade their colleagues to bring them back. If an entire team leaves, send the individual on your team who has the strongest relationship with them (possibly the Good Guy) to bring them back immediately. Do not allow a breakdown to continue if the consequence of no deal is worse than the last deal that was on the table. If a breakdown cannot be remedied internally, then you may need to call a third party, such as a conciliator, a mediator, or an arbitrator.

87 Do not insist on an apology when order has been restored.

ORCHESTRATING ▶ A BREAKDOWN

Since one of Joe's objectives was to protect his supply line with Kim's company, walking out was a poor way to deal with a frustrating situation. The future relationship was undermined by Joe's outburst. It would have been better to bring in a third party to mediate.

CASE STUDY

Joe went to Taiwan to reclaim money from Kim's company for a shipment of bicycles that Joe's employer claimed were faulty. Joe knew there were other suppliers happy to provide him with bikes, but he was unwilling to disturb Kim's well-established supply line. Kim had no power to financially compensate Joe; she could only replace the bikes. Joe said that would not be enough to restore his company's reputation with purchasers of faulty goods.

Joe was booked on a plane leaving in three hours, and saw nothing to be gained from listening politely to Kim's stonewalling for that time. He stood up angrily and left the room. Kim was embarrassed, but did not want to lose face by asking him to return.

Joe now buys his bikes in the US, and Kim's company has suffered as a result.

88 Contact the other party immediately after a walkout.

89 Agree a date for future talks to limit damage.

HANDLING INTENTIONAL BREAKDOWNS

There are occasions when one party actively wants negotiations to break down. If your team comes up with an unexpected bit of information that completely undermines the opposition's case, they may choose either to give in on the spot, ask for an adjournment, or manipulate a breakdown in the negotiation. While this is not helpful, they may feel strongly that continuing will be harmful to their case. If this occurs, stay calm, and try to amend the situation by effecting a reconciliation.

USING A MEDIATOR

When you have explored all the avenues, and the parties involved in a negotiation have still not reached an agreement, a mediator may be necessary. By agreeing to use a mediator, all parties are expressing a desire to resolve the situation.

90 View the use of a third party as a positive step, not a failing.

91 Think twice before using mediation – it is expensive.

ROLE OF A MEDIATOR ▼
The ideal mediator is unbiased, considers all angles, is acceptable to both parties, understands the issues, helps parties to find their own solutions, and prepares recommendations quickly.

UNDERSTANDING THE PROCESS OF MEDIATION

Mediation is the process in which deadlocked parties consider the suggestions of a third party, agreed upon in advance, but are not bound to accept the mediator's recommendations. The mediator acts as a referee between the negotiating parties and tries to find common ground among their agendas. Once some common ground is established, the mediator can begin to find mutually acceptable routes out of the deadlock.

Helps opposing parties to understand each other

Helps parties to create their own solutions

Considers problem from all angles

Suggests other solutions

Is impartial at all times

Explains issues to each side

CHOOSING A MEDIATOR

A mediator has to be acknowledged by both parties as unbiased, and must also be sufficiently knowledgable and informed about the points at issue to be able to make sensible recommendations that are relevant to both parties.

It is tempting to appoint a person in a position of authority (a former senior employee with experience in the field or a retired diplomat, for example) as a mediator. Although their authority may influence the final outcome, a mediator's capacity to adjudicate effectively is limited if they do not have the ability to recommend a solution. Consider using a less obvious person to mediate: someone, for example, who can think laterally, who has no preconceptions about the deadlock, and who can come up with a variety of creative suggestions for the best solutions to a stalemate.

92 Ensure mediators act while the parties are still keen to proceed.

93 Consider unconventional suggestions to resolve a deadlock.

DEVELOPING THE ROLE OF NEGOTIATOR-AS-MEDIATOR

You can help the smooth running of a negotiation by adopting a dual role from the very beginning. In the first role, you are a negotiator with specific objectives; in the second role, you are a mediator attempting to reconcile your objectives with those of the other party. In short, try to achieve your own objectives while finding common ground and presenting recommendations that are mutually acceptable to both parties.

It is essential to match a versatile and diplomatic personality to the role of negotiator-as-mediator. Ask yourself if you have a personality that is naturally suited to this dual role: do you look for balance in your life, and do you tend to make "we" statements as opposed to "I" statements? Avoid using forceful or aggressive members of your team in this role – they may be better at holding the floor and making proposals, but will need to stand aside if negotiations break down.

BALANCING ▶ ROLES
The role of negotiator-as-mediator requires you to be unbiased to ensure that the best interests of both parties are met.

GOING TO ARBITRATION

I*f a negotiation breaks down, you can resolve the dispute by using arbitration. This involves introducing a third party to help break the deadlock. Under the rules of arbitration, both sides are required to abide by the final decision given by the arbitrator.*

94 It is worth paying as much as you can afford for good arbitration.

95 Ensure that you fully understand the process of arbitration.

CHOOSING ARBITRATION

If you need to go to arbitration, there are several options open to you. Use your industry's semi-permanent arbitration bodies or procedures for settling disputes, if it has them. Alternatively, ask an independent tribunal, individual, or professional body to arbitrate for you. However, as this requires the involvement of qualified experts and the establishment of formal agreements, such arbitration is slow and expensive – so make sure that there are no other options available to you.

AN ARBITRATOR'S ROLE ▼
The ideal arbitrator is unbiased, respected by all parties, empowered to enforce judgments, and discreet about findings.

Helps both parties to reach their solutions

Remains impartial during negotiations

Is knowledgable about all issues

Adjudicates between both parties

Considers problems that cause deadlock

Reaches decisions enforceable by law

THE ADVANTAGES OF USING AN ARBITRATOR

The arbitrator's role in proceedings is to decide on a fair agreement between the negotiating parties, and then to enforce this ruling. Arbitration effectively bars negotiators from leaving the table without an agreement, although in extreme cases, the courts can be asked to implement a decision.

Collect all the information available from both sides in the dispute to enable the arbitrator to assess your case in detail. You will benefit from this process since the arbitration service works independently – the case for each party is heard in confidence, and the final decision is released only to the parties concerned. In commercial disputes this is particularly important – many firms will go to great lengths to avoid the publicity that accompanies the majority of court judgments.

96 Choose an arbitrator that both sides can trust completely.

97 If necessary, ask a third party to appoint an arbitrator for you.

USING THE COURTS TO IMPLEMENT DECISIONS

The courts are a last resort for negotiating teams – after they have failed to reach agreement among themselves and if the judgments of independent third parties are not acceptable, through either mediation or arbitration. Any legal process is likely to be expensive, and to bring the dispute into the public arena. This often exposes negotiators to new and undesirable pressures, so always take legal advice before instituting judicial proceedings. For example, a company with a short-term cash-flow problem should try to reach private rescheduling agreements with its creditors. If these problems end up in court, it is in grave danger of being declared bankrupt, in which case, both the company and its creditors could come out with nothing.

Implementing Decisions

Once you have reached an agreement, either independently or with the help of a third party, your final decisions need to be implemented. Draw up a plan of action, and appoint appropriate members of your organization to put this plan into effect.

98 Agree an order in which the action agreed on should be fulfilled.

99 Draw up a final schedule for implementing the action agreed on.

Agreeing on Action

Whenever agreement is reached between parties in a negotiation, the terms should be recorded and signed as an indication of multilateral approval and acceptance. Next, you must agree on how to implement the decisions. You may feel that it is appropriate to appoint a joint team to put the plans into action, or, alternatively, you may prefer to ask an independent party to oversee the project. Decide early on in the planning stage whether you wish for sanctions to be applied if the agreed action is not carried out to your deadlines – such measures can take the form of legal action or financial penalties. Unexpected problems will often arise at the implementation stage of an agreement, so appoint a team leader to monitor the process rigorously.

CASE STUDY

Stefan ran a small design practice and won a pitch to refurbish a large office building. He negotiated an agreement on the timing and cost of the work, and set a completion deadline of six months hence.

Knowing that he could not complete the work by himself, Stefan then hired an interior designer to procure the soft furnishings for the building, and an administration assistant to oversee the daily running of the project. This freed him to concentrate on restructuring the building itself.

As the work progressed, it became apparent that Stefan did not have time to deal with the teams of plumbers and electricians working in the building. He handed over this responsibility to his assistant, briefing her very carefully and issuing a schedule of tight deadlines for her to adhere to. The work was completed early and within budget.

◀ **UTILIZING A TEAM WELL**
Once he had negotiated his agreement, Stefan made the best use of the talents of his team by allocating them specific responsibilities. When he rethought his tactics, he briefed his assistant thoroughly and gave her a strict deadline to complete the work on time.

ASSIGNING A TEAM

The people assigned to implement any negotiated agreement may not have taken part in the actual discussions. For them, the provision of clear and accurate information is vital. When appointing a team and allocating specific tasks, pay special attention to the brief. Who is best suited to each task, and who needs to know what? How will team members receive information, and from whom? When will they receive updates, and how long will they be given to act on the information?

> **100** Decide who needs regular updates on the progress of your agreement.

> **101** Make a good last impression. It can be as important as the first one.

SCHEDULING IMPLEMENTATION

A negotiated decision is not considered a success until it has been enforced, so build deadlines and a plan of action into any agreements made around the negotiating table. Check the progress of your plan of action frequently – any slippage in the schedule may affect the agreed package, especially if major concessions were granted on the basis of meeting set targets. If other problems arise, resolve them by holding further negotiations.

◀ **REACTING POSITIVELY**

Engender good will around a negotiating table by reacting positively and enthusiastically when a final agreement on how to implement decisions is reached. Smile, shake hands, and congratulate each other warmly.

ASSESSING YOUR ABILITY

E*veryone is frequently involved in negotiation at work and at home, but in order to be truly successful at it you need to assess your skills. Evaluate your performance by responding to the following statements, and mark the options that are closest to your experience. Be as honest as you can: if your answer is "never", mark Option 1; if it is "always", mark Option 4; and so on. Add your scores together, and refer to the Analysis to see how you scored. Use your answers to identify which areas need improving.*

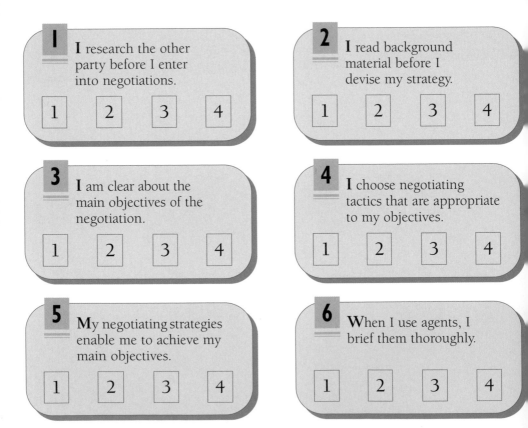

1 I research the other party before I enter into negotiations.

1   2   3   4

2 I read background material before I devise my strategy.

1   2   3   4

3 I am clear about the main objectives of the negotiation.

1   2   3   4

4 I choose negotiating tactics that are appropriate to my objectives.

1   2   3   4

5 My negotiating strategies enable me to achieve my main objectives.

1   2   3   4

6 When I use agents, I brief them thoroughly.

1   2   3   4

7 When I use agents, I aim to give them as much authority as they need.

1   2   3   4

8 I have a flexible attitude towards negotiations.

1   2   3   4

9 I believe negotiations to be an opportunity for both parties to benefit.

1   2   3   4

10 I enter into negotiations determined to reach a satisfactory agreement.

1   2   3   4

11 I communicate my points in plain language.

1   2   3   4

12 I communicate my points logically and clearly.

1   2   3   4

13 I consciously use body language to communicate with the other party.

1   2   3   4

14 I avoid exposing the other party's weaknesses.

1   2   3   4

15 I am polite at all times during the negotiation.

1   2   3   4

16 I create deadlines that are realistic and determined by the negotiation.

1   2   3   4

17 I use my instincts to help me understand the other party's tactics.

1 2 3 4

18 I have enough power to make decisions when necessary.

1 2 3 4

19 I am sensitive to any cultural differences of the other party.

1 2 3 4

20 I work well as a member of a negotiating team.

1 2 3 4

21 I am able to be objective and put myself in the position of the other party.

1 2 3 4

22 I know how to guide the other party into making an offer.

1 2 3 4

23 I avoid making the opening offer.

1 2 3 4

24 I make progress towards agreement via a series of conditional offers.

1 2 3 4

25 I approach my final objectives step by step.

1 2 3 4

26 I show emotion only as part of a tactical move.

1 2 3 4

27 **I** regularly summarize the progress that has been made during negotiations.

| 1 | 2 | 3 | 4 |

28 **I** use adjournments tactically to give me time to think.

| 1 | 2 | 3 | 4 |

29 **I** introduce third parties when the negotiations break down.

| 1 | 2 | 3 | 4 |

30 **I** employ a mediator as an effective way of breaking a stalemate.

| 1 | 2 | 3 | 4 |

31 **I** ensure that any agreement is signed by each party.

| 1 | 2 | 3 | 4 |

32 **I** prefer to negotiate a win/win situation whenever possible.

| 1 | 2 | 3 | 4 |

ANALYSIS

Now you have completed the self-assessment, add up your total score and check your performance by reading the corresponding evaluation. Whatever level of success you have achieved when negotiating, it is important to remember that there is always room for improvement. Identify your weakest areas, and refer to the chapters in this section where you will find practical advice and tips to help you establish and hone your negotiating skills.

32–64: Your negotiating skills are weak. Learn to use and recognize the strategies and tactics essential to successful negotiation.
65–95: You have reasonable negotiating skills, but certain areas need further improvement.
96–128: Your negotiations are successful. Continue to prepare thoroughly for every future negotiation.

MAKING PRESENTATIONS

INTRODUCTION

W hether you are a seasoned orator or a novice speaker, you can improve your presentation skills and enhance your credibility through planning, preparation, and practice. This section contains essential information on every aspect of public speaking, from the researching and writing of your material to overcoming tension and dealing with questions from an audience. Practical advice, for example on choosing the best audio-visual aids, will furnish you with the confidence to handle real-life situations professionally and help you to develop and perfect your skills. Further vital information is included in the form of 101 concise tips, which appear throughout the section, while a self-assessment exercise allows you to evaluate and chart your progress following each presentation you give.

PREPARING A PRESENTATION

There are two secrets to making a good presentation: preparation and practice. Take the time to prepare properly, and your chances of success will increase enormously.

DEFINING YOUR PURPOSE

What do you want to communicate to your audience? Before you start to prepare your presentation, decide what you want it to achieve. Focus on the purpose of the presentation at every stage to ensure that your preparation is relevant and efficient.

 1 Once you have written your speech, cut it, cut it, and cut it.

POINTS TO REMEMBER

● Your presentation should be relevant, simple, and to the point.

● Your audience will be impressed by the depth and breadth of your knowledge rather than a show of false intellect and wit.

● Your positive attitude, energy, and enthusiasm for the subject will speak volumes. They will be remembered by your audience long after the details of your speech have been forgotten.

CONSIDERING YOUR AIMS

The first points to think about are what you intend to tell your audience and how best to communicate your message. Your strategy will depend on three things: the type of message you wish to deliver; the nature of the audience; and the physical surroundings of the venue.

Review the purpose of your presentation, and ask yourself whether it is simple enough or too complex. Think about who might be in your audience and how they might receive your speech. Then ask yourself if this is how you want your speech to be received. If not, modify your purpose.

ASSESSING ABILITIES

Unless you are a trained actor, it is difficult trying to be anyone other than yourself. Concentrate on defining and utilizing your best assets. For example if you have a good, clear voice, use it to your advantage; if you have a talent for such things, tell a humorous but relevant short anecdote. Next, confront your fears and anxieties about the presentation, so that you can make sure that you are prepared for them on the day.

2 Group similar ideas together to establish themes.

**SPEAKING ▶
CONFIDENTLY**
Use techniques that you are comfortable with in your presentation. This will help you control your nerves once you are standing in front of the audience.

REDUCING YOUR FEARS

COMMON FEARS	PRACTICAL SOLUTIONS
EXCESSIVE NERVES You cannot relax. You forget what you are trying to say and dry up.	Prepare by rehearsing in front of a mirror and, if possible, at the venue. Make sure that you can see your notes clearly at all times. Take a deep breath, and smile.
BORED AUDIENCE The audience loses interest, and fidget and talk among themselves.	Ensure that the point you are trying to make is relevant – if not, cut it. Be enthusiastic. Vary the pace of your presentation, and maintain eye contact with the audience.
HOSTILE AUDIENCE You are heckled. Questions from the floor are aggressive in tone.	Remain polite and courteous. If your audience has specialist knowledge of your subject, defer to them. Redirect difficult questions back to the audience.
BREAKDOWN OF VISUAL AIDS Equipment fails to work, or you cannot remember how to use it.	Avoid using any technology with which you are not thoroughly familiar. Immediately before the presentation, check all the equipment that you will be using.

KNOWING YOUR AUDIENCE

Find out as much as you can about who will be attending your presentation. Have you invited some of the audience? Does it consist of colleagues? Once you know who will be attending, structure your speech to elicit the best response from them.

3 Make sure that the audience leaves the venue feeling informed.

QUESTIONS TO ASK YOURSELF

Q What is the expected size of the audience?

Q What is the average age of the audience?

Q What is the ratio of males to females in the audience?

Q Is the audience well informed about your subject?

Q Has the audience chosen, or been asked, to attend?

Q What do the members of the audience have in common?

Q What prejudices does the audience hold?

Q What is the cultural make-up of the audience?

Q Does everyone or anyone in the audience know you?

4 Always remember to talk *to* your audience, rather than *at* them.

EVALUATING AN AUDIENCE

To communicate your message effectively, you need to take account of the cultural values and opinions held by your audience. Consider how they might react to any sensitive issues raised in your speech, and be aware that this could affect the rest of your presentation. If the audience members are known to hold strong opinions on your chosen subject, be wary of introducing contentious issues without supporting your point of view, and remember that humour can easily cause offence, so use it sparingly in your speech.

FINDING OUT MORE

The primary source of information about your audience will be the organizer of the event at which you are speaking. If your presentation is to be included as part of a conference, ask for a list of the delegates in advance. If you are making a presentation to a potential new client, ask your contacts in the appropriate industry what they can tell you about them. Before addressing a public meeting, take the time to read the local press to see what concerns your audience might have. Use this prior knowledge to your best advantage – a speech that connects directly with members of the audience and shows that you have done your background work will be well received.

BEING ADAPTABLE

The size of the audience will have a significant impact on the way you structure your presentation. With small groups there is plenty of opportunity for two-way interaction – you can answer questions as you go along, or you can ask your audience for their opinions about the questions and issues you are raising. With large groups, the communication is almost entirely one-way, and a very different approach is required by the speaker. It is vital that your material is clear, precise, and easy to follow so that the audience's interest is held throughout.

5 Involve your audience in the presentation as much as possible.

ADJUSTING YOUR PRESENTATION TO AUDIENCE SIZE

AUDIENCE SIZE	PRESENTATION STYLES	TECHNIQUES
SMALL AUDIENCE A group of fewer than 15 people is considered a small audience. Most people will be asked to address an audience of this size at some point in their working career.	**FORMAL** Follow formal procedures in committee meetings, sales pitches to prospective clients, and interdepartmental presentations.	● Establish eye contact with each member of the group at an early stage. ● Face your audience at all times – this will help hold their attention.
	INFORMAL Use informality to break the ice when presenting new products to known suppliers and when presenting to colleagues.	● Interact with the audience by soliciting questions. ● Allow individuals to have a say, but keep it brief.
LARGE AUDIENCE A group of 15 or more people constitutes a large audience. It is easier to address this size of audience if you already have previous presenting experience. 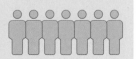	**FORMAL** Follow formal procedures when giving a speech at a conference or at the annual general meeting of a public company.	● Make sure that all of the audience members are able to hear you clearly, especially at the back of the venue. ● Link, sum up, emphasize, and repeat main points.
	INFORMAL Use informal procedures when making a spontaneous presentation from the floor at a formal conference.	● Speak slowly, and enunciate at all times. ● Keep your message broad, general, and simple. Go into more detail only if asked.

DEALING WITH LOGISTICS

O nly meticulous organization can ensure that your presentation will be effective. Careful planning of the practical details in advance will free you nearer the time to concentrate on perfecting your presentation, rather than dealing with unforeseen hitches.

6 Visit the venue in advance to become familiar with its layout.

CONSIDERING KEY POINTS AT THE START

LOGISTICS

Who is organizing the event? → Find out, and obtain full details.

How will you be travelling? → Plan and check travel arrangements.

VENUE

What size and shape is the room? → Request a floor plan from the organizer.

What equipment will be available? → Find out if you have to supply anything yourself.

TIMETABLE

Who is speaking before you? → Find out if you will have chance to listen to them.

Who will be introducing you? → Make sure they are briefed in advance.

ORGANIZING YOUR SCHEDULE

At an early stage, think through the event in its entirety. If the venue being used is not local, you will need to plan your travel arrangements and organize accommodation well in advance. Try to allow about three hours on the day of the presentation, or the evening before, to prepare yourself for it – both mentally and physically. You should also set aside about an hour to think through your speech and, if possible, rehearse on arrival at the venue. Plan what clothes to wear, and ensure they are clean and pressed. If you are the first (or only) speaker, check that any equipment you will be using is in working order.

7 Compile a schedule of preparations for the day.

PLANNING TRAVEL

Calculate your departure time carefully to avoid arriving late at your venue and not having sufficient time to prepare. Work backwards from the time you want to arrive, adding together journey times, then add at least one hour as a safety factor. Allow for delays, and if travelling by plane, include the time of the journey from the airport. Build enough time into your schedule to rest, and to overcome jet-lag if you are travelling over a long distance to give your speech.

8 Take work with you to occupy journey time.

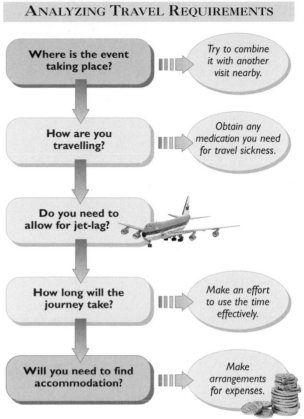

ANALYZING TRAVEL REQUIREMENTS

Where is the event taking place?
→ *Try to combine it with another visit nearby.*

How are you travelling?
→ *Obtain any medication you need for travel sickness.*

Do you need to allow for jet-lag?

How long will the journey take?
→ *Make an effort to use the time effectively.*

Will you need to find accommodation?
→ *Make arrangements for expenses.*

MAKING TIME TO PREPARE

The casual, seemingly effortless presentations that are most successful are invariably the result of a great deal of preparation, research, and hard work. A company chairperson's annual speech to shareholders may take several speechwriters weeks of drafting and redrafting before it is of a suitable standard, whereas an induction for new trainees may take considerable work initially but then require only a little last-minute reworking. Start preparing at least four weeks before your presentation to allow time to formulate ideas and gather any necessary reference material. As you gain experience, you may find that you need less time.

9 For every hour of presentation, put aside 10 hours for preparation.

Making Itineraries and Checklists

Even the most organized speakers have many practicalities to remember before giving a speech. Making an itinerary and listing all the materials and props that you require for your presentation are as essential to preparation as rehearsing your speech. The safest way to do this is to make a checklist, noting down points as you think of them. Work through your checklist, and try to foresee any potential hitches. If the presentation is taking place away from your place of work, make sure that you leave a contact number with your colleagues in case they need to get in touch with you during the day. Be sure they know the time of the presentation, and ask them not to disturb you just before or during it – except in a real emergency.

10 Confirm all the details of the event in writing with the organizers.

11 Always check the expertise of guest speakers carefully.

Points to Remember

- Potential venues should always be checked out for suitability.
- Size of audience plays a crucial role in the choice of venue.
- In most cases, personal opinions should not influence choice of guest speakers.
- A list of alternative speakers should be made in case your first choice cannot attend.
- Whenever possible, professional rivalries between guest speakers need to be avoided.
- Direct questions or comments from members of the audience should always be channelled through the chairperson.
- Details of dates, venues, order of proceedings, and other speakers must be circulated in advance.

Organizing a Presentation Yourself

If you are asked to organize a presentation yourself, there are several important decisions to make early on concerning the venue, speakers, and size of audience. Draw up a list of possible venues to compare the advantages and disadvantages of each, bearing in mind costs, location, capacity, and facilities. Select a venue to suit the size of your audience and the style of the presentation. Pass on all these details to the other speakers so that they can organize their presentations accordingly. Keep an alternative venue in mind in case your first choice is not available on the date you require or falls through after it has been booked. When considering guest speakers, check their credentials thoroughly to ensure that they have the necessary expertise. Give them plenty of notice, and reconfirm the details before the presentation. As with venues, keep alternative speakers in mind.

ORGANIZING A GROUP PRESENTATION

If you are going to organize a group presentation, you need to consider some additional points. The secret of a successful group presentation is to keep a tight hold on the proceedings, since events can easily degenerate into chaos if people speak out of turn. Discuss beforehand the order in which the panel members will speak, and draw up an agenda well in advance so that each member of the panel is aware of this running order. It is important to adhere to this, so appoint a strong chairperson to regulate the proceedings strictly.

When organizing a group presentation, research the background of your chosen speakers carefully – it is vital to have the right balance among the participants. If they are too like-minded, there will be little discussion generated by their speeches; if their ideas clash, they may react to one another with hostility while on the podium. If necessary, build in time for a final question-and-answer session between the panel and audience.

THINGS TO DO

1. Book a venue with the facilities to cope with group presentations.
2. Check that there are no personal animosities between proposed speakers.
3. Invite the speakers, and confirm their attendance.
4. Discuss the running order of the speeches.
5. Draw up a rigid timetable.
6. Appoint a strong individual to act as chairperson.

12 Research your audience before sending invitations to a presentation.

INVITING AN AUDIENCE

When thinking about who should attend a presentation, bear in mind the following points:
- Who would benefit from hearing the information in the presentation?
- What would you like the audience to learn from the presentation?
- How can you reach the target audience?

Planning your publicity is an integral part of the organizational process. Once you have decided on your target audience, ensure that advertising is placed where they will see it – for example, in an appropriate trade publication. The time, date, and venue should be clearly visible. Have personal invitations sent to anyone you wish to attend.

223

KNOWING YOUR VENUE

*I*f possible, visit your chosen presentation *venue in advance to check out the layout. If this is not practical, ask the organizers to send you a detailed floorplan showing all the facilities. Consider the lighting, acoustics, seating, and power supply carefully.*

13 Assess all details of a venue, no matter how minor they may appear.

ASSESSING THE VENUE

The venue will set the mood of your presentation. An informal gathering in a sunny room on a university campus will put an audience in a very different frame of mind than will the sterile conference hall of a large hotel. If you visit the venue in advance, note down as many details as possible – including its atmosphere and size. Assess your venue at the same time of day as your presentation will be given so that you will be able to make informed decisions about the seating and lighting. Take the opportunity to check out the locations of doorways, power points, light switches, and refreshment facilities.

Keep area around doorway clear for easy entry and exit

Position refreshments at the rear of the venue to avoid possible distractions

Locate power points, and check whether you need extension leads

Lower window blinds to shut out light when projecting visual aids on to screen

14 Locate the light switches so that, if necessary, you can dim the lights to use your visual aids.

▲ ASSESSING THE BASICS
When visiting a venue in advance, try to assess whether there are any awkward obstructions that might hide you from the audience. Check the positions of doorways, power points, and other facilities, and get a feel for the atmosphere of the room.

15 Decide on the positioning of any visual aids well in advance.

CONSIDERING THE DETAILS

When assessing a venue, take careful stock of its location – is it accessible to your audience? Is it near an airport, railway station, or underground? Is the venue on the flight path of a major airport, or next to a noisy restaurant? Are there immovable features that could restrict the audience's view? If so, plan your seating around these. Can you control the heating or air conditioning? If so, adjust the temperature to just below what is comfortable, since considerable warmth will be generated by a large number of people being together in one room.

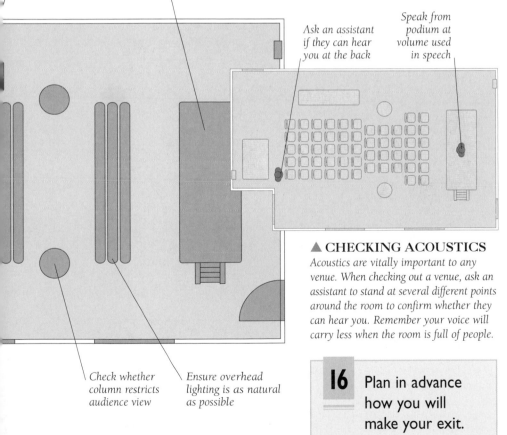

Provide a place for audience to collect handouts after presentation

Make sure stage is well-lit

Ask an assistant if they can hear you at the back

Speak from podium at volume used in speech

Check whether column restricts audience view

Ensure overhead lighting is as natural as possible

▲ CHECKING ACOUSTICS

Acoustics are vitally important to any venue. When checking out a venue, ask an assistant to stand at several different points around the room to confirm whether they can hear you. Remember your voice will carry less when the room is full of people.

16 Plan in advance how you will make your exit.

SEATING THE AUDIENCE

It is important to get the right balance when seating your audience. Comfort is an obvious factor to consider, but you must ensure that your audience is not so comfortable that they fall asleep, or so uncomfortable that they start fidgeting before you reach the end of your presentation. Ideally, chairs should be upright and of equal size. If you can adjust the seating, place chairs far enough apart to allow people to put their bags and briefcases on the floor beside them. Spacing the chairs out in this way will also prevent the audience from feeling claustrophobic. If you think your audience will want to take notes during your presentation, provide chairs with armrests on which to balance notepads. To ensure that the seats in the front of the auditorium fill up first, remove seats from the rear. Keep a number of accessible spare seats in reserve to put out for any latecomers. Finally, be sure to comply with the venue's fire safety regulations with regard to seating arrangements.

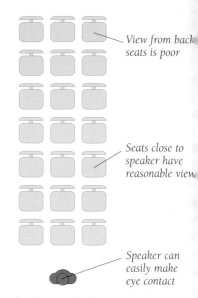

View from back seats is poor

Seats close to speaker have reasonable view

Speaker can easily make eye contact

▲ PLAN ONE

A series of straight, narrow rows allows the speaker to make eye contact with all of the audience. However, this layout does not provide a good view or acoustics for people seated at the back of the venue.

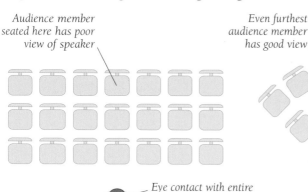

Audience member seated here has poor view of speaker

Even furthest audience member has good view

Eye contact with entire audience is difficult

▲ PLAN TWO

Here an audience of the same size as that in Plan One is seated closer to the speaker. The majority of the audience has a good view of the speaker and is near enough to hear the presentation clearly. The speaker has to work hard to make eye contact with everyone.

Speaker can see entire audience

▲ PLAN THREE

This semi-circular layout is popular as it provides the optimum arrangement for acoustics and visibility – but the disadvantage is that it takes up more space than Plans One and Two. The speaker can maintain strong eye contact with all members of the audience.

CHECKING THE VENUE'S AUDIO-VISUAL FACILITIES

If you intend to use audio-visual elements in your presentation, you must check that the appropriate facilities are available at the venue, and that they function correctly. Familiarize yourself with each piece of equipment to avoid any delays or mistakes during the presentation. Large venues will require the use of a basic public address system (PA) comprising speakers, an amplifier, and one or more microphones. If a PA is not available, you will have to bring and install your own – they can be hired. Make sure is it powerful enough for the venue room. Ensure that there is a screen on which to project any images, checking that the size of the screen is appropriate to the size of the venue, and that it is in view of the whole audience.

17 Ensure that you know how the public address system functions.

18 Keep spare seats in reserve for any latecomers.

USING A MICROPHONE

A microphone is needed only when you are speaking to a large audience, or if you are speaking in the open air. If you need to use one, always test it in advance, making adjustments for volume and background noise. Hand-held or podium microphones tend to restrict movement, so if you will need to demonstrate visual aids use a wireless hand-held model. Clip-on microphones allow you to use both hands while presenting your speech, but always be sure to position them correctly otherwise they can exaggerate noises such as breathing or turning pages.

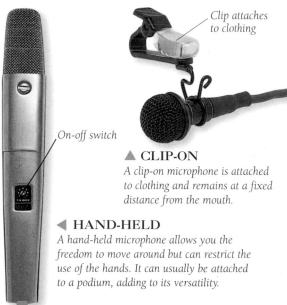

Clip attaches to clothing

On-off switch

▲ **CLIP-ON**
A clip-on microphone is attached to clothing and remains at a fixed distance from the mouth.

◀ **HAND-HELD**
A hand-held microphone allows you the freedom to move around but can restrict the use of the hands. It can usually be attached to a podium, adding to its versatility.

CLARIFYING OBJECTIVES

Before you prepare for a presentation, it is important that you think about your objectives. Do you want to entertain the audience, pass on vital information, or inspire them to rush off and take immediate action as a consequence of your speech?

19 Structure your speech around three or four main points.

SETTING THE TONE

The general tone and style of your presentation can reinforce the purpose of your speech. If you want to pass on information, then you need to take a logically consistent, well-structured approach to your subject matter. If your main purpose is to entertain, include some jokes, anecdotes, and funny stories. If you want to inspire the audience, keep the content of your speech positive and pitched at a level at which they can respond personally and emotionally.

20 Keep the audience interested by including a few relevant anecdotes.

ENCOURAGING RESPONSES

Every speaker wants to give a successful and well-received presentation, but many do not know that there are practical methods to achieve this. By structuring your speech in certain ways, you can elicit the response you want from the audience. For example, if you are providing your audience with new information, you may want them to ask questions at the end of your speech. Whet their appetites for the subject by not telling them everything they need to know immediately, but encouraging them to be inquisitive.

▼ USING THE THREE Es
Each successful presentation has three essential objectives. The first aim is to educate: the audience should learn something from your speech. The second is to entertain: the audience should enjoy your speech. The final element is to explain: all parts of your speech should be clear to your audience.

Educate → **Entertain** → **Explain**

USING YOUR KNOWLEDGE

The main objective of making a presentation is to relay information to your audience, and nothing is more likely to capture and hold their attention than your enthusiasm for the subject. Do not get too carried away with your preparation – plan to lead your audience with your enthusiasm rather than overwhelm them with it. Authoritative knowledge usually speaks for itself, so there is no need for you to drop names or academic references if you really know your subject. You will gain credibility if you handle audience questions adeptly, so be well-informed and well-prepared.

21 Make sure you deliver the main concepts of your presentation clearly.

22 Summarize your main points in one sentence.

SELECTING KEY POINTS

Every adult audience has a limited attention span of about 45 minutes. In that time, they will absorb only about a third of what was said, and a maximum of seven concepts. Limit yourself to three or four main points, and emphasize them at the beginning of your speech, in the middle, and again at the end to reiterate your message. Try to find a catchy title that sums up your speech, but avoid being too clever or too obscure. "The Role of TQM in BPR" is fine for managers in your company who know that you are intending to talk about the concepts of total quality management and business process re-engineering, but it is no use making your title so cryptic that you confuse even the most informed audiences. Your audience will be most open to you if they have a clear idea of the subject of your speech.

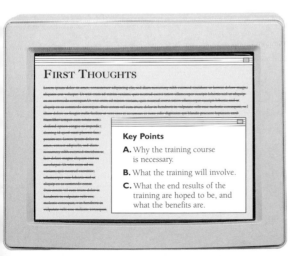

FIRST THOUGHTS

Key Points

A. Why the training course is necessary.

B. What the training will involve.

C. What the end results of the training are hoped to be, and what the benefits are.

▲ CHOOSING YOUR MAIN POINTS

Clarify your ideas by summarizing the main ideas from your notes into succinct points. Limit yourself to three or four points to keep your message simple and memorable.

FINDING MATERIAL

A successful presentation always begins with careful background research. This requires initiative and hard work, and can be time-consuming. Allocate sufficient time for your research, and explore as many sources as possible, from press cuttings to the Internet.

23 Keep your main objectives in mind while researching your material.

A. Why the training course is necessary.

B. What the training will involve.

C. What the end results of the training are hoped to be, and what the benefits are.

▲ USING YOUR MAIN POINTS

When you begin your research, keep the three or four main points in mind. As you find material relevant to your speech, organize it into separate files for each main point until you have enough to fill out your presentation.

FINDING SOURCES

A good starting point for research is to review one of the leading books on the subject of your presentation, and to look at its bibliography. From there you should be able to find a large amount of relevant reference material. For newspaper or magazine articles, consider using a press-cuttings agency, which, for a fee, will supply you regularly with a package of articles on virtually any subject that you care to name. This will provide you with the free time to explore the many other sources of information available, for example:

● Management reports, government papers, and professional journals;

● Friends, family, and other personal contacts;

● Videos, CD-ROMs, and the Internet.

RESEARCHING MATERIAL

At the beginning of your research, allow yourself enough time to consider thoroughly the advantages and disadvantages of every source of information you intend to use. Be realistic about what you hope to find out from each source, and think about how best to use the information in your speech. Always consult your personal contacts for any leads; there is nothing more frustrating than spending days in a library only to find that a friend of a friend is the greatest living expert on your subject.

24 Try different sources to see which you find the most helpful.

FRESHENING UP YOUR RESEARCH

Be open-minded when starting on your research, and seek out fresh fields of research to enliven your presentation. Do not rely on dusty old books – explore new reference sources on the Internet to glean the latest information on your subject. Your speech will be all the more appealing to the audience if it sounds innovative rather than like a rehash of old information from oft-quoted sources. Make the audience feel that you are feeding them new knowledge by providing fresh information around your basic facts and figures.

▲ MAKING GOOD USE OF YOUR TIME

It is important to decide very quickly whether or not a particular avenue of research is worth pursuing. Once you begin to find relevant information, note its source and its main points. Is it the most up-to-date material on the subject? Is the information accurate? Is it giving you any new leads or areas of research? Persevere only with the material that fills your research criteria.

▲ EXPLORING WEB SITES

Each Web site on the Internet holds a wealth of information that can be accessed, saved, or printed out, and used as reference material. One of the chief advantages of this mode of research is that the information Web sites hold is usually more frequently updated than the same information in print.

USING NEW TECHNOLOGY

The Internet brings an international electronic library right on to your desk. Use well-chosen key words to search for relevant reference material from the extraordinary range of information available on the Internet – new sites are springing up daily. The more specific your key words are, the more chance you have of finding the data you require within a reasonable length of time. Store large amounts of material on computerized data bases, which can be purchased as ready-made software packages or designed specifically for your purposes.

25 Do not ignore a good source just because the information is not immediately accessible to you.

STRUCTURING MATERIAL

The order in which you present the main points of your presentation, and the emphasis each point is given, will affect the message that your audience takes away. Use the most appropriate structure in your speech to give your audience the right message.

26 Decide how many points you intend to make in your presentation.

CHOOSING A STRUCTURE

There are several ways in which you can present your three or four main points. You may choose to introduce them separately, either one after the other in order of importance, or chronologically, or in any other sequence that makes sense. If you want one particular point to give the strongest impression, present it first, and follow it with supporting points – or any other points that you are making. Alternatively, interweave your points to highlight their equal significance. The structure most commonly used by speakers is to overlap the main points that are being made. This way, an idea can be left open and referred back to in response to subsequent ideas in the presentation.

27 Make sure that your presentation ends on a strong, positive point.

1   2   3   4

▲ MAKING SEPARATE POINTS
Here ideas that do not necessarily flow into each other can be presented separately and given equal weight. Remember, an audience may assume that the first point has greater significance.

1   2   3   4

▲ EMPHASIZING ONE POINT
If one point is of greater significance than the others, put it first and allow it the most time so that you can discuss it fully. Back it up or complement it with your secondary or supporting points.

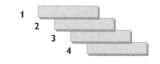

▲ OVERLAPPING POINTS
In practice, the most frequently occurring structure is the one in which each point overlaps and depends to some extent upon the others. The second point has to be partially unveiled in order to explain the first, and so on. Each subsequent point can be referred to in relation to the earlier points, linking all the main points together.

MATCHING PRESENTATION STRUCTURE TO MATERIAL

TYPES OF STRUCTURE	PRACTICAL USES
MAKING SEPARATE POINTS Points are presented in a sequence that suits the particular subject.	Formal presentations, such as a serious educational talk or a lecture on management theory, can benefit from this presentation structure. If the audience members are taking notes, the speaker can assist them by summarizing each point after it has been made and providing a brief introduction to lead into the following point.
EMPHASIZING ONE POINT The main point is followed by several other points.	Examples of this type of presentation might include a talk given to staff about the need for improved customer service. The structure is emphatic and is suitable for use when the audience is well-informed about the subject matter and can grasp a high level of detail. It is also useful if you want to present another aspect of the same subject.
OVERLAPPING POINTS Points are referred back to or reintroduced for emphasis.	This structure is most suitable for informal talks given in front of a small audience. It is often used in meetings attended by close colleagues, who are familiar with the subject matter and can cope with a relatively complex presentation. Overlapping points encourage debate and audience intervention as different ideas present themselves.

USING NARRATIVE

The basic technique of narrative is to give your subject a recognizable beginning, middle, and end. The most common use of this technique is in storytelling. For your presentation to be a success, it is important that you follow this basic format when composing your speech. The introduction to your presentation is the beginning; the middle section consists of your central themes and ideas (using whichever structure you decide best suits your purpose); while the end is formed by your conclusion, referring back to your main themes, and then taking questions from the audience if necessary. Remember that it is important to give the audience clear signposts at the beginning and end of each stage of your presentation.

▲ **USING SYMBOLS**
Think laterally when structuring your speech. Choose familiar images to support your ideas, such as a cat to show instinctive behaviour. Look outside your original field of research for analogies that illustrate points vividly.

USING AN OUTLINE

It is helpful to prepare a written outline of the material that you wish to present. This will help to clarify the structure of your presentation while you are writing it and can be used to jog your memory while you are making the presentation. Think of your three or four main points as A, B, C, and D, and then put subheadings under each one (1, 2, 3). Label any secondary subheadings as i), ii), iii), and so on. When writing these notes, keep them simple so that they are easy to read at a glance.

A. Why training is needed.
  1. Staff benefit from refresher course.
  2. New staff will learn correct procedures.

Main points are labelled alphabetically

B. What training involves.
  1. Improving performance.
    i) Tests of skill level.
    ii) Gaps in knowledge.
  2. Practicalities.

Subheadings are labelled with Arabic numerals

C. Expected end results.
  1. Improved efficiency.
  2. Greater productivity.

Secondary subheadings are labelled with Roman numerals

▲ OUTLINING A STRUCTURE
Make up a rough outline of the structure you are planning for your presentation, as in the sample above. Use this as a basis from which to expand on your theme while you are researching and preparing your presentation.

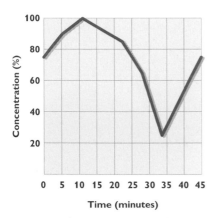

▲ AUDIENCE ATTENTION SPAN
This chart shows a typical audience's attention span, based on a 45-minute presentation. Audiences are most alert just after the start of a presentation, reaching a peak at about 10 minutes. Attention fades until 30–35 minutes have passed, then increases as the presentation nears its end.

OPENING EFFECTIVELY

It is essential to make a good impression at the beginning of your presentation, and one of the best ways to do this is for you to appear positive and confident. This means you must first be well-prepared. Seasoned presenters who prefer not to use notes invariably write out their first sentence or two. That way, they can concentrate more on the impression they are giving, and less on the words they are speaking. Plan an effective opening that provides the audience with an outline of the presentation you are about to give, informing them briefly of the points you will be making during your speech. Use anecdotes to break the ice and draw the audience into your speech in a familiar way. Always remember, however, that the audience is not at its most alert at the very beginning of your speech, so save your strongest point for a few minutes into the presentation.

LINKING AND SUMMING UP

It is important to incorporate clear signposts into your presentation. Plan a logical flow of ideas and themes to help the audience follow your presentation easily, and introduce new subjects by making clear links between the old and new ideas. Listen to professional speakers on radio and television, and note the techniques they use to link together the points or themes of their speeches and sum up each point before introducing a new one. These links and summaries are as important as the main points themselves, so plan them well.

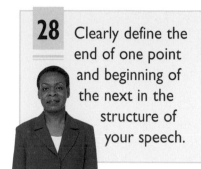

28 Clearly define the end of one point and beginning of the next in the structure of your speech.

29 Do not change the tone of your voice too often; this can sound false.

USING REPETITION

Recapping information during your presentation is an effective way of reinforcing the main points of your argument. When structuring your speech, build some repetition into its framework at the end of each main point and in the conclusion. However, simply repeating the information you have already delivered in the main body of your speech is not enough. Use different wording to keep the ideas sounding fresh, yet familiar.

ENDING MEMORABLY

Structuring a strong ending to your presentation is as important as planning a good beginning – it is vital to signal to your audience that the end of your speech is approaching. Insert phrases such as "for my final point..." or "in conclusion..." to alert the audience to the fact that you are about to summarize all that you have said. They will be grateful for the opportunity to catch up on any points they may have missed during your speech.

▼ REINFORCING POINTS
It is important to reinforce the main points of any presentation. You can do this by first giving the audience a "contents list" of your speech, then discussing the issues you are raising, and finishing off with a summary.

| Tell them what you are going to tell them | Tell them | Tell them what you have told them |

WRITING A PRESENTATION

It is important to be aware that written material can sound very different when it is delivered to an audience in spoken form. Learn to write your prose in a natural oral style that follows natural speech patterns and is suitable for verbal presentation.

30 Remember that writing a speech is different from hearing it read.

STARTING TO WRITE

Once you have completed all your research and outlined the structure of your presentation, you are ready to start writing. Try to imagine your words as you would like your audience to hear them. Spend some quiet time alone thinking about what you will write, then compose a first draft by writing down – without stopping – everything that you think you would like to include. If you are unsure about how to write for speech, prepare by assessing the difference between spoken and written language.

31 Find different ways for expressing the same idea. Use the most natural one.

ADAPTING WRITING STYLES FOR SPEECH

SENTENCE STRUCTURE	SPEAKING RATHER THAN WRITING
GRAMMAR Try to avoid sentences that are grammatically correct but sound stilted when spoken. To sound direct, use the first and second person (*I* and *you*) and active verbs.	*Say*: "The accounting system I work with", *not* "The accounting system with which I work".
	Say: "You must recognize these ploys for what they are", *not* "It is important that these ploys are recognized...".
SYNTAX Always put the most important or interesting facts first. Do not begin a sentence with a subordinate clause or with any statement that could be put in parentheses.	*Say*: "Lower costs and increased output – that's what we need", *not* "We need to reduce costs and increase output".
	Say: "This can make all the difference", *not* "Although this may seem a minor detail, it can make all the difference...".

STREAMLINING MATERIAL

Once you have produced the first draft of your presentation, you can begin to hone down the material. Read through your draft to ensure that you have prioritized the facts correctly and included all the essential information. Fill in your material with relevant examples to reinforce your main points. Finally, use items of particular interest or appeal, which are not essential but will enhance audience enjoyment of your presentation, to add humour and topicality to your speech.

32 Be particular about what you include in the presentation.

▼ PRIORITIZING LEVELS OF INFORMATION

Before you begin, write down every point relevant to the theme of your presentation, and put each in one of these categories.

Must know ➡ **Should know** ➡ **Nice to know**

WRITING TO SOUND NATURAL

The best starting point for giving a successful presentation is that you feel confident and relaxed about the words you are delivering, so when you are writing your speech, keep your sentence construction simple. Think about your audience as a single person – this will help to create an atmosphere of intimacy. Speakers who succeed in doing this make every member of the audience feel that their message is directed uniquely at them, which holds their attention. If you are not sure whether you sound natural, tape-record yourself reading a draft of your speech, then listen and amend your text where necessary.

DO'S AND DON'TS

✔ Do use simple, direct sentences.

✔ Do use the pronouns "you" and "I".

✔ Do use active verbs (run, go, do, use, etc.).

✔ Do sprinkle your speech liberally with adjectives.

✔ Do prepare and rehearse phrases to avoid stumbling.

✔ Do include examples and analogies to illustrate your points.

✘ Don't use jargon or inappropriate language.

✘ Don't fill your speech with irrelevant points.

✘ Don't feel that you have to write out the speech word for word.

✘ Don't overwhelm the audience with too much detail.

✘ Don't patronize your audience.

✘ Don't try to imitate someone else's style; it will sound false.

33 Make sure the written structure of your presentation is not too complex, or it may be confusing.

CONDENSING A PRESENTATION INTO NOTES

If you choose to deliver a presentation using notes, begin by writing a full draft of the presentation, including all your main points and the examples you will use to illustrate and explain them. This script is the starting point from which you can begin to condense your prose into notes. Using clearly numbered note cards, pick out the key words and phrases from your script, and write them legibly on one side of card. Do not write too much on each card, and keep the information simple and unambiguous.

◀ **PREPARING A DRAFT**

Having decided on the structure of your presentation and then compiled your research material, write (or type) the speech out in full. Edit and re-edit this draft until you are satisfied with the flow and pace of the speech.

◀ **PREPARING NOTES**

Extract the major points from the final draft, and write them on numbered cards. Limit your notes to two points per card for clarity.

PACING A SPEECH

Think about what makes a good speech work well. More often than not, it is the timing. The silent parts of a speech – in other words, the pauses – are just as important as the spoken words in communicating the content of the speech, since they provide aural punctuation. When writing your speech, consider how it will sound to your audience. Whether you choose to read the presentation from notes or as a full script, write "pause" wherever you feel a break is necessary – for example, where a point requires emphasis, or to mark a break between one clear idea and another. Include these pauses when rehearsing. Using silence takes courage: a scripted pause should last about three seconds – much longer than a pause in your normal speech.

34 Print your speech on one side of the page only, and use a large typeface.

35 Always number the pages of a full, written speech.

PREPARING NOTE CARDS

Regard using notes during a presentation as an insurance against forgetting your speech – you do not have to read from them parrot-fashion, but you have the security of knowing that they are there if your mind goes blank. Notes are meant to provide a series of cues to remind you what you want to say, and in what order, allowing you to talk to the audience instead of reciting your presentation to them. There are a number of useful techniques you can use if speaking from notes, such as condensing a preprepared outline, writing key sentences, or noting key words – but write out quotations and jokes in full unless you are sure you know them. Use a system of colour coding to mark text that you can cut from your speech without compromising the integrity of your message if, for instance, you run over your allotted time. For example, write essential text in blue ink, and write text that can be cut in green ink.

> **36** Make notes on firm paper or index cards.

▲ USING PROMPTS
Transfer key words and phrases from your presentation on to cards. Be straightforward in what you write down so that you are able to remember the point of each prompt.

PREPARING A WRITTEN SCRIPT

If you choose to use a written script in your presentation, it is essential to arrange it carefully. Use large type and double line-spacing so that the text is easy to read. Set out the headings clearly so that it is easy to keep your place. Use a variety of different styling methods, such as emboldening or italicizing, to highlight the text that you want to emphasize. Finally, print the finished document on to sturdy paper, and keep a spare copy.

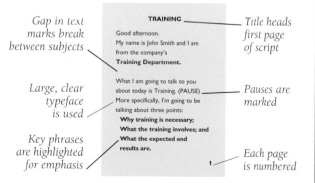

Gap in text marks break between subjects

Large, clear typeface is used

Key phrases are highlighted for emphasis

Title heads first page of script

Pauses are marked

Each page is numbered

TRAINING

Good afternoon.
My name is John Smith and I am from the company's
Training Department.

What I am going to talk to you about today is Training. (PAUSE)
More specifically, I'm going to be talking about three points:
Why training is necessary;
What the training involves; and
What the expected end results are.

1

▲ LAYING OUT A WRITTEN SCRIPT
Highlight emphases and pauses when laying out your script – this will help you to speak naturally and confidently to your audience, which is essential for a smooth-running presentation.

USING AUDIO-VISUAL AIDS

Audio-visual (AV) aids can be central to a presentation, as they are often able to illustrate difficult concepts more easily than words. Always ask yourself if using AV aids will contribute to your presentation, and never be tempted to use them unnecessarily.

37 Always rehearse your presentation using your chosen audio-visual aids.

USING DIFFERENT AUDIO-VISUAL AIDS

TYPES OF AUDIO-VISUAL AID	EXAMPLES

LOW COMPLEXITY
The advantage of these aids is their simplicity, and in the fact that no power supply is needed for them to work. Information can be prepared in advance, leaving little to set up on the day. Handouts can be prepared for any size of audience, but boards and flip-charts need to be visible and are best for small audiences.

HANDOUTS
Distribute these before giving your presentation, preferably during a break. Make sure that you give the handouts a purpose by referring to them during your presentation.

MEDIUM COMPLEXITY
This group contains some of the most commonly used AV aids, which achieve good effects without involving too much technical hardware. The aids themselves need setting up on the day of your presentation, but the information and any slides used in conjunction with them can be prepared in advance.

SLIDE PROJECTOR
Arrange the slides you need to illustrate your arguments in a carousel prior to your speech. Practise operating the projector before you give your presentation.

HIGH COMPLEXITY
These aids involve the very highest level of technical capability and may require a specialized team to set them up. The impact achieved using high-complexity AV aids can be stunning and well worth the work, but there is more opportunity for breakdown or failure the more complex the AV aid.

VIDEO
Use video to show short, live-action images or a taped message from a speaker who is not able to attend the presentation in person.

CHOOSING AV AIDS

There is a range of AV aids to suit different types of presentation. Such aids can sometimes distance you from the audience, however, so use them only if they are appropriate and helpful. AV aids have varying levels of complexity. Many require a source of electricity, which can lead to problems if the power fails; others may need to be designed or installed by specialists and may be difficult to use.

38 Pause when you first ask your audience to look at a visual aid.

WRITING BOARD
Use a writing board to illustrate your points in an informal presentation to a small audience. Make sure that your writing is legible to the people sitting at the back of the audience.

FLIP-CHART
Prepare any number of sheets in advance, using charts and diagrams to highlight your arguments. Emphasize key points with colour, and ensure that the flip-chart can be seen by everyone in the audience.

OVERHEAD PROJECTOR
This is the best way of presenting charts and tables. Use a pointer to draw attention to particular graphs or numbers without obscuring the audience's view of the image.

AUDIO SYSTEM
An audio system with headphones is vital if you have to provide simultaneous translation facilities. A microphone, amplifier, and speakers are also handy for large audiences.

MULTIMEDIA
Use CD-ROM packages with moving images and an audio track on a large monitor with speakers. Alternatively, employ a software engineer to create a package to your specific requirements.

COMPUTER GRAPHICS
Software can be used to display graphs, charts, or three-dimensional images on screen. Moving graphics can be used to show how statistics will change over time.

CONSIDERING AUDIENCE SIZE

Different AV aids suit different sizes of audience, but if your resources are limited you can adapt your AV aids to suit any audience. For example, if you are using computer graphics but want to avoid losing definition of images by enlarging them too much, provide each member of the audience with handouts of the computer graphics you are showing on-screen. Alternatively, if you are presenting to a large audience, project the images on to several large screens.

◀ **VIEW FROM A SMALL AUDIENCE**
When presenting to a small audience sitting close to you, your visual aids will be clearly visible to everyone – whichever type you choose to use.

39 Number your slides to avoid any confusion.

VIEW FROM A ▶ LARGE AUDIENCE
Visual aids that work for a small audience are unlikely to work for a large one. An audience sitting far away may be unable to discern much from them.

PREPARING AV AIDS

All AV aids require considerable preparation, but whereas a writing board can be set up relatively quickly and then used over again, a multimedia demonstration can take a long time to prepare. Generally speaking, the higher the complexity of the AV aid, the more preparation is required.

If you do not have the time, the knowledge, or the creative talent to prepare your own AV aids, enlist somebody to do it for you. Use support staff, a colleague, or an external design agency. Choose your helper carefully, and present them with a tight brief to prevent any misinterpretation regarding the desired final product.

POINTS TO REMEMBER

● Audiences read on-screen material faster than you can speak it, so do not read it out loud for their benefit.

● While one half of the audience will be looking at your visual material, the other half will be looking at you. Stand still when you want the audience to concentrate on visual material.

● If you plan to re-use your AV aids, make sure you arrange to have them collected after your presentation.

MAKING AN IMPACT

During your preparation time, you may find that you can make information easier to understand and express abstract ideas more clearly by adding design elements to visual aids. Keep all visual aids simple and uncluttered, and use design elements consistently. Use bold colours – subtleties between pastels do not carry across a crowded room. The sections on a pie diagram can be completely lost if the colours used are not sufficiently contrasting.

When using video, show long segments that illustrate and complement your points, rather than short bursts, which can distract the audience's attention from the essence of your speech.

40 Use cartoons to make serious points lighter.

41 Write notes on the frames of overhead projector slides.

ASSEMBLING TOOLS

Think carefully about which items you may need in order to make proper use of your chosen AV aids. For example:

- A laser pointer to indicate items on screens, writing boards, or flip-charts;
- Two sets of chalk or special marker pens to use on writing boards;
- Blank acetate sheets for use with an overhead projector;
- Spare flip-chart;
- Extension lead;
- Back-up disks and spare cable for multimedia presentations;
- Copies of videos or slides;
- Adapters, if taking electrical equipment abroad.

KNOWING YOUR AV AIDS

By the time you actually come to give your presentation, you should be fully aware of how to operate any high-complexity AV aids you have chosen to augment your subject matter. Even if you do not enjoy working with multimedia or video aids, there are instances in which the effort (and the additional expense of creating them) is worthwhile, even for a small audience.

On rare occasions when using high-complexity AV aids, you may be unlucky enough to experience technical problems. If you do not have the requisite expertise to deal with these hitches, ensure that someone who does will be present at the venue to help you out. Always take along a series of low-complexity aids, such as handouts, as a back-up, or be prepared to go without any AV aids at all.

42 Take duplicates of all audio-visual materials that you know you cannot do without in your speech.

REHEARSING

Rehearsal is a vital part of preparing for a successful presentation. It is an ideal opportunity to memorize and time your material and to smooth over any rough edges in your delivery. Practise with your AV aids, and allow time for questions at the end.

43 Practise losing your place in your script or notes – and finding it again.

POINTS TO REMEMBER

● You cannot rehearse too much. If you are confident with your material, your audience will have confidence in you.

● The time you will have to speak includes time you will spend using AV aids and answering questions from the audience, so allow for this when rehearsing.

● Rehearsals should rely less and less on the script each time.

● Sample questions should be prepared beforehand, so you can practise answering them and estimate timing.

PRACTISING ALOUD

The main point of a rehearsal is to memorize your material and the order in which you are going to present it. This is your best opportunity to fine-tune the content of your speech, and to ensure that all your points are delivered with the weight and significance you intend. Start rehearsals by simply reading through your full script. Once you are comfortable with the material, begin to practise in front of the mirror, and switch to notes if you are using them. The first attempt may make you feel slightly nervous and uncomfortable, but your confidence should build with each rehearsal, so that you are well-prepared when you stand before your real audience and begin your presentation.

DEVELOPING SPONTANEITY

Only when you are freed from slavish reliance on your script or notes can you begin to feel and sound spontaneous. Speaking off the cuff to an audience is a very different discipline to presenting a rehearsed speech. However, it need not be such a daunting task. Develop the trick of apparent "spontaneity" by knowing your subject inside out. In doing this, you give yourself confidence to add details or examples that have not been written into your speech, thus making your presentation sound fresh, off-the-cuff, and unrehearsed.

44 Practise speaking clearly both in normal tones and at volume.

INVITING FEEDBACK

When you feel ready, begin to practise your speech aloud in front of a friend or colleague, and ask for honest and constructive criticism. Invite your "audience" to point out areas where they feel improvements could be made and to suggest how you can make them. Your audience should bear in mind the context in which the presentation is going to be made, so explain it to them clearly. Try to reproduce the conditions of the presentation, especially the distance between you and the front row of your audience, as closely as possible. That way you can get a sense of how well your voice will carry. Learn to control your voice so that it will sound the same to the audience whether you are presenting in an auditorium or to a small group in a meeting room.

45 Vary the pace of your speech, and decide which pace is most effective.

Use hand gestures that reinforce your message

Audience should watch for any distracting mannerisms

Use notes less as you rehearse and memorize material

Note whether body language of audience indicates interest

◀ **PRACTISING WITH AN AUDIENCE**
Rehearsing in front of a friend will build your confidence. Ask their opinion of both your vocal and physical delivery; enjoy their praise, but acknowledge any criticisms or advice for improvement that they might suggest.

PREPARING YOURSELF

It is as important to prepare yourself as it is to prepare your speech. The overall impact of your presentation will be determined as much by how you appear as by what you say.

BELIEVING IN YOURSELF

A positive self-image is all-important for delivering a successful presentation. Identify your strengths, and make the most of them. Except in very rare cases, the audience is as keen as you are for your presentation to be interesting and successful.

46 An audience is your ally. Its members want to learn from you.

THINKING POSITIVELY

Repeat positive and encouraging thoughts to yourself as you prepare for your presentation and just before it to help boost your confidence and allay any last-minute fears and nerves. For example, try some of the following phrases:

❝ My presentation is interesting and full of great ideas. The audience will love it. ❞

❝ I know my subject inside out. The audience will discover that for themselves early on. ❞

❝ The audience is sure to be enthusiastic. My presentation is strong, and I'm well prepared. ❞

❝ My rehearsals went really well. I can't wait to see the reaction of the audience. ❞

VISUALIZING SUCCESS

When preparing for a presentation, train yourself to visualize the scenario positively. Picture an enthusiastic audience loving your successful presentation. You have a message to convey to the audience, and you are being given the perfect opportunity to do so. Imagine your audience taking notes, laughing at any jokes or anecdotes that you may use, and asking interesting and constructive questions at the end. Visualize the body language of the audience's positive response, and imagine yourself making eye contact with members of the audience to encourage the positive rapport developing between you.

> **47** Behave naturally, and an audience will warm to you.

> **48** Think of a large audience as if it were a small group.

▼ **PICTURING PERFECTION**
Increase your confidence by imagining yourself giving a perfect presentation. Visualize the enthusiastic, interested faces of the audience listening to your speech.

You know your material so well that you do not constantly need to refer to your notes

Audience is interested and attentive

Audience enjoys and applauds your presentation

You look your best and inspire confidence by taking an authoritative stance

ANALYZING APPEARANCE

Your audience will be greatly affected by the way you look, but it is not always easy to judge your own appearance and the impression you are creating. Ask friends or colleagues to comment on your image and help you to adjust it to suit your audience.

49 Study yourself in a mirror to see what impression you make.

POINTS TO REMEMBER

- A good night's sleep is essential before the day of your presentation.
- A hair brush, toothbrush, travel iron, clothes brush, and shoe buffer are useful items to take to the venue, so that you can look your best for your presentation.
- Zips and buttons should be fastened, and your shirt should be tucked in before you enter the presentation room.
- A jacket can be worn to hide any marks that may appear, if perspiration is a problem.

MAKING AN IMPRESSION

First impressions are strong, and very hard to change. Think about how quickly you make judgments about people you meet for the first time. Signals can be picked up very quickly from the way people dress, the way they walk, and even from the way they stand. Before you reach the lectern, your audience will have formed an opinion of you based on these first impressions. It is important to decide on the image you want to convey to your audience early on. Making the right first impression may be vital to the success of your presentation, so dress appropriately, and walk, speak, and stand with confidence, to achieve the right first impression.

KNOWING THE AUDIENCE

Your message will be best received if the audience can identify with you, so it is important always to be aware of the audience's perception of the image you present. If you know a little about your audience, it is easier to decide on the impression that you want to create. Remember, particular styles of dress can communicate specific messages to each different audience. For example, consider how a factory manager will be perceived who addresses the shopfloor workforce wearing a suit in comparison to one dressed in overalls.

50 Do not wear anything that may distract the audience.

AVOIDING PITFALLS

Check the clothes that you are going to wear in advance to prevent the problem of having to wear ill-fitting or unlaundered clothes at your presentation. If you want to look your absolute best for the presentation, bring the outfit with you, and change into it before you begin your last-minute preparation. Check that changing facilities are available at the venue before you arrive.

> **51** Keep your hands out of your pockets during the presentation.

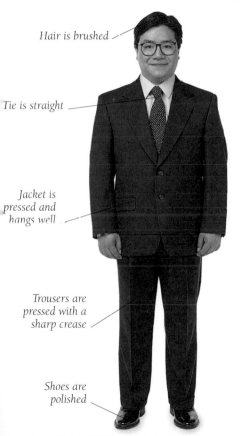

Hair is brushed

Tie is straight

Jacket is pressed and hangs well

Trousers are pressed with a sharp crease

Shoes are polished

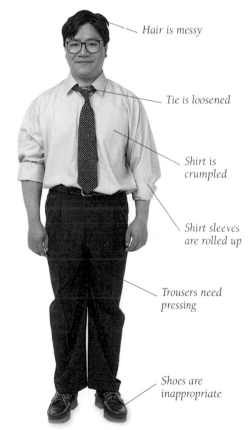

Hair is messy

Tie is loosened

Shirt is crumpled

Shirt sleeves are rolled up

Trousers need pressing

Shoes are inappropriate

▲ LOOKING WELL GROOMED

It is not always necessary to wear a suit, but it is always necessary to look well groomed. Make sure that your clothes are all clean and well pressed, your shoes are polished, and your hair is tidy.

▲ LOOKING UNKEMPT

If you do not take time to groom yourself, you will look unprepared, and the audience may assume that you are not an expert on your subject. An unkempt appearance may distract people from your message.

ENHANCING BODY IMAGE

As much as two thirds of communication between people is totally non-verbal, transmitted either through hand gestures, facial expressions, or other forms of body language. Good body image begins with posture – the way you hold your skeleton.

52 Make sure your body language reflects what you are saying.

ANALYZING YOUR STANCE

The best posture in which to begin your presentation is upright with the feet slightly apart, and the body weight divided equally between them. Your arms should be relaxed by your sides. This is the most non-committal posture and conveys neutral body language. You can build on this to create different impressions if you understand the ways in which various stances are interpreted. Leaning slightly forwards, for example, appears positive and friendly – as if you are involving and encouraging the audience. Leaning backwards, however, may appear negative and possibly aggressive.

53 Learn to relax your facial muscles – and smile!

Head is held high and straight

Shoulders are pulled back and level

Back is straight

Stomach is held in

Arms are relaxed and hang by sides

Bottom is held in

Hands are relaxed; fingers are loose

Legs are straight

Knee joints are loose, not locked

Feet are evenly spaced

◀ **STANDING CORRECTLY**
Holding yourself upright and straight not only has physical benefits, such as improved vocal clarity, but can enhance your mental outlook as well. Standing properly increases your stature, which can give you greater self-confidence.

AVOIDING BAD HABITS

To improve your posture and avoid bad habits, practise in front of a mirror or video-tape your rehearsal, and watch for any unconscious mannerisms. Ask a colleague to watch you practising and comment on distracting gestures or stances.

Speaking into podium muffles voice

Eye contact with audience is lost when you look at podium

Slouching looks unprofessional

Standing with your back to an audience detracts from your speech

Visual aid blocked by body

Crossing your legs makes your stance less stable

◀ **BLOCKING THE VIEW**

Avoid the temptation to lean across visual aids as you use them. Prepare them in advance, and use a pointer so you do not block the audience's view.

▲ **BEING UNBALANCED**

Avoid standing on one leg or crossing your legs. These stances are unstable and also lack authority – an unbalanced body can be an indication of an unbalanced mind.

IMPROVING YOUR STANCE

The muscles in your body are there to hold the skeleton in an upright position. If you use them correctly, your body language will say "I am a well-balanced, confident person". If your muscles relax too much, your body will slouch. To improve your stance, practise standing in an upright position until you are confident that it looks and feels as natural as your usual relaxed standing position. Imagine that you are taller than you are, or that you are gently being pulled upwards by a thread leading from the top of your head, to help achieve and maintain this stance.

54 Always wear comfortable shoes when presenting.

55 Make sure your hair does not fall across your face.

IMPROVING YOUR VOICE

The tone and volume of your voice have a critical effect on a presentation. Understanding how the vocal system works, and how you can control it to manipulate the sound of your voice, is a key part of preparing yourself for a successful presentation.

56 Suck a mint or honey-flavoured sweet just before you begin to speak.

BREATHING CORRECTLY

Breathe slowly and deeply to improve the flow of oxygen into the body and thus the flow of blood to the brain. This will help you think more clearly, which, in turn, will help you order your thoughts when speaking in front of an audience. Taking in more oxygen also improves the flow of air to your vocal chords, allowing you to speak clearly, reducing nervousness, and helping you to remain calm.

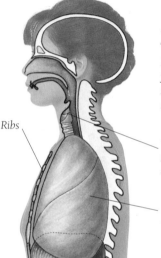

Ribs

◀ **BREATHING FROM THE DIAPHRAGM**
Learning how to breathe from your diaphragm will give more support to your breathing and strengthen the pitch of your voice.

Vocal chords produce sound when they vibrate as air passes over them

Lungs expand and contract with movement of ribs and diaphragm

Diaphragm separates chest from abdomen

57 Consider doing yoga exercises to improve the depth of your breathing.

CONTROLLING YOUR VOICE

Sound is produced when air passes over the vocal chords, making them vibrate. Thus the first requirement for speaking clearly is a good supply of air to the lungs. You can learn to improve your intake of air by practising a simple breathing exercise (see right). The second requirement is a properly functioning larynx, or voice box, which houses the vocal chords. Make an effort to rest your larynx the day before your presentation by limiting how much you speak.

USING THE RIGHT PITCH

In many languages, the only difference between asking a question and making a statement lies in the intonation. A statement such as "the managing director's office is over there" can be understood as a question if the pitch goes up at the end of the sentence. Your audience should understand the exact meaning of your words, so use intonation and pitch carefully to transmit the right message.

58 Practise changing the intonation of a few sentences.

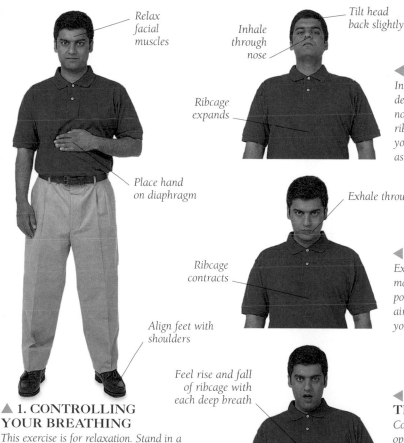

Relax facial muscles

Place hand on diaphragm

Align feet with shoulders

Inhale through nose

Tilt head back slightly

Ribcage expands

◀ **2. INHALING**
Inhale slowly and deeply through the nose, feeling your ribcage expand. Hold your breath for as long as it is comfortable.

Exhale through mouth

Ribcage contracts

◀ **3. EXHALING**
Exhale through the mouth as deeply as possible, pushing all the air out of your lungs as your ribcage contracts.

Feel rise and fall of ribcage with each deep breath

▲ **1. CONTROLLING YOUR BREATHING**
This exercise is for relaxation. Stand in a balanced position with your weight evenly distributed. Place your left hand on your diaphragm, listen to your breathing, and feel the rise and fall of your ribs as you breathe.

◀ **4. REPEATING THE EXERCISE**
Continue to exhale, opening your mouth widely as you do so. Repeat the exercise, pausing briefly between each breath taken.

ELIMINATING TENSION

When you are nervous your muscles become tense. This is because your body is preparing them in an instinctive way for "fight or flight", the basic choice people face when confronted with danger. Simple exercises can help to eliminate this tension.

59 Stretch yourself and imagine that you are taller than you really are.

REDUCING TENSION

Tension building up in your muscles can have some undesirable effects on your body during a presentation. Tension can spoil your posture, making you hunch your shoulders and look defensive. It can also prevent your larynx from functioning smoothly, giving you voice that familiar quiver identified with nervousness. Being tense for any length of time is tiring in itself and can detract from the impact of your presentation. By using a series of simple exercises to help reduce muscular tension, you can make sure that you have more control over your body.

Relieve tens in hand by gripping an relaxing

▲ HAND SQUEEZE

This simple exercise can be done anywhere at any time. Squeeze and release a small rubber ball in your hand. Repeat the exercise several times.

Push head into hands

FRONT VIEW

Keep elbow pushed back

Hands join behind head at base of skull

BACK VIEW

◄ NECK PUSH

To relieve tension in your head and neck, join your hands at the base of your skull, keeping your elbows back. Push your head back into your hands as hard as you can. Hold this stretch for about 10 seconds, release, and repeat.

EXERCISING WHILE SEATED

It is possible to exercise even while you are sitting down – whether at your desk, stuck in a traffic jam, or at home. Follow the simple exercises below to keep your body supple and to help eliminate muscular tension. They do not require a high level of strength or fitness, and are most effective when practised on a daily basis. By taking the time to stretch your body for a couple of minutes each day, you can help prevent the onset of muscle tension and related conditions such as headaches, neckache, and backache.

60 Try to relax in an upright position for 10 minutes without moving.

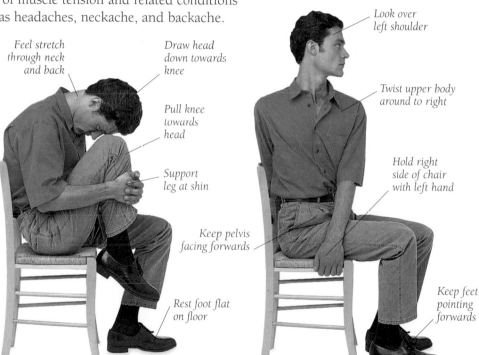

Feel stretch through neck and back

Draw head down towards knee

Pull knee towards head

Support leg at shin

Keep pelvis facing forwards

Rest foot flat on floor

Look over left shoulder

Twist upper body around to right

Hold right side of chair with left hand

Keep feet pointing forwards

▲ **STRETCHING THE BODY**

This stretch relieves tension in the neck, back, and hamstrings. Sit facing forwards in an upright chair, and pull your right knee towards your chest, supporting it with your hands joined across the shin. Lower your head, and hold the stretch for about 10 seconds. Repeat three times with each leg.

▲ **STRETCHING THE SPINE**

To relieve tension in your spine and shoulders while sitting down, hold the back of a chair seat with your right hand, turning to hold the right side of the chair with your left hand. Keeping your hips, legs, and feet facing forwards, look over your left shoulder. Hold for about 10 seconds, then repeat on the other side.

DELIVERING A PRESENTATION

The key to good delivery is to be yourself, to be natural. Anything else looks and sounds false – unless you have considerable acting talent.

CONTROLLING NERVES

All but the most experienced of speakers will feel nervous just before making a presentation. Nervousness prevents you from being natural, so you need to do everything you can to control your nerves in order to give the most effective presentation.

 61 List the factors that make you nervous about presenting.

POINTS TO REMEMBER

- Checking that all your props and audio-visual aids have arrived at the venue enables you to concentrate on preparing yourself.
- Thorough preparation for your presentation should give you the confidence that everything is going to go right.
- Heavy eating or drinking before a presentation makes you feel and sound sleepy.
- Practice makes perfect.

IDENTIFYING NERVES

To deal with nerves effectively, you need to be able to anticipate and identify the signs of nerves that usually affect you. There are many symptoms; one of the most common is the feeling of having "butterflies in the stomach". Others signs include dryness of the mouth, the appearance of a twitch in the corner of an eye, trembling hands, sweaty palms, fidgeting with hair or clothing, and rocking from one side to the other, as well as general tension in various parts of the body. Everyone is affected differently, but it is quite common to experience more than one symptom at a time.

BEING PREPARED

One of the chief causes of nerves is the fear that something will go wrong during a presentation. By reducing the chances of this happening, you can minimize that fear, and your nerves will be calmer. The key is to prepare yourself thoroughly, and leave nothing to chance. Every time you think of something you wish to double-check, write it down. Accustom yourself to using a checklist each time you prepare to make a presentation. Some of the points you should remember to check are:

- That the pages of your script or notes are numbered, in case you drop them;
- That your AV aids will be understandable from the back of the venue;
- That all the electrical equipment you intend to use is functioning properly;
- That the venue and your appearance are confirmed, and that you have the right date.

62 Smile only when it feels natural to do so. A forced smile always looks false and unconvincing.

DEFUSING NERVES

To make a strong, effective presentation, you must be relaxed beforehand. Even if you do not feel tense, about 30 minutes before you are due to speak, try to find a quiet place to gather your thoughts and relax. If you know you do have a tendency to feel nervous, try to be positive about these feelings – in time they will become familiar, so welcome their arrival as if they were old friends, and try to use them. Rethink your attack of nerves – and rename it "anticipation".

CALMING YOURSELF

PREPARATION
Remind yourself how thoroughly you did your preparation, and look through your notes for the presentation

REHEARSING
Remember the time you spent rehearsing the presentation, and reflect on what you learned during the rehearsals

RELAXATION
Work through your relaxation exercises five minutes before you begin – and meanwhile, relax

63 Get a good night's sleep the night before, so that you feel alert.

64 Follow the same last-minute routine before each speech.

65 Imagine yourself delivering a first-class speech.

ESTABLISHING A RITUAL

It can be helpful to follow a ritual in the last few minutes before you begin your presentation. This should come after the preparations described on the previous page, and should consist of taking a few moments to gather your thoughts, exercising the facial muscles as shown opposite, and doing a few breathing exercises. This should take your mind off the things that make you nervous. There is also something very comforting in following a sequence of undemanding actions before a stressful event. People who are afraid of flying find it helpful to follow a similar routine in the minutes before their plane takes off.

REASSURING YOURSELF

Before your presentation, reassure yourself by running through your last-minute calming ritual, and remind yourself of the following:

- Unless the waiting audience is hostile for some reason, remind yourself that people want to see a successful presentation. In other words, they are on your side;
- Despite the fact that most people are nervous before giving a speech, an audience will assume that you are not;
- You have a message to pass on to your audience – in the form of factual information, personal insights, or both. The audience wants to hear this message, otherwise they would not have given up the time to come and listen to your presentation. Take heart from this knowledge; use it to your advantage to boost your confidence and counteract your nerves;
- Be wary of being over-confident. This can make you sound like a know-all, and there are very few audiences, however interested in a topic, that will warm to such an individual.

POINTS TO REMEMBER

- Nerves can add extra, positive energy to your presentation.
- The audience is more interested in what you are saying than in how you are feeling.
- Your enthusiasm and sincerity will help win over the audience.
- A short exercise regime can help to reduce last-minute nerves.
- Time spent relaxing at the last minute helps you to concentrate during your presentation.
- The more presentations you make, the more opportunities you have to perfect your skills.

66 Use some of your nervous energy to enliven your speech.

ELIMINATING TENSION

Take time before you start your presentation to ease the tension that accumulates in the face and upper body. Rid your facial muscles of nervous tension by following the simple exercises shown below. This will help in the articulation of your presentation, as you will be less likely to trip over your tongue or stutter. Repeat all three exercises several times each, until your face feels relaxed.

67 Take a deep breath, relax, smile, and start your speech slowly.

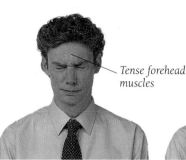

Tense forehead muscles

Purse lips tightly together

Stretch jaw as wide as possible

Open eyes wide

▲ FACIAL SQUEEZE

Try to squeeze your face as though it is being compressed between your chin and forehead. Start with a frown. Relax and repeat.

▲ FACIAL SCRUNCH

Tightly close your eyes, purse your lips, and scrunch up your face as if there is sideways compression. Hold for 30 seconds, then relax.

▲ MOUTH STRETCH

Open both your eyes and mouth as wide as possible, stretching the muscles in your face. Repeat two or three times as required.

REDUCING LAST-MINUTE NERVES

Simple last-minute breathing exercises can help you reduce nerves by giving you better control over your body and voice. By concentrating on your breathing, you can also calm your thoughts and dispel feelings of tension and anxiety, enabling you to focus clearly. Follow the exercise on the right, shutting your eyes and taking a series of controlled, deep breaths.

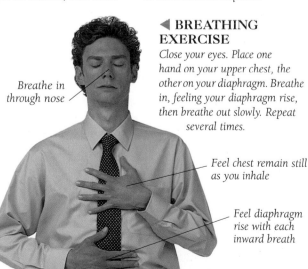

Breathe in through nose

◀ BREATHING EXERCISE

Close your eyes. Place one hand on your upper chest, the other on your diaphragm. Breathe in, feeling your diaphragm rise, then breathe out slowly. Repeat several times.

Feel chest remain still as you inhale

Feel diaphragm rise with each inward breath

259

SPEAKING CONFIDENTLY

The delivery of a presentation has as much impact as the message itself. It is essential to start strongly. After that, use tone of voice, pace, and your body language to enhance your audience's understanding of what you have to say.

68 Scan your notes in small sections, then concentrate on fluent delivery.

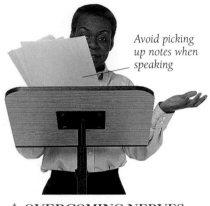

Avoid picking up notes when speaking

▲ OVERCOMING NERVES

Check the height of the lectern before you start a presentation to ensure it is at a comfortable level. If you feel nervous, it is tempting to hide behind your notes; train yourself to keep them on the lectern.

BEGINNING CONFIDENTLY

Make sure that you are introduced properly to the audience. A good introduction will establish your credibility and can provide the audience with a clear expectation of what you are about to tell them. Find out who will be introducing you, and brief them thoroughly. Make sure that your expertise in the subject of the presentation is mentioned if it would be helpful. Start speaking confidently and at a natural pace, and try to deliver your first few points without referring to your notes. This will reinforce an air of confidence, openness, and authority, and at the same time will enable you to establish eye contact with the audience. Try to glance at the whole audience at the start so that they feel involved.

PACING A PRESENTATION

Varying the pace of your delivery will keep the audience interested, but you should avoid speeding up and slowing down just for the sake of it. Remember to pause between your main points, and take the opportunity to make eye contact with the audience. This will also give you a chance to gauge their reactions to your speech. As you progress through the stages of your presentation, speak slowly and emphatically when you want to highlight important points.

69 Pause briefly each time you make an important point.

USING BODY LANGUAGE

At every moment of your waking life, you are sending out non-verbal signals about your feelings and intentions. It is possible to use this body language in a presentation to help to reinforce your message. Keep an open posture at all times, avoiding crossing your arms or creating a barrier between you and the audience. Use hand gestures selectively for emphasis – do not gesture so much that your hands become a distraction. If you are relaxed, your body language will reinforce your message naturally, but using the appropriate gestures can help you to disguise your nerves.

70 Tell a favourite, relevant anecdote; its familiarity will put you at ease.

Eye contact establishes positive rapport with audience

Relaxed body language conveys confidence

Open jacket presents an image of honesty

Gaze includes entire audience

Open hand gestures emphasize key points

▲ **SPEAKING AUTHORITATIVELY**
This confident stance suggests a thorough grasp of subject matter, and will establish authority and credibility with the audience.

▲ **LOOKING AND FEELING RELAXED**
Once audience rapport has been built, the speaker visibly relaxes and the audience focuses more readily on what is being said.

▲ **USING THE RIGHT GESTURES**
The speaker makes good use of open-handed gestures to emphasize his integrity and draw the entire audience into his presentation.

USING EYE CONTACT

Eye contact is a very powerful tool that establishes a degree of intimacy between people. It is important to establish this intimacy with an audience during a presentation. Sweep your gaze right across the audience, remembering to engage with the people at the very back and far sides, as well as those at the front. Although it is tempting to increase the frequency of eye contact with audience members who appear enthusiastic and interested, do not neglect those who appear neutral or negative. Audience members who feel excluded by the speaker are more likely to respond negatively to the speech than those who feel involved.

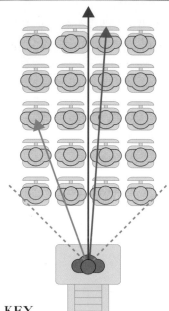

LOOKING AT THE AUDIENCE ▶

Sweep your gaze across the entire audience, remembering to include the back row. Establish initial eye contact with a friendly face, rather than looking over the heads of your audience when speaking.

KEY

---- Limit of speaker's
     sightlines

→ Sightline fixed on friendly
    face in audience

→ Sightline fixed on back
    row of audience

→ Sightline fixed on
    middle distance

> **71** Make your initial eye contact with someone whom you consider to look approachable.

USING GESTURES

Perspective changes in relation to the size of the audience, and you have to adapt your gestures accordingly. Large audiences require greatly exaggerated movements to achieve the same visual effect that a "normal" gesture would for a small audience. For example, a gesture emphasizing two points "on the one hand...and on the other hand..." needs to start from the shoulder, rather than from the elbow or wrist, to have the right visual impact on a large audience. Although gesturing in this exaggerated style may at first feel awkward, it will look natural to the audience.

72 Make eye contact with somebody in the audience at every available opportunity.

DEVELOPING STYLE

As you become more experienced you will be able to use the various tools you have at your disposal – your voice, your demeanour, and the words you use – to create different impressions. Usually you will want to use all the tools at the same time to work towards the single goal of keeping the attention of the audience. For example, if you want to emphasize a point, use concise sentences, stand upright, and raise your voice. To give the audience the impression that you are going to share an exciting revelation with them, lean forwards and lower your voice. They will make sure that they hear you because you have made it seem so interesting. These tools are an essential element of any presenter's success, and with practice their use will become second nature. Always use a style that is appropriate to each particular audience – what works well for one group of people may not work at all with another.

DO'S AND DON'TS

✔ Do use simple, concise language wherever possible, for clarity.

✔ Do use eye contact to obtain feedback from the audience. Their body language will reveal their reactions to your presentation.

✔ Do keep pauses specific and emphatic. Use them to allow your audience to absorb what you say.

✔ Do glance at a wall clock to check on the time rather than looking at your watch.

✘ Don't apologize to the audience for your lack of speaking experience.

✘ Don't mumble or hesitate. If you have lost your place, stay calm until you find it.

✘ Don't drop your voice at the end of a each sentence. It will sound as if you are not sure of what you are saying.

✘ Don't lose sight of the message that you are giving, or you will find that you lose your concentration as well as your audience.

73 Repeat key numbers: "15 – one-five – weeks."

74 Do not be afraid to use big gestures and long pauses.

LIMITING YOUR SPEECH TIME

Tell your audience how long you will be speaking for so they know how long they need to concentrate: "We've only got 20 minutes, so let me go straight in…". Later you can remind them again that your eye is still on the clock: "We've only got five minutes left, so I'll sum up by saying…". Do not be diverted from your prepared presentation by a member of the audience who wishes to ask a question or appears to disagree with a point you are making. Tell them when you will be answering questions from the floor, and continue your speech.

CLOSING EFFECTIVELY

It is vital to have a strong conclusion to your presentation, since this helps form the impression that audience members take away with them. Always reiterate the major points made in your speech to bring them to the attention of the audience again.

75 Do not leave visual aids on display too long – they distract the audience.

SIGNPOSTING THE END

During the course of your presentation, give the audience verbal signposts to indicate how many more points you have to make, and when the end of your speech is approaching. Use phrases such as: "now the third of my four points…" or "and now, to sum up briefly before I answer your questions…". By informing the audience that the end is near, you will be sure of having their full attention before you summarize your main points. It is important that your summary covers all the major points and ideas from your presentation, so that the audience has a final chance to recap on your subject matter. This gives them a chance to consider any questions that they want to ask you.

THINGS TO DO

1. Tell the audience how many points you want them to take away with them.
2. Make sure you stick to your allocated time.
3. Work out which points can be cut if you run over your allotted time.
4. If you forget anything, leave it out rather than adding it to the end of your speech.

76 Do not rush off as if you are in a hurry to leave.

77 Always close with a good, strong summary.

LEAVING AN IMPRESSION

It is the final impression that you leave in the minds of your audience that lingers the longest, so make sure that it is a good one. Before delivering the presentation, spend time working on the final sentences of it so that you can deliver them perfectly. Combine pauses, intonation, and verbal devices such as alliteration in your summary to create a memorable "package" for the audience to take away with them. In this way, your message will get across – and your reputation as a speaker will be enhanced.

DRAWING TO A CLOSE

Avoid adopting a dogmatic tone when delivering the conclusion to your presentation. Concentrate on presenting accurate, well-researched facts, and do not be tempted into giving personal opinions on your subject matter. Base your conclusion firmly on the facts you have presented throughout your speech. If your presentation is to be followed by a question-and-answer session, remember that the impact of your own carefully prepared final sentences may be diluted. In such a case, you may choose to accept a series of questions from the audience and then make a short, concise summing up speech reiterating your major points.

Use open hand gestures to show enthusiasm

DELIVERING YOUR SUMMARY ▶
As you are about to begin summing up your presentation, move to the front of any visual aids you are using so that the audience can see you clearly. Stand confidently, and deliver your closing sentences authoritatively.

78	Use alliteration to make an impact when summing up.

79	Pause between your summary and the question-and-answer session.

FINISHING STRONGLY

It is important to create a strong and memorable finish. To help you to do this, there are several tips that you should bear in mind:

● Encapsulate your presentation in one or two sentences. It is important to be brief when summing up; short, powerful sentences hold the attention of the audience far more effectively than a 10-minute monologue.

● Emphasize key words. Pausing after key words and phrases adds emphasis to them. It is also a good idea to emphasize the word "and" as you approach your final main point.

● Use alliteration. The use of several words beginning with the same letter helps make a summary memorable. Restrict the alliteration to a maximum of three words.

265

HANDLING AN AUDIENCE

A presentation is made for the benefit of an audience, not for that of the presenter. Be sure that you know how to read an audience's response and how to handle its reactions.

JUDGING THE MOOD

Try to arrive at the venue early enough to assess the mood of the audience. Has the audience just come in from the pouring rain? Are they likely to be hostile to what you want to tell them? Has a previous speaker made them laugh?

80 Listen to as many of the previous speakers as you possibly can.

INVOLVING AN AUDIENCE

Judge the mood of your audience – by assessing their reactions to previous speakers, for example. You can then decide on a strategy to deliver your message effectively. If any members of the audience appear bored or drowsy, stimulate them by asking questions that can be answered by a show of hands. "How many of you phoned your office before coming here? Only three? Well then, how many of you *thought* of phoning your office?" If the audience is hostile, you could start the presentation with a joke, but make sure that your body language is giving out positive signals.

81 Let audience members know that you are aware of their feelings.

LOOKING FOR SIGNALS

You will have rehearsed your own body language as part of your preparations for a presentation. Now you have to learn to read the body language of the members of the audience. Watch for signs, and do not expect everyone to be expressing the same thing. Some may be straining forwards eagerly to ask a question, while others may be sinking into their seats, wishing they were somewhere else.

82 Involve members of the audience by asking questions at regular intervals.

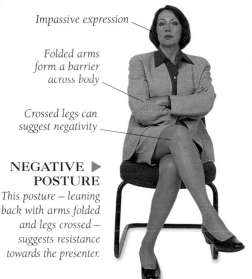

Impassive expression

Folded arms form a barrier across body

Crossed legs can suggest negativity

NEGATIVE ▶ POSTURE
This posture – leaning back with arms folded and legs crossed – suggests resistance towards the presenter.

SPOTTING NEGATIVITY

There is a wide range of ways in which members of an audience can indicate disapproval or hostility. Watch out for people leaning over and criticizing your speech to a neighbour. Alternatively, look for people frowning directly at you with their arms folded, or looking in the air as if the ceiling is more interesting than anything you have to say. Remember that looking at one piece of body language in isolation – such as crossed legs – may give a false impression, so look at the whole picture before coming to a conclusion.

SEEING SIGNS OF INTEREST

Stances indicating interest are easy to spot – look for people smiling or nodding, or leaning forwards in their seats and watching you intently. The expressions on their faces may reveal faint frowns of concentration. People manifesting any of these signs can probably be won over to your point of view, so make sure that you involve or engage them in your presentation.

Frown of concentration

Torso leans forwards

Clasped fingers indicate thoughtfulness

◀ QUIZZICAL POSTURE
Leaning forwards, with elbows on knees, and chin resting on clasped hands, suggests that this person is considering a point that the speaker is making.

READING FACIAL SIGNS

In terms of body language, the face is most expressive. If you are close enough to the members of your audience, you will be able to pick up a multitude of small signals – from the movements of eyebrows and the look in the eyes to the sloping of lips. As with general body language, always remember to read the face as a whole. One sign taken in isolation may not be a true indication of what the person is feeling.

> **83** Watch for a hand stealthily moving up to stifle a yawn.

Neutral facial expression indicates unformed opinions

Chin resting on hand shows concentration

Crossed legs suggest contemplation

NEUTRAL ▶ POSTURE
This familiar relaxed posture suggests an open mind. This person has yet to be swayed either way by the argument and is willing to hear more.

READING HAND AND ARM GESTURES

Hand and arm movements are helpful in adding to the impact of speech and can tell you a lot about the person using them. During question-and-answer sessions, note the hand and arm gestures of the people asking questions. If you cannot see them clearly, ask individuals to stand up when speaking. The gestures people use have a strong cultural content, so bear this in mind when interpreting body language. For example, if northern Europeans gesticulate emphatically, they are probably agitated, but such gesturing accompanies most conversations among southern Europeans.

DEALING WITH UNFORESEEN CIRCUMSTANCES

Would you know what to do if there was a loud explosion in the middle of your presentation? Or if a member of the audience suddenly had a seizure? Although the chances of such an event are remote, it is as well to go over in your mind the steps you might follow if you were faced with an unexpected incident such as this. Ask yourself if you know where to turn on the lights, where to find a first-aid kit, how to summon medical help, and where the fire exits are. If you do not know where you might find these things, make sure you get this information before your presentation.

USING YOUR EARS

You do not need to have all the lights on to pick up your audience's body language; much of it can be picked up aurally. You can hear the rustle of people fidgeting or the sound of whispering, both of which may indicate that your audience is bored or confused. It is easy to block yourself off when you are concentrating on presenting, but it pays to be alert to noise at all times – it is a valuable clue for judging the mood of your audience.

WATCHING LEGS

The position into which someone puts their legs says a lot about their attitude. For example, if an audience member has crossed legs, it may indicate that they are still contemplating your speech. Legs placed together, however, can indicate total agreement. If your audience is seated, movement will be limited and you may be able to see only those in the front row, but their leg movements should give you an indication of how the rest of the audience are reacting to your presentation.

84 Be aware of tapping feet – a strong indication of impatience.

Position of chin on knuckles indicates eagerness to learn

Arrangement of legs indicates alertness

◀ **INTERESTED POSTURE**

This posture expresses interest. The body leans forwards, and the chin rests on the hand. The leg positions also reinforce the positive stance of the upper body.

Leaning forwards demonstrates agreement

AGREEMENT ▶ POSTURE

The relaxed position of the hands, the parallel legs, and the frank, open expression of the face indicate that the listener agrees entirely with your presentation.

NOTICING HABITS

Most people unintentionally reinforce their body language with habitual fidgeting with their personal props, such as glasses, watches, earrings, or cufflinks. Looking at a watch can betray boredom or even impatience, while chewing on a pen or glasses suggests contemplation. On the positive side, sitting still and an absence of any of these habits can often indicate total involvement and agreement with the content of your presentation.

DEALING WITH QUESTIONS

Many a fine presentation has been ruined by poor handling of questions raised by the audience afterwards. Learn to deal with difficult and awkward questions during your preparation, and you will handle anything you are asked with confidence.

85 Practise answering some impromptu questions put to you by a friend.

86 Remain calm, whatever the tone or intention of the questioner.

POINTS TO REMEMBER

- Question-and-answer sessions can be as important as the main body of the presentation itself.

- It is possible to anticipate most questions when researching presentation material thoroughly.

- Most questions taken from the audience will be intended generally, and should not be taken personally.

- Nerves may tempt you to a hasty response. Always think about your answer before you begin to speak.

- Some questions may need clarification from the questioner.

- Questions should always be answered one at a time.

PREPARING WELL

It is important that you go into your presentation fully prepared to answer any questions thrown at you by the audience. The key to this is in careful research and rewriting. Once you have finished drafting your speech, read it through thoroughly several times, note any unanswered questions that it raises, and try to fill in any gaps. Having done this, read your presentation to friends or colleagues, and ask them to raise any queries. Deal with their points, adding extra information as necessary. Be aware that, despite this preparation, there may be somebody who asks an awkward question you have not thought of.

APPEARING CONFIDENT

Just as a good presentation can be ruined by a poor question-and-answer session, a mediocre one can be saved by a confident performance at the end. Answer questions as loudly, clearly, and succinctly as you delivered the presentation. This is especially important if you have had to sit down or move to another location for questioning. If appropriate, stand up when answering questions, and keep your voice level. Do not fidget with you hands or use negative body language, such as crossing your arms in front of your chest, which will make you appear defensive.

STAYING IN CONTROL

Never allow more than one person to talk at once, otherwise the occasion may rapidly head out of control. Establish that you can only handle one question at a time: "If we could hear your question first, John, then I'll come back to you, Laura, immediately afterwards". Never be drawn into a protracted discussion of minor aspects of your presentation; if matters become too involved, arrange to continue the discussion afterwards.

87 Say "Good point!" to encourage a questioner who is shy or nervous.

88 Divert hostile questions back to the questioner or the audience.

HANDLING QUESTIONERS

Questioners come in a variety of guises, so it is important to be able to recognize and deal with them accordingly. Exhibitionists like to try and demonstrate that they know more than you do, while drifters wander around the subject and never seem to ask a direct question. Each requires careful handling. Bring the drifter back to the issue by saying, "That's a good point, and it raises a question about...". Exhibitionists may cause trouble if antagonized, so treat them politely at all times.

TYPES OF QUESTION TO EXPECT FROM AN AUDIENCE

There are certain typical queries that come up over and over in question-and-answer sessions. Learn to recognize these so that you can deal with them successfully:

- The Summary Question: "What you seem to be saying is... Am I right?" This is an effort to recap on proceedings.
- The Straight Question: "Can you tell me about the services you offer in Brazil?" This is a direct appeal for information.
- The Me and Mine Question: "When my mother tried, she found the opposite.

How do you explain that?" Personal experience is used to make a point.
- The Cartesian Question: "How can you say X, yet insist on Y?" Here logic is being used to defeat the speaker.
- The Raw Nerve Question: "When are you going to get back to 1995 levels?" This is an ill-natured dig.
- The Well-Connected Question: "Have you talked to my good friend Bill Clinton about this problem?" Name dropping is used to emphasize power.

ANALYZING QUESTIONS

You only have a brief moment to analyze the nature of each question you are asked. Are you being asked to recap on your presentation? Is it a simple request for further information on your subject matter? Are you being led into a trap? Some people want to make a point rather than ask a question – if their input is positive and reinforces your argument, it is courteous to acknowledge them. However, if the point is irrelevant, thank the speaker and move on to the next question.

GAINING TIME

If you find yourself faced with a particularly difficult question, remain calm and give yourself a little time to think carefully before you reply. When tackling a question that requires careful thought, do not be afraid to refer back to your notes – you will still appear to be in control if you tell the audience what you are doing and why. If absolutely necessary, use a stalling tactic, such as taking a sip of water, coughing, or blowing your nose. This will help you to avoid looking as though you are lost for words.

89 Address answers to the whole audience, not just the questioner.

POINTS TO REMEMBER

- Answering questions from the audience can increase your credibility by demonstrating a wider knowledge of your subject.
- The audience needs to know whether you are voicing personal opinions or facts.
- It is crucial not to be drawn into argument with a questioner, regardless of how unacceptable his or her assumptions are.
- All questions should be handled with respect and courtesy.
- Some really difficult questions may have to be researched and answered at a later date.

RESPONDING TO UNANSWERABLE QUESTIONS

There are a number of standard replies you can use in response to difficult questions. If you do not know an answer, try to offer a satisfactory reply to show you have not ignored the question. If a questioner persists, throw the question open to the audience.

❝ I don't know the answer, but I can find out for you. If you leave me your address, I will get back to you. ❞

❝ I need to think about that one. Could we come back to it later? Next question, please. ❞

❝ I'm not sure I know the answer to that one. Perhaps we could discuss it after the session. ❞

❝ There really is no right or wrong answer to that. However, my personal belief is... ❞

DEALING WITH HIDDEN AGENDAS

Beware of loaded questions designed to show up serious weaknesses in an argument, embarrass the speaker, and undermine your case. Questions that have little to do with your presentation may be an attempt by a member of the audience to show off. Alternatively, they may stem from a desire to destroy your credibility by making you appear ill-informed. Try to have a few stock answers at your disposal, such as: "I was not intending to cover that aspect of the subject today", or "That is a separate issue that I do not have time to discuss now", which, though evasive, will ease the pressure on you.

90 Win over your audience with your knowledge.

91 Take care not to patronize your audience.

SPEAKING OFF THE CUFF

On occasions, you may find that somebody in the audience asks a probing question that needs a great deal of discussion about one aspect of your presentation. If this is not of general interest, ask the questioner to contact you after your presentation has finished. However, if you feel that the entire audience would benefit from hearing more detail – and you are sure of your facts – you may chose to launch into an unrehearsed mini-presentation. Keeping it brief, structure your impromptu speech clearly, and present it as fluently as the main body of the presentation.

BEING HONEST WITH THE AUDIENCE

There are going to be times when, for various reasons, you simply do not know the answer to a question. If this happens, be honest with the audience. If you do not know the facts, it is best to admit this straight away rather than hedging around the issue. Do not respond with phrases like "I will be covering that point later", because the audience will resent any attempt to fool them, and you may lose credibility.

Assess whether the required reply is purely factual or also a matter of personal opinion. If it is the latter, you are on firmer ground, since you can admit to not knowing the facts but still give a reasonable and considered answer based on past experience or personal opinion.

92 Prepare one or two lengthy answers in advance for questions you are sure will be raised.

COPING WITH HOSTILITY

A presentation may occasionally give rise to strong feelings or violently opposed viewpoints among members of the audience. When faced with such a situation, you must be able to cope with both overt outbursts of hostility and a silent reception.

93 Remember that hostility is aimed at your opinions, not at you.

94 Avoid prolonged eye contact; it may cause aggravation.

RECOGNIZING DISRUPTERS

Learn to recognize the types of disruptive audience members you may face, and you will be able to deal with them more effectively. Attention-seekers may respond to a speech with sarcasm just to make themselves look clever, while others may respond unwittingly to a rhetorical question, for example, without intending you any malice. The most disruption is likely to be caused by hecklers in the audience – people who disagree with what you are saying, and who actively want to cause trouble.

Illuminate points with interesting example

Sum up main points so far

Pause to take a drink of water, and renew eye contact since this can change the course of events

Start off strongly

Drop notes on floor

Heckler shouts "Rubbish!"

Tell a joke at your own expense

Presentation degenerates into chaos

DEALING WITH HECKLERS

Hecklers appear in all sorts of situations, harassing speakers with awkward comments and interruptions. To deal with hecklers you must be polite but firm. Your goal should be to get the rest of the audience on your side. This is not always easy, and underestimating hecklers can be costly if you allow them to undermine your presentation. Hecklers often have a genuine concern, which, if not addressed properly and quickly, may be taken up by other members of the audience.

If someone denounces something that you have said, do not enter an argument with them. If you are stating fact rather than opinion, make this clear and present the evidence. If you are stating personal opinion, be frank about it; this is your presentation. Give hecklers an opportunity to speak afterwards.

POINTS TO REMEMBER

- Losing your temper will gain you nothing.
- Everyone deserves a fair hearing even if you cannot agree with their point of view.
- Any points of agreement with hecklers should be emphasized.
- It is important to repeat your case at the end of the presentation.

95 If you are stating facts, back them up with evidence.

Respond well to questions from audience

Conclude with clear summary

▲ KEEPING ON TRACK

This illustration shows two possible courses of a presentation – a negative outcome and positive outcome. Despite a strong start, there may be hecklers and mishaps. This could cause a presentation to end in chaos. To stay on course, stay calm, deal with mishaps as they occur, and move on with composure and aplomb. Hold the audience's interest and you can make a success of any situation.

DEALING WITH CONFLICT WITHIN AN AUDIENCE

If a serious disagreement between members of an audience disrupts your presentation, remember that you will be assumed by the audience to be the mediator. Defuse the tension by reassuring everyone that they will get a chance to speak, and restore equilibrium as soon as possible. Get everyone back on to the right path by reminding the audience of the presentation's purpose. In all cases, aim to convey to your audience that you are in control. If the situation deteriorates any further, enlist some help from the organizers, or bring the presentation to an end.

96 If you are giving your presentation sitting down, stand up in order to assert your authority.

97 Try to find some common ground with the audience.

98 Guide questioners to other sources of information.

FACING AN UNRESPONSIVE GROUP

Although an unresponsive audience is not necessarily a hostile audience, many people would prefer to deal with outright hostility than silence. In such a situation, it is easy to imagine that the audience has no questions because there is no interest in your talk. This is unlikely to be the case – they are probably just unresponsive people. If a chairperson is present, you should have no worries. He or she will invite questions from the audience and, if there are none, start with questions of their own. If there is no chairperson, try asking the audience a few general, direct questions to encourage them to respond to you.

DEALING WITH HOSTILITY

An audience might be hostile for a number of reasons, including fundamental disagreement with the point of your presentation, anger at a previous speaker, or resentment at having to sit through your speech when they really came to hear someone else. One technique you can use to deal with hostility is to acknowledge it. Try to disarm a hostile audience by being open, then ask them to be fair and non-judgmental while you give your presentation. Another possibility is to plant a friend or colleague in the audience with a question with which to open the discussion. Your "plant" can ask an apparently awkward question, to which you can respond with a strong, preplanned answer – winning over some audience members.

99 Wait for questions, even if there are none forthcoming.

CULTURAL DIFFERENCES

Sometimes a speaker can unwittingly generate hostility in an audience by making a cultural *faux pas*. When making a presentation, pointing with the index finger to emphasize a remark is considered acceptable by most Westerners. However, many Asians cultures consider this rude, and prefer gestures of indication to be made with the whole hand.

100 Tell the truth, because an audience will quickly recognize insincerity and your authority will be undermined.

DEALING WITH THE MEDIA

If you have to speak at a public meeting or represent your organization at a press conference, it is important to handle the media confidently. Always answer queries calmly, politely, and intelligently, and be careful not to let journalists put words into your mouth.

66 *I have already stated my point of view during my presentation. I don't think I have anything more to add at this juncture...* 99

66 *No, that is not what I am saying at all. I would like to reiterate that what I am actually saying is...* 99

66 *You have certainly made a valid point, but I prefer to think that...* 99

66 *Whereas I appreciate what you are saying, I feel that I must emphasize that...* 99

LEARNING FROM YOUR EXPERIENCE

Dealing with awkward questions and general hostility during a presentation requires skills that can take a long time to develop. Learn from your mistakes, and draw on other situations in life when you have been faced with such difficulties. How did you cope? Did you think the situation through before responding? Did you defuse the situation tactfully? What if an audience resorts to derisive laughter in an attempt to undermine your credibility? The best response in this situation is to employ humour – never use sarcasm, which may only serve to exacerbate the situation.

If you know that your presentation is likely to provoke antagonism – for example, when making an unwelcome speech to shareholders or at a public meeting – try to anticipate the hostility. Practise fielding aggressive comments successfully by asking colleagues to fire difficult questions at you. The more experience you have, the better you will become at responding confidently.

POINTS TO REMEMBER

- Remaining calm when faced with hostility from the audience can help defuse a negative situation.
- Only the question that has been asked should be answered, not one that you would have preferred.
- Answers should be kept relatively short, especially if you know that there are other questioners waiting to be heard.
- There may be a hidden agenda behind aggression or hostility.
- Silence can be used to provoke an audience to ask questions.

 101 Stay relaxed but alert, and enjoy your presentation.

ASSESSING YOUR ABILITY

Remember that practice makes perfect when preparing for a presentation: regard each presentation as a chance to practise for the next. Evaluate your performance by responding to the following statements, and mark the options closest to your experience. Be as honest as you can: if your answer is "never", mark Option 1; if it is "always", mark Option 4; and so on. Add your scores together, and refer to the Analysis to see how you scored. Use your answers to identify the areas that need improving.

OPTIONS

1 Never

2 Occasionally

3 Frequently

4 Always

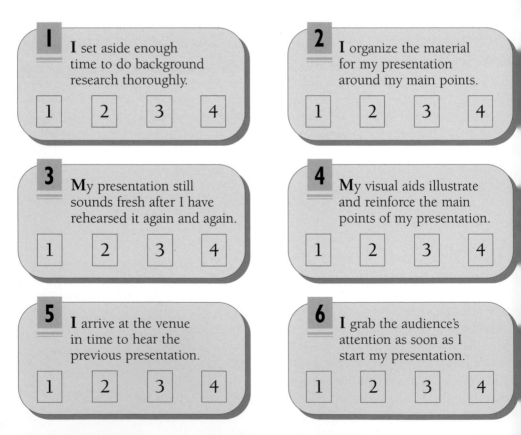

1 I set aside enough time to do background research thoroughly.

1   2   3   4

2 I organize the material for my presentation around my main points.

1   2   3   4

3 My presentation still sounds fresh after I have rehearsed it again and again.

1   2   3   4

4 My visual aids illustrate and reinforce the main points of my presentation.

1   2   3   4

5 I arrive at the venue in time to hear the previous presentation.

1   2   3   4

6 I grab the audience's attention as soon as I start my presentation.

1   2   3   4

7 I speak at a volume and pace that appears to suit the audience.

1 2 3 4

8 I speak fluently and confidently throughout the presentation.

1 2 3 4

9 I make eye contact with all sections of my audience throughout the presentation.

1 2 3 4

10 My presentation interests the audience and provokes questions from them.

1 2 3 4

11 I remain calm when responding to awkward or hostile questioners.

1 2 3 4

12 My replies are to the point and hold the interest of the audience.

1 2 3 4

ANALYSIS

Now you have completed the self-assessment, add up your total score and check your performance by reading the corresponding evaluation. Whatever level of success you have achieved during your presentation, it is important to remember that there is always room for improvement. Identify your weakest areas, and refer to the chapters in this section where you will find practical advice and tips to help you establish and hone those skills.

12–24: Use every opportunity to learn from your mistakes, and take more time to prepare and rehearse for each presentation that you give from now on.

25–36: Your presentation skills are generally sound, but certain areas need improvement.

37–48: You have good presentation skills, but do not become complacent. Continue to prepare well.

MARKETING SUCCESSFULLY

282

INTRODUCTION

Marketing is an essential business discipline, and its vital contribution to the success of an organization is widely recognized. Successful marketing results in stronger products, happier customers, and bigger profits. Whether the whole marketing function within your business is your responsibility, or whether it is a peripheral activity, Marketing Successfully will show you how to take a strategic approach to the task. Stay on course with helpful hints, advice, and information and evaluate your skills with a self-assessment exercise. Covering basic concepts such as the marketing mix, essential skills including direct mail, and the fundamentals of marketing strategy, this book is an invaluable guide to improving your marketing performance.

PUTTING CUSTOMERS FIRST

Marketing is key to the success of any business and must be customer-driven in order to be effective. Make customers your prime focus and reap the rewards.

UNDERSTANDING MARKETING

Marketing is often confused with publicity and promotion, but these are just part of the discipline. Understand all the components of marketing, particularly the central role that customers play, and you will be a step closer to business success.

1 Design your whole business around your customers' needs.

2 Gather as much information as possible on the requirements of potential new customers.

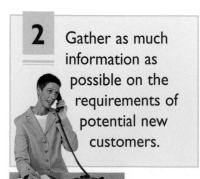

DEFINING MARKETING

Effective marketing is often described as "making what you can sell, not selling what you can make". Organizations that sell what they can make are product-led: they make the product first, consider customers afterwards, and see marketing simply as a means of persuading customers to buy. The most successful organizations make what they can sell. They are customer-led, creating products and services in response to customer need.

TAKING MARKETING SERIOUSLY

Focus on every aspect of marketing, not just on promotion and sales techniques, to persuade customers to buy. By taking the discipline seriously and acknowledging its influence, you will reap all the benefits that effective marketing has to offer: satisfied, loyal customers, a growing customer base, popular and successful products, increased turnover, more recommendations and repeat business, as well as fewer complaints. The end result of all this is bigger profits, which is one of the most powerful reasons for improving marketing performance. You are also far more likely to enjoy overall business success, and be the envy of your competitors.

FOCUSING ON CUSTOMERS

Research is conducted into customers' wants

↓

Product or service is designed to meet need

↓

Product or service is made public

↓

Customers buy product or service

↓

Product or service meets customers' need

↓

Customers buy product or service again

3 Try to develop an outward-looking approach to marketing, as opposed to an insular one.

IDENTIFYING MARKETING COMPANY TYPES

TYPE OF COMPANY	CHARACTERISTICS
FOREFRONTER Consistently anticipates customers' needs and gets its products to the market first.	Innovative and proactive. This type of organization truly understands marketing. It invests in research and product development and devises innovative solutions.
FOLLOWER Dislikes taking risks. Prefers to play it safe and see which way the market will go before deciding whether to take any action.	Lacks pioneering spirit. This type of company might attain success, but its attitude will always limit achievement. A more proactive approach would improve marketing success.
FOSSIL Has always conducted business in the same way and sees no reason to change.	Conservative, insular, and complacent. Such organizations need to develop a more outward focus. Activity must be driven by customer need, not company habit and tradition.

ANALYZING THE MARKETING MIX

The marketing mix is a very simple and successful recipe to follow. Blend its key ingredients – product, price, place, and promotion – in the correct proportions, and you will reap the many benefits of effective, strategic marketing.

4 Look at each element of the mix and determine its importance.

5 Create the right balance between price and quality.

6 Concentrate your efforts on the key elements of the mix.

UNDERSTANDING THE MIX

The marketing mix of product, price, place, and promotion is known as the "Four Ps". Marketing involves developing the right product (one that meets customer need); setting the right price (one that delivers a profit and keeps customers happy); getting the product to the right place (where customers can buy it); and promoting it (to encourage customers to buy it). The ingredients of the mix are the same for all organizations, only quantities vary. Where customers are price-conscious, for example, price dominates the mix and setting the right price is vital.

COMPARING ▶ DIFFERENT MIXES

Two hotels can have very different marketing mixes. For a five-star hotel, product (excellent restaurant, health club facilities, and superior rooms) is the principal ingredient of the mix. Guests expect luxury and accept that they must pay a price for it. For a budget hotel, cost is paramount. Its customers want to be able to stay at an affordable price.

FIVE-STAR HOTEL   **BUDGET HOTEL**

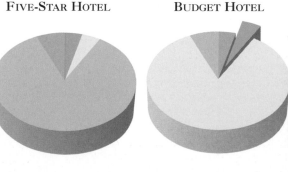

Key ▮ Price ▮ Product ▮ Place ▮ Promotion

EXAMINING PROPORTIONS

Devise the right marketing mix and you will maximize profits. Focus on each element of the mix to determine its importance to your business. Remember that the mix is not static; the perfect proportions today may not produce the desired results next year, or even next week. From time to time you will need to vary the recipe, by reducing prices during quiet periods, for example. There is an interrelationship between the four ingredients of the mix. If a product's price is high, customers will have high expectations. If advertising and promotional activity is significant, these costs will have to be recouped in the price.

7 Re-examine your marketing mix from time to time.

8 Compare your mix to that of your competitors.

CREATING THE RIGHT MARKETING MIX

KEY ELEMENTS	FACTORS TO CONSIDER
PRODUCT OR SERVICE Bought by customers to meet a need. The need may be practical (to get rid of stains), emotional (to feel good), or basic (to satisfy hunger).	● Products and services usually fulfil a number of needs, and it is important to identify which ones your products and services satisfy. ● A product or service may satisfy a need that consumers did not even realize they had.
PRICE A crucial part of the mix, the price must be right if customers are to buy a product in sufficient quantities to ensure a profit.	● The right price for quality goods is a fair one. Price and quality must be balanced successfully. ● Fair does not necessarily mean cheap – set the price of a product too low and customers may assume that its quality is inferior.
PLACE The "bridge" connecting customers and products, such as a wholesaler, retail outlet, or other distribution system.	● For some niche businesses, place is not an issue – enthusiasts and collectors, for example, are willing to travel long distances to shop. ● The Internet provides a new mechanism for bringing customers and company together.
PROMOTION Promotional activity, such as advertising and direct mail, that informs customers what you have to offer and persuades them to buy.	● For most enterprises, promotional activity is essential for attracting customers. ● For businesses that rely on passing trade, promotion is less important, since the right location and products will ensure success.

SETTING THE RIGHT PRICE

Price is the most flexible element of the marketing mix, since you can change it quickly and easily. But your profits depend on getting it right. Selling at low prices means tight profit margins and an over-reliance on high sales volume. A downturn in your market can put you out of business. There is no fixed link between price and cost: you can raise prices even if your costs have not increased, and lower them without a cost decrease. Monitor competitors' prices so that you know exactly what is happening in the marketplace, and aim to understand what your competitors' strategies are. Then develop your own pricing strategy. Supply and demand will inevitably affect what you can charge, but aim at a Goldilocks pricing strategy: not too cheap, not too expensive, but just right.

POINTS TO REMEMBER

- Low price is often equated with low quality. Customers might prefer to pay more for an identical product because they are convinced that it is better than a cheaper one.

- Customers do not buy a product simply because it is cheap; they buy because of need. However inexpensive your lawnmowers, you will not sell one to someone without a garden.

- Customers can be less "price aware" than you might expect. Test to see. Find out more about your customers' buying habits and whether they shop around for the best price.

9 Make sure you know what price your competitors are charging.

10 Employ market research to find out how you are perceived by your clients.

SELLING ON VALUE

Consider selling on value rather than price. Price-based sales pitches attract price-sensitive customers who are already in the market for what you are selling. A value-based pitch can woo customers who did not realize they needed your product. For example, a £300 mattress will appeal to customers who are looking for a new mattress at a good price. A mattress guaranteed to ease back pain will open up a new market by appealing to bad back sufferers who were not even considering such a purchase.

QUESTIONS TO ASK YOURSELF

Q What is the value of our offering in terms of saving customers time and effort?

Q Is our offering giving value by enhancing beauty or status?

Q Are we demonstrating that a purchase is not a cost but a good investment?

Q Have we asked what customers most value about our products?

FITTING PR INTO THE MIX

Public relations (PR) is often regarded as the fifth "P" of the marketing mix, standing for perception. A good image is a prerequisite for successful marketing. An attractive product at the right price will not guarantee a sale. Customers do not like to buy from companies with poor reputations. Use PR techniques to enhance your image and shape positive customer perceptions. Consider ways of boosting your image: perhaps your organization could support or sponsor a charity, a worthwhile cause, or local venture, for example. Take the opportunity to build a strong profile by publicizing your achievements in the media.

11 Involve PR staff in marketing decision-making.

12 Use research rather than gut feeling to assess customers' needs.

CREATING THE RIGHT IMAGE

Look at the various aspects of your business that customers use to form their view of you. These might include your premises, the telephone manner of staff, and your publicity materials. Examine each of them in detail and work out what kind of image is being conveyed to your customers. Is that the image you want to put across? If not, draw up a plan of action for bringing your desired image into line with your actual image.

◄ CONVEYING A GOOD IMAGE

Attractive physical surroundings, committed staff, and well thought-out procedures are all important in conveying a caring and friendly image and giving an organization an edge over its competitors.

GETTING TO KNOW YOUR CUSTOMERS

G*ood customer information is key to boosting profit, so it is vital to build up a clear picture of who your customers are. Watch them, talk to them, ask them questions, and find out all that you can in order to give them what they want and keep them happy.*

13 Avoid gathering facts for the sake of it – look only for what you can use.

14 Collect information on an on-going basis by asking new customers a few marketing questions.

COLLECTING DATA

Many organizations have huge customer bases, but it is those who respond to customers' needs to be treated as individuals who are most likely to succeed. By collecting and processing customer data to produce a customer profile and identify customer segments, you can tailormake products and services for particular groups of key customers. Meet identified customer need and you will sell more products and lose fewer customers. A better understanding of your customers will also enable you to target publicity more accurately.

PROFILING CUSTOMERS

A customer profile provides a picture of your typical customer. Some companies require an in-depth profile, detailing sex, age, income, lifestyle, address and type of accommodation, number of children, and so on. For others, a simpler profile will suffice. Decide which common characteristics it would be useful to look for in your customers. Business-to-business organizations, for example, may wish to analyze factors such as company size, vehicle fleet size, turnover, and location. Identify the kind of data you need, then plan how to uncover it.

QUESTIONS TO ASK YOURSELF

Q What age groups are our customers in, and what is the male/female split?

Q Where do our customers live, and do they travel far to buy?

Q Do they make one-off purchases, or is there an on-going relationship?

Q How much do they spend each month/year?

IDENTIFYING SOURCES OF INFORMATION

SOURCE	FACTORS TO CONSIDER
COMPANY RESOURCES Includes invoices, dispatch notes, mailing lists, and sales statistics.	Existing information can often provide valuable marketing intelligence, such as size of purchase, date of last purchase, and geographic location of customers.
CUSTOMER INTERACTION Includes face-to-face surveys and focus groups.	A good way of eliciting qualitative information about your customers' motivations. Explain that their insights will help you to develop products and services to meet their needs.
CUSTOMER FEEDBACK Includes comment cards and feedback via your Web site.	Create as many channels as possible for customers to give you their views. Ask what they think about your products and services, but also seek relevant data about them.
STATUTORY BODIES Regulatory bodies holding data on company performance and finances.	Use statutory sources of information to build a company profile of your typical customer based on factors such as size or turnover. Use this data to target similar companies.

SEGMENTING CUSTOMERS

Break your customer base into segments. You may have low-value regular or occasional customers, or high-value regular or occasional customers. Identify your principal segments and target marketing activity accordingly. High-value customers, for example, may merit more attention, while loyalty schemes or discounts may persuade low-value customers to buy more and more often.

15 Turn low-value occasional clients into high-value regular ones.

16 Identify which factors will help you target new customers.

USING THE INFORMATION

Influence your marketing decisions with profiling and segmentation. A profiling exercise might reveal that products aimed at one group are actually bought by another. If a men's underwear company finds that 75 per cent of its customers are female, this suggests that men leave their underwear-buying to mothers, wives, and girlfriends. In such a case, use mail shots and other advertising to target women, not men.

UNDERSTANDING CUSTOMER BUYING

F ind the key to why customers buy and
you have unlocked the secret of how
to sell to them. Discover what your
customers buy, how often, when, and why.
Then use this important information to
influence your marketing decisions.

17 Emphasize your
buying points
in publicity and
sales pitches.

18 Ensure that both
buying and selling
points coincide.

IDENTIFYING SELLING POINTS

A selling point is a powerful factor that you
identify internally as helping to clinch a sale.
To determine your strongest selling points, you
must understand what a customer looks for when
making a sale. This is known
as a buying point. To ensure
success, the points you
highlight when selling should
be the same factors that
customers most value when
buying. You may, for example,
decide that being "established
for a century" is a good selling
point because your company
takes pride in this. But your
customers' key buying point is
likely to be quite different.

◀ **ANALYZING BUYING**
*In a large shopping mall, where stores
compete for the same customers, those
that promote customers' key buying points
– such as good prices – as their selling
points are more likely to succeed.*

UNDERSTANDING THE BUYING PROCESS

KEY STAGES	CUSTOMER ACTION
RECOGNITION Becoming aware of a need.	Prospective customer realizes that something is required: more space at home, for example.
APPRAISAL Investigating what is available to fufil need.	Customer reads brochures, magazine articles, looks for information on price, durability, etc.
NEGOTIATION Approaching supplier of produce or service.	Having made a choice, customer asks supplier for quotations, looks at warranties, etc.
PURCHASE Buying preferred option.	A decision is made and the customer goes ahead with purchase.
RECOMMENDATION Commending product or service to others.	Customer evaluates the product and, if happy, recommends it to friends, colleagues, etc.

BEING ADAPTABLE

If your customer is a company, as opposed to an individual, bear in mind that its buying process will probably be very specific. This means that to succeed in selling to a company, particularly a business customer, you must understand what its buying process is and adapt your approach to suit. Ask the following questions:

- "Do you consult a list of approved suppliers? If so, how can we get on that list?"
- "Do you ask for tenders? If so, how can we get on the tender list?"
- "Do you always shop around for the best deal?"
- "Do you go by recommendation or use contacts?"
- "Do you always use the same supplier? What would persuade you to try a different one?"

Time spent getting to know how other people's customers buy is time invested in learning how to turn them into your own customers.

QUESTIONS TO ASK YOURSELF

Q How often do our customers buy?

Q What is the average transaction size?

Q Which payment methods do they use?

Q Which customers are most profitable?

Q Which customers are least profitable?

19 When dealing with a company, find out who influences key buying decisions.

USING SURVEYS

Work out some reasons why customers might choose to buy goods or services from you, then use survey techniques to discover the facts. Ask customers to rank the factors you have identified in order of importance, as well as adding their own. Your list might include:

- quick or free delivery;
- competitive price;
- excellent after-sales support;
- easy payment terms;
- friendly staff.

Self-completion questionnaires are an excellent way of reaching customers quickly and cheaply.

20 Collate buying information as an on-going task.

21 Set a deadline to encourage the return of mailed questionnaires.

MAKING THE MOST OF SURVEY TECHNIQUES

TECHNIQUE	USING IT EFFECTIVELY
MAILED QUESTIONNAIRE An excellent way of reaching a large number of geographically spread customers quickly and cheaply.	• Boost return rates by enclosing a stamped addressed envelope and use a follow-up mailing to encourage non-responding customers. • Make sure that questionnaires have an attractive layout and, above all, are easy to complete.
ONE-TO-ONE INTERVIEW Although time-consuming, this is seen as the best type of survey and tends to elicit the best response rate.	• Look at location options carefully: would interviews in the street serve your purpose better than interviews in a hotel, or in your customers' homes or workplaces? • Rapport is important, so ensure that interviewers explain the purpose and value of the survey.
CUSTOMER PANEL Comprises a group of your customers with a strong interest in your organization or products.	• Use customer panels as a sounding board for new ideas and a source of valuable feedback. • Ensure that panels retain their objectivity: if they become too integral a part of the organization's structure, customers can feel more like employees.
FOCUS GROUP A small discussion group led by a facilitator. Its aim is to uncover attitudes, motivations, and qualitative insights.	• Ensure that focus group members are representative of your customers and that the facilitator encourages them to add their input. • Remember that, although structured, these should be less rigid than questionnaire-based interviews.

UNDERSTANDING MOTIVATION

Usually there will be a combination of several motivating factors to buy, not just one. Easy payment terms might prove to be the clinching factor, but friendliness of staff, or the availability of the product from stock, may also influence the decision to buy from you. It is important to learn what motivates your customers and find ways to build on this knowledge.

MOTIVATING FACTORS ▶

These three customers use the same wine bar, although their reasons for doing so are very different. Being able to identify the principal selling points allows for more effective marketing.

Phil is a regular because the bar serves an extensive range of quality French wines

Tracy uses the bar because it is convenient, just two minutes' walk from her office

Aziz travels some distance to the bar because it operates a no-smoking policy

CALCULATING LIFETIME VALUE

Use a simple formula to calculate roughly what the average regular customer is worth to you during your relationship. You can then decide whether to treat high-value customers in a special way, for example by inviting them to special events. The example here shows that although the average sale is only £40, the customer is, in fact, worth £3,200 to the company.

A	Value of average sale (divide annual sales in £s by number of transactions)	£40
B	Number of transactions each regular customer makes annually	4
C	Average number of years a customer buys from you	5
D	Average number of referrals/recommendations a customer makes annually	3
E	Sales per customer per year (A x B)	£160
F	Sales per customer over a lifetime (E x C)	£800
G	Potential gross sales from referrals (F x D)	£2400
	TOTAL VALUE OF CUSTOMER (F + G)	**£3200**

BUILDING RELATIONSHIPS

Selling to existing customers is far cheaper and easier than finding new ones. Use marketing to nurture customer loyalty through good service and quality products, backed up by a strong, lasting, mutually rewarding relationship.

22 Examine every area of customer service and seek to improve it.

MONITORING FOR QUALITY OF SERVICE

Review all aspects of your working practices

↓

Set measurable standards so that quality is not left to chance

↓

Make sure that staff are trained to be able to meet standards

↓

If necessary, issue staff with a customer service manual

↓

Measure performance to check that quality is being attained

↓

Review standards to keep improving customer care

DELIVERING SERVICE

Customers today expect first-class service, and rightly so. Think about how you felt when you last received poor service. Disappointed? Angry? Cheated? This is exactly how your customers feel when they experience similar treatment. Compare this with how you feel when you receive exceptional service. Remember that customers are not an irritation standing in the way of you and your work, they are your work. Without them you have no business. List areas where you feel that you can improve customer service. Look at how staff interact with customers, how orders are processed, and how correspondence is dealt with. Tackle each area for improvement in turn.

QUESTIONS TO ASK YOURSELF

Q Do we answer the phones quickly and courteously?

Q Are our staff smart, helpful, friendly, and knowledgeable?

Q Are our premises clean and comfortable?

Q Do we reply to mail promptly?

Q Do we provide good after-sales service?

Q How swiftly are orders processed?

Q Could we do more to eliminate ordering errors?

Q How many compliments or complaints do we receive?

TACKLING COMPLAINTS

Complaints should always be taken seriously. Some companies have found that customers who have complained, and have had their complaints dealt with to their satisfaction, are more loyal than customers who have never complained. This underlines the importance of handling complaints well. Devise a fair and efficient procedure, set timescales for responding to complaints, and never let a complaint drift on. If you are in the wrong, admit it, apologize, and, if necessary, compensate the customer. Learn from errors and revise procedures so that mistakes are not repeated.

23 Remember that an existing client is more valuable than a potential one.

24 Ask dissatisfied customers how you can win them back.

▼ RESOLVING COMPLAINTS

This illustration shows two outcomes following a customer complaint. When the case is handled badly, the customer not only feels poorly treated enough to take her business elsewhere, but discusses her bad experience with others. When prompt remedial action is taken, the customer feels that her business is valued. Fair, courteous treatment also helps to ensure her continued loyalty.

Customer feels satisfied with the way the complaint has been resolved and is happy to leave her business where it is

Staff member takes call from customer who complains that her order has been delivered late

Staff member apologizes and promises an immediate investigation

Offers to refund 50 per cent of the invoiced amount

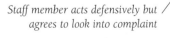

Puts complaint to one side and forgets all about it

Staff member acts defensively but agrees to look into complaint

Unhappy customer tells everyone about the poor service she has received, and takes her business elsewhere

KEEPING IN TOUCH

When a customer places an order, it is not the end of selling, it is just the beginning. Turn that one-off purchase into repeat sales by developing a relationship with your customers. Relationships do not sustain themselves. They take effort, and all the responsibility lies with you. Your customer may not even want a relationship. You have to take the initiative, not them. Find excuses to remind customers that you are there. Tell them when their maintenance contract is due for renewal, offer them upgrades, invite them to exclusive previews, give them special discounts, and make sure they are among the first to hear about new developments. Devise valid reasons for communicating and so keep your company's products or services fresh in their minds.

THINGS TO DO

1. Call customers with news and developments.

2. If you cannot get in touch with customers by phone, send an e-mail.

3. Drop in on business clients, if necessary, having checked first that your visit will be convenient to them.

4. Devise new ways of keeping customers informed of special offers or events, sales, and improvements in service.

---

25 Maintain healthy relationships with customers by being helpful and pleasant at all times.

▼ **USING CUSTOMER CONTACT CARDS**
Sustain relationships by mapping out planned customer contact. Keep records of the contact made with each customer, any follow-up required, and the outcome.

Customer Contact Card

Customer name: Thelma Driver, Trepark Limited

Due	Action	Completed	Outcome
21st April	Call to check that new system is working well	✔	System working well. Agreed to meet for lunch
3rd May	Call to arrange date for lunch	✔	Met and discussed new projects. Have promised to send free tickets to the next trade exhibition
16th July	Send complimentary tickets to the trade exhibition	✔	Thelma visited trade exhibition with Trevor James, a friend from Davis Company. Have added Trevor's details to mailing list
20th August	Send copy of customer newsletter	✔	

TESTING THE STRENGTH OF RELATIONSHIPS

There are two tests of a relationship's strength: is a customer satisfied enough to remain loyal?, and is a customer happy to recommend you to others? Find out by asking them. A good way to elicit honest answers is to use a questionnaire, or try an after-sales phone call to customers. Some companies ask these questions on the product guarantee registration card. If customers plan to use a different company next time, or are unwilling to recommend you, discover why.

26 Thank people for their custom to make them feel valued – the human touch can make all the difference.

NURTURING LOYALTY

Customers need a reason to remain loyal. They may expect more than simply excellent products or services. How do your competitors nurture customer loyalty? Could you introduce ways to show customers actively how much you value their business? Loyalty or reward schemes have been proven to work for many businesses. Give people a card that records their custom with you. After a number of transactions, or after reaching a certain total, they can qualify for special treatment, free gifts, discounts, or other perks. In a competitive market, where customers tend to shop around for the best deal, a voucher offering a reduction off their next order can help attract repeat business. A discount that escalates with each order, while still making a profit for you, might make you irresistible to otherwise fickle customers.

ADVOCATE

If really happy, client becomes an advocate who recommends you to others

CLIENT

If happy, the customer makes repeat purchases and becomes a regular client

CUSTOMER

New customer makes a one-off purchase

PROSPECT

Prospective customer is considering buying, possibly from you, or possibly from a rival

TARGET

Target customer receives information (advertising, sales visit, or other)

UNKNOWN

Unknown customer is not familiar with your company or products

▲ MOVING PEOPLE UP THE LOYALTY LADDER

Successful marketing can turn a casual customer into a committed advocate of your company. Aim to advance everyone to the top of the loyalty ladder.

WINNING NEW CUSTOMERS

Customer loss is inevitable: people move house, change job, and, of course, they die. Losses may be gradual and easy to overlook, but the effects are cumulative. Maintain a thriving business by finding new customers faster than you lose them.

27 Consider setting up a special introductory offer for new customers.

28 Provide incentives for your sales team to help them improve their overall selling performances.

UNDERSTANDING CUSTOMER LOSS

You are sure to be losing some customers, even if you have a full order book. But is this due to natural loss, or could you be driving customers away? Contact former customers and ask them. If losses are due to your own underperformance, take action to correct it. If your traditional customer base appears to be a dying breed, your business is heading for terminal decline. The only cure is to find a new market and possibly also to develop new products or services. Replacing customers is an endless task, but an essential one.

FINDING NEW BUSINESS

It is vital to go out and find customers, since they cannot be relied upon to come to you. Plan how you are going to win new business. Follow up all leads and get in touch with people who have made an enquiry or requested information. Contact former customers in a bid to win them back. Identify potential customers and let them know how you can help. Approach competitors' customers and make them an offer they cannot refuse. Review your publicity strategy to see if there is a better way of reaching potential customers. Would cold calling or a direct mail campaign be useful in attracting new business?

QUESTIONS TO ASK YOURSELF

- Do we know how many customers we lose?
- Do we know the reasons why customers desert us?
- Are there any compelling reasons why customers should remain loyal to us?
- How do we show our customers that we value them and their loyalty?
- Could we do more to retain our customers?

INCREASING YOUR CUSTOMER BASE

There is a well-established technique, known as member-get-member, or MGM, that many businesses use to good effect in the endless challenge to win new custom. Try to get each of your existing customers to provide just one productive lead. You can literally double the size of your customer base using this method, but obviously your customers will be willing to participate only if they feel happy with your products and your organization generally. Use incremental incentives to encourage customers to provide leads.

▼ TURNING CUSTOMERS INTO YOUR SALES FORCE

Happy customers can do as good a job for you as the most highly trained sales force, and at a fraction of the cost. Harness the enthusiasm of satisfied customers and ask them to help you spread the word to their friends and family. An easy-to-complete card sent to regulars can result in valuable leads.

USING INCENTIVES

Ask customers for details of colleagues/friends who might like to be on your mailing list

Offer a small incentive, such as a prize draw entry, to encourage customers to supply leads

Send your mailing to leads, explaining that a friend recommended them

If necessary, offer a bigger incentive, such as a free gift, if a lead places an order

---

Flag up the incentive in the headline

You may want to ask customers for additional details, but remember that the more information you ask them for, the less likely they are to respond

Include your address on the card just in case the reply-paid envelope is lost

RECOMMEND US AND ENTER OUR PRIZE DRAW

As a loyal customer you already know how great our products are. Don't keep it a secret! If you have friends or family who might like to find out what we have to offer, please complete their details and we will make sure they receive a copy of our latest catalogue free of charge. In return for your help, we will enter you into our PRIZE DRAW for the opportunity to win a case of champagne. If your friend goes on to place an order with us, we will also send you a COMPLIMENTARY BOX OF CHOCOLATES as a thank you.

Your name and address:

Your friend's name and address:

Please return this card, in the reply-paid envelope, by March 30th to qualify for the prize draw. Send to Garden Tools Limited, Unit 17, Anytown Industrial Estate, Anytown.

Make the incentive incremental, with a small incentive for supplying details and a larger one if the prospective customer places an order

Make it easy for respondents to reply by, for example, using prepaid envelopes

Include a reply-by date to encourage customers to act

BUILDING STRONG PRODUCTS

Quality products, backed by a strong brand, are vital for success. To keep your customers and stay ahead of competitors, you must develop first-class new products and improve existing ones.

IMPROVING PRODUCTS

Products generally have some kind of life-cycle: some age and die, while others need restyling to remain fresh. Change, enhance, repackage, rebrand, remodel, or upgrade your products to ensure that they appeal to today's market.

29 Tell former customers about improvements to your products.

30 Use comment cards to elicit useful feedback.

31 Regard feedback from customers as valuable marketing intelligence.

ENHANCING PRODUCTS

Before investing considerable time and effort in developing new products, look at your current range. It is important to avoid creating new products at the expense of existing ones. For the best ideas on how to improve your products, consult the experts: your customers. Seek their opinions and suggestions using questionnaires, comment cards, focus groups, or customer panels, so that you can introduce real enhancements based on customer demand. Keep products fresh by introducing new variants, limited editions, add-ons, special recipes, and improved versions.

32 Always look for ways to improve your products.

33 Always thank your customers for their comments, even if they are negative.

PROMOTING PRODUCT IMPROVEMENTS

Whenever you introduce product improvements, tell your customers. You can use this as an excuse to write, telephone, or visit them. Ensure that your adverts mention the enhancements and use product packaging to draw attention to them. You can also highlight improvements in your publicity material. Brief your sales team on new features so that they are able to promote them. If there is a news angle, issue a press release to attract positive media coverage. Significant improvements to products will provide a launch pad for renewed promotional activity aimed at reviving sales.

LEARNING FROM YOUR COMPETITORS

Study your competitors; you may find that some of their ideas or working practices are worth copying or adapting. As a member of the public, sample any improvements they make to their products and services. Send for their publicity material. Phone their switchboard. Read their adverts. Call in at one of their outlets. Examine organizations in other sectors. Is there anything they can teach you? Which of their good ideas are transferable or adaptable? Look out for ideas that you can adopt, adapt, borrow, or steal. Aim to improve existing products by taking the best of the rest and incorporating them to create a product that cannot be beaten.

▼ **MONITORING COMPETING PRODUCTS**
An easy way to compare your product with rival products is to search the Internet and see what other companies are offering. Make sure you monitor the competition periodically, not just once.

Manager looks at competitor's brochure

Colleague checks competitor's Web site

DIFFERENTIATING YOUR PRODUCTS

Few products are unique. Often the challenge lies in finding a way to differentiate your products from a rival's near-identical offerings. Make use of a combination of techniques to give you an advantage over the competition.

34 Review company processes to make them more customer focused.

35 Ask customers what your unique selling point is.

36 Identify something you offer that your rivals do not.

UNDERSTANDING COMPETITIVE EDGE

When your products are better than those of your competitors, and when customers recognize this superiority, you have a real advantage. Few organizations are in this position. Most find that there is little or nothing to distinguish their own products from a competitor's. To gain competitive advantage, uncover not just differences but also attributes that customers value. Make sure the differences are meaningful to customers, so that your product is preferable to the others available.

RECOGNIZING WHAT IS IMPORTANT

Often it is the little things that count. Customers may choose your product over a competitor's identical product simply because they prefer your packaging, or because you give them coffee while they wait. Pay attention to details that could make a difference. A genuine customer-centric approach will differentiate you from competitors. Show your commitment to customers and ensure that staff are empathic. Review company systems and processes to make them more customer focused.

QUESTIONS TO ASK YOURSELF

Q Why should customers buy from us rather than from our competitors?

Q What makes us different from our competitors?

Q How are we better than our rivals?

Q What strengths do we have that we can effectively capitalize on?

ADDING VALUE

When there is nothing intrinsically different about your product, look to your strengths as an organization to find your competitive edge. A combination of the following may differentiate you from your rivals:

- free/same-day delivery
- products held in stock
- free trial
- on-site demonstration of product
- choice of payment terms/ interest-free credit
- free parking
- personal service from trained staff
- better warranty
- good after-sales service/ on-site repairs
- freephone customer helpline

37 Gain advantage over your competitors by achieving total customer satisfaction.

IDENTIFYING USPS

Even an indistinguishable product can have a claim to uniqueness, and you may still have a unique selling point (USP). Perhaps you are the only local company to offer such a service, or were the first to make it available. You may be the newest, the nearest, or the largest. You might be the most experienced, the only family-owned firm, or the longest-established. Perhaps you are the only supplier to have achieved a coveted award, or maybe your staff have all reached a certain level of training or experience. Scrutinize your company for a claim to uniqueness. Check that none of your competitors is making a similar claim. Even a weakness can be turned into a strength. Being the smallest, for example, could be a USP. It means that you can offer a more personal, flexible service.

CASE STUDY

anessa and Susan ran two ower shops, which were situated only a short distance apart in the same street. Both florists had to compete for the same customers, and since their stock and prices were similar, there was no strong reason for customers to favour one florist over the other. Searching for a way to increase business, Vanessa came up with the idea of making special bouquets to

co-ordinate with interior colour schemes. It was not more expensive for Vanessa to offer this new service, nor did customers have to pay any more to use it, yet the scheme gave Vanessa the competitive advantage she was looking for. Customers were delighted and made a point of returning to Vanessa's shop rather than to her rival's. Just over a year later, the shop managed by Susan closed, increasing Vanessa's trade even further.

◀ CREATING AN ADVANTAGE

By differentiating her own business from her near-identical neighbouring competitor, Vanessa succeeded in making her florist's shop far more profitable. Her idea was simple but clever: adding value for customers without increasing cost. Creative thinking is free, but can result in significant business gains.

PROVIDING INCENTIVES

Even without uniqueness you can still build a competitive edge. Ask yourself, "Why would a customer choose us rather than one of our competitors?". If you cannot come up with at least one compelling reason, consider using incentives. These can encourage customers to opt for you over a rival. Be sure to work out costs and benefits very carefully before taking this route. If you offer an expensive incentive, you or your customer will end up paying the price; it needs to be cheap to you but attractive to the customer. Choose a relevant incentive, such as a free tie with every suit, or free on-site servicing with every photocopier.

UNDERSTANDING THE BUYING PROCESS

Select incentive

Discard incentive

Will incentive persuade customer to buy from you rather than from a competitor?
YES   NO

Will incentive result in a boost to sales sufficient to cover extra costs incurred?
YES   NO

Go ahead with incentive and carefully monitor results

38 Choose an incentive that will enhance your reputation; tawdry gifts may tarnish your image.

SEEKING ENDORSEMENTS

Endorsements can be powerful persuaders, providing customers with a strong reason to buy from you. Who could resist saucepans promoted as the professional cook's favourite? Or the home computer that programmers choose? Or the holiday resort where travel agents take their vacation? Customers like the safety and security that an endorsement provides. A relevant endorsement can result in a dramatic sales boost.

CULTURAL DIFFERENCES

Before using endorsements and testimonials to differentiate your products, check the relevant guidelines or legislation. In the UK, for example, The Advertising Standards Authority issues strict rules about the use of both testimonials and endorsements. Advertising regulations in the United States are governed by law, while the regulatory body in Australia also issues codes.

Using Testimonials

Testimonials serve exactly the same purpose as endorsements, but the difference between them is that a testimonial quotes a named person who has used the product and wishes to recommend it. Famous faces, relevant professionals and experts, and even ordinary people can provide testimonials. Customers are more likely to believe third-party testimony than to accept your company's claims of excellence. Testimonials reproduced in your publicity material in a handwritten form appear to be more persuasive and believable than typewritten ones. Always get written consent before using any testimonial, and make sure that the views expressed in it can be supported by independent evidence.

39 Ensure that views expressed in testimonials can be supported.

40 Choose an incentive that is relevant to the product.

41 Brief your sales team to highlight product benefits, not features, when talking to customers.

Evaluating Features and Benefits

When promoting products, companies have a tendency to focus attention on a product's features. But customers do not look for features; they want to see benefits. Regard features merely as a way of creating benefits. Start by listing the features for each of your products and then add the benefits that customers derive from them. Make sure that all your publicity material and packaging highlights the latter.

Comparing Features and Benefits

FEATURE	BENEFIT
"Uses the latest microchip technology"	"Never again burn a slice of toast"
"In-built moisture reader"	"Transforms stale bread into fresh toast"
"Audible toast-completion alert"	"Bell lets you know when the toast is ready"

DEVELOPING A BRAND

S trong, well-known products provide companies with a real competitive advantage. Use the power of branding to imbue your products with personality and meaning, ensuring they achieve a prominent position in the marketplace.

42 Establish trust in your brand and customers will remain loyal.

NAMING PRODUCTS

The right name helps to sell products and services. It bestows individuality and personality, enabling customers to identify with your offerings and to get to know them. It makes products and services tangible and real. Choose names that enhance your company image and that are appropriate for the product and its positioning in the marketplace. Check that the name is available and register it so that it cannot be used by others. If your market is international, ensure that the name is pronounceable in other languages and does not translate into a rude word or one with negative connotations. Aim for a name that is short, apt, easy to spell, and memorable. Strict rules govern the naming of organizations, so check them out with the relevant official body.

▼ **TESTING YOUR BRAND NAME**
Show your shortlist of product names to target customers and ask them what images each name conjures up. Use their feedback to help select a name with the most positive associations.

International customer considers whether names will be appropriate in her country

Regional customer rejects two names because they have negative connotations in her area

Target customer gives his view on the appeal of suggested product names

COMPARING BRAND ATTRIBUTES

SERVICE ATTRIBUTES

Friendliness

Creativity

Courtesy

Helpfulness

Knowledgeability

PRODUCT ATTRIBUTES

Durability

Reliability

Usefulness

Value for money

Aesthetic value

---

43 Extend branding across your entire product range.

Manager asks selected customers for feedback on new product names

HARNESSING BRAND POWER

An effective way of differentiating your products from those of your competitors is to use branding. Branding means developing unique attributes so that your products are instantly recognizable, memorable, and evoke positive associations. Some brands have a solid and reliable personality, others are youthful and fun. Choose your company and product name, corporate colours, logo, packaging, and promotional activity to help convey a personality and build a brand. Branding conveys a complex message quickly. A customer should be able to look at one of your products and assimilate all that you stand for in a second by recalling the brand values.

44 A strong brand is not a substitute for quality, but an enhancement to it.

45 Look out for opportunities to reinforce your corporate identity.

46 Maintain corporate identity consistently by issuing written guidelines for staff.

PROMOTING A CORPORATE IDENTITY

The creation of a corporate identity is a vital element of branding. Present an integrated, strong, instantly recognizable, individual image that is regarded in a positive way by your customers, and seize every opportunity to strengthen your corporate identity. Devise a distinctive logo and corporate colours, and use them on stationery, packaging materials, and for your vehicle livery. Work the branding into the the design and layout of your premises. Big hotel chains, for example, reinforce their corporate identity through colour co-ordinated staff uniforms, carpets, soft furnishings, and towels. They also have napkins, coasters, crockery, and cutlery bearing the company logo.

▲ **CREATING A STRONG IDENTITY**
Utilizing distinctive corporate colours and logos on company vehicles helps to build a strong identity. This ensures that an individual company is easily distinguishable from others that may offer very similar services.

POINTS TO REMEMBER

● A logo forms a central part of your corporate identity and should convey something about your business.

● It may incorporate a strapline – a summary of your mission or your business.

● A logo can be typographical or a design in its own right.

● The logo's colours will become your corporate colours.

47 Be aware that colours can have cultural or political connotations.

48 Keep corporate colours to a minimum to keep printing costs low.

49 Ensure all aspects of company behaviour reflect brand values.

COMMISSIONING A VISUAL IDENTITY

If your organization lacks a strong visual identity, or has an outmoded image, consider a restyle. Give a full brief of your brand values and positioning to a graphic designer whose style you like, and ask them to produce some ideas. Explain how you intend using your new corporate identity. Will it be placed on vehicles, for example, or on shop fronts? Ask to see your proposed new visual identity on mock-ups of items on which it will ultimately appear: product packaging, stationery, and so on. Test your short-listed design on a focus group comprising your key audiences, such as customers and suppliers. Find out what associations it produces. Take time to develop a new identity; you will have to live with it for a long while.

MAINTAINING BRAND VALUES

Having established a brand, work to maintain its positive values. Use patents, trademarks, design rights, and other devices to protect your brand and prevent others from cashing in on its success. Live up to your projected image. Ensure that standards of customer care, service, and product quality remain high, giving real substance to the brand. It can take years to create a successful brand yet seconds to destroy it. Check regularly that the brand values are still relevant, since brands can become outdated. Gently reposition the brand over time where necessary, or opt for a major repositioning and use media exposure to promote your new image.

▼ GAINING RECOGNITION

Successful brands have such a strong visual identity that they are instantly recognizable, even when seen in a foreign language. Companies can often charge more for winning brands, since customers feel, often subliminally, more confident in the value of the product.

ACHIEVING GROWTH THROUGH PRODUCTS

Selling more products is the most effective strategy for ensuring big increases in profitability. Achieve growth in this way by expanding your share of the existing market, finding new markets, developing new products, or diversifying.

50 Use the Internet as a vehicle for reaching global markets.

51 Be prepared to restructure in order to grow.

52 Use related products to expand your product range safely.

PENETRATING THE MARKET

One way to ensure growth is to achieve a larger share of the market. This strategy is widely used because it is considered a "safe" way to grow. Security lies in the fact that you are dealing with two known entities: your offerings, i.e. your products, and the market. You have already spent time getting to know this market and refining your products to meet customer need, so you avoid the need to invest in new research, or in new product development. Your aim is simply to make contact with previously unreached potential customers.

DEVELOPING THE MARKET

Market development involves finding new markets for your existing products. Start by drawing up a list of possible new markets. Conduct research to check whether they would be interested in your offerings and that you could satisfy potential new customers with your existing products. Some product remodelling may be necessary if you are to appeal to your new market, but remember that you are not looking at totally new products. Finally, plan how you will reach your new markets.

POINTS TO REMEMBER

- It is possible to increase sales by simple but valued product improvements.
- You may combine, for example, product development with market penetration.
- It is a good idea to develop new products that will be bought in the same transaction as your existing products.

IMPLEMENTING GROWTH STRATEGIES

GROWTH STRATEGY	IMPLEMENTION METHODS
MARKET PENETRATION Improving share of market by reaching previously unreached potential customers.	● Use heavy advertising, promotional offers, direct mail campaigns, or cold calling to find new customers matching the profile of existing ones. ● Focus on winning customers from competitors.
MARKET DEVELOPMENT Identifying and breaking into new markets to increase sales of existing products.	● Use targeted advertising, direct mail, and the Internet. ● Consider internal restructure, such as setting up a sales arm to deal with large companies, or remodel products to appeal to new markets.
PRODUCT DEVELOPMENT Introducing new product lines or add-ons to existing products to appeal to current market.	● Research new product ideas, ask customers for opinions, and examine successful rival product lines. ● Examine your market carefully to ensure that it is not already over-saturated.
DIVERSIFICATION Expanding through the development of new products to be sold to new markets.	● Remember that the rules applying to setting up a new enterprise also apply to organizations seeking to diversify. ● If you decide to diversify, you will need to develop a separate marketing strategy.

CREATING NEW PRODUCTS

Achieve growth and keep risk to a minimum by introducing new product lines to your existing market. Products introduced to an existing range can be very successful. A curtain manufacturer, for example, may add co-ordinating bed-linen to its range of curtains. Customers will often buy an existing product (a mobile phone) and a new one (a colourful, snap-on cover) in the same transaction.

53 Ask customers what new products they would like to see on the market.

DIVERSIFYING

The riskiest growth strategy – diversification – involves developing totally new products to sell to new markets, and it is a journey into the complete unknown. Essentially you are embarking on an undertaking not dissimilar to a complete new business start-up. This is not often a first choice for boosting profits, but it can be – and has been – done. Do explore all the alternatives first.

54 Be sure to explore all the alternatives before risking diversification.

MAXIMIZING PUBLICITY

To buy from you, customers must know what you have to sell, which is why promotion is a vital part of the marketing mix. Learn to make the most of publicity to boost sales and profits.

PLANNING A CAMPAIGN

A successful publicity campaign can lead to an enhanced profile, increased sales, and improved profits. Before embarking on a campaign, map out exactly what you wish to achieve so that you can choose the right method to attain your goals.

55 Use diaries and desktop giveaways to keep your name in view of clients.

56 Use directories and yearbooks as publicity tools.

57 Use launches and previews to reach customers.

SETTING OBJECTIVES

The first step of a publicity campaign is to consider the outcome you desire and then set one or more clear, specific, measurable, time-framed objectives to achieve it. Avoid vague outcomes, such as "to attract more orders", and be explicit, for example, "to attract orders valued at £100,000 within four weeks" or "to attract 5,000 enquiries, leading to 1,000 sales in two months". Only by setting measurable objectives will you be able to identify what works and what does not. This will allow you to concentrate your publicity budget where it will produce the best results.

EVALUATING KEY METHODS

By far the most popular methods of gaining publicity are press and radio advertising, direct mail, and the Internet, since these have high impact and are affordable for most businesses. When considering which method to use, bear in mind the following:

- Advertising in print allows excellent targeting, since most publications have detailed readership profiles.
- Radio adverts are easier to digest than print adverts, but they are more transient.
- Direct mail is highly effective, provided that it is efficiently targeted, although it does have a rather poor image.
- The Internet is a booming growth area with a vast potential for publicity.

ORGANIZING A SUCCESSFUL CAMPAIGN

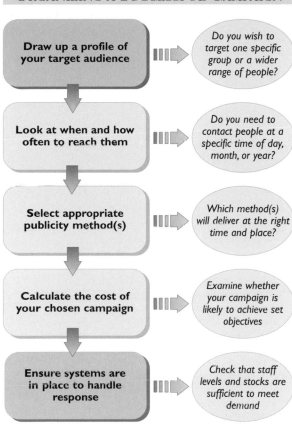

Draw up a profile of your target audience — Do you wish to target one specific group or a wider range of people?

Look at when and how often to reach them — Do you need to contact people at a specific time of day, month, or year?

Select appropriate publicity method(s) — Which method(s) will deliver at the right time and place?

Calculate the cost of your chosen campaign — Examine whether your campaign is likely to achieve set objectives

Ensure systems are in place to handle response — Check that staff levels and stocks are sufficient to meet demand

COMBINING METHODS

The best way to obtain maximum publicity is to organize an integrated campaign combining several methods. This allows optimum penetration of the market: one technique builds upon the work achieved by another. A software company targeting business start-ups, for example, could place a coupon response advert in the national press offering a free business software pack to business start-ups. This would bring in names and addresses of target customers, to whom direct mail and publicity could be sent with the free packs.

POINTS TO REMEMBER

- Check that any claims made in your publicity materials can be substantiated.
- Avoid making false or exaggerated claims.
- Ensure publicity is both accurate and unambiguous.
- Be sure that publicity does not mislead or deliberately give the wrong impression.

GETTING THE MOST FROM ADVERTISING

Advertising is a paid-for, persuasive promotional activity that uses the media and other publicity channels, such as the Internet. Use it to build and maintain awareness; to publicize special offers, sales, and events; to promote new products and services; to announce price changes, revised opening hours, or product modifications; to invite enquiries and to find new customers. Above all, use it to sell. Direct response advertising (incorporating a response device, such as a coupon or fax number) brings you and your customers together.

58 Ensure relevant staff know which adverts are appearing when.

CALCULATING COST ▶

Use a simple formula to check that an advertising campaign will produce results. When adding up the total cost of your campaign, include every item, not only the cost of buying space or airtime. If forecast sales exceed the break-even figure (C), success is likely. Allow a margin of error: response rates are a guideline and not a guarantee.

(A) **Total cost of campaign**	£1,000
(B) **Profit per sale**	£20
(C) **Number of sales needed to break even** (A) ÷ (B)	50
(D) **Mailing quantity, circulation figures, or listening/viewing statistics**	5,000
(E) **Expected response rate** (based on figures supplied by publication/station)	80
FORECAST SALES	62.5

DEFINING THE KEY STEPS TO SUCCESSFUL PUBLICITY

KEY STEPS	HOW TO TACKLE THEM
GRAB ATTENTION	Use a striking design, a hard-hitting headline, strong colours, large lettering, powerful photography, or other devices to get noticed.
HOLD INTEREST	Devise an appealing, persuasive proposition that will make potential customers sit up and pay attention.
STIMULATE DESIRE	Make your offer irresistible: show how good the deal is and highlight valuable extras, such as easy payment terms or quick delivery.
GAIN CONVICTION	Convince customers that they need what you are selling by giving powerful reasons that will appeal to them.
PUSH FOR ACTION	Urge customers to act using words such as "time-limited offer". Make action easier with coupons, freephone numbers, credit card payment, etc.

USING EXPERTS

If you are planning a major campaign, or intend to move into a specialist area, such as television or cinema advertising, consider calling in the experts. Media professionals should be able to run a campaign more effectively on your behalf, and sometimes for less money than you would pay, and usually more quickly. If you plan to spend a lot on advertising, it could be to your advantage to use an advertising agency. Agencies earn a commission for buying media space or airtime, and this may cover their creative and account management costs. This effectively means that you are receiving their services for nothing. Approach a few advertising agencies and find out how they structure their fees.

MAKING IT LEGAL

Strict industry and legal codes govern advertising in the United Kingdom and the United States. In the UK, for example, over 150 statutes and regulations relate to issues including data protection, advertising claims, trade descriptions, consumer protection, consumer safety, and a host of other issues. Break them and you will not only face a fine, but also damage your reputation with consumers.

---

59 Investigate using an outside company to handle the extra work for you.

PREPARING TO RESPOND

Be ready for the response to your campaign by ensuring that there are plenty of staff to answer telephone calls as well as process, pack, and dispatch orders. Organize extra telephone lines, if necessary. Check that you have sufficient stock, packaging materials, brochures, or information packs to fulfil responses. Delays will reflect badly on your company and may lead to customer loss. If you cannot cope with a big response, stagger your advertising. Target one geographic area or customer group, fulfil orders, then place your next batch of advertisements. Alternatively, employ a specialist fulfilment house to handle all the extra work on your behalf.

◀ **BEING PREPARED**
Be ready for the increase in customer response once your marketing takes effect. If necessary, employ more telephone staff and ensure they are fully briefed.

ADVERTISING IN PRINT

*P*ress advertising offers the cheapest way to
reach a large audience, and is highly
effective for direct response advertising, where
the public buys straight off the page. Choose
the right publication, craft your adverts
carefully, and negotiate the best deal.

60 Bear in mind that spaces between paragraphs will increase readership.

61 Avoid too much small print; it is difficult to read.

62 Keep your idea or proposition as simple as possible.

REQUESTING MEDIA PACKS

Draw up a list of possible publications in which
to advertise, and ask each one to send a media
pack, with information on readership profiles and
circulation details. Choose the best title for your
product and target audience. Details and dates of
special features contained in the pack will help
you to decide the best time to place your advert.
Try to book space for the time when your chosen
publication is running a feature on your market
sector. The pack will set out the deadlines for
placing an advert, as well as technical data
explaining the form in which to supply artwork.

NEGOTIATING THE BEST PRICE

Never agree to pay the quoted rate card price for
advertising space without first trying to negotiate
it downwards. It is almost always possible to
arrange some kind of reduction. Various factors
affect cost, including the time of year, demand,
the size and position of your advert, circulation
of the publication, and whether the advert is in
black type or colour. If demand for space is slack,
a discount is usually available. Even if you cannot
get the price reduced, try to negotiate a bigger
advert for the same price, a second advert at half
price, or a more prominent position for it.

QUESTIONS TO ASK YOURSELF

Q What do we hope to achieve as a result of advertising?

Q Whom do we want to reach and what do we want to say to them?

Q Which publications do our target customers read?

Q How often do we need to advertise to get our message across successfully?

Q How large will our advert need to be?

USING THE RIGHT PUBLICATION

TYPE OF PUBLICATION	ADVANTAGES AND DISADVANTAGES
FREE LOCAL PAPERS Usually weekly, these contain editorials on the local area and are delivered free through the door.	● These rely solely on advertising for income, so there are many more adverts competing for attention. ● It is cheap to advertise in these papers, and easier to get away with less sophisticated adverts.
"PAID-FOR" PAPERS Daily and weekly, local and regional, these are generally paid-for titles serving local cities and communities.	● Good for local organizations, or national ones, wishing to target areas where they have outlets. ● Short lead-in times. ● Daily papers have a short shelf-life.
NATIONAL NEWSPAPERS These are daily publications, usually with a Sunday title or a Sunday sister title.	● Good for reaching a mass audience, because readership profiles allow wide socio-economic targeting. ● National advertising can be prestigious. ● Expensive and with a short shelf-life.
CONSUMER MAGAZINES This huge range of publications includes women's, lifestyle, music, health, and sports titles.	● Good for targeting special interest groups. ● High reader interest so more likely to be read. ● Longer lead-in times. ● Competitors are likely to be advertising in them, too.
PROFESSIONAL PUBLICATIONS These include publications for particular professions and trades, from architects to pig farmers.	● Excellent for targeting a particular professional group. ● Often retained for reference, extending their shelf-life. ● Often passed around the workplace and read by more than one person.

TARGETING ▶ ADVERTS

Andrew found that advertising in the wrong place produced no new leads, whereas a well-placed advert generated a steady stream of new work. He learned that an advertising campaign in itself will not necessarily produce an upturn in sales. For his adverts to be effective, they needed to reach the right target. Readership profiles helped him to pinpoint the right publication – the one that was read by his potential customers.

CASE STUDY

Andrew ran an architectural practice in a large city, working on domestic projects. He first advertised in an architectural magazine but realized that it was the wrong vehicle for him, since only those in the trade were reading it. Andrew then drew up a profile of the clients he wanted to reach: reasonably well-off people who lived within a 50-mile radius of the city in which he practised. He placed an advert in the regional glossy lifestyle magazine for his area. The readership profile stated that the magazine was bought by relatively affluent property owners interested in homes and interiors, and they all lived within reach of the city. The profile was perfect. Andrew's first advert produced 15 enquiries, which led to nine commissions. He decided to advertise there monthly and gained 80 per cent of his work this way. As a result, turnover increased by 60 per cent.

WRITING A PRESS ADVERT

Make sure that the elements making up your advert – style of language, tone, colours, graphics, photographs, and illustrations – are chosen with your target reader in mind. Check competitors' adverts, too, to see how they promote their products. Do you want to take a similar approach, or a radically different one? Create a clear, simple proposition, and avoid complex ideas that require hard work from readers. Ensure that all the elements of your advert work in harmony. Use text to reinforce any photos or illustrations, and eye-catching design to hold the various aspects together, thereby creating an unmissable and persuasive advert that makes readers act.

63 Give a small advert a heavy dashed border to increase its impact.

▼ MAKING YOUR PRESS ADVERT WORK

When readers see an advert for the first time, their eye follows a set route. Take account of this route when designing your advert. Readers tend to look first at the picture, then at the headline, bottom right-hand corner, captions, subheads, and body copy, in that order.

Use the headline to attract attention; remember that 80 per cent of people will stop reading at this stage

MAIN HEADING
Subhead

The body copy expands on the headline and photograph to tell the story. About 80 per cent of readers will not get this far. However, those who are still reading at this point are genuinely interested.

Readers quickly scan subheads and crossheads, illustrations, and graphs

An illustration or photo is the first element readers look at, and it will encourage them to read further

Body copy must be readable, informative, persuasive, and directive, but also simple

Captions on photos attract twice the readership of the main text

The caption for the picture

Please send me your brochure.
Name
Address

Telephone   Fax

Post now to: Van Village, Freepost, Anytown AN 1 1AA
NBI22

logo

A reply device such as a coupon response makes it easy for customers to take action

Code coupons so that you know which publications produced the best response and on which days

Readers expect to see a company logo here, which helps to reinforce corporate identity

PRETESTING ADVERTS

Before spending your budget on buying media space, ask your staff, passers-by in the street, or, best of all, your target audience what they think of your adverts. Discover whether they find the adverts attractive, the copy readable, and the proposition persuasive. See which of two adverts they like best. Both adverts might be yours; or one could be your competitor's. After the adverts have appeared, you can then assess their effectiveness using objective measures, such as the number of enquiries generated, the number of sales, or the percentage upturn in people through your doors. Measuring outcomes can occur only after an advert has been placed.

64 Appeal directly to readers by using the "first person" in advertising copy.

65 Use colour adverts to attract twice the readership of mono ones.

ANALYZING DIFFERENT TYPES OF HEADLINE

HEADLINE TYPE	EXAMPLE	WHEN TO USE IT
DIRECT Presents your proposition in a direct and concise form.	"Any van serviced for just £80 at Van Village"	To present a simple proposition requiring little or no explanatory body copy.
FILTER Shows the relevance of your advert by flagging up the target audience.	"Attention all van owners"	To attract the right prospective customers and ensure that they do not overlook your advert.
CRYPTIC Attracts the reader's curiosity but makes no sense as a stand-alone headline.	"It's what everyone's talking about"	To hook your readers and lure them into your body copy, providing you with an opportunity to persuade them.
COMMAND Issues the reader with an instruction that cannot be ignored.	"Contact us today to arrange your cheap van service"	To prompt readers to take action and respond to your advert.
QUESTION Poses a query to which the answer should be "yes".	"Want to save money servicing your van?"	To engage readers' interest and push them towards accepting your proposition.

ADVERTISING ON RADIO

Since customers listen to the radio at home, at work, and in their cars, it is an effective way of plugging your message. Weigh up the pros and cons of using local and national commercial radio, investigate what is involved, and carefully assess costs.

66 Find out if the radio station can help with production.

67 Ask to listen to adverts that agencies have already produced.

QUIZZING A STATION REPRESENTATIVE ▼

Have a list of questions ready to ask the representative. Find out what the listener profile is, whether it changes at night, and what costs are involved. Remember that the representative wants to sell airtime to you, so may be economical with the truth.

MAKING GOOD ADVERTS

The most successful radio adverts induce listeners to prick up their ears. Sound, music, voices, accents, both a male and a female voice for extra rhythm, and a conversational style in which speakers talk directly to the listener are all elements of a good advert. Since a studio and specialist equipment are needed, appoint an advertising agency, or commission the radio station's in-house creative team to script and produce the advert for you. Look at the station's listener profile and think of a real person you know who fits that profile. Try the advert out on them. Would they like it? Would they be persuaded to buy?

Radio representative provides information about the station and its listeners

Manager asks questions from a prepared list

Colleague notes facts and sales points

ADVANTAGES

DISADVANTAGES

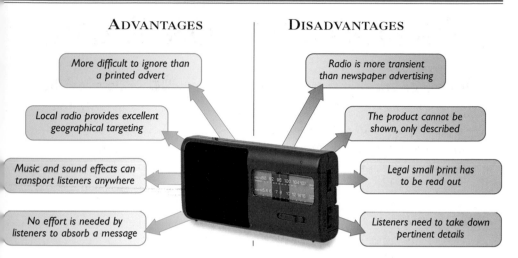

- More difficult to ignore than a printed advert
- Local radio provides excellent geographical targeting
- Music and sound effects can transport listeners anywhere
- No effort is needed by listeners to absorb a message

- Radio is more transient than newspaper advertising
- The product cannot be shown, only described
- Legal small print has to be read out
- Listeners need to take down pertinent details

PLANNING COSTS

There is more to radio advertising than buying airtime, so it is important to budget for extra costs. You may need to pay a copywriter to write the script for your advert, as well as actors or voice-over artists. If you commission your own music or jingle, you will need to pay a composer, musicians, and singers. Existing music will require permission to play and involves air-play royalties. Studio time, technicians, and sound effects all have a cost, too.

▲ WEIGHING UP THE BENEFITS
Consider both the pros and cons of radio advertising. You may find that spreading your advertising budget over a range of mediums will be more effective.

68 Remember that radio adverts are heard, not seen.

ADVERTISING ON TELEVISION

It is possible to produce radio adverts without using an advertising agency, but television advertising is far more specialist and technical. Commission an agency to advise on where, when, and how to advertise, as well as coming up with creative ideas and overseeing production. Contact at least three agencies with a written brief explaining what you wish to achieve. Ask each to do a presentation outlining their credentials, explaining how they would approach your assignment, and detailing costs. Look at examples of their work and ask for their client list. Select your agency on their experience and ability, creativity and approach to the campaign, their understanding of your needs, enthusiasm, and total cost.

MASTERING DIRECT MAIL

Direct mail is a form of advertising that delivers targeted, individually addressed communications through the post. Select the contents of your mail shot carefully, ensure it hits its target, then test the effectiveness of the campaign.

69 Make sure you keep your mailing list up to date at all times.

70 Ensure that people's names are correctly spelt.

IDENTIFYING USES

Direct mail has many marketing applications. Use it to find and convert new prospects, to distribute product samples or newsletters, and as a selling tool targeting current customers. Launch new products, win back lapsed customers, and announce changes to your service or forthcoming sales, events, and special offers – all via the post. Use the technique to build and maintain customer relationships. Keep in touch with clients, send them Christmas cards, tell them all the latest news and developments. Send out questionnaires and gather valuable marketing information.

UNDERSTANDING DIRECT MAIL ▼

Direct mail is a carefully targeted mail shot sent only to people with a proclivity to buy the product or service being promoted. Junk mail is irrelevant mail sent to the wrong people.

DIRECT MAIL RECIPIENT

A regular skier, recipient reads about promotion offering cut-price skiing equipment with keen interest

JUNK MAIL RECIPIENT

Recipient has never skied, has no intention of doing so, and barely glances at the mail shot

TARGETING YOUR MAIL SHOT

Your mail shot is only as good as the address printed on it, which is why a good mailing list is essential if you are to target customers effectively and maximize your returns. Mailing people who have moved house or changed job, who hate direct mail, or who are just not interested is a waste of your marketing budget. Existing customers are three times as likely to respond to a mailing as cold prospects, so make them the basis of your list and then start looking for names to add. People who have enquired in the past and former customers could be worth testing, as could people whose business cards you have collected.

71 Write "you" in your mail shots – it is a strong lure.

CULTURAL DIFFERENCES

Some countries operate mailing, telephone, and fax preference schemes that allow consumers to opt out of receiving direct mail, so-called "junk" faxes, and cold calling on the telephone. Before embarking on a direct mail campaign, check the legislation and codes that affect direct mail in your country, including any laws relating to the use of information on databases.

HIRING A LIST

When seeking new customers, you may wish to approach a list broker who can provide names and addresses of people who match the profile of your existing customers. Note that mailing lists are usually hired, not bought; you buy permission to use the list a certain number of times. If you attempt to use it more often, be warned: brokers plant "seed" names to check that their lists are not reused without permission. The names you hire are called "cold prospects". However, if they respond to your mailing, they become "warm prospects" and you can legitimately add them to your own mailing list and contact them again. Make sure you ask the broker the following questions:

● How was the list compiled?
● When was the list last updated?
● How has the list performed?
● What are typical response rates for others who have used it?
● Can we have the list in a form that suits us, such as on disk or sticky labels?

IDENTIFYING ITEMS TO INCLUDE IN A MAIL SHOT

A mail shot can comprise nothing more than a simple postcard with a printed message. More usually, it is made up of an envelope containing one or more of the items shown:

- covering letter
- leaflet, brochure, or catalogue
- promotional video
- customer newsletter
- product sample

- free gift
- money-off voucher
- order form
- coupon response device
- reply-paid envelope

USING ENVELOPES

The envelope is a vital ingredient of your mail shot and has an important job to do. If you cannot encourage people to open the envelope, it is not worth spending money on what is inside. Some companies have found that envelopes resembling regular mail are most successful because customers tend to open a mail shot that looks like an ordinary letter. Other organizations have found that undisguised mail shots bring better results. Printed envelopes that urge the recipient to open the mailing, or that highlight the offer inside, are also effective. Innovative envelopes have novelty value and can attract attention, as can unusual sizes, shapes, textures, or colour combinations, or unexpected materials such as foil, rubber, or plastic. Use gimmicky envelopes such as inflatables, or unusual fastenings such as Velcro. All can boost response rates, although they may be more expensive.

72 Make it easy for clients to update their details for your mailing list.

Unusual envelope and amusing free gift prompt recipient to read mail shot

ATTRACTING ATTENTION ▶
Regard your envelope as more than just a container for your mail shot. Consider using an unusual envelope which, although more expensive, can boost response rates.

CREATING THE PERFECT MAIL SHOT

Maximize your marketing budget by developing the perfect mailing. You can achieve this by testing what works best, working with one variable at a time. Try out different mailing lists to find the best one, experiment with different offers to ascertain which is most attractive to customers, send mailings at different times to identify the best timing for a mail shot, and try out a variety of response devices to see which produces most replies. You can also use a technique known as split test mailing. If, for example, you want to test whether a price reduction produces a greater response, send half of your mailing list the standard offer and the other half the discounted offer. Then compare the take-up from each half.

73 Think about expanding your mailing list into a database.

▼ GAUGING COST
A standard method of accurately measuring the impact of a direct mail campaign is known as "cost per response", which tells you how much you are paying to elicit each response.

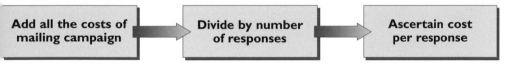

| Add all the costs of mailing campaign | Divide by number of responses | Ascertain cost per response |

74 Use bullet points to make benefits stand out from the main text.

75 Read your covering letter aloud. If it sounds stilted, rewrite it.

MEASURING CONVERSION

In addition to the "cost per response", there is another measurement that provides an insight into the effectiveness of a campaign. The "cost per conversion" tells you how much it costs to attract each sale. Divide the total cost of the mailing by the number of sales. At the outset, establish an allowable cost per conversion. Only you can decide what is acceptable. If an average customer spends £10,000 a year with you, £100 appears an acceptable investment to win such a customer. However, £100 is too much to pay if the annual transaction value per customer is only £35. If your allowable cost per conversion is £100, and you mail 10,000 packs (which cost £1 each), you will need to make 100 sales to break even.

USING THE INTERNET

Everyone seems to want a presence in cyberspace and more organizations are getting on-line daily. Make sure that you stay ahead of the competition by developing your own Web site, and learn how to use the Internet as a powerful sales channel.

76 Avoid hyphens in domain names; they complicate a Web address.

77 Visit competitors' sites and collect useful ideas for your own.

78 On-screen reading is harder on the eye, so keep text legible.

DEVELOPING A WEB SITE

Since your Web site may be the first point of contact for customers, it is very important that it reflects the right image. Templates enabling you to build your own Web site are available to download from the Internet, but it takes an expert to design a well-executed site. Professional web designers know all the tricks. They can help ensure that your site pops up when potential customers use a search engine to hunt for you, and link you to other sites. They can also advise on domain names, as well as securing and registering one for you, and they will, for a fee, maintain your site and keep it up to date on your behalf.

THE PROS AND CONS OF INTERNET SELLING

ATTRIBUTES	LIMITATIONS
Conveys a massive amount of information.	Fraud presents problems for buyers and sellers.
Provides a gateway to new markets.	Buying on-line concerns some customers.
Enables instant feedback from customers.	Hacking and viruses are an ever-present threat.
The number of "hits", or visitors, attracted can be measured.	It is impossible to go to consumers; they must come to you.
Available 24 hours – the Internet never sleeps.	Not everyone is on-line.

MAKING THE MOST OF YOUR WEB SITE

Consider carefully how you will use your site and have it constructed around your needs. Think about how the Internet will fit into your overall marketing plan. It should be tackled not in isolation but as a component part of a much wider-ranging strategy. Your site can be used for:

- interactive publicity;
- customer support via e-mail;
- maintaining relationships with existing customers and attracting new clients;
- generating interest in and building awareness of your product, service, or organization;

- conducting market research;
- selling products and services online;
- providing product information and current availability.

◀ **VESTING CONTROL**
Traditional publicity is relatively passive: organizations push it at consumers. The Internet is a proactive medium: customers pull the information that they want.

ADVERTISING IN CYBERSPACE

Advertising on the Internet continues to develop. It is inexpensive and measurable, interactive, sometimes fun, and can be viewed anytime, night and day. Use it to reach new markets locally, nationally, and globally. Make your Web site a promotional tool in its own right, so that it acts as an interactive brochure. Advertise on others' sites, perhaps with banner adverts, which are the main advertising vehicle on the Net, or animated or static adverts, often found on search engine sites, which, if clicked on, lead viewers directly to your site. Sponsor other related sites that can provide a route to your own site. Web brokers will offer demographic information to help you decide where and how to advertise on the Net, and they will also negotiate the space for you.

POINTS TO REMEMBER

- Your Web site should be designed to reflect your corporate image.
- A Web site should be easy and quick to navigate.
- Prospective clients may leave your site and visit those of competitors if your pages are elaborately designed and take ages to download.
- It should be possible to return to the home page with one click.
- Including an e-mail link will allow visitors to get in touch easily.
- Registering with directories may help publicize your site.
- A site needs maintaining to keep it fresh, current, and relevant.

CREATING A VIRTUAL SHOP

E-commerce is a major growth area because it provides a fast, cost-efficient, "open all hours" way of selling. Setting up shop on the Web is a very different undertaking from simply having a Web site. Once you begin to sell on-line, you are entering a new world, and internal restructuring will be needed. Set about establishing an order management system, comprising interactive order forms, order handling and tracking, a safe and secure payment environment, automated invoicing, and order fulfilment and delivery systems – orders may arrive from anywhere in the world. Some products do not lend themselves well to on-line selling (those that need to be touched or felt), while others are made for it (music or software, which can be downloaded direct from the Net). Consider how an on-line shopfront will affect your existing selling channels.

79 Register with Net directories to ensure your site is publicized.

▼ ANALYZING WEB SITE USES

A Web site can have numerous marketing applications. Use it to build and maintain customer relationships via e-mail, for selling, promoting awareness of products or services to a wider market, giving up-to-date information, and so on.

80 Update the information on your site regularly.

81 Decide whether your products are suitable for selling on-line.

QUESTIONS TO ASK YOURSELF

Q Are our customers on-line?

Q Is our product or service suitable for on-line sales?

Q Do we want to limit our on-line presence to the publicizing of our venture?

Q Are our competitors on-line?

Q Do we have the skills to create and maintain our site?

Q Do we want to sell via the Internet and could we handle the extra orders?

E-MAILING CUSTOMERS

While ill-targeted direct mail is called junk mail, the e-mail equivalent is known as "spam". Mass e-mailing (or spamming) to cold prospects is bad Netiquette and will only result in damage to your reputation. However, e-mail contact with customers and warm prospects can work to your advantage. E-mail provides an extremely cheap way to maintain a lasting relationship. Ask visitors to your Web site if they want to receive e-mailed updates, information, special offers, or details of new products; many will say yes. Ask current customers for their e-mail details. Always keep an up-to-date e-mailing list and find legitimate excuses to get in contact. Remember to include a simple opt-out so that customers can ask to be removed from your e-mailing list if they wish.

REASSURING VIRTUAL CUSTOMERS

The Internet is no longer new, yet there is still wariness about Internet shopping. Scare stories about fraud and unfulfilled orders abound. Give customers confidence in your Web site. Explain how credit card payments can be made securely and safely. Create a customer charter or statement of rights to reassure people that it is safe to buy on-line from you. Explain clearly what your refunds policy is. Publish your complaints procedure. Include an address, telephone and fax number, and a contact name, so that customers have other means of getting in touch if necessary.

82 Create a short domain name that is easy to spell and remember.

Customer is impressed that he is able to exchange goods bought on the Internet at one of the supplier's retail outlets

INSTILLING ▶ CONFIDENCE
Where possible, allow customers to use both your virtual shop and high-street outlets, if you have them. If customers buy on the Net, let them exchange goods through your retail stores.

DEVELOPING A STRATEGY

A strategy gives businesses a defined route to follow and a clear destination. Build a marketing strategy and you will ensure that marketing is a long-term way of working, not a one-off activity.

THINKING STRATEGICALLY

When devising a marketing strategy, getting started can be the hardest part. Bring together a strong team to help plan your approach, and make sure that everyone understands the strategic elements that contribute to marketing success.

83 Allow plenty of time so that key decisions are not rushed.

84 Work on your marketing strategy when it is quiet to aid concentration.

GAINING FROM A STRATEGIC APPROACH

A marketing strategy provides organizations with a shared vision of the future. All too often, an organization will perform a marketing task, such as a direct mail shot, then sit back and see what happens. Or, as a knee-jerk reaction to falling sales or competitor activity, it might follow it up with a promotional offer, almost as if the organization is making up marketing as it goes along. A strategic approach will ensure that you maximize returns on your marketing spending and boost the profits of your organization.

STRATEGIC MANAGER

Has a clear picture of the future

Anticipates changes in the market

Works towards clear, long-term goals

NON-STRATEGIC MANAGER

Lives day to day without planning

Reacts to changes in the market

Has only short-term objectives

BUILDING A TEAM

Producing a marketing strategy from scratch can be daunting, especially if you are not a marketing specialist. Pull together a marketing strategy team from a range of departments to assist with drawing up future plans. Involve people whose function touches on marketing, and those whose job involves considerable customer contact. Before embarking on your marketing strategy, establish common ground by agreeing definitions and purpose. Build team unity, perhaps by organizing an away day at a pleasant venue to discuss shared marketing issues and concerns. Show that you recognize the contribution each team member can offer. Establish your authority as team leader by chairing meetings and overseeing follow-on activity.

▲ BEING AN EFFECTIVE MARKETING MANAGER

A successful marketing manager is strategic in outlook, ensuring maximum returns on marketing spending and boosting profits. A non-strategic manager has no clear, long-term strategic objective in mind.

85 Choose team members for their range of skills.

External consultant is able to offer impartial advice

USING A ▶ FACILITATOR

Consider bringing in an external facilitator or a marketing expert to work with the team and to keep you focused.

ANALYZING YOUR SITUATION

Planning your future marketing strategy is much more effective if you begin by examining the present. Study all aspects of your organization: your products and services, your customers, your market, and your competitors. Look closely at the marketing activity you currently undertake as well as the reasoning behind it. Ask yourself why you adopt certain working practices. Are there strong reasons for undertaking marketing activity in the way you do, or is it merely force of habit? What are your marketing successes? What about your failures? Examine your position in the marketplace, and see how you compare with your competitors. Build up a realistic picture of your organization as it is today. Now you are ready to look to tomorrow.

PLANNING YOUR APPROACH

Work out how long you will need to develop the strategy, bearing in mind all the stages involved. Ensure that everyone on your team can dedicate the necessary time to the task. Map out a process for producing the strategy. This may comprise weekly team meetings, with individual tasking/follow-up work in between. Set a deadline for the completion of the strategy to keep the momentum going. Agree dates in advance for all the meetings you will need and enter them into diaries to ensure that there is little excuse for non-attendance. Keep notes of meetings and principal decisions and circulate these to team members.

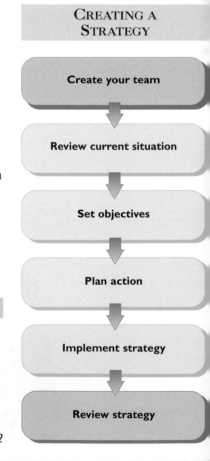

CREATING A STRATEGY

Create your team

Review current situation

Set objectives

Plan action

Implement strategy

Review strategy

QUESTIONS TO ASK YOURSELF

Q Is there anyone else I should really have on the team?

Q Will we need to report to anyone higher up the ladder, such as the chief executive?

Q How long should I allow for the planning process?

Q Would it be helpful to engage an external marketing expert to help guide the planning process?

PERFORMING A SWOT ANALYSIS

The acronym SWOT stands for Strengths, Weaknesses, Opportunities, and Threats. Analysis of these four factors provides information on how to shape your marketing strategy. Devise objectives aimed at strengthening weak areas, exploiting strengths, seizing opportunities, and anticipating threats. To help your analysis, list your strengths, then ask the following questions:

- Do you use your strengths to full advantage? Could you do more to capitalize on them?
- Are there current or future opportunities you could exploit? Are new markets emerging or are there existing, untapped customer groups?
- What threats do your competitors pose? What threats exist in the wider marketplace?
- What lets you down? What are you not good at? What do your competitors do better?

86 Set a deadline for the completion of your strategy.

87 SWOT analyze competitors to see how you compare.

▼ **STEPPING STONES TO MARKETING SUCCESS**

All marketing strategies comprise three main stages: first, determine what you want to achieve; next, adopt the right approach or method to achieve that aim; finally, measure performance to gauge the level of success.

Aim ➤ **Act** ➤ **Assess**

INVOLVING ▶ COLLEAGUES

Ellie was in charge of sales for a small firm making sofa beds. Although not trained in marketing, she was also given overall responsibility for the company's marketing activity. She discovered the benefits of involving colleagues in major marketing initiatives.

CASE STUDY

Without consulting her colleagues, Ellie decided to launch a Web site to attract new business. It was an enormous success, with 40 orders received on the first day. Unfortunately, these were from different parts of the country, which posed distribution problems (the company's orders had previously come from local retailers, making deliveries quick and simple). Given that the production department already had an order of 500 sofa beds for a new hotel, they were unable to meet all the delivery dates, and the new customers were disappointed. This embarrassing situation made Ellie realize that she had to include members of the production and dispatch departments in the planning of any future promotional activity, so that they could share important information about busy periods, existing commitments, and distribution problems with her.

SETTING OBJECTIVES

A strategy is a plan of action devised to meet certain objectives. Draw up your objectives carefully, because your entire marketing strategy will be structured around them, and ensure that they are measurable so that you can evaluate their success.

88 Take time to plan your marketing objectives carefully.

89 Set objectives that are challenging yet achievable.

PLANNING OBJECTIVES

Analyze current position

↓

Specify ideal and modify to incorporate reality

↓

Define measurable short- and long-term objectives

↓

Seek advice or views of colleagues

↓

Modify and finalize objectives

TAKING STOCK

Objectives are goals that are drawn up to take your organization from its current position to where you would like it to be in the future. Short-term objectives can be staging posts on the way towards fulfilling long-term goals. Analyze your situation and then ask: "What if we do nothing?". Will products become out of date? Will your customers remain loyal to a company stuck in a time warp? Will your competitors grow more powerful? Spend time asking "what if?" to help you realize the effects of not keeping up with customer needs and competitors' activities. It can serve to spur action.

CREATING A VISION

Ask yourself where, in an ideal world, you would like your organization to be in five years' time. What position would you like to attain in the marketplace? Would you like to achieve significant growth in your customer base and profitability? Would you like to be the brand leader? Paint a picture of the perfect scenario. Now bring a little reality to bear. Think about likely economic, legal, technological, social, and political changes. Will they pose opportunities or threats? Modify the ideal situation to take account of the realities of the market. What is achievable if you work really hard at it? Keep a record of your ideas.

DEVISING OBJECTIVES

The framework for your objectives has already been created in your vision of the future. Now take each of your goals for the future and translate it into an objective. Remember that an objective simply states what you want to achieve, not how you will achieve it. Each one should have both a quantity and a timeframe. These will help you to tighten the focus of your objective and to measure success. Some objectives will be achievable in the near future: these are your short-term goals. Others will be longer term. Organize objectives into short- and long-term so that you can manage the workload that goes with turning aims into reality. Phrase them so that they are clear and unambiguous.

▼ **MAKING OBJECTIVES MEASURABLE**
Underneath your vision, list your objectives, then quantify each one and set out a date or timescale within which the objective will be achieved. This enables you to evaluate progress and measure success far more effectively.

Future Vision

To be the premier player in our field

Objectives	Quantity	Timeframe
To increase our customer base	By 25 per cent	Within 12 months
To widen our product range	With the introduction of two new lines	By the end of January
To raise our customer profile	So that consumer awareness of the organization and products is boosted by 20 per cent	Nine months into the profile-raising campaign

90 Set at least one objective that can be achieved imminently.

91 Discuss objectives with colleagues to ensure their support.

GAINING AGREEMENT

Once you have devised a set of objectives around which to build your marketing strategy, seek agreement for them from across the organization. Marketing is a discipline that cuts through many departmental boundaries. Marketing activity will have a knock-on effect in various parts of the operation so, for it to be effective, you will need the support of colleagues. Ensure they understand the need for these objectives and the impact they may have on their work. Listen to any objections they may have and assess their validity. It is better to spend time discussing objectives at this stage, so that they can be modified where necessary before you invest considerable effort in devising ways of achieving your goals.

ACHIEVING YOUR GOALS

Having established your objectives, now work out how you are going to attain your ultimate goal. Investigate constraints, such as time and money, and then create a timetable of activity to give you a working marketing plan.

92 Encourage full participation at brainstorming sessions.

93 Try brainstorming away from the workplace; it may be more effective.

BRAINSTORMING IDEAS

Coming up with ideas for achieving your objectives is a creative process. The best technique for freeing creativity is brainstorming. Display an objective on an overhead, whiteboard, or piece of flipchart paper. Next, ask your strategy team to suggest ideas for helping achieve that objective. Write all ideas on a flipchart. Do not comment on, assess, discuss, or evaluate ideas at this stage. Simply record all suggestions. Aim to attract as many ideas as possible, and encourage all group members to participate.

DEVISING SOLUTIONS ▼

Discuss each suggestion put forward during a brainstorming. If an idea seems unworkable at first, encourage the team to think of innovative solutions rather than discarding it without consideration.

Team member suggests sending written product briefing to all customers each month

Colleague questions whether idea would be affordable in terms of time and money

Team member suggests e-mail briefing would be both easy and cheap

Manager agrees that modified idea is good and agrees to implement it

SETTING BUDGETS

Look at your marketing ideas and work out the cost of each. Remember that marketing involves meeting customer need at a profit. To be justified, marketing activity should have a positive impact on the balance sheet. Examine not only the cost but also the benefit. An advertising campaign may cost a lot of money, but if it reaps profits amounting to several times its cost, it is cheap. Avoid setting an overall marketing budget to start with. Instead, work out costs and outcomes, decide what is justified, then calculate the budget.

94 Determine costs and outcomes before setting a budget.

▼ SETTING OUT A PLAN

Some marketing ideas will require little time or money to implement. Others will be costly and/or complicated. List your ideas and give them a high, medium, or low priority. Then assign start and completion dates. Consider implementing low priority ideas immediately if they are quick, cheap, and easy.

TIMETABLING ACTIVITIES

Prioritize activities and then organize them into a logical order. Put a date alongside each activity. When assigning dates, consider the importance of timing. Some ideas are best undertaken when there is an obvious marketing link. For example, if you manufacture apple pies, aim to tie in your promotion with a significant or high-profile event, such as National Apple Day. When timetabling, bear in mind the impact that your marketing activities will have on internal resources. Avoid time-intensive activities during periods of high staff absence, such as during the summer holidays. Remember that this timetable is your working marketing plan.

MARKETING PLAN

ACTIVITY	PRIORITY	START DATE	COMPLETION DATE
Organize lunch for top ten customers	Medium		by end February
Produce new brochure	High	mid-January	end March
Update mailing list ready for new brochure	High		end March
Mail new brochure	High	early April	

EFFECTING THE STRATEGY

Producing a marketing strategy is a means to an end; results will come from implementing it. Assign tasks to staff, provide any support they need, then review progress, measure performance, and periodically revise objectives.

95 Ask for regular progress reports, specifying which facts you need.

96 Make sure that staff inform you of implementation delays and difficulties.

ASSIGNING ACTIVITIES

Some organizations invest considerable effort in developing a strategy, but enthusiasm and energy wane when it comes to implementation. Ensure that your marketing strategy is put into action, not left to gather dust on a shelf. Assign each task or activity due for implementation within the next 12 months to a named person. Check that anyone given responsibility for an activity has the time, knowledge, expertise, budget, and authority to complete the task. Give clear instructions on what is expected and by when. If necessary, ask for regular progress reports, so that you are assured everything is running according to plan.

◀ REVIEWING PROGRESS
The general marketing forum might be open to a large number of staff. In addition to this you will need a smaller review group. This might comprise the original marketing strategy team. Meet at least quarterly, possibly more often. The remit for this group is to compare progress against planned activity.

ACTIONING THE PLAN

Make sure you allow staff to get on with their marketing tasks, but, equally, make sure you do not neglect them. Create a forum for those involved in the creation and implementation of the strategy so that problems and difficulties can be discussed. Work together at devising solutions. Build a supportive atmosphere, rewarding those who are staying on course and encouraging those who are not. Although staff may be involved in implementing only a small part of the strategy, an inclusive forum will enable them to see the bigger picture. Use the forum to receive and discuss progress reports. By sharing these with staff, you will help them to see the benefits of marketing activity and strengthen their commitment to implementing a successful strategy.

QUESTIONS TO ASK YOURSELF

Q Have profits increased since the strategy was implemented?

Q Have we seen an increase in our customer base?

Q Have we attracted a greater number of orders, or larger individual orders?

Q Has the number of product/service enquiries risen?

Q Has awareness of our organization and its products or services increased?

▼ REVISING OBJECTIVES

The world is not static. Things within your organization or within your market are likely to change over time. If they do, you might need to redefine your objectives. Review objectives six-monthly or annually to check that you are still on track.

97 After delegating a task, try to avoid interfering unless there is a risk that objectives will not be met.

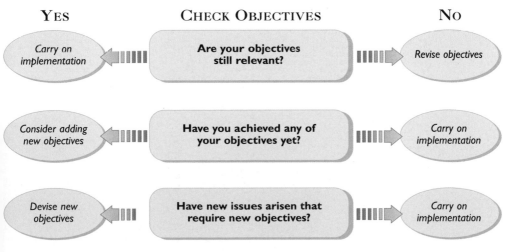

YES	CHECK OBJECTIVES	NO
Carry on implementation	Are your objectives still relevant?	Revise objectives
Consider adding new objectives	Have you achieved any of your objectives yet?	Carry on implementation
Devise new objectives	Have new issues arisen that require new objectives?	Carry on implementation

GAINING SUPPORT

M*arketing has a vital role to play in every organization, but its contribution is not always recognized. As part of your strategy, build support within the workplace. Break down departmental barriers and help create a marketing organization.*

98 Explain how marketing can support colleagues in their work.

99 Make colleagues aware of marketing successes.

100 Cultivate the support of all your colleagues.

WINNING ALLIES

Marketing managers often complain that their departments are always blamed when things go wrong and are never credited when they go well. It can be difficult for staff at the sharp end of the business to see the relevance of marketing. Win the support, understanding, commitment, and collaboration of your non-marketing colleagues, including the chairperson and chief executive. Tell them of your organization's marketing successes. Show them what effective marketing can achieve, and use hard data to demonstrate its benefits.

BECOMING A MARKETING ORGANIZATION

If staff across the organization can see the relevance and benefits of marketing, their co-operation will follow naturally. They may offer sales leads, provide constructive feedback on marketing materials, or come up with workable ideas for improving customer service. Involve all staff in marketing activities. Ask for ideas and show that you value their contribution. As well as telling them about your work, become acquainted with their work, too.

▼ **SHARING SUCCESSES**
Explain to colleagues how marketing techniques can be used to support them in their work. Involve relevant staff from other departments in marketing planning. Give them a stake in its success.

SHARING INFORMATION

Keep colleagues informed of any marketing activity. Staff sometimes grumble that they are the last people to hear about what the marketing department is doing; the first they may know about a new advert is when customers or friends tell them. When this happens, staff feel stupid, embarrassed, or ill-informed. Use memos and e-mails to brief colleagues. Let them feel that they have insider knowledge. Tell staff the day before a new press advert appears or a new radio advert is broadcast. Tip them off that a direct mail campaign is about to get underway. Obviously you will not wish to publicize commercially sensitive information, but there is no harm in keeping staff up to date and involved.

▲ SUPPORTING OTHER DEPARTMENTS

Find out what colleagues in different departments do from day to day and see if your marketing skills can help them provide a better service to customers.

POINTS TO REMEMBER

- Cross-organization support is required for effective marketing.
- The marketing department cannot operate in a vacuum.
- Colleagues should not be given an opportunity to question your value and contribution.

101 Be prepared to justify your existence in a positive way.

HANDLING SCEPTICISM

It is not unusual for employees to criticize other departments within their organization, and marketing often attracts more than its fair share of adverse comment. If people outside of the marketing department are heard complaining that "we do not know what marketing finds to do all day", or "marketing does not understand the realities of our work", you are working in a compartmentalized organization. If this is the case, do all that you can to cultivate the support and respect of colleagues in other departments. In a true marketing organization, all members of staff are able to see the direct benefit of marketing and are fully aware of how the marketing team contributes to its overall success.

ASSESSING YOUR MARKETING ABILITY

A good understanding of basic marketing theory, combined with experience of techniques, will ensure your ability to implement an effective marketing programme. This questionnaire will test your approach to marketing. Answer the questions as honestly as you can. If your answer is "never", mark Option 1, and so on. Add your scores together, and refer to the Analysis at the end of the questionnaire.

OPTIONS

1 Never

2 Occasionally

3 Frequently

4 Always

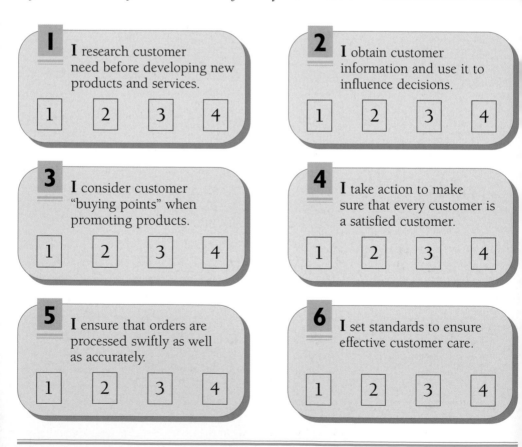

1 I research customer need before developing new products and services.

1   2   3   4

2 I obtain customer information and use it to influence decisions.

1   2   3   4

3 I consider customer "buying points" when promoting products.

1   2   3   4

4 I take action to make sure that every customer is a satisfied customer.

1   2   3   4

5 I ensure that orders are processed swiftly as well as accurately.

1   2   3   4

6 I set standards to ensure effective customer care.

1   2   3   4

7 I measure performance against the standards of customer care.

1 2 3 4

8 I take the complaints of customers very seriously.

1 2 3 4

9 I monitor the number of customer complaints that we receive.

1 2 3 4

10 I try to see if there is anything I can learn from a customer's complaint.

1 2 3 4

11 I find reasons to keep in touch with customers.

1 2 3 4

12 I try to turn one-off customers into regular ones.

1 2 3 4

13 I keep a record of key customer contact.

1 2 3 4

14 I ask customers whether they will recommend us.

1 2 3 4

15 I show customers that their business is valued.

1 2 3 4

16 I try to find out why we have lost a customer.

1 2 3 4

17 I attempt to win back lost customers.

1   2   3   4

18 I am on the lookout for new customers.

1   2   3   4

19 I try to nurture customer loyalty.

1   2   3   4

20 I seek customer comment and feedback.

1   2   3   4

21 I listen to what customers say.

1   2   3   4

22 I pay attention to the little details that make all the difference.

1   2   3   4

23 I try to add value to our products and services.

1   2   3   4

24 I emphasize benefits, not features.

1   2   3   4

25 I use public relations techniques to boost marketing effectiveness.

1   2   3   4

26 I draw up a pricing strategy for every new product marketed.

1   2   3   4

27 I set objectives for publicity campaigns.

1   2   3   4

28 I carefully target mail shots.

1   2   3   4

29 I take care to select the right envelope for a direct mail campaign.

1   2   3   4

30 I test mail shots to find the most successful combination.

1   2   3   4

31 I measure the overall effectiveness of a publicity campaign.

1   2   3   4

32 I keep non-marketing colleagues informed of key marketing activity.

1   2   3   4

ANALYSIS

Now that you have completed the self-assessment, add up your total score and check your performance. Whatever level of success you have achieved, there is always room for improvement. Identify your weakest areas, then refer to the relevant sections of this book, where you will find practical advice and tips to help you establish and hone your marketing skills.
32–64: You need to take a more organized, planned, methodical, and measured approach to improve your effectiveness.
65–95: Some of your marketing activity is a success, but you need to develop your skills to become wholly effective.
96–128: You have adopted a thoroughly professional, strategic approach to marketing and are running successful marketing campaigns. Keep up the good work to stay ahead of the competition.

PROJECT MANAGEMENT

INTRODUCTION

To be successful in today's competitive business world, managers must deliver results on time and within budget. By applying the processes, tools, and techniques shown in Project Management *you will maximize performance and ensure optimum results every time. Suitable for managers at all levels, this book equips you with all the know-how you need to lead any project, large or small, to a successful conclusion. From starting a project with a flourish to motivating a team and overcoming problems; every aspect of professional project management is clearly explained. There is a step-by-step guide to project planning, while 101 tips offer further practical advice. Finally, a self-assessment exercise allows you to evaluate your ability as a project manager, helping you to improve your skills and your prospects for the future.*

UNDERSTANDING THE BASICS

Project management provides structure, focus, flexibility, and control in the pursuit of results. Understand what running a project entails and how to improve the likelihood of success.

DEFINING PROJECTS

A project is a series of activities designed to achieve a specific outcome within a set budget and timescale. Learn how to distinguish projects from everyday work and adopt the discipline of project management more widely to improve performance.

1 Greet a new project as an opportunity to develop your skills.

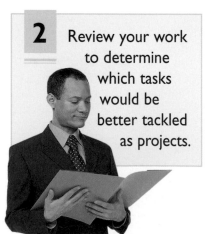

2 Review your work to determine which tasks would be better tackled as projects.

WHAT IS A PROJECT?

A project has clear start and end points, a defined set of objectives, and a sequence of activities in-between. The activities need not be complex: painting the staff restaurant is as valid a project as building a bridge. You may be involved in a project without realizing it – for example, if you work in a special team, perhaps outside the normal business schedule, to a deadline. Routine work, on the other hand, is usually on-going, repetitive, and process-oriented. Some everyday work may lend itself to being managed as a project – tackling it as such will greatly increase your efficiency.

WHY USE PROJECT MANAGEMENT?

In today's competitive business environment, a flexible and responsive approach to changing customer requirements is essential. Project management enables you to focus on priorities, track performance, overcome difficulties, and adapt to change. It gives you more control and provides proven tools and techniques to help you lead teams to reach objectives on time and within budget. Organizing activities into a project may be time-consuming initially, but in the long term it will save time, effort, and reduce the risk of failure.

IDENTIFYING THE KEY FEATURES OF PROJECTS

FEATURES	POINTS TO NOTE
DEFINED START AND END All projects have start-up and close-down stages.	● Some projects are repeated often, but they are not processes because they have clear start and end points. ● Routine work can be distinguished from projects because it is recurring, and there is no clear end to the process.
ORGANIZED PLAN A planned, methodical approach is used to meet project objectives.	● Good planning ensures a project is completed on time and within budget – having delivered the expected results. ● An effective plan provides a template that guides the project and details the work that needs to be done.
SEPARATE RESOURCES Projects are allocated time, people, and money on their own merits.	● Some projects operate outside the normal routine of business life, others within it – but they all require separate resources. ● Working within agreed resources is vital to success.
TEAMWORK Projects usually require a team of people to get the job done.	● Project teams take responsibility for and gain satisfaction from their own objectives, while contributing to the success of the organization as a whole. ● Projects offer new challenges and experiences for staff.
ESTABLISHED GOALS Projects bring results in terms of quality and/or performance.	● A project often results in a new way of working, or creates something that did not previously exist. ● Objectives must be identified for all those involved in the project.

EXAMINING KEY ROLES

Projects can involve a wide range of people with very different skills and backgrounds. However, there are several pivotal roles common to all projects, and it is important to understand the parts that each of these key people play.

3 Draw up a list of all the people who might be able to help you.

UNDERSTANDING ROLES

As project manager, you are in charge of the entire project. But you cannot succeed alone, and establishing good relations with other key players is vital. Important project people include the sponsor, who may also be your superior, and who provides backing (either financial or moral); key team members, who are responsible for the overall success of the project; part-time or less senior members, who nevertheless contribute to the plan, and experts or advisers with important roles. There will also be stakeholders, or people with an interest in the project, such as customers, suppliers, or executives in other parts of your organization.

INVOLVING STAKEHOLDERS

Aim to involve your stakeholders at an early stage. Not all stakeholders will be equally important, so identify those who could have a significant effect on the project; and when you draw up the project plan later, consider how regularly they should be consulted. When stakeholders are enthusiastic and strongly supportive of the project, seek their assistance in motivating others. Make sure that you forge strong alliances with those stakeholders who control the resources. Finally, check that everyone understands the reason for their involvement in the project and what its impact on them will be.

4 Build up a good rapport with your main stakeholders.

5 Make sure that your core team consists of people you really trust.

IDENTIFYING KEY PLAYERS AND THEIR ROLES

KEY PLAYER	ROLES
SPONSOR Initiates a project, adds to the team's authority, and is the most senior team member.	• Ensures that the project is of real relevance to the organization. • Helps in setting objectives and constraints. • Acts as an inspirational figurehead. • May provide resources.
PROJECT MANAGER Responsible for achieving the project's overall objectives and leading the project team.	• Produces a detailed plan of action. • Motivates and develops project team. • Communicates project information to stakeholders and other interested parties. • Monitors progress to keep project on track.
STAKEHOLDER Any other party who is interested in, or affected by, the outcome of the project.	• Contributes to various stages of the planning process by providing feedback. • Might only be involved from time to time. • May not be a stakeholder for the entire project if his or her contribution is complete.
KEY TEAM MEMBER Assists the project manager and provides the breadth of knowledge needed.	• Makes a major contribution in examining feasibility and planning a project. • Lends technical expertise when needed. • Is directly responsible for project being completed on time and within budget.
TEAM MEMBER Full or part-time person who has actions to carry out in the project plan.	• Takes responsibility for completing activities as set out in the project plan. • Fulfils a specialized role if involved as a consultant, or as an individual who is only needed for part of the project.
CUSTOMER Internal or external person who benefits from changes brought about by the project.	• Strongly influences the objectives of the project and how its success is measured. • Dictates how and when some activities are carried out. • Provides direction for the project manager.
SUPPLIER Provider of materials, products, or services needed to carry out the project.	• Can become very involved with, and supportive of, the project. • Delivers supplies on time and provides services or goods at a fixed cost, agreed with the project manager at the outset.

IDENTIFYING THE ESSENTIALS FOR SUCCESS

To achieve the desired outcome, a project must have defined and approved goals, a committed team, and a viable plan of action that can be altered to accommodate change. Abide by these essentials to keep you on course for success.

6 Make sure that people understand what you are aiming to achieve.

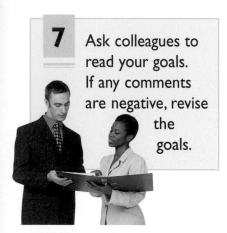

7 Ask colleagues to read your goals. If any comments are negative, revise the goals.

HAVING CLEAR GOALS

To be successful, a project must have clearly defined goals. These goals must be agreed by all involved, so that everyone proceeds with the same expectations. The scope of the project must remain consistent so that it achieves what it set out to accomplish. Whoever agreed to the initiation of the project, usually the project sponsor or customer, should not need to make significant changes to its scope or extent. People who are key to the success of the project must commit their time to it, even if their involvement is only on a part-time basis.

GAINING COMMITMENT

A keen, skilled, and committed team is vital to the success of any project. To this end, the motivational and people-management skills of the project manager are paramount. As project manager, it is your responsibility to develop the best team that you can, guide it in the right direction, and ensure that members benefit from the experience. Choose your team carefully and provide training, if necessary. The ongoing support of your superior, sponsor, and other interested parties must also be gained from the outset.

QUESTIONS TO ASK YOURSELF

Q Could I respond to a customer's demand by initiating a project?

Q Whom should I approach to get the project under way?

Q Am I confident that key people will lend their support to make this project successful?

Q Do the overall aims of the project seem achievable?

PLANNING AND COMMUNICATING

For a project to run smoothly, the resources required must be available at the time you need them. This demands effective front-end planning, taking into account not only people, but also facilities, equipment, and materials. A detailed, complete plan guides the project and is the document that communicates your overall objectives, activities, resource requirements, and schedules. It is also vital that you keep everyone involved fully informed of the plan and update them whenever it changes.

8	Expect to revise and enhance your project plan at least several times.

◀ **ACTING EARLY**
Check with your superior that a sufficient budget and realistic timescale have been agreed for the project from the outset. This avoids the success of your project being threatened later because time or money has run out.

BEING FLEXIBLE

In a rapidly changing business environment, the ability to think ahead and anticipate can make the difference between achieving project objectives or not. You must be prepared to change your plans in a flexible and responsive way. It is unlikely that your original plan will be the one you follow all the way, since circumstances and requirements generally change as the project unfolds. This means that you will have to re-evaluate the plan regularly and adapt it accordingly. If your project is to succeed, you must be able to anticipate and recognize the need for change, implement it, and measure its impact effectively.

9	Learn to accept the inevitability of change.

10	You can hope for the best, but always plan for the worst.

DEFINING THE STAGES

There are five stages to a project: initiation, planning, motivating, monitoring, and closing. Start with a flourish, end positively, and recognize the different techniques and skills required to negotiate the three key stages in-between.

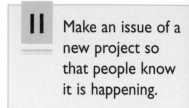

11 Make an issue of a new project so that people know it is happening.

PLANNING A PROJECT

Whether you initiate a project yourself, or your manager or a customer suggests it, the first step in the planning process is to agree a vision of the project, stating exactly what it will achieve. To do this, you will bring together your core team members and people with a close interest in the project's result, known as stakeholders. Having defined a vision, you can identify objectives, agree on actions and resources, order and schedule tasks, and finally validate the plan with all concerned and gain their commitment to it.

IMPLEMENTING THE PLAN

The success of the implementation phase rests with the project team and, ultimately, your ability to lead them. You will have to think about team selection, understand how the team will develop as the project progresses, encourage teamwork, agree on key decisions, and adopt different leadership styles to inspire and motivate different personalities. To gain the commitment of all concerned, make sure that you start with a well-prepared flourish, using the authority of your sponsor, manager, and customer to focus everyone on the plan. You must ensure that everyone has access to key project information, and keep communication flowing at all times.

12

Monitor the project consistently from start to finish – problems can occur anywhere along the way.

MONITORING PERFORMANCE

Once the project is under way, you will need to assess how it is faring against objectives and time targets. An efficient monitoring system is vital if you are to deal with problems and changes before they throw a project off course. During this stage, you will be asking for regular progress reports, organizing team meetings, and identifying milestones that will measure your progress. Once you have identified potential problems and threats, you can then use logical processes to overcome them, and to manage and incorporate changes to the plan when required. Finally, you will gain maximum benefit for your organization by recording your experiences for future reference.

UNDERSTANDING PROJECT DEVELOPMENT

Initiators of project agree a vision

Key people outline project purpose and objectives

Activities and resources are agreed and prioritized

Project plan is approved by all involved

Project manager executes plan, guiding team to achieve goals

Progress is monitored and plan revised as necessary

Project is successfully completed on time and within budget

Project manager greets new colleague with enthusiasm

◀ MAKING AN IMPRESSION

Bring the project team together as early as possible to introduce them, and yourself, informally. It is important to start off on a good footing, so be positive and stress how much you are looking forward to working together as a team.

CHECKING FEASIBILITY

Before starting on a project, you need to be certain that there is a good probability that it will be successful. Take the relevant steps to find out whether a project is appropriately timed, feasible, and worthwhile before going ahead with it.

13 Make sure you are not undertaking a task that cannot be achieved.

14 Find out where a project is in danger of failure.

15 Examine whether a given schedule is realistic.

TIMING IT RIGHT

However promising and desirable a project may seem, always examine carefully whether it is the right time to initiate it. Take into account other projects that have already started. Some organizations have so many projects in place that it is not possible for them all to succeed, so you may have to consider postponing the new project or curtailing those that are unlikely to produce valuable results. Since all projects require access to limited or even scarce resources, it is vital that each has a clear reason for existing and that now is definitely the right time for it to happen.

IDENTIFYING DRIVING RESOURCES

Every project is driven by the needs of the organization. The stronger these driving forces, the more likely the project is to succeed. If, for example, a project involves winning back lost customers, the driving force is very strong. To create a list of driving forces, or reasons why your project should go ahead, decide which business concerns the project will have an impact on, and then compare your project with other projects. For example, if there is a driving force behind two projects to increase sales, then the one that, say, doubles sales is more likely to succeed.

QUESTIONS TO ASK YOURSELF

Q Are there any on-going projects with a higher priority than my own that are taking up key resources?

Q Are my project goals in line with the long-term objectives of my organization?

Q How will the outcome of the project affect the performance of the organization?

Q Could this project damage the chances of another project being successful?

IDENTIFYING RESISTING FORCES

There are always reasons why projects may not be completed. Such forces include people's resistance to change, the weight of the current workload, lack of information or resources, or a dearth of people with the necessary skills. Identify these resisting forces early on so that you can overcome them, or change the timing of the project. A strong resisting force emerges in organizations that frequently initiate projects to change the way people carry out their jobs but fail to see the projects through. If people view a project as simply another management initiative, it will take great skill to motivate them to make it happen.

▼ SEEKING EXPERT ADVICE
Ask a key team member with technical expertise to help you identify reasons why your project may not be successful. They may be able to pinpoint flaws that you had not previously considered.

▼ USING FORCEFIELD ANALYSIS
Create a simple diagram, such as the example below, to compare driving and resisting forces. List the driving forces against a vertical grid, and give each column a number between one and five. Do the same with the resisting forces but give them a negative measurement.

PREDICTING SUCCESS

A useful technique, known as forcefield analysis, will help you to decide whether the driving forces outweigh the resisting forces, and, consequently, whether the project has a good chance of success. By creating such an analysis, you will be able to see at a glance whether the balance is weighted towards success or failure. To assess the relative impact of each force, remember that drivers range from "one", a weak driver, to "five", an essential need. "Minus one" describes a resisting force that is not much of a threat to the success of the project, while "minus five" shows a force that is very strong, and that, unless you can minimize its impact, is likely to hinder you in achieving the desired project results.

Resisting forces					Driving forces				
	Lack of budget								
	Current workload								
				Loss of revenue					
				Current staff frustration					
-5	-4	-3	-2	-1	0	1	2	3	4	5
Strong					Weak					Strong

PRIORITIZING PROJECTS

When managing several projects, you must evaluate which is the most important to your organization in order to allocate time and resources. Seek advice from key people and use the discipline of a master schedule to prioritize effectively.

16 Put your projects in order now and avoid damaging conflicts later.

17 Check that project and organizational priorities align.

SETTING PRIORITIES ▼

In this example, the project manager is assigned several projects by her superior. By prioritizing effectively, she is able to complete all the projects successfully. A failure to prioritize, however, leads to disorganization, resulting in none of the projects achieving their intended value.

CONSIDERING VALUE

Before starting a new project, consider how many people and what resources it needs to meet its objectives. Your aim is to deploy the organization's resources to projects that offer the greatest value in their results. Discuss with your superior, and/or the project initiator, the relative importance of your project. You may wish to hold meetings with your customer or other project team members. The more complex the project, the more important it is to seek the opinion of others before you prioritize.

Project manager reviews projects but cannot decide which is most important

Project manager takes responsibility for three new projects

SCHEDULING PROJECTS

To help you decide early on how best to tackle a string of projects, create a form known as a master schedule. You need not identify all the resources in detail at this stage but write down an estimate. This will enable you to see where there are potential resource clashes between projects and confirm or deny the feasibility of a new project. If, for example, two projects require a crane at the same time, and you only have one available, you must reschedule one project to ensure that the crane is available for both.

Master Schedule

	JAN	FEB	MAR	APR	MAY	JUNE	JULY
Project 1							
Project 2							
Project 3							
RESOURCES							
Project manager	1	2	2	3	2	2	1
Engineers	2	4	4	5	4	1	0
Installation staff	0	3	3	4	2	2	1
Computers	3	5	5	7	4	3	2
Low loader	0	1	2	2	0	0	0
Heavy crane	0	0	1	2	0	0	0

▲ **CREATING A MASTER SCHEDULE**
Create a series of monthly (or, for complex projects, weekly) columns running to the right of the form. List all your on-going projects and underneath, detail the resources (people, equipment, materials) you think you are likely to need.

Project manager seeks superior's opinion on which projects should take priority

Project manager completes all three projects successfully

Project manager falls behind with projects because she has failed to prioritize

THINGS TO DO

1. Decide which projects offer the greatest potential value to your organization.

2. If in doubt, seek advice from a superior or the project initiator.

3. Create a master schedule to outline the resources each project requires.

4. If available resources are in conflict, rethink priorities.

PLANNING A PROJECT

An effective plan maps out your project from start to finish, detailing what needs to be done, when, and how much it will cost. Prepare your plan well, and it will guide you to success.

DEFINING THE VISION

Having a clear idea of what a project will achieve is essential if you are to ensure that it will accomplish something of perceived value. With your key team members and sponsor, produce an overall statement that describes the project vision.

18 Be as ambitious as you can, but avoid committing to the impossible.

19 Create a precise vision to avoid ambiguous results.

20 See if others agree with your vision of the future.

DEFINING DESIRABLE CHANGE

Ensure that everyone knows exactly what a project is expected to attain by summarizing its aims. With your key team members and sponsor, create a statement that describes the project vision. For the statement to explain your proposal properly, it must answer the question, "What are we going to change and how?". Check the vision statement with your customers, who may help to refine it by describing what they would expect from such a project. If the project creates something of value for the customer, that is a good indicator of its desirability.

Examining the Ideal

To help you outline your vision, try to define what would be ideal. Start from a blank sheet of paper and ask the team to describe what, in an ideal world, the project would change. Avoid being held back by the situation as it is now. While you must remain realistic, you must also be creative in your thinking. Do not allow the way in which you have always done things to deter you from coming up with alternatives. If you involve the customer in this process, avoid giving them the impression that this is how the world will be, but how you would like it to be. Check how feasible the ideal is to arrive at your vision.

CREATING A PROJECT VISION

```
Identify a need
for change
        ↓
Meet with key team
members and sponsor
        ↓
Define what the project
would ideally change
        ↓
Assess the likelihood of
attaining ideal vision
        ↓
Produce a feasible
vision statement
```

Do's and Don'ts

✔ Do compromise on the ideal if that is what it takes to arrive at the vision.

✔ Do make the vision statement explain why the project is needed.

✘ Don't ignore obstacles at this stage – they may prove to be major stumbling blocks.

✘ Don't involve too many people this early in the process.

AGREEING A VISION ▶
Encourage team members to question every aspect of the vision to check that it is truly workable and achievable. Make sure that everyone agrees on the way ahead, so that they are committed to attaining the vision.

21 Check at this stage that the vision is clearly worth attaining.

SETTING OBJECTIVES

Once you have agreed the project vision, you must set clear objectives that will measure the progress and ultimate success of the project. Expand the vision to clarify the purpose of the project, list the objectives, and then set priorities and interim targets.

22 Gain agreement on objectives from everyone involved in the project.

23 Make sure that your objectives are measurable.

24 Think how relevant an objective will be when it is achieved.

DEFINING PURPOSE

Expand the vision statement to explain what you are going to do, how long it will take, and how much it will cost. Your statement of purpose should reflect the relative importance of time, cost, and performance. For example, if you aim to create a product that competes with the newest solutions available, the key purpose is performance. Time-scale is the key driver if you must install a new system before starting international operations. Cost is the key purpose if you cannot, under any circumstances, spend more than last year's budget.

DEFINING OBJECTIVES AND INDICATORS

List the specific objectives you wish to achieve, covering the areas of change that the project involves. Avoid listing an activity, such as "complete a pilot", instead of an objective, which would be to "demonstrate that the project will achieve the planned business impact". Ensure that progress against objectives is measurable by setting an "indicator" against each one. For example, if your objective is to increase sales of a new drink, use the indicator of sales volume to measure success. If you are having difficulty in arriving at the indicator, ask the question, "How will we know if we have achieved this objective?".

▼ RESEARCHING STANDARDS

Nominate a team member to read up on industry standards. These will provide a benchmark for your own indicators and a check on your competitiveness.

Team member studies competitors' brochures

SETTING PRIORITIES AND TARGETS

It is unlikely that all the objectives will be equally important to your organization. Give each a priority of one to ten, where one is the least important. It will probably be obvious which objectives are significant and which are not, but priorities of those falling in-between will be less clear. Discuss and agree these with the team. Then set targets. These may be simple, such as increasing sales by 50 per cent, or they may be more complex. If, for example, your objective is to improve customer satisfaction, and the indicator is based on complaints, you must count the number of complaints you now receive, and set a target for reducing them.

▼ DECIDING ON PROJECT EMPHASIS

Write down your objectives, indicators, priorities, current performance, and targets. This will help you to decide which aspects of the project require most effort and resources.

POINTS TO REMEMBER

● Objectives should always be appropriate for the whole organization, not just your own area or department.

● It will be easier to identify targets if you discuss them with others, including your customers.

● Well-defined and appropriate targets will enthuse and motivate team members, encouraging good team morale.

25 Be prepared to drop any objective that has a low priority.

Key objectives that determine project's success

Priority of objective

Objective	Indicator	P	Current	Target
Improve sales of non-standard products	Increase volume of orders	10	5 million	7.5 million
Improve the speed of decision-making	Reduce time taken to respond to a customer request for a quotation	8	8 weeks	4 weeks
Improve efficiency of preparing customer quotations	(a) Reduce time spent on preparing quotations (b) Cut number of days spent on product training courses	6	(a) 4 days per month (b) 5 days per year	(a) 2 days per month (b) 0 days per year
Improve management accountability for proposals	Make a single manager accountable for producing each customer proposal	6	Not done	In place

Measure of the objective's success

Current level of performance

Desired level of performance

ASSESSING CONSTRAINTS

Every project faces constraints, such as limits on time or money. Occasionally, such constraints may even render the project unfeasible. Make sure that team members understand the constraints in advance, and that they are able to work within them.

26 You can overcome most constraints by planning how to get around them.

▼ LIMITING CHANGE

Talk through any changes you wish to make with your superior, but be prepared to accept that some will not be approved. There may be valid reasons for keeping certain processes or practices intact.

PROTECTING WHAT WORKS

There is little point in change for the sake of it if you can work within the constraints of what currently exists. Even if you identify an area for improvement, it may be better to include the change in a later project, rather than deal with it immediately. This is because too many changes can put a project at risk as people try to cope with too fluid an environment. Also, by taking on too many changes, there is the danger that you will not be able to identify those that have resulted in the success of the project, or indeed, its failure.

ASSESSING TIME CONSTRAINTS

A fast-moving business environment often gives projects a specific window of opportunity. If you are facing a competitor who is to deliver a new product into the shops for the autumn season, you must work within that time constraint. You will not benefit from working hard to deliver a competitive product if you cannot launch the new range in time for your customers to place orders. Whether you like it or not, the time constraint has been set and you must work within that boundary.

27 Face up to constraints in a logical fashion.

28 Do your best to find short cuts to success.

EXAMINING RESOURCE LIMITATIONS

Most organizations work within limited resources and budgets, and projects are subject to similar constraints. A new project may entail an extravagant use of resources, so you will need to make sure that they really would be available. But if the success of your project depends on a level of resources that is unlikely to be forthcoming, think again, and alter the objectives of the project. For example, if you can complete the project with fewer resources, then you should make that your plan. Alternatively, if you are in a position to negotiate for more time and money to enable the project to go ahead, do so.

THINGS TO DO

1. Assess whether time is of the essence.
2. Analyze what resources you will need and whether you can afford them.
3. Look into using existing processes or resources.
4. Identify any external constraints, such as legal or environmental regulations.
5. Decide whether to proceed within the given constraints.

29 Explain the constraints to all who agree to take part in the project.

USING EXISTING PROCESSES

In order to reduce project timescales, look at what currently exists. For example, other departments may have plans for change in an associated area that you could capitalize on, product parts that would shortcut design, or current technologies that would avoid the need to invent something new. It is important to consider these issues and reuse as much as possible. It is rarely a good idea to start from scratch, no matter how appealing that may seem.

CASE STUDY

Robert was asked to create a Web site for his department. Since he did not have the expertise to do this alone, he asked two outside companies that specialized in setting up and maintaining Web sites to quote for the work.

Robert's sponsor thought that both quotations were too high, and advised Robert to look at the Web sites already created by other departments within their organization.

Robert particularly liked the site designed and maintained by Anne-Marie, who showed him how to use the software she had bought in especially to create her site.

As a result, Robert was able to create the Web site for his department. In doing so, he not only saved the money that had been allocated specifically for that purpose but also made further use of the software investment originally made by Anne-Marie.

◀ **CAPITALIZING ON INVESTMENTS**
By studying systems in other departments within your organization, you can capitalize on internal expertise and experience, at the same time saving your organization money.

Listing Activities

Having identified your objectives and constraints, you can now plan in greater detail. List all the activities needed to achieve the objectives and divide them into groups to make it easier to assess what must be done, when, and by whom.

30 Make sure that you consult widely when creating your activity list.

Why List Activities?

Breaking the project work down into smaller units, or activities, makes it much easier to see how work overlaps, and how some activities may affect the timing or outcome of others. Since the list can be long, it helps to divide activities into groups so that each set of tasks becomes more manageable and easier to track when monitoring performance and progress. Grouping activities also helps you determine how they fit into a logical sequence for completion, which aids scheduling and enables you to assess the number of people and the skills that will be needed. Listing activities in this way also reduces the risk of misunderstandings, since everyone knows what their tasks are.

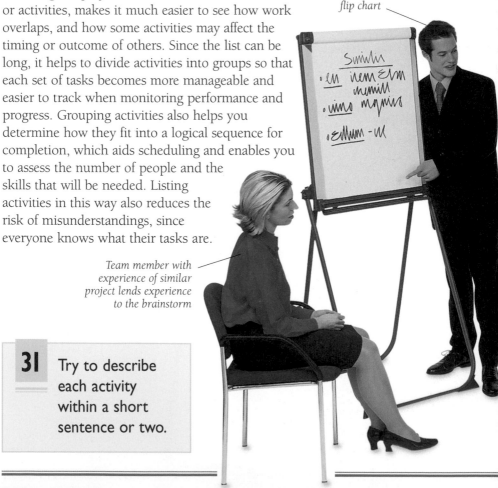

Team member records each activity on a flip chart

Team member with experience of similar project lends experience to the brainstorm

31 Try to describe each activity within a short sentence or two.

DRAWING UP A LIST

Start the process by brainstorming a list of activities. You may need to include more people at this stage. It is often useful, for example, to ask various stakeholders for their views on what it will take to complete the project, especially if it is a complex one. You may also wish to consult other potential team members. Such consultation makes sensible use of other people's expertise and experience. Ideally, if someone in the organization has previously completed a similar project, consult the original project manager and use the previous plan as a checklist. At this stage it is not necessary to concern yourself with the order in which the activities will occur; this comes later.

32 Keep checking your list to see if anything is missing.

PLANNING PROJECT ACTIVITIES

Brainstorm a comprehensive list

Group activities into a logical order

Check that nothing has been missed

Give each group and activity a unique identifying number

Document the activity list

Project manager guides team but does not judge contributions

Team member feels free to suggest an activity

Colleague is aware that this is not the time to pass comment

◀ BRAINSTORMING ACTIVITIES

Use a brainstorming session to generate ideas on all the activities needed to complete the project. Note every activity suggested, no matter how inconsequential. Your aim is to draw up a comprehensive list that can be refined later.

GROUPING ACTIVITIES

Break down your long list of activities into smaller, more manageable units by putting the activities into logical groups. You can ask the team to help you or, as project manager, you can do it yourself. Most groups will be obvious. Perhaps certain activities are all concerned with one event occurring later in the project, or some may all involve the same department or people with similar skills. If an activity does not fit into a group, question whether it is really necessary, or leave it as a separate entity.

GROUPING ACTIVITIES ▶

To group activities effectively, consider the logical order in which they will have to happen. One group, for example, may not be able to start before another is complete. The extract shown lists groups of activities involved in bringing a new product to the manufacturing stage.

33 Present your activity list so that it is clear and easy to understand.

ACTIVITIES AND GROUPS

1 **Conduct analysis**
1.1 Interview customer representatives
1.2 Consolidate findings into a report
1.3 Present report to board
2 **Agree product outline**
2.1 Hold discussions with departments
2.2 Gain budget approval
3 **Complete design**
3.1 Take first draft to representative customers
3.2 Amend to answer customer comments
3.3 Gain top level agreement to design
4 **Arrange logistics**
4.1 Order materials
4.2 Train personnel
4.3 Engage subcontractors

34 Ask specialists for advice when grouping activities.

35 Put the list away and review it a week later with a fresh perspective.

IDENTIFYING TYPICAL GROUPS

Every project has a start-up phase, or a group of activities that signifies the launch of the project, introduces team members, and records what each person has committed to achieving. Similarly, there should be a group of activities marking the project's close-down, involving final checks on performance indicators and finalizing project records for the benefit of subsequent project managers. Finally, most projects need a group of communications activities, for example issuing weekly progress reports or holding a presentation shortly before a planned pilot scheme goes live.

CHECKING FOR GAPS

Review your list of activities and groups to ensure that it is complete. If you miss out this step now and realize later that you have overlooked something, it could have serious implications on the project's budget, schedule, or other resources. Have you identified every activity needed in each group? Go through the planned activities step-by-step: is there anything missing; are you assuming that something will have happened in between activities that you have not actually listed? Once you are confident that each group is complete, give each group and each activity within the group a unique identifying number.

QUESTIONS TO ASK YOURSELF

Q If we complete all the activities listed, will we have done everything required to meet the project's objectives?

Q Will the activities ensure that we hit our indicator targets?

Q Does our activity list reflect the priorities we originally set for each objective?

Q Have we written down all our activities in sufficient detail?

Q Are all of the activities listed really necessary?

PLANNING A PILOT

Another group of activities that features in many projects, especially when the purpose is to create something entirely new, is a pilot implementation. Typical activities include choosing a limited number of people as a pilot team, implementing the whole project on a limited basis, and keeping records of the experience. By building a pilot phase into the plan, you will have a far less stressful and error-prone time when it comes to rolling out the entire project.

Choose your people for the pilot scheme carefully and make them aware that they are, for this particular project, guinea pigs. Make sure you communicate your thanks to them after the project, since their agreement to be involved at an early stage probably caused them some problems.

RUNNING A TRIAL ▶
Testing a new idea, even one as complex as an automated production line, allows problems to be solved before a new system is introduced more widely.

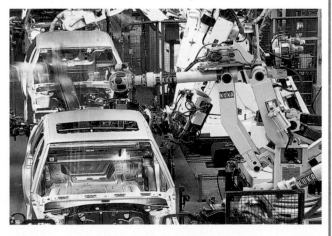

COMMITTING RESOURCES

Before starting to implement a project, you must study resource requirements and budgets. The feasibility of the project depends on you and your team being able to justify the expenditure by comparing it favourably with the proposed benefits.

36 Estimate costs carefully – once approved, you are bound by them.

ESTIMATING MANPOWER

Think about who needs to be involved in each activity and for how long in actual man days. A team member may need to work on a project for a period of ten days, but if he or she has to work on it for only 30 minutes per day, the total commitment is just five hours. If the member can usefully work on other projects for the rest of the time, the cost to your project will be a fraction of the member's ten-day earnings or charge. But if he or she can make no contribution elsewhere, then your project's budget must bear the full cost.

37 Provide the best supplies, facilities, and equipment you can afford.

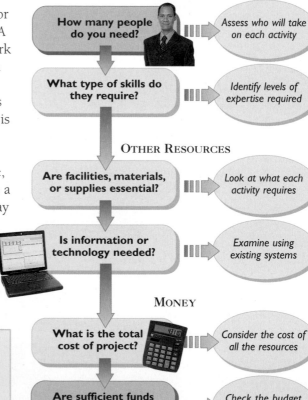

CONSIDERING KEY RESOURCES

PEOPLE

How many people do you need? → Assess who will take on each activity

What type of skills do they require? → Identify levels of expertise required

OTHER RESOURCES

Are facilities, materials, or supplies essential? → Look at what each activity requires

Is information or technology needed? → Examine using existing systems

MONEY

What is the total cost of project? → Consider the cost of all the resources

Are sufficient funds available? → Check the budget that was agreed

IDENTIFYING OTHER RESOURCES

While the major cost of a project is generally the people, there are other resources that will have an impact on the budget. For example, you may have to commission market research. Facilities, equipment, and materials may also involve expenditure. Failure to identify all the costs will mean that you lose credibility when others examine the project to balance its costs against its benefits. A comprehensive estimate of costs at this stage also reduces the risk that you will have to request extra funds once the project is up and running.

QUESTIONS TO ASK YOURSELF

Q Can I estimate costs or resources more accurately by asking someone with relevant expertise for advice?

Q Is there another way to achieve the goals that would not require expenditure on particular resources?

Q Is the cost estimate that I have drawn up realistic rather than optimistic?

38 Ensure that the budget will allow you to complete all your activities.

EXAMINING THE DETAILS

It is not enough to know that the team will need a training room for a month during the project, you will also need to know how large that room needs to be and what kind of equipment you should install in it. The better the detail at this stage, the more likely you are to avoid problems during the implementation. This will enable your team to focus on achieving objectives rather than on fixing matters that were poorly planned.

CHOOSING A COSTING METHOD

Whatever resources you consider, you can calculate their cost in one of two ways: absolute costing or marginal costing. Absolute costing means calculating the exact cost of the resource. If, for example, a new computer is essential for the project, the amount you pay for it becomes a project cost. If you can use an existing computer, allocate a proportion of its cost to the project. Marginal costing means that you only allocate costs to the project if they would not be incurred if the project did not take place. For example, if an existing computer, which is not being used, is required, the marginal, or extra cost, of the computer is nil. The cost of the computer should not be in the project budget. With practice, marginal costing is easy to calculate and is generally a more accurate measure of the cost of a project to an organization.

MAKING COMPROMISES

In an ideal world, you would gain approval for all the resources you need. In reality, you will probably have to cope with less. The person you most want for a certain task may be unavailable, or the best premises for the project occupied, and you will have to make compromises. Look for compromises that will not threaten the overall aims and objectives of the project. For example, you may be able to recruit a highly skilled worker part-time and allocate the remainder of the work to a less experienced, yet able, team member.

39 Avoid cutting back on tools that the team really needs.

40 If resources are scarce, consider your alternatives.

41 Refine a resource plan until anyone could work from it.

DOCUMENTING RESOURCES

The key to ensuring that the resources you require will be available when you need them is to produce a document that all the stakeholders can agree to. This is known as a commitment matrix, because it can be used to remind people of their commitments. Check that the matrix is complete and that every group of activities is comprehensive so that you can be sure that you have identified all the necessary resources.

**CREATING A ▼
COMMITMENT MATRIX**
When you have identified all the resources and estimated costs, document these on a commitment matrix and seek your stakeholders' agreement to it.

Activity as identified by number on activity list

Team members assigned to carry out activity

Resources required to carry out activity

Total cost involved

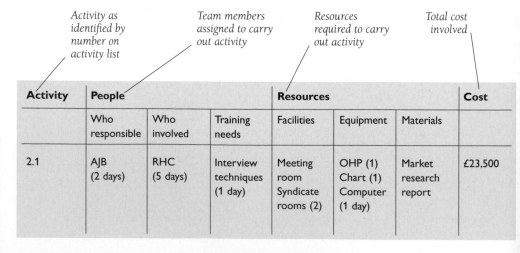

Activity	People			Resources			Cost
	Who responsible	Who involved	Training needs	Facilities	Equipment	Materials	
2.1	AJB (2 days)	RHC (5 days)	Interview techniques (1 day)	Meeting room Syndicate rooms (2)	OHP (1) Chart (1) Computer (1 day)	Market research report	£23,500

USING OUTSIDE RESOURCES

While many resources will come from within your team or organization, you will need to go outside for others. Make sure that you get competitive quotations from potential suppliers and reach an agreement on costs and performance that makes it easy for both parties to monitor progress tightly. You may need to brush up on your negotiating skills beforehand to ensure that you can win the best deal. While it may seem unnecessary to go into such detail at the outset, the tighter the agreement, the more likely you are to avoid conflict.

MAKING CONTACTS ▶
Ensure that you meet with several potential suppliers and keep their details on record. Even if you decide not to use them this time, an extensive network of contacts could well prove useful for future projects.

GETTING SIGN-OFF

Before you can obtain the official go-ahead for a new project, it must be proven that it is still a business priority and that its benefits to the organization considerably outweigh its costs. This is known as investment appraisal, or cost-benefit analysis, and it is a discipline used widely in many organizations which often have formal systems for the process. If the costs are the same or more than the benefits, the sponsors have three alternatives: they can proceed with the project regardless (although this is seldom desirable unless the strategic value of the project is very important to the long-term aims of the organization); they can modify the objectives and change the activities in a way that reduces costs; or they can cancel the project because it is considered unfeasible.

POINTS TO REMEMBER

- If your organization has an official system for obtaining sign-off for a project, this should be followed.
- Finance departments can provide useful feedback on your estimates by comparing your project's costs with others.
- The benefits of a project should never be exaggerated – promises will be expected to be delivered.

42 Be prepared to justify your choices, dates, and budgets.

ORDERING ACTIVITIES

Not all activities can, or need to, start at the same time to meet the project's planned completion date. Put activities into a logical sequence, estimate the duration of each, and then use clear documentation to help you devise a project schedule.

43 Remember that activities can be carried out in parallel.

44 Ask whoever is responsible for an activity to give you their estimated start and end dates.

CONSIDERING ORDER

Having completed a list of the activities required to complete the project, look at how they interrelate. Decide which activities should start immediately or first, which need to be completed before moving on to the next, and work through all the activities until the end of the project. Some activities will be the culmination of a number of others. For example, the team will probably need to complete several activities before it can make a presentation to the people involved in a pilot scheme. Important activities will be review meetings.

ESTIMATING ACTIVITY TIMES

To draw up an effective schedule, you need to know how much time each activity is likely to take. It is important to estimate these durations accurately, since poor guesswork may throw the entire project off course. Team members should also have input to ensure that they agree with the estimated activity times and will be able to work to the schedule that you produce. If there is major doubt as to how long an activity could take, estimate best and worst case scenarios and work out a compromise between the two. If a project is under time pressure this will help to identify where you could reduce the overall timescale.

QUESTIONS TO ASK YOURSELF

Q Do I have time to do a trial run of an activity to test how long it might take?

Q Could I estimate the duration of an activity more reliably if I sought expert advice?

Q Have I looked at previous project plans to see how long similar activities took?

Q Could I ask other project managers for their advice?

Q Am I confident that my estimates are realistic?

45 Get expert help to draw the first network diagram.

WORKING WITH A NETWORK DIAGRAM

A network diagram shows the relationship between activities, and which ones depend on the completion of others. The diagram may be simple or highly complex, according to how many activities there are and how they interrelate. Where there are several routes through a network, there is a chance to complete tasks simultaneously. Indicate the duration of each task and add up the total time required to complete each route to find the longest route through the network. This longest route is known as the critical path, which shows the shortest possible duration for the project.

Key

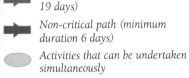

Critical path (minimum duration 19 days)

Non-critical path (minimum duration 6 days)

Activities that can be undertaken simultaneously

Activity that can only start once previous activities are complete

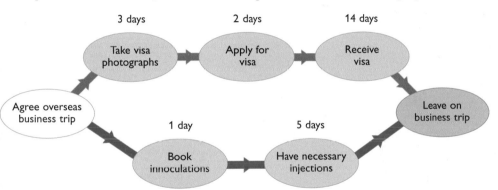

3 days — Take visa photographs

2 days — Apply for visa

14 days — Receive visa

Agree overseas business trip

Leave on business trip

1 day — Book innoculations

5 days — Have necessary injections

LOOKING FOR SLACK

You can also use the the network diagram to find opportunities for shortening the project schedule. This involves looking at where you can cut the amount of time it takes to complete activities on the critical path, for example, by increasing the resources available to that activity. Take another look at the diagram to identify where any other routes might have some slack. You may then be able to reallocate resources to reduce the pressure on the team members who are responsible for activities on the critical path.

▲ CREATING A NETWORK DIAGRAM

The network above sets out activities to be completed before a business trip. Progress on the critical path must be monitored closely, since a delay in carrying out these activities will affect the project end date.

46 Keep to the critical path to stay on schedule.

AGREEING DATES

Having identified how the activities follow on from one another, and worked out the minimum duration of the project, you can now set real dates. Plot these carefully, taking any potential conflicts into account, and then agree them with the team.

47 Start non-critical tasks as early as possible to free up resources later.

48 Remember to keep your Gantt chart up to date at all times.

CALCULATING DATES

Use the network diagram to help you calculate start and end dates for each activity. Begin with the first activity and work through all the others, starting each as early as possible to allow as much time as you can. If an activity is not on the critical path, start and end dates can be more flexible, since these will not necessarily affect the overall project duration. Finally, plot the dates against a timeline to produce a Gantt chart. These charts are useful for early schedule planning, for showing individual timescales on complex projects, and for comparing progress to the original schedule.

USING A GANTT CHART ▼
This Gantt chart lists tasks on the left and the project timescale in weeks across the top. The bars show when tasks start and finish, providing a clear visual overview of project tasks and timings.

Timescale shows length of project

Each activity is listed separately

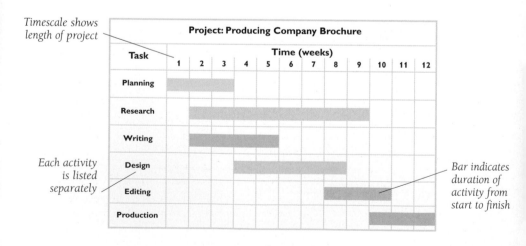

Bar indicates duration of activity from start to finish

LOOKING FOR OVERLAP

To check that the dates you have calculated are realistic, refer to your Gantt chart, commitment matrix, and master schedule. The Gantt chart shows you immediately where project activities overlap. Where an overlap exists, the commitment matrix will reveal whether an activity requires the same resource at the same time. In these circumstances, you will have to amend that activity's start and finish dates. The final piece of information comes from looking at the master schedule, which will tell you whether there is any overlap in resources between two projects or more.

49 Encourage your team members to be realistic about dates.

GAINING AGREEMENT

Discuss the dates you have set with the key people to make sure that they are truly available at the time they are needed. You may have to hold discussions with their managers if they are being held to other commitments elsewhere in the organization. On long projects, remember to allow for the fact that team members will not necessarily be available every day, even if they are theoretically working full-time on the project. The percentage of time they will be available is often around two-thirds of the calendar year, or 240 days. Use that number to check that you have allowed time off for holidays, sickness, and training.

◀ PLANNING HOLIDAYS
Ask team members to book in their holiday time as early as possible in order to avoid last-minute alterations to the schedule. Use a wallchart to show the team's holiday commitments.

VALIDATING THE PLAN

No matter how well you have written your plan, the unexpected is bound to occur and circumstances are certain to change. It is vital to work closely with the team and stakeholders to anticipate and pre-empt potential problems.

50 Make a point of discussing the final plan with your customers.

51 Use other project managers' experience to identify threats.

IDENTIFYING THREATS

Now that you have a schedule for all the activities needed to complete the project, brainstorm a list of potential threats and analyze each for its impact on your plan. People outside the team can be very helpful in this process, which also encourages the team to defend the plan against constructive criticism, making them more determined to overcome any obstacles. Deal with every threat in turn, paying most attention to those that have an impact on activities on the critical path so that you can work out your best counter-attack in advance.

ANTICIPATING ▼ PROBLEMS

Bring together a representative group of stakeholders, particularly customers, and those with relevant experience, and ask what could, in their opinion, go wrong.

Customer identifies potential problem

Sponsor weighs up impact on project

Project manager suggests a way of overcoming threat

Team member notes threats and suggested counter-attacks

PRE-EMPTING PROBLEMS

Now get the team to focus on preventing the problems from occurring. The question is, "What can we do to reduce the probability that each potential problem might occur?". If the plan is dependent on the weather, for example, you may change the timing of the work schedule. If key materials are in short supply or there is the possibility of industrial action in your own organization or that of your supplier, you must consider ways to address these problems early on.

52 If you suspect that someone may be promoted off the team, take steps to train a replacement.

53 Check contingency plans with whoever supplies resources.

54 Table the plan, with contingencies, at a review meeting.

CONTINGENCY PLANNING

It is not possible to pre-empt every eventuality that could harm the project. Get the team to consider what it will do if certain threats occur, and how to minimize the impact of the threats. If the project needs a new piece of software, for example, look at what you could do if it were to be delivered late. If the software is late, and you need a contingency system, it will probably add to the cost of the project. Bring this to the attention of those in control of budgets. You may then have to revisit your cost-benefit analysis.

COMPLETING THE PLAN

From the list of threats and the discussion on pre-empting problems and contingency planning, you will be able to decide what changes to make to the plan. Make these alterations and the plan is complete. The team has its "baseline" or starting point. It knows what the situation is now, and what will be the result of implementing the plan. Remember, though, that you must ensure that the team is prepared for the fact that the planning and implementation process is rarely sequential. It is likely they will have to recast some of the plan as activities are carried out and changes occur.

POINTS TO REMEMBER

- The more stakeholders who validate a plan, the more likely it is to be implemented.

- If there is a strong likelihood that a contingency plan will be needed, that course of action should become the actual plan.

- Time spent validating the plan and preparing for problems in advance is rarely wasted.

- The entire plan should be double-checked by the project manager before implementation.

IMPLEMENTING A PLAN

The success of a project plan relies on the people who execute it. Equip yourself with the leadership skills necessary to build a strong, committed team and guide it to the desired outcome.

EXAMINING YOUR ROLE

To successfully implement a project plan, it is important to understand what is involved at the outset. Familiarize yourself with the key tasks, responsibilities, and skills involved, and you will be better prepared to lead a project team successfully.

55 Know the project plan inside out and answer questions authoritatively.

56 Keep the business priorities in mind, especially when the project goal is to make a profit.

DEFINING YOUR RESPONSIBILITIES

As project manager, you have overall responsibility for the project's success. Having negotiated the planning process, you must now translate the plan into action. This involves selecting the right team members, focusing and motivating them to achieve project goals, and helping them to develop both as individuals and as team workers. The project manager must also build good relationships with stakeholders, run team meetings effectively, administrate and co-ordinate, and communicate clearly on all levels every step of the way.

TAKING THE LEAD

A successful project manager is both a manager and leader. Leaders command authority and respect, follow up plans with actions, and are able to inspire and motivate others. They also adopt different leadership styles as circumstances dictate. You can develop these skills through training and experience: try practising outside work by taking office at your local sports club. Mainly, you develop leadership skills by taking responsibility for objectives. You may have to start by becoming accountable for a group of activities before you can take on an entire project.

Select final team members and allocate responsibilities

Launch the project successfully

Motivate and focus team on objectives

Organize information systems

Communicate key information

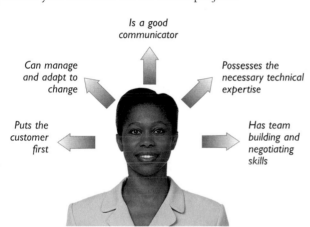

Is a good communicator

Can manage and adapt to change

Puts the customer first

Possesses the necessary technical expertise

Has team building and negotiating skills

◀ **EVALUATING SKILLS**
To be an effective leader, you must develop several important attributes. This example shows some of the essential qualities of a successful project manager.

QUESTIONS TO ASK YOURSELF

Q Are you willing to stay with the project for its entire term?

Q Are you interested in developing people and helping them to become leaders?

Q Do you have a real interest in working on the project?

Q Can you delegate objectives to the team as well as tasks?

ASSESSING YOURSELF

If you are not sure whether you have what it takes to be a leader, ask someone whose opinion you respect for objective comments. For example, you could talk to people with whom you have worked in the past to ascertain how they regard you. If they plainly feel that they could work for you, then that is a good indicator. Once you have gathered the facts, you can create a picture of where you want to be in the future, and put together a plan for developing the necessary skills.

BUILDING A TEAM

Having planned the project with a core team, now ensure that you have the full complement of people with the right mix of skills and personalities to see it through. Choose your team carefully, bearing in mind the vital team roles that should be covered.

57 Try not to have preconceived ideas about people – judge as you find.

QUESTIONS TO ASK YOURSELF

Q How much do I know about a potential team member and do I trust him or her?

Q Will I be able to work comfortably with him or her?

Q Am I confident that all the team members will get along with one another?

Q Does the team member have the necessary skills and talent to do the job – or will training be required?

ASSESSING AVAILABILITY

Refer back to your commitment matrix to identify the skills and people needed to complete the project. The chart will tell you who is required, for how long, and when. Draw up a list of candidates who might be suitable for each part and find out whether they are available. You may need to negotiate with other managers if you wish to appoint staff working in different areas of the organization. Your own project is almost certainly not the only one in progress, so you may also need to talk to whoever is co-ordinating the resources deployed on all of the projects.

CHOOSING THE RIGHT PEOPLE

Apart from having the necessary skills, the people you want to attract are those who will come willingly. It is much easier to work with people who are enthusiastic about the project, so it pays to hold discussions with potential team members to find out whether they are keen to work on the project. Think also of the team as a whole. Will each team member fit in with the others? Is there any conflict between potential members? You will, of course, help them to form a team under your leadership, but it is better to start off with people who are sympathetic to each other.

58 Be frank with potential team members – ask if they identify with the project's aims.

59 Build a team that takes advantage of each individual's skills without overburdening their weaknesses.

CONSIDERING ROLES

In any team you will look for people to carry out a team role as well as their functional role. To operate efficiently you, as the team leader, will want someone to perform the roles of critic, implementer, external contact, co-ordinator, ideas person, team builder, and inspector. Most team members will fit strongly into one or more of these roles. You need them all, and if one is not present, you will have to take the role on yourself. If, for example, you see that no one is challenging the team's standards, quality, and way of working, you are lacking a critic. Keep challenging the team yourself until you see someone else leaning towards this role. Discuss these roles in an open manner, encourage friendly conversations, and you will build one of the most important qualities of a group – team spirit. Remember that only as a team will you be able to achieve the project's objectives.

DO'S AND DON'TS

✔ Do allow people to settle into roles without being pushed.

✔ Do double or treble up on roles when a project team only has a few members.

✔ Do ask a stakeholder to take on a role if it is not being played.

✘ Don't attempt to shoehorn a personality into a particular role.

✘ Don't expect people to continue playing a role if they become uncomfortable in it.

✘ Don't take on a role yourself if it means appearing insincere.

KEY TEAM ROLES

CO-ORDINATOR
Pulls together the work of the team as a whole.

CRITIC
Guardian and analyst of the team's effectiveness.

IDEAS PERSON
Encourages the team's innovative vitality.

IMPLEMENTER
Ensures smooth running of the team's actions.

EXTERNAL CONTACT
Looks after the team's external contacts.

INSPECTOR
Ensures high standards are maintained.

TEAM BUILDER
Develops the teamworking spirit.

60 Encourage criticism, but ask the critic to supply alternatives, too.

STARTING POSITIVELY

Once you have the right team in place, it is important to launch a new project in a positive manner. Encourage teamwork by inviting everyone to an informal gathering at the outset, and record the project's existence formally to clarify its purpose.

61 Ask the most senior person possible to attend a project launch.

62 Listen to reactions from newcomers and be prepared to review activities.

STARTING ACTIVELY

At an early stage, gather the team together for a full initiation session to let them know exactly what the project is all about. Explain what the targets and constraints are, let everyone know how the project will benefit them, and establish ground rules relating to the sharing of information and decision-making. Keep the session two-way so that people can ask questions. By the end of the meeting, everyone should understand what needs to be done, and feel motivated to achieve it.

USING YOUR SPONSOR ▼
The first team meeting offers your sponsor an important platform. Invite him or her to address the team and express belief and commitment in the project. This is invaluable for encouraging team spirit.

Team member learns of the project's importance

Team member is impressed by sponsor's confidence in the project manager and team

Colleague feels valued in his new role

Sponsor greets team with positive enthusiasm

WRITING A START-UP REPORT

A start-up report should make everyone aware of the vision that has inspired the project and the measures of success the team will be aiming for. You may also document the resources allocated to the project, and give some indication of the risks that are involved. Finally, it is a good idea to name all the stakeholders so that everyone knows who they are, and ask key people who are underpinning the project to endorse it by adding their signatures to the document. These will include the project manager and project sponsor.

63 Keep reports free of jargon and complex language.

64 Ask for signatures to the plan as a formal agreement.

STRUCTURING A START-UP REPORT

PARTS OF A REPORT	FACTORS TO INCLUDE
VISION An explanation of the overall aim of the project.	• Clarify exactly why the project has been initiated and what it is setting out to achieve. • Spell out the benefits of the project to the entire project team and to the organization as a whole.
TARGETS A summary of indicators, current performance, and target figures.	• Provide clear information on how the success of the project will be measured. • Explain what business results are expected to have been achieved by the end of the project.
MILESTONES Special events or achievements that mark progress along the way.	• Summarize milestones to remind everyone of what they will have to deliver at each stage of the project • Set out your milestones so that they divide the project into logical, measurable segments.
RISKS AND OPPORTUNITIES A list of the potential risks and additional opportunities.	• Explain what needs to be avoided when team members carry out their roles. • Highlight any areas where improvements could be made in order to gain even greater benefit from the project.
LIST OF STAKEHOLDERS A directory of all the stakeholders involved in the project.	• Name all interested parties and list their credentials to add to the credibility of the project. • List all your customers, and state what each customer expects to gain from the project.

LEADING EFFECTIVELY

There are many different styles of leadership, but because projects rely on good teamwork, it is important to favour a consensus-building, rather than a dictatorial, approach. To lead a project well, you must be able to motivate your team.

65 Be a manager whom people want to seek out, rather than avoid.

66 Show your enthusiasm for the project, even when under pressure.

UNDERSTANDING STYLES

There is a spectrum of possibilities in leadership styles, and you will need to adopt them all at certain points in the project. While your approach may need to vary from a dictatorial style to a consensus-seeking one, the predominant style you adopt should depend on your organization, the nature of the project, the characteristics of the team, and your own personality.

CHOOSING A LEADERSHIP STYLE

LEADERSHIP STYLE	WHEN TO USE IT
DICTATORIAL Making decisions alone, taking risks, being autocratic and controlling.	This style may be appropriate if the project faces a crisis, and there is no time to consult. However, since it discourages teamwork, it should be used sparingly.
ANALYTICAL Gathering all the facts, observing and analyzing before reaching decisions.	This style, which requires sound analytical skills, may be used when a project is under time pressure or threat, and the right decision must be made quickly.
OPINION-SEEKING Asking for opinions from the team on which to base decisions.	Use this style to build team confidence and show that you value people's views, as well as to impress stakeholders, who like to be consulted.
DEMOCRATIC Encouraging team participation and involvement in decision-making.	This is an essential style to be used on a regular basis to empower team members, and help strengthen their commitment to a project.

CULTURAL DIFFERENCES

Project managers in the UK often create an inner circle of key team members to speed up decision-making, while in the US, the entire team is brought together frequently. In Japan, decisions are reached by consensus, in which unanimous agreement is reached through a laborious process.

CHANGING STYLES

Be prepared to change your leadership style to suit the circumstances and the team, even if you feel uncomfortable for a while because the style you are adopting does not come naturally. For example, some managers find consultation annoying and time-wasting, while other managers are so intent on gaining consensus that decisions take too long, and the project suffers as a result. The key to making good consensus decisions is to listen carefully to everyone before indicating which way they are leaning. A decision is then reached accordingly, unless someone can argue most convincingly that it is the wrong move.

LEADING APPROPRIATELY

Each member of a team has a unique personality and style. Take time to study each individual and understand what motivates them so that you can provide the level of guidance they need. Some team members will prefer to be set objectives, with the project manager delegating responsibility to them for how they should be tackled. Others will react better to being given specific tasks. Use the appropriate style for each individual.

▼ ADOPTING A HANDS-OFF APPROACH
Motivate an experienced, capable team member by allowing them to use their own initiative. Provide support and guidance but avoid interfering too heavily.

◀ BEING HANDS-ON
Explain clearly what you expect from a new or less confident worker, who will need close supervision and encouragement.

OBTAINING RESULTS

There are two major factors to consider when deciding which style of leadership to use. If the project is under time pressure, there may be no alternative to the dictatorial style because you do not have the luxury of time to consult. If you want to gain commitment, you must involve others in the key decisions to increase their willingness to make the decision work. Whichever style you choose, the quality of the decision is vital. Before you impose a decision, ensure that you have all the facts to prove that it is the right thing to do.

POINTS TO REMEMBER

- The team should not be expected to do everything your way, provided that their results are satisfactory.
- When a small point is important to a member of the team, it is wise to give way – you should be trying to win the war, not every single battle.
- If, in your view, the success of the project is in any way threatened, that is the time to be assertive.

67 Look for ways to use conflict constructively.

RESOLVING CONFLICT

Personality clashes are inevitable when many people work together. There may be differences of opinion or disputes that arise from people having different standards on quality of work, or there may be one or two team members who simply do not get on. If team members are in disagreement, find a way of resolving the conflict either by taking on the role of decision-maker yourself or by using diplomacy in talking to the people concerned.

Conflicts can sometimes arise as a result of schedules. For example, one team member might want more time for a group of activities, which a colleague feels is unnecessary. Work through the schedule with both parties to arrive at a solution that suits everyone.

◀ BEING A DIPLOMAT

When a conflict between team members threatens the project's success, you will have to mediate. Look for a solution that brings some source of satisfaction to each party. Such a compromise will allow the project to move on.

CASE STUDY

Sally, a key member of the project team, was responsible for leading a small team of her own. As the project got under way, Tom, the project manager, was surprised to see that Gerald, one of Sally's most competent and confident team members, was contributing very little to team meetings. He took Gerald aside informally and asked how he was getting on. Although Tom was reluctant to criticize Sally, by listening carefully, Tom realized that Gerald had been used to far more involvement in making decisions on other project teams he had worked for. It was evident that Gerald found Sally too abrupt. Tom approached Sally and asked her to think about her leadership style with Gerald. As a result, she spent more time discussing issues with him, and Gerald went on to play a far more active part in team meetings once again.

◀ **LEADING WISELY**

Sally's abrupt approach and her tendency to make all the decisions was very demotivating for Gerald, who liked to be able to use his initiative. Rather than take matters into his own hands, Tom asked Sally to consider the matter and take any action she deemed appropriate. Sally decided to make a point of involving Gerald more to make him feel valued. As a result, his performance soon began to improve.

STANDING BACK

It can be a hard lesson to learn that a good leader will allow people to make a mistake. You may, from your experience, know that the team is taking a decision that is not in the best interests of the project. But if you take control, you are not necessarily helping them to improve. If they never see the effects of their decisions, they will never learn which ones led to difficulties. Obviously, you must use your discretion as to when to step back. The team's development is important, but not as vital as achieving the objectives of the project.

68 Show your team respect, and they will show it to you.

69 Introduce new ideas to maintain the team's interest.

EXERCISING LEADERSHIP SKILLS

To lead your team effectively, you must:

- Ensure that everyone is working towards agreed, shared objectives;
- Criticize constructively, and praise good work as well as find fault;
- Monitor team members' activities continuously by obtaining effective feedback, such as regular reports;
- Constantly encourage and organize the generation of new ideas within the team, using techniques such as brainstorming;
- Always insist on the highest standards of execution from team members;
- Develop the individual and collective skills of the team, and seek to strengthen them by training and recruitment.

DEVELOPING TEAMWORK

F or a team to be successful, people must learn to pull together. Encourage teamwork by promoting a positive atmosphere in which people compete with ideas rather than egos, and recognize the team's changing needs as it progresses through the project.

70 When individuals perform well, praise them in front of the team.

CULTURAL DIFFERENCES

Project managers in the US often use rousing speeches and rhetoric to motivate staff and build team spirit. In the UK, an eloquent speech will also strengthen commitment, but the approach has to be far more subtle. In Japan, managers seek to build strong ties of loyalty by emphasizing the importance of the project to the company.

ENCOURAGING TEAMWORK

Make sure that each member of the team recognizes the value that everyone else is bringing to the project. Encourage them to appreciate one another's skills and capabilities, and to work together to achieve the highest standards. Praise the team as well as individuals so that everyone feels that they are doing a good job. If everyone understands who is playing which role and who has responsibility for what, there should be no reason for conflict and uncertainty. As project manager, you must be seen to be fair to everyone, since showing any favouritism can also lead to dissent. Use project review meetings to strengthen teamwork and help build team confidence.

UNDERSTANDING TEAM DEVELOPMENT

All teams go through a series of stages as they develop, described as forming, storming, norming, and performing. Your aim is to move the team on to the performing stage, where they are working well together, as quickly as possible. With strong leadership, the difficult initial stages of bringing the team together and settling them into the project can be negotiated smoothly. Use your authority to swiftly defuse any conflict and put a stop to any early political manoeuvring.

POINTS TO REMEMBER

- Not every team member will be equally committed to the project at the outset.
- It should be expected that everyone will have to go through the storming stage, but this can be creative if managed positively.
- It is important to develop creative team members rather than conformists.
- People need to be comfortable to work well together.

DEALING WITH STAGES IN THE LIFE OF A PROJECT TEAM

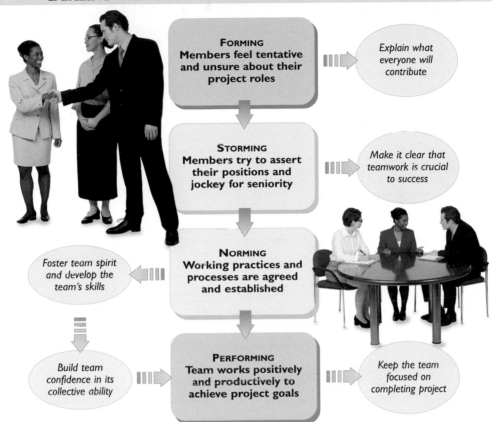

FORMING
Members feel tentative and unsure about their project roles

Explain what everyone will contribute

STORMING
Members try to assert their positions and jockey for seniority

Make it clear that teamwork is crucial to success

Foster team spirit and develop the team's skills

NORMING
Working practices and processes are agreed and established

Build team confidence in its collective ability

PERFORMING
Team works positively and productively to achieve project goals

Keep the team focused on completing project

MAINTAINING MOMENTUM

There are two more stages that occur in a team's long-term life, known as "boring" and "mourning". The first applies to a project lasting a long time, where team members may stop looking for new challenges or new and improved ways of doing things. Put in effort at this stage to encourage innovation. Mourning occurs when a team has bonded well and reacts to a member's departure by grieving their loss. Decide how to replace that person and reassure remaining team members that you have every confidence in their ability.

71 Help people to define problems for themselves.

72 Remember that relationships will change over time.

MAKING TEAM DECISIONS

When mapping out the future course of the project, quality decision-making is paramount. To ensure that you make the right decisions as a team, establish a logical process that you follow every time. Then use feedback to double-check quality.

73 Ensure that you know all the facts before making a decision.

- Using a decision-making process may take time initially, but speed will improve with experience.

- The decision-making process can be clearly explained to sponsors and stakeholders.

- People implement decisions more willingly when they have participated in them.

USING A LOGICAL PROCESS

Following the same process in making every decision has several benefits. The team becomes faster at decision-making, since if everyone knows the process, they quickly eliminate invalid options and come to the most sensible alternative. The quality of decisions improves because using a process removes some of the guesswork and, finally, any team members who might initially have been against a decision are more likely to accept it if it has been reached via a process of consensus.

DEFINING THE IDEAL

The team must agree on the criteria against which they wish to measure a decision and the ideal performance against each criterion. Suppose, for example, you are looking at two options for a supplier of services to the project. Ask team members to brainstorm what an ideal solution would look like. Ask the questions: "What do we want this solution to do for us?", and "What benefits should we look for?". This list then gives the team a way of filtering options and comparing the alternatives.

▼ **AGREEING CRITERIA**
Brainstorm a list of criteria against which you will measure decisions, and ask a team member to record each suggestion on a flipchart so that everyone is using the same wording to describe the ideal.

EVALUATING OPTIONS

With the team's help, identify which criteria are the most important. You may find that three or four stand out as being vital. Now measure all your options against the ideal agreed for each criterion. The process is logical, but good creative thinking is still needed to evaluate the options effectively. Having carried out this evaluation, you may find that the decision is obvious. If not, take the next most important criterion and repeat the exercise. Continue until one option stands out, or until the team is certain that, say, two options have nothing between them. Where that is the case, choose the option you believe will be the most acceptable to your sponsor and other stakeholders.

74 Encourage debate on all the options to gain a wider perspective.

75 Ask an objective critic to look at your decision and give you feedback.

MAKING SAFE DECISIONS

What would be the impact if you made a wrong decision? If it would be catastrophic, you may want to think again and find a less risky route. Finally use the acronym SAFE to validate the choice. SAFE stands for:

- Suitable: is the decision really the most suitable one, given the current state of the project?
- Acceptable: is the decision acceptable to all the stakeholders who have an interest in it?
- Feasible: will it be practical and feasible to implement the solution, given the project's time and resource constraints?

- Enduring: will the solution endure to the end of the project and further into the long term?

Remember that the SAFE test can be applied as a quick and useful check for any decision made by teams or individuals.

VALIDATING DECISIONS ▶
Check that you have made the right decisions by asking your sponsor or other stakeholders, such as customers or suppliers, for their views.

MANAGING INFORMATION

*E*veryone must have easy access to key *project information whenever they need it. You can ensure that all the project data is kept up to date and recorded efficiently by setting up a knowledge centre and appointing a co-ordinator to manage it.*

76 Keep notes of errors made and lessons learned for future reference.

77 Index information clearly to make it more accessible.

78 Check that data is being updated on a regular basis.

ASSESSING INFORMATION

During the life of a project you will produce a wealth of data. Each item of information should be regarded as potentially valuable, either to your own project or to a subsequent one. It will be obvious what must be stored, but try to think more widely. If, for example, a project involves researching a benchmark for productivity, remember that this may be of interest to other parts of the organization. Any work undertaken on risk management, new techniques used, or even the way in which the team has been structured could prove valuable in the future.

ORGANIZING DATA

Project data can be grouped into two types: general planning information, such as the vision statement, objectives, master schedule, and network diagram; and general data, such as any background information that might be needed to carry out activities. It may be a good idea to divide activity information into three further groups: completed activities; activities currently in progress; and activities still to be started. In this way, everyone will know exactly where to look for the information they need. Beware of amassing lots of unnecessary data, however, because this will simply clog up what should be an efficient, easy-to-use system.

THINGS TO DO

1. Explain to the team what type of information is to go into the knowledge centre.

2. Ensure that the knowledge co-ordinator has the necessary software tools to run the centre efficiently.

3. Ask the co-ordinator to remind people of deadlines for completing activities and progress reports.

APPOINTING A CO-ORDINATOR

In projects where the information flow is limited, you will probably be able to manage the data yourself. However, in a large project with a mass of information, it will pay dividends to put a team member in charge of the knowledge centre, either full-time or part-time. Such a person is known as the knowledge co-ordinator, and the most likely candidate for the job is the team member who most takes on the role of co-ordinator. He or she will keep the planning documentation up to date and collect, index, and make available all the important project information gathered by the team.

CULTURAL DIFFERENCES

Business organizations in North America tend to lead the way when it comes to saving information and making it available to the organization as a whole. Most organizations in the US employ knowledge co-ordinators at several levels, meaning that project managers are able to access information quickly and easily. Knowledge co-ordinators are gradually making their presence felt in Europe as their importance becomes recognized.

Team member updates co-ordinator on progress of an activity

Co-ordinator records information for knowledge centre

◀ UPDATING PROJECT INFORMATION

The knowledge co-ordinator plays an important role as the administrator of the project plan, collecting progress reports, updating network diagrams, Gantt charts, and activity reports.

COMMUNICATING CLEARLY

The better the communication, the more smoothly a project will flow. Make sure that everyone who needs it has easy access to project information, and that you encourage two-way communication by listening and asking for feedback.

79 Avoid sending any message that could hinder, rather than help, your project.

80 Tell the team what they want and need to know.

81 Meet often with team members on a one-to-one basis.

SHARING KNOWLEDGE

Consider who needs what information, in what format, and when. Refer to the list of stakeholders in the start-up report to ensure that no-one is forgotten. Concentrate on people whose access to information will be crucial to the project, but do not ignore others with less significant roles. Plan how you are going to make the information available, bearing in mind that these activities should take up as little time as possible. Your knowledge co-ordinator must know what the priorities are. For example, if a customer changes requirements, the team needs to know urgently.

USING INFORMATION TECHNOLOGY

Make the most of new technology to improve communications. E-mail is an extremely useful time-saving device, provided it is handled correctly. The main point to remember is that you receive as many e-mails as you send, which means that you should think carefully before writing each message. Is it absolutely vital to send a message now? Is it the most effective means of communication for the current situation? As a guideline, send as few e-mails as possible to do the job well, and you will get the best out of electronic communication. Take care too, with compatibility. E-mailing an electronic file to someone who does not have the same software results in an immediate communication breakdown. This wastes time.

ENCOURAGING TWO-WAY COMMUNICATION

The team is the primary conduit for information between the customer, other stakeholders, and you, the project manager. It is important to encourage honest feedback. Use open questions, such as the ones below, to ascertain their real feelings and opinions.

How do you think we could improve the way we are working on this project?

How are our customers reacting to the work we are doing – do they appear to be satisfied?

Having completed that activity, is there anything you would change if you had to do it again?

Are you aware of any negative reactions concerning the progress of the project?

LISTENING TO OTHERS

Encourage the project team to be open and honest with you by showing that you value their opinions and are willing to listen to them. Make it clear that even negative feedback is viewed as a positive opportunity for improvement, and ensure that team members are not intimidated by fear of any repercussions when they do express criticisms. Keep your door open for stakeholders, too – it is important that they feel they can approach you with queries or problems. Always listen to people carefully – because only through listening can you determine whether your messages have really been understood.

| **82** | Be interested both in what people say and how they are saying it. |

Colleague provides both negative and positive feedback

Team member feels free to voice an honest opinion

◀ INVITING FEEDBACK

Take team members aside, either individually or in small groups, and solicit feedback by asking for their comments on how they think the project is progressing.

MONITORING PERFORMANCE

Effective monitoring keeps a project on track in terms of performance, time, and cost. Focus on your plan while acting fast to tackle problems and changes in order to stay on course.

TRACKING PROGRESS

Even the best-laid plans can go awry, which is why it is crucial to have an early-warning monitoring system. Make sure that you understand what effective monitoring involves and how to set up a process that will highlight potential problems.

83 Keep comparing current schedules and budgets against the original plan.

84 Never relax control, even when all is going to plan.

85 Ask the team for ideas on speeding up progress.

MONITORING EFFECTIVELY

Keeping control of a project involves carefully managing your plan to keep it moving forward smoothly. Effective monitoring allows you to gather information so that you can measure and adjust progress towards the project's goals. It enables you to communicate project progress and changes to team members, stakeholders, superiors, and customers, and gives you the justification for making any necessary adjustments to the plan. It also enables you to measure current progress against that set out in the original plan.

MONITORING SUPPLIERS

External suppliers can be a threat, since you do not have direct control over their resources. Remember to ensure that you monitor their progress, too. Make them feel part of the team by inviting them to meetings and informal gatherings. This will help you to track their progress throughout their involvement in the project, rather than only when they are due to deliver.

USING REPORTS

Anyone responsible for an activity or a milestone must report on progress. Encourage the team to take reports seriously, and to submit them on time. Reports should record the current state of the project, achievements since the last report, and potential problems, opportunities, or threats to milestones. As project manager, you review the reports and summarize the current position for your sponsor and stakeholders. Having gauged the importance of issues reported, use a red, amber, and green status system to help you draw up your review meeting agenda, so that the most urgent items, or those with red status, take priority.

UNDERSTANDING THE MONITORING PROCESS

Team members prepare progress reports

Project manager summarizes for sponsor and stakeholders

Items for discussion are listed on regular review meeting agenda

Regular review meeting is held to resolve issues and assess progress

Periodic meetings are held to monitor milestones

Plans are updated if necessary to keep project on track

POINTS TO REMEMBER

- If the project is a large or complex one, reports will be required more frequently.

- When a project involves tackling issues for the first time, tight and frequent controls should be established.

- If team members are used to working on their own, too frequent monitoring may be counterproductive.

CONSIDERING TIMING

Think about how often you will need progress reports and review meetings. You may require weekly or even daily reports, depending on the potential harm a problem could do to the project were it not detected and reported. Regular review meetings provide an opportunity to resolve issues, discuss progress and review performance. You should hold reviews at least once a month, and probably more often on a complex project, or one going through a particularly demanding phase.

HOLDING REVIEW MEETINGS

Review meetings are held throughout the life of a project to discuss progress and achievements and mark milestones. Run these meetings effectively to encourage teamwork and provide all involved with an accurate picture of how the project is faring.

86 Encourage team members to speak out on any aspect of the project.

87 Ensure that review meetings are not tediously long.

88 If progress has been made, praise people's efforts.

PLANNING A REVIEW

There are two types of review meeting. A regular formal review occurs at least monthly to monitor detailed achievements and issues in implementing the plan. An event-driven review, to which stakeholders, such as your sponsor, will be invited is held as certain milestones are arrived at. These meetings are concerned with the business objectives of the project. They may be called to check that the project is meeting certain criteria. It is sometimes true that if the criteria are not met, the future of the project will be in doubt.

SELECTING ATTENDEES

You will need your sponsor at some meetings, but probably not all. Key team members will almost certainly attend all reviews, while other members should attend only if there is a valid reason for their attendance, or their time will be wasted. If someone need only be present for one or two items, estimate when you will reach those items and ask them to arrive a few minutes earlier. If you need to make a decision, ensure that the person with the authority to make the decision is present and that all the necessary information is available.

QUESTIONS TO ASK YOURSELF

Q Will every attendee have a valid contribution to make?

Q Are there some team members who only need to attend part of the meeting?

Q Is this team member attending the meeting because they have always done so, rather than for a specific purpose?

Q Does the absence of anyone pose a threat to the project?

Use progress report to compile agenda	→	Decide who needs to attend review	→	Circulate agenda to participants

CHAIRING A REVIEW

The key to chairing a review meeting successfully is good discipline. Summarize the objectives at the outset and allocate time to each item on the agenda. Focus the team on appraisal rather than analysis, using questions such as "How is the project going?" and "What new issues have arisen since the last meeting?". Your aim is to keep everyone up to date with progress and give them a shared understanding of what is happening.

ESTABLISHING ▶ DISCIPLINE
Be prepared to be tough on late-comers. Make it clear from the outset that such behaviour is unacceptable, stressing the fact that one person's lateness wastes everyone's time.

89 Remind people of the agenda when they stray from it.

90 Always seek to end a meeting on a positive note.

▲ PREPARING FOR MEETINGS
Key decisions are made at review meetings, so it is essential to prepare for them well. Send out agendas in advance to give the team time to do preparation work, too.

Team member arrives late for meeting

Project manager sets standards for punctuality in future

REINFORCING OBJECTIVES

Ensure that you return to the objectives throughout the meeting, recording which have been achieved, which remain, and how the meeting is going against the time plan. If people are straying from the point or talking irrelevantly, bring the discussion back to the main issue by saying, for example, "We are not here to discuss that today – let's get back to the point." At appropriate moments, summarize the views and decisions made. As objectives are achieved, consider releasing those people who are no longer needed.

OVERCOMING PROBLEMS

However sound the project plan, once you start to operate in the real world, problems will occur. Encourage team members to raise concerns, and use the discipline of problem-solving techniques to tackle difficulties as they arise.

91 Look at every aspect of a problem before trying to resolve it.

92 Remember that forewarned is forearmed.

93 Ask team members to bring you solutions as well as problems.

RAISING CONCERNS

Your primary aim is to identify problems early enough to prevent their becoming crises. It is far more difficult to take action when a problem has become urgent. Although you may create extra work by examining problems that do not ultimately occur, it is better to err on the side of caution than to find that a problem has escalated without your knowledge. With experience, the team will get better at judging whether and when to raise a concern. You should be particularly concerned to see that problems with a high impact on the project are spotted and action taken before they become high urgency as well.

CASE STUDY

John was put in charge of a new project to improve the inventory control system in his organization's main warehouse. However, once the project was under way, he was approached by Tom, the warehouse manager, who told John that he and his warehouse staff were having to spend an inordinate amount of time chasing up deliveries deemed to be late by a member of the project team. Tom explained that most of the queries raised by the team member were unnecessary, because the goods were generally delivered only a few hours late, and so asking warehouse staff to chase them seemed pointless. John called Tom and the project team together to agree when a query really needed to be raised. This reduced the strain on warehouse staff, and gave everyone more time to chase up deliveries that really were late.

◄ HANDLING TENSIONS

Since projects tend to be carried out alongside regular business operations, problems often result when the two are ongoing. In this case, the project members were trying to make improvements by identifying late deliveries. But by raising concerns too early, they were disrupting the usual warehouse work. By agreeing when to raise concerns, both teams were able to do their jobs more effectively.

DEALING WITH PROBLEMS

> Listen to concerns raised by team members

> Discuss their impact and, if significant, look at the options with the team

> Take an overview and make a final decision

> Update the plan if the decision involves altering course

> Send updated plan to knowledge co-ordinator

RESOLVING DIFFICULTIES

A useful problem-solving technique is to home in on four areas to find out which is causing difficulty. For example, if production is falling short of target, consider which of the following four P's could be the culprit:

- **People** Is the problem occurring because people do not have the right skills or support?
- **Product** Is there something wrong in the design of the product or the production method?
- **Process** Would an improvement in one of your business processes cure the problem?
- **Procurement** Is it something to do with the products and services we buy?

DO'S AND DON'TS

✔ Do keep in constant touch with suppliers who may be causing you problems.	✘ Don't start to resolve an issue until you have understood the whole problem.
✔ Do correct a recurring problem by changing a process.	✘ Don't assume that team members have problem-solving skills

UPDATING THE PLAN

Ask your project co-ordinator to document on-going problem-solving activities in the knowledge centre as open items, and assess them at your regular review meetings. Major issues may result in the need to make significant changes to the plan. It is even possible that new information or a change in the external environment will invalidate the project as it stands. Suppose, for example, that a competitor brings out a new product using components that makes your project irrelevant. This would be unfortunate, but since your priority is to deliver value to your organization, the best value may lie in scrapping the project.

94 Keep stakeholders informed if you change the plan.

95 Identify the cause of a problem to prevent it from happening again.

DEALING WITH CHANGE

Change is inevitable on projects, so flexibility is vital. Whether customers revise a brief or senior managers alter the scope of a project, you must be able to negotiate changes, adapt the plan, and keep everyone informed about what is happening.

96 Look at alternatives before changing a major component of the plan.

97 Explain the benefits of change to those affected by it.

98 Seek approval for any changes as quickly as possible.

UNDERSTANDING CHANGE

Some changes will be within your control, such as shortening the schedule because you and your team are learning how to complete activities more quickly as you work through the plan. Other changes will be imposed upon you, such as when a customer asks for something different, or a superior decides to poach two of your key team members to do another job. Alternatively, your monitoring system may have highlighted the need for a change to avoid a potential problem or threat. Whenever the need for change arises, it is vital to be able to adjust the project plan as necessary. You must also be able to measure whether the desired effect on the project has been achieved, so that you will know if the change has been successful.

◀ **DISCUSSING CHANGE**
Bring the team together to evaluate how changes might affect the project plan, looking at the proposed alterations against your original goals, order of activities, budget, people, resources, and time.

ASSESSING IMPACT

Before you commit to making any changes, assess their impact on the project. Ask the team to review how they will affect the schedule, budget, and resources. Examine the alternatives: is there another way to accomplish the project's objectives? If changes have to be made for the project to move forwards, document them on the original plan, and gain approval from superiors, sponsors, and stakeholders before implementing them.

RESISTING UNNECESSARY OR DETRIMENTAL CHANGES

When change is dictated, perhaps by a superior or sponsor, it may not always make sense. Determine whether carrying out the change will affect the eventual outcome of the project. If the change seems to be frivolous, or will have a negative impact on the project, make those imposing it aware of the benefits that will be lost. Be prepared to fight your corner, or to offer alternative solutions that will ensure your project still meets its objectives.

TACKLING CHANGE EFFECTIVELY

Discuss impact of change with the team

↓

If change has a major impact, look at the alternatives

↓

Document necessary changes on original plan

↓

Seek approval from stakeholders and superiors

↓

Inform everyone on the project of changes as soon as possible

THINGS TO DO

1. Talk to the team about how changes will affect them.
2. Explain the rationale behind the changes and why they had to happen.
3. Redefine new objectives, timescales, or roles.
4. Discuss issues individually if anyone is still unhappy about the changes.

COMMUNICATING CHANGE

If your team has been working hard to achieve one set of objectives and is suddenly told that the goal posts have changed, people will inevitably feel demotivated. Talk to the team about change as soon as possible, particularly if roles are affected. Focus on the positive aspects of change, and be frank about why it is happening. Take people's concerns seriously, listen to their ideas, but stress the need to adapt as quickly as possible. Finally, spell out clearly any new expectations, schedules, or objectives in writing, so that everyone understands what should happen next.

MAXIMIZING IMPACT

As a project draws to a close, it is important to evaluate exactly what has been achieved and what can be learned for the next time. Take your project through a formal close-down process that ties up all loose ends and marks its success.

> **99** Evaluate this project well to better manage the next one.

QUESTIONS TO ASK YOURSELF

Q Is the sponsor satisfied that the original aims and business objectives of the project have been met?

Q Is the customer satisfied that he or she is receiving an improved service?

Q Have we spoken to all our stakeholders about final results?

Q Have I thanked all the contributors to the project?

Q Have all new insights and ideas been recorded?

SEEING PROJECTS THROUGH

Inevitably towards the end of a project, some team members will start to move to new assignments. It is important to keep remaining team members focused on final objectives until the very end of the project, when you write a formal close-down report and hold a final meeting. You may have to protect your resources from being moved off the project too early, particularly if you want to avoid an untidy ending where the benefits are dissipated because final activities are completed haphazardly. Finally, you want your organization to learn as much as possible from the exercise and to ensure that the results you predicted are delivered in full.

LEARNING FROM PROJECTS

Talk to your knowledge co-ordinator about publishing a report explaining what the project achieved, and detailing relevant information such as facts gathered and processes used. If the project is likely to be repeated, meet with team members to go through the project from start to finish. Ask people to point out where, with hindsight, they could have made improvements. Your organization may benefit significantly if you produce a template for such a project plan, including an outline network and Gantt chart.

> **100** Ensure that you have not left any jobs unfinished.

> **101** Publicize the achievements of the project team.

COMPILING A CLOSE-DOWN REPORT

PARTS OF REPORT	FACTORS TO CONSIDER
PERFORMANCE INDICATORS A comparison of what the project has achieved against the original targets set.	● Explain in full the reasons for any variances between targets and actual achievements. ● Word the comparison in a way that validates the original investment appraisal.
RESOURCE UTILIZATION An assessment of the resources planned and those that were actually used.	● If the project used more or fewer resources than expected, state the reasons why. ● Include any information that will validate the budget allocated to the project.
STRENGTHS AND WEAKNESSES An appraisal of what went well on the project and what went wrong, or caused problems.	● Ask team members for input in order to conduct as thorough an analysis as possible. ● Make sure that the information recorded enables others to learn from this experience.
SUCCESS FACTORS A record of the top 10 factors judged to be critical to the success of your project	● List your success factors with the help of the team, sponsor, and stakeholders. ● Create a list that will provide focus for future project managers.

THANKING THE TEAM

It is important that all the members of the team go their separate ways feeling as positive as possible, especially since you may want to work with the same people on subsequent projects. Indeed, good relationships should be kept up with all the stakeholders. Talk to everyone individually to thank them for their contributions. Hold a final meeting at which your sponsor can confirm that the project has indeed brought benefits and thank the team for its efforts. Your customers, in particular, may welcome an opportunity to express how they have found the results of the project.

▼ **CELEBRATING SUCCESS**
Mark the end of a project with a celebration in recognition of the team's hard work and effort. This allows people to say their farewells and realize their achievements in a convivial atmosphere.

ASSESSING YOUR PROJECT MANAGEMENT SKILLS

*E*valuate your ability to think strategically by responding to the following statements, marking the option closest to your experience. Be as honest as you can: if your answer is "never", circle Option 1; if it is "always", circle Option 4, and so on. Add your scores together, and refer to the Analysis to see how well you scored. Use your answers to identify the areas that most need improvement.

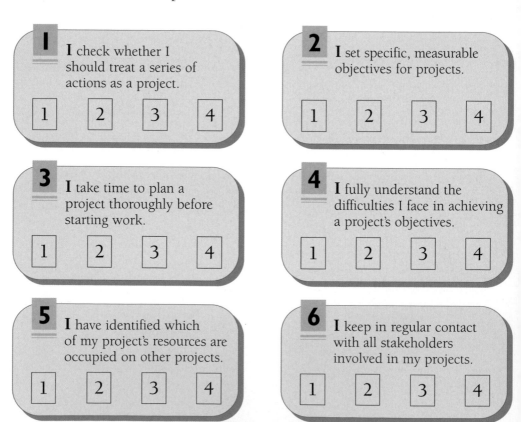

1 I check whether I should treat a series of actions as a project.

1   2   3   4

2 I set specific, measurable objectives for projects.

1   2   3   4

3 I take time to plan a project thoroughly before starting work.

1   2   3   4

4 I fully understand the difficulties I face in achieving a project's objectives.

1   2   3   4

5 I have identified which of my project's resources are occupied on other projects.

1   2   3   4

6 I keep in regular contact with all stakeholders involved in my projects.

1   2   3   4

7 I always consider what the ideal outcome of a project would be.

1 2 3 4

8 I ensure that everyone clearly understands the project's objectives.

1 2 3 4

9 I set business targets for each part of a project.

1 2 3 4

10 I check that a project will not unnecessarily change what already works.

1 2 3 4

11 I compile a full list of project activities before I place them in correct order.

1 2 3 4

12 I calculate manpower time and elapsed time of all project activities.

1 2 3 4

13 I make sure all the key people have approved the plan before I start a project.

1 2 3 4

14 I liaise with the finance department to check the costs of a project.

1 2 3 4

15 I generally start project implementation with a pilot.

1 2 3 4

16 I keep a network diagram up to date throughout a project.

1 2 3 4

17 I inform all interested parties of changes to project resource requirements.

1   2   3   4

18 I prepare contingency plans for all major risks to the project.

1   2   3   4

19 I adapt my leadership style to suit circumstances and individuals.

1   2   3   4

20 I consider how best to develop my teams' skills.

1   2   3   4

21 I consider how well new team members will fit in with the rest of the team.

1   2   3   4

22 I make sure each team member knows exactly what is expected of them.

1   2   3   4

23 I use my sponsor to help motivate my team.

1   2   3   4

24 I have documented and circulated the primary milestones of the project.

1   2   3   4

25 I ensure that every team member has access to the information they need.

1   2   3   4

26 I avoid keeping secrets from the project team and stakeholders.

1   2   3   4

27 I ask people to attend review meetings only if they really need to be present.

1   2   3   4

28 I use the same standard method of reporting progress to all stakeholders.

1   2   3   4

29 I prepare the objectives and agenda of meetings.

1   2   3   4

30 I use a logical process to make decisions with my project team.

1   2   3   4

31 I keep my sponsor fully up to date with progress on the project plan.

1   2   3   4

32 I use problem-solving techniques to arrive at decisions.

1   2   3   4

ANALYSIS

Now you have completed the self-assessment, add up your total score and check your performance by referring to the corresponding evaluation below. Whatever level of success you have achieved, there is always room for improvement. Identify your weakest areas and refer to the relevant sections to refine your skills.

32–64: You are not yet sufficiently well-organized to ensure that a complex project will achieve its objectives. Review the planning process thoroughly and make sure that you follow it through step-by-step.

65–95: You are a reasonably effective project manager, but need to address some weak points.

96–128: You are an excellent project manager. Be careful not to become complacent or to let your high standards slip.

UNDERSTANDING ACCOUNTS

INTRODUCTION

F*inance is probably the most important function in any organization, and an understanding of the fundamental figures and financial statements is key to successful* management. Understanding Accounts *shows you how to master the language of finance, enabling you to contribute more effectively to overall business performance and improve your leadership skills. This book clearly explains how accounts are compiled and shows you how to uncover a wealth of information about financial activity within your own, or a competitor's, organization. Packed with helpful hints, 101 tips, real-life case studies, and practical advice and information, it provides an indispensable guide to using and interpreting a set of accounts.*

UNDERSTANDING THE BASICS

Accounts are produced periodically to measure how well an organization is performing. Learn how they are prepared and what they reveal about your own, or a competitor's, business.

EXPLAINING ACCOUNTS

A set of accounts provides an invaluable insight into business performance. Learn what the three key financial statements are and how they link together to give an overall picture of just how well an organization is faring.

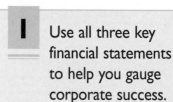

1 Use all three key financial statements to help you gauge corporate success.

2 Regularly set aside time to review your organization's financial performance.

PRODUCING RELIABLE ACCOUNTS

When Italian monk Fra Pacioli first invented double-entry book-keeping some 500 years ago, he introduced the civilized world to reliable accounting. Transactions were recorded twice (once to show where an item came from, and then to show where it went), so that nothing could be missed. Accountants today use the same principles – as well as following standards laid down by their own profession – to produce meaningful financial statements that summarize both the past and current financial position of an organization.

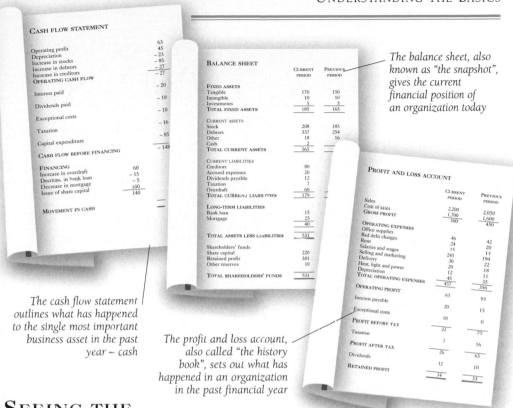

CASH FLOW STATEMENT

Operating profit	63
Depreciation	45
Increase in stocks	– 23
Increase in debtors	– 85
Increase in creditors	– 27
OPERATING CASH FLOW	– 27
	– 20
Interest paid	– 10
Dividends paid	– 10
Exceptional costs	– 16
Taxation	– 85
Capital expenditure	
CASH FLOW BEFORE FINANCING	– 148

FINANCING

Increase in overdraft	60
Decrease in bank loan	– 15
Decrease in mortgage	– 5
Issue of share capital	100
	140
MOVEMENT IN CASH	

BALANCE SHEET

	CURRENT PERIOD	PREVIOUS PERIOD
FIXED ASSETS		
Tangible	170	150
Intangible	10	10
Investments	5	5
TOTAL FIXED ASSETS	185	165
CURRENT ASSETS		
Stock	208	185
Debtors	337	254
Other	18	16
Cash	2	
TOTAL CURRENT ASSETS	565	
CURRENT LIABILITIES		
Creditors	80	
Accrued expenses	20	
Dividends payable	12	
Taxation	7	
Overdraft	60	
TOTAL CURRENT LIABILITIES	179	
LONG-TERM LIABILITIES		
Bank loan	15	
Mortgage	25	
	40	
TOTAL ASSETS LESS LIABILITIES	531	
Shareholders' funds		
Share capital	220	
Retained profit	301	
Other reserves	10	
TOTAL SHAREHOLDERS' FUNDS	531	

The balance sheet, also known as "the snapshot", gives the current financial position of an organization today

PROFIT AND LOSS ACCOUNT

	CURRENT PERIOD	PREVIOUS PERIOD
Sales	2,200	2,050
Cost of sales	1,700	1,600
GROSS PROFIT	500	450
OPERATING EXPENSES		
Office supplies	46	42
Bad debt charges	24	20
Rent	15	14
Salaries and wages	245	194
Selling and marketing	30	22
Delivery	20	18
Heat, light and power	12	11
Depreciation	45	35
TOTAL OPERATING EXPENSES	437	356
OPERATING PROFIT	63	91
Interest payable	20	15
Exceptional costs	10	0
PROFIT BEFORE TAX	33	76
Taxation	7	16
PROFIT AFTER TAX	26	63
Dividends	12	10
RETAINED PROFIT	14	53

The cash flow statement outlines what has happened to the single most important business asset in the past year – cash

The profit and loss account, also called "the history book", sets out what has happened in an organization in the past financial year

SEEING THE TRUE PICTURE

Each time you examine the financial statements that make up a set of business accounts, keep some key points in mind. First, since all businesses have different accounting policies and adding-up methods, no two sets of accounts will be the same. Second, different business formats (partnerships or limited liability companies, for example) and types (such as manufacturing or service organizations) will operate in different ways, with the result that some accounts are straightforward and others complex. Accounts may also be produced for a variety of reasons, such as calculating tax liability, assessing investment potential, or establishing a value for sale. Remember this when you interpret the figures.

▲ IDENTIFYING THE KEY FINANCIAL STATEMENTS

There are three financial statements that will help you assess the success of a company. Broadly, the profit and loss account reveals the income less expenses, the balance sheet shows the assets less the liabilities, and the cash flow statement records the increase or decrease of cash.

3 Understand that accounts do no more than reflect financial reality.

WHO USES ACCOUNTS?

*A*ccounts are of interest to everyone associated with the organization that produces them and to outsiders such as competitors and tax authorities. Add to your understanding of accounts by learning how to look at them from different points of view.

4 Recognize that accounts are produced for different purposes.

5 Be clear on why it is vital to examine your company's accounts.

WHO NEEDS ACCOUNTS?

There are two main groups of people who use accounts: those who are interested in the financial performance of an organization (such as investors, shareholders, lenders, or suppliers), and those who take a broader view (often for taxation, regulatory, or legal reasons). The latter are more interested in general issues such as compliance with appropriate legislation than in the detailed financial analysis.

DEFINING PERSPECTIVES

In addition to annual reports and accounts for external consumption, most organizations produce internal, or management, accounts. These are used only within the organization and are helpfully flexible in measuring different (sometimes non-financial) aspects of performance because they are not subject to the rules and regulations that govern the preparation of external figures. However, because internal accounts do not have to adhere to any rules, they often bear little or no resemblance to annual external accounts. The internals can simply be wrong, causing problems for managers who are using them to drive the business forwards.

Manager wants to know where performance can be improved

INTERNAL ACCOUNTS

Tax official checks that correct tax has been paid on profits

EXTERNAL ACCOUNTS

LOOKING AT DIFFERENT ACCOUNTS ▶
External accounts show consistency and comparability. Internal accounts need not follow any rules and can be more flexible and useful to a business, but also more open to error.

Identifying Users of Accounts

Users of Accounts	What They Look For
Owner Has a vested interest in the organization's future and success; tends to be financially cautious.	● How well the business is doing compared with previous years and with competitors. ● Reassurance that the family source of income is safe and secure.
Investor/Shareholder Invests money or has shares in an organization; their analysis is often detailed and ruthless.	● Information on an organization to allow comparisons with other businesses, with a view to choosing between them. ● Indications that returns will be maximized.
Lender Advances loans; needs to know that the interest is affordable and that the debt can be repaid.	● Evidence that an organization will be able to pay the interest on any debts. ● The worth of an organization should the debt be unpaid and the business wound up.
Competitor Has an interest in the relative financial performance and business statistics of rivals.	● Growth in sales, market share, net profits, and overall business efficiency. ● Information about the cost structure and operations of competitors.
Manager/Employee Works for and is paid by the organization on a full-time or regular basis.	● Reassurance that the organization will continue to operate competitively. ● End-of-year figures that reflect his/her competence favourably.
Customer/Supplier Needs to know whether he/she is dealing with financially sound and reputable organizations.	● Continuity of supply and business without disruption to the flow of goods or services. ● Ability of an organization to pay for goods and deliver on time.
Taxation Official Reviews financial statements for accuracy and reasonableness, then checks the amount of tax payable.	● Properly prepared and computed accounts and profit and loss statements. ● Validity of accounts when compared with similar businesses.

EXAMINING REGULATIONS AND PRACTICE

The drawing up of accounts is governed both by strict legal requirements and by more informal guidelines created by the accounting profession. Understand the principles and the influences that have shaped the way in which accounts are prepared.

6 Understand the impact of the law and the accounting profession.

7 Accept that minimal information is usually disclosed.

8 Keep up to date with accounting methods.

FOLLOWING THE LAW

In most countries the primary rules for producing accounts are laid down by law. This states exactly what must be done in creating, managing, and closing down a company – in short, the law establishes the overall framework, or "skeleton", for producing accounts. While the law is usually clear on the "what" and "when" of accounts, it is often vague on such issues as "How should stock be valued?" or "How should profit be recognized on a particular transaction?". This detailed level of accounting is usually left to accountants.

ASSESSING GUIDELINES

For those accounting issues where the law gives insufficient guidance, accountants have established their own set of guidelines and standards known as Generally Accepted Accounting Principles (GAAP). Country-specific, GAAP advises how certain key transactions are best treated. Because GAAP is not compulsory, compliance with it may be less than perfect, which is why abuse of the system is possible. Additional rules may also apply to certain businesses, depending on company size, ownership, and listing rules of stock exchanges.

QUESTIONS TO ASK YOURSELF

Q What size of business am I looking at, and what level and detail of accounting disclosure should I expect to see?

Q What does the law require the accounts to contain, and how informative will I find this?

Q Are the accounting policies of the organization typical and reasonable for a business of its size and type?

COMPARING PRACTICE IN DIFFERENT COUNTRIES

The rules governing the preparation and structure of accounts are unusual. Strict legal requirements laid down by a country's law, together with generally accepted but more informal practice typically created by the accounting profession of that country, may be either strong or weak, depending on the country. Countries with strong "codified" law and tax regimes (Continental Europe in general) tend to have weaker GAAP, and vice versa. Strong and open stock exchanges typically have strong GAAP, since, unlike laws, GAAP guidelines can be drawn up relatively quickly in response to real-life issues.

CHOOSING POLICIES

Operating within both the law and GAAP, organizations choose how they will treat certain financial transactions. Known as accounting policies, these are generally selected by the directors of an organization and their business advisers as being the most appropriate to the company's current circumstances and also the best way of fairly presenting their results and financial position. Since no two organizations are the same, they will obviously all add up their accounts in a slightly different way.

9 Realize that adding-up methods vary around the world.

▼ **DEFINING INFLUENCES ON ACCOUNTS**
Of the five key influences on accounting statements, company law and accounting practice have most impact on the form that accounts take, followed by regulatory and taxation bodies, and international rules.

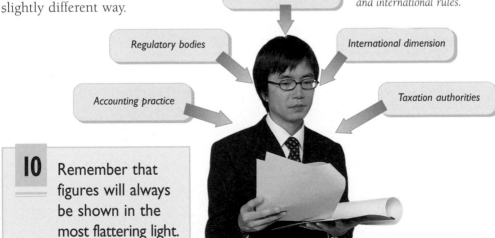

Company law

Regulatory bodies

International dimension

Accounting practice

Taxation authorities

10 Remember that figures will always be shown in the most flattering light.

425

DEFINING KEY CONCEPTS

There are certain fundamental themes or concepts, such as accruals, prudence, consistency, and viability, that are seen as the cornerstones of good accounting. In order to understand accounts it is vital to appreciate the importance of these.

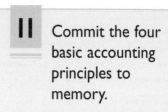

11 Commit the four basic accounting principles to memory.

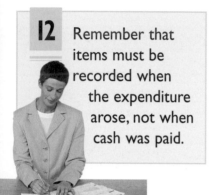

12 Remember that items must be recorded when the expenditure arose, not when cash was paid.

USING ACCRUALS

The principle of accruals, or matching, sets out when a transaction should appear in the accounts. An item is always recorded when the income (or expenditure) arises – not when cash is received (or paid). For example, even when a sale is made on credit terms and cash may not be received until the next accounting period, the sale must still be recognized now. While applying this fundamental accounting principle is commonsense, it nevertheless causes most accounting problems.

SHOWING PRUDENCE AND CONSISTENCY

Financial statements must be prudently or conservatively presented, which means that profits must not be overstated, and costs must be realistically and fairly estimated. In other words, figures should be on the pessimistic side. Prudence addresses the question: "How much should an amount be?" and is the most important of the key concepts. Accounts should also be produced using consistent assumptions and treatments. This means that an organization should use similar principles year-on-year, so that accounts can be compared sensibly. Changes to assumptions and treatments can, of course, be made but the financial implications must be highlighted and quantified.

POINTS TO REMEMBER

● The accruals principle asks the question: "In which accounting period?" or "When should the impact of a transaction be shown?"

● Prudence, or financial conservatism, effectively overrides all other accounting principles in importance.

13 Know that prudence governs fair accounting.

Assuming Viability

When producing a set of accounts it is necessary to assume that the organization will be in business, or a going concern, the following year. This is a silent assumption, since it would be almost impossible to produce accounts if the business were likely to fail. The value of stock in a warehouse, a plant, a piece of equipment, or any other item in the accounts would be affected if the business were to cease to exist.

 14 Be aware that any change in adding up often indicates something to hide.

Explaining Key Terms

Key Term	Definition
ASSET	Anything owned by an organization that has a monetary value, from plant and machinery to patents and goodwill.
AUDIT	Independent inspection of accounts, according to set principles, by accountants who are qualified auditors.
DEPRECIATION	Annual cost shown in the profit and loss account of writing off a fixed asset over its expected useful life.
EQUITY	Share capital and reserves of a company, which represent what shareholders have invested in the organization.
FIXED ASSET	Asset used in a business and not held for resale, typically with a life of more than one year.
LIABILITY	Amount owed at a set time, often split into short term (less than one year) and long term (more than one year).
RESERVES	Profits made by a business, which have been invested in the business rather than paid out in dividends.
WORKING CAPITAL	Capital available for daily operations of an organization, usually expressed as current assets less current liabilities.

MASTERING ACCOUNTS

Mastering accounts means understanding the three key financial statements: the profit and loss account, the balance sheet, and the cash flow statement. Learn how they all fit together.

UNDERSTANDING A PROFIT AND LOSS ACCOUNT

The profit and loss account is an organization's statement of earnings; it shows all the income less expenses over the year. Make sure that you know how the profit and loss account is structured and what type of items are included.

15 Check how the accounting policies show that profit is measured.

16 Remember only "revenue" items appear in a profit and loss account.

RECORDING THE PAST

The profit and loss account is a "history book" of the past year. It tells how well a business has performed, listing all the "ins less outs", or sales less costs. Working on the accruals principle, only items arising during the year are shown. They must also be of a "revenue" nature (goods, services, and general annual expenditure), never items of a "capital" nature (purchase or sale of fixed assets such as equipment and machinery).

READING THE LINES

A profit and loss account measures various levels, or "lines", of profit. First is gross profit: sales (sometimes called gross income or fees billed) less cost of sales (the costs of providing goods or services). Next is operating profit: gross profit less all the expenses supporting the infrastructure and administration of an organization. Profit before tax is the operating profit less interest incurred on borrowings for the year, plus interest received. Profit after tax is calculated by deducting the tax due as a result of trading for the year. Retained profit is the after-tax profit less any dividend paid to the shareholders.

PROFIT AND LOSS ACCOUNT

	CURRENT PERIOD	PREVIOUS PERIOD
Sales	2,200	2,050
Cost of sales	1,700	1,600
GROSS PROFIT	500	450
OPERATING EXPENSES		
Office supplies	46	42
Bad debt charges	24	20
Rent	15	14
Salaries and wages	245	194
Selling and marketing	30	22
Delivery	20	18
Heat, light, and power	12	11
Depreciation	45	35
TOTAL OPERATING EXPENSES	437	356
OPERATING PROFIT	63	94
Interest payable	20	15
Exceptional costs	10	0
PROFIT BEFORE TAX	33	79
Taxation	7	16
PROFIT AFTER TAX	26	63
Dividends	12	10
RETAINED PROFIT	14	53

DECIDING WHAT COUNTS

Items included in the profit and loss account must all have passed the accruals test, but there are times when deciding what should be counted as sales or expenses is tricky. For example, should a sales invoice be included in the accounts if the work has not been completed? Accountants use various signposts to help them recognize what and how much to include, and when to do so. These signposts include the following:

● Completion: is the work substantially completed?
● Ownership: has ownership passed from the vendor to the customer?
● Measurement: can the profit be accurately and prudently estimated?
● Irrevocability: could the customer cancel the sale, causing the loss of profit?

▲ RECOGNIZING THE FORMAT

A typical profit and loss account is consistently structured into set rows and columns to show the profit or loss for the year; that is, the difference between income and expenditure.

17	Understand what the main headings in a profit and loss account mean.

LOOKING AT GROSS PROFIT

The gross profit, or first line of profit, provides an important early measure of a business's wellbeing. Ensure that you understand which type of expenses are deducted to calculate gross profit and what the gross margin can tell you.

18 Remember that the gross profit percentage should not be falling.

19 Compare your company's accounts year-on-year and with competitors'.

20 Be aware that gross profit measures a company's basic viability.

RECORDING SALES

The first item on a profit and loss account records a business's overall volume of activity and is called either sales, turnover, income, or fees billed. This is the full amount of all the sales invoices raised during the accounting period that have met the correct accruals criteria for being included on the statement. These are stated less any sales-related taxes (since tax belongs to the Internal Revenue Service, not the organization itself).

▼ **DETECTING GROSS PROFIT**
The first three lines of a profit and loss account show an organization's fundamental financial performance in black and white. From it, the wellbeing of the business can be determined.

The previous period's figures are shown so that they can be easily compared with this period's results

PROFIT AND LOSS ACCOUNT

	CURRENT PERIOD	PREVIOUS PERIOD
Sales	2,200	2,050
Cost of sales	1,700	1,600
GROSS PROFIT	500	450
OPERATING EXPENSES		
Office supplies	46	42
Bad debt charges	24	20
Rent	15	14
	245	194

Gross profit is the key result of a business and the first figure that investors or owners are likely to be interested in

DEDUCTING COST OF SALES

There are two types of costs in the profit and loss account and these are deducted separately. The first group is known as cost of sales (COS), sometimes referred to as cost of goods sold (COGS). These are all the costs expended to make or produce the product or service that is being sold, and usually include materials, production staff, production premises, and machinery costs – typically "factory" costs.

21 Look beyond the figures to the type and structure of the organization.

PROVIDING A MEASURE

While gross income, or the full amount of sales, is an important sign of life for a business, gross profit, or the full amount of sales less COS, is more informative about its health. This "factory result" is often more usefully expressed as a percentage of sales. Since different businesses have different COS, they will have different gross profit percentages. These must be looked at in relation to what would be expected from the type of business.

PERFECT PRINTERS
PROFIT AND LOSS ACCOUNT

	CURRENT PERIOD	%	PREVIOUS PERIOD	%
Sales	2,200	100.0	2,050	100.0
Cost of sales	600	27.3	560	27.3
GROSS PROFIT	1,600	72.7	1,490	72.7
OPERATING EXPENSES	46	2.1		
Office supplies				

▲ COMPARING GROSS PROFIT MARGINS

Gross profit margins vary significantly between different types of business, and a low margin is to be expected from a business with a high cost of sales, such as a supermarket or travel agency. On the other hand, a service business with a lower than normal cost of sales will have a higher than average gross profit margin.

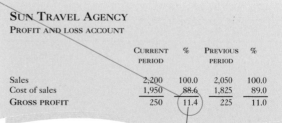

SUN TRAVEL AGENCY
PROFIT AND LOSS ACCOUNT

	CURRENT PERIOD	%	PREVIOUS PERIOD	%
Sales	2,200	100.0	2,050	100.0
Cost of sales	1,950	88.6	1,825	89.0
GROSS PROFIT	250	11.4	225	11.0

Profit margins for low cost of sales businesses are typically between 50 and 90 per cent; for high cost of sales businesses they rarely exceed 10 per cent

DETERMINING OPERATING PROFIT

T*he second line of profit is operating or trading profit, which is a clear measure of a business's performance after all its operating costs have been deducted. Identify which costs apply and so ascertain how successfully a business has been managed.*

22 Examine operating costs to gauge management efficiency.

23 Look at trends in certain costs to anticipate any future problems.

**CALCULATING ▼
OPERATING PROFIT**
Operating profit is struck after the remainder of costs in a business have been deducted. It is usually expressed as a percentage of sales.

DEDUCTING OTHER COSTS

The second type of costs in the profit and loss account, which are now deducted to determine operating profit, are called selling, general, and administration (SG&A) costs, or operating expenses. These cover any expenses not listed in the cost of sales category. SG&A includes marketing and advertising under "selling", while "general and administration" costs cover head office, accounting, information technology, marketing, personnel, directors, and central costs. All costs must be either COS or SG&A.

Sales		
Cost of sales	1,700	1,600
GROSS PROFIT	500	450
OPERATING EXPENSES		
Office supplies	46	42
Bad debt charges	24	20
Rent	15	14
Salaries and wages	245	194
Selling and marketing	30	22
Delivery	20	18
Heat, light, and power	12	11
Depreciation	45	35
TOTAL OPERATING EXPENSES	437	356
OPERATING PROFIT	63	94
Interest payable	20	15

Total operating expenses are deducted from the gross profit

Operating profit made from trading, before the deduction of taxes, interest, and dividends

UNDERSTANDING DIFFERENT CYCLES

All businesses have two cycles – an operating cycle and a capital investment cycle. The operating cycle is straightforward: a business buys goods or services in order that they can be sold on at a profit. The capital investment cycle, on the other hand, is a measure of how much is invested in the fabric of a business (such as the plant, tools, or machinery) in order that a business may carry out its operating cycle. More than one operating cycle is generally needed to fund one capital cycle. A set of accounts simply reflects how much money is tied up in an organization at any time in both these cycles.

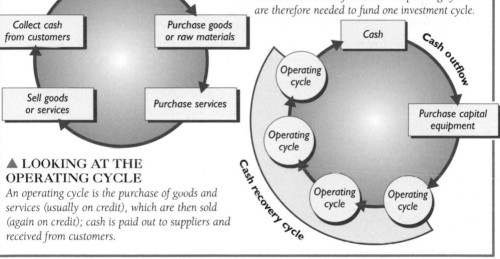

▼ REVIEWING THE CAPITAL INVESTMENT CYCLE

Capital investment, or the purchase of one-off items needed for an organization to trade, involves a substantial cash outflow. Several operating cycles are therefore needed to fund one investment cycle.

▲ LOOKING AT THE OPERATING CYCLE

An operating cycle is the purchase of goods and services (usually on credit), which are then sold (again on credit); cash is paid out to suppliers and received from customers.

REACHING A SUBTOTAL

Deducting SG&A costs from gross profit gives the subtotal of operating profit. This is effectively the end of the "first half" of the profit and loss account, which measures how well a business has performed in its core operations. Operating profit is often more usefully expressed as a percentage of sales – a typical range being between zero and 10 per cent.

24 Compare operating profit percentages between organizations.

EVALUATING THE BOTTOM LINE

T*he second half of the profit and loss statement, down to the "bottom line", relates to other expenses, including taxation and interest. It is vital to learn how to interpret these items, since their financial impact can often be significant.*

25 Determine whether an interest bill is really affordable.

26 Check if one-off costs are warning signs of problems.

LOOKING AT INTEREST

Below the operating profit the next deduction to be made is the amount of interest incurred on all loans and borrowings over the period covered by the profit and loss account. This is often an issue because the amount payable can call into question the viability of an entire business. Affordability can be calculated by comparing the interest charges for the year to the operating profit. For example, if operating profit is £63 and interest £20, the interest could be paid about three times over and interest cover is said to be "three". There is no absolute target; what is important is the trend in interest cover, which can change from year to year.

REACHING THE ▼ BOTTOM LINE
The difference between operating profit and retained profit will be due to varying amounts of interest, exceptional items, taxation, and dividends.

TOTAL OPERATING EXPENSES		356
OPERATING PROFIT	63	94
Interest payable	20	15
Exceptional costs	10	0
PROFIT BEFORE TAX	33	79
Taxation	7	16
PROFIT AFTER TAX	26	63
Dividends	12	10
RETAINED PROFIT	14	53

Profit after tax is what is left for shareholders after interest, exceptional costs, and taxes have been deducted

After paying shareholders' dividends, the business reinvests the retained profit

EXAMINING EXCEPTIONAL COSTS

Occasionally you will come across other items of a one-off, non-recurring nature, and traditionally these are shown separately to the core gross and operating profit figures so as not to distort them. Such items are referred to as exceptional items and typically include provisions for large future events (recognizing costs now even though the event will happen in the future), currency movements, gains and losses on sales of assets or businesses, and pensions. Assess whether these seem reasonable, or if they indicate problems.

EXAMINING TAXATION

The operating profit minus interest gives profit before tax (PBT), which is subject to taxation; the profit and loss account details the tax bill on the year's profits. The amount is unlikely yet to have been paid in full to the Internal Revenue Service and is also probably a best estimate. Whatever the annual tax charge is computed to be, it is deducted from PBT to give profit after tax, or PAT, which, in principle, belongs to the shareholders. PAT also provides a basis for calculating shareholder measures such as earnings per share.

27 Investigate a tax bill if it is not the expected rate.

28 Spot the trend in, and sufficiency of, retained profits.

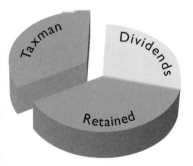

▲ SPLITTING PROFIT BEFORE TAX

For a quoted company, profit before tax is split three ways. One-third represents tax (where corporate tax rate is approximately 30 per cent), one-third is typically paid to shareholders by way of dividend, and the final one-third is retained in the business.

PINPOINTING RETAINED PROFIT

At the bottom line of the profit and loss account, once declared dividends have been deducted, are retained earnings. These represent the profit kept behind by an organization in order to help it grow. Bear in mind that profits make a balance sheet grow, so the amount of retained profit should correspond to the increase in the balance sheet. However, in large companies this simple accounting truth may be obscured by technical shuffling. It may also be unclear exactly where the retained profit will be; it is hoped that it would be in cash form in a successful organization, rather than in a less liquid item, such as stock.

UNDERSTANDING BALANCE SHEETS

The balance sheet is effectively a listing of everything a business owns less all that it owes. Learn how this key financial statement is structured and how the figures work to provide you with a picture of the total net assets of an organization.

29 Think of the balance sheet as an aerial photograph.

BALANCE SHEET	CURRENT PERIOD	PREVIOUS PERIOD
FIXED ASSETS		
Tangible	170	150
Intangible	10	10
Investments	5	5
TOTAL FIXED ASSETS	185	165
CURRENT ASSETS		
Stock	208	185
Debtors	337	254
Other	18	16
Cash	2	10
TOTAL CURRENT ASSETS	565	465
CURRENT LIABILITIES		
Creditors	80	109
Accrued expenses	20	18
Dividends payable	12	10
Taxation	7	16
Overdraft	60	0
TOTAL CURRENT LIABILITIES	179	153
LONG-TERM LIABILITIES		
Bank loan	15	30
Mortgage	25	30
	40	60
TOTAL ASSETS LESS LIABILITIES	531	417
Shareholders' funds		
Share capital	220	120
Retained profit	301	287
Other reserves	10	10
TOTAL SHAREHOLDERS' FUNDS	531	417

▲ READING THE BALANCE SHEET
The balance sheet lists assets and liabilities comparing both previous and current accounting periods, grouping them into meaningful subtotals and totals that explain what is happening financially within an organization.

EXAMINING HOW BALANCE SHEETS WORK

The balance sheet shows the present financial performance of a business. It can be compared to a snapshot of an entire organization taken at the close of business on a specific day, and it is therefore correct only at that one precise moment. The snapshot shows everything that the business owns – its assets – and all that it owes – its liabilities. Balance sheets are generally drawn up each year at the same time as the profit and loss account. But bear in mind that pictures can be flattering. If, for example, a fashion retailer's balance sheet is done after the summer sales (when there is plenty of cash in the bank and stocks are low), it will look particularly good.

QUESTIONS TO ASK YOURSELF

Q Does the year-end fit the annual nature of the business?

Q Would a different accounting date alter the balance sheet?

Q Have there been major changes in any sums year-on-year?

Q Have assets shown at current value been estimated fairly?

GROUPING FIGURES

The balance sheet is split into sections, according to strict accounting rules. The first section lists an organization's assets split between fixed (or long-term) and current (or short-term) assets. The second section itemizes liabilities (again split between fixed and current). The third shows shareholders' funds, or money invested in the business by its owners.

30 Understand the importance of how liabilities and assets are grouped.

Accountant also notes that the company has excess stock

Fleet manager informs team that new vans are needed

Colleague reminds fleet manager that their major client has unsettled bills

Senior manager decides that it is too risky to purchase new vans at present

USING THE ▲ BALANCE SHEET

As a manager, it is important to look at, understand, and act upon what the balance sheet tells you. In this way you will be able to make better-quality financial decisions.

31 Appreciate that balance sheets show cost and not value.

INTERPRETING THE TOTAL

All assets and liabilities are generally shown on the balance sheet according to an accounting convention called historic cost, which means that they are shown at their original cost to the business. The balance sheet total, also referred to as total net assets, is arrived at by adding up the cost of all assets and then deducting the total of short- and long-term liabilities. Remember that the balance sheet normally shows only costs, and it should not be seen as an indication of an organization's market value. Nothing could be further from the truth, yet it remains a popular misconception.

EXAMINING FIXED ASSETS

Fixed assets are used by a business on a permanent basis to create wealth in the normal course of operations. Learn to recognize the three types of fixed assets (tangibles, intangibles, and investments) and understand the concept of depreciation.

32 Investigate any significant additions in unusual fixed assets.

33 Scrutinize closely any asset that is shown at current value..

UNDERSTANDING ▼ FIXED ASSETS

Fixed assets are generally grouped into tangible, intangible, and investments held for the longer term. They are listed in order of the frequency in which they are encountered. Amounts are stated after depreciation.

RECOGNIZING TANGIBLE FIXED ASSETS

Assets needed for a business to be in a position to trade are known as fixed assets. These are typically tangible items with a life of more than 12 months (otherwise they would be shown as a cost on the profit and loss). Spending on fixed assets is called capital expenditure, and this reflects how much is invested in the fabric of a business in order that it may carry out its operating cycle. Typical fixed assets are land, buildings, equipment, machinery, computers, fixtures and fittings, and vehicles. Manufacturers generally have high fixed assets and are capital-intensive. Service businesses have low fixed assets and are not capital-intensive.

BALANCE SHEET	CURRENT PERIOD	PREVIOUS PERIOD
FIXED ASSETS	170	150
Tangible	10	10
Intangible	5	5
Investments	185	165
TOTAL FIXED ASSETS		
CURRENT ASSETS	208	185
Stock	337	254
Debtors	18	16
Other	2	10
Cash	565	465
TOTAL CURRENT ASSETS		

Total fixed assets shows how much is invested in a business to enable it to trade

ANALYZING DEPRECIATION

Fixed assets are shown at cost less depreciation, known as net book value. Depreciation writes off the cost of the asset (less any anticipated residual value, often assumed to be nil) over its effective useful life. For example, assuming a computer costs £900 and has a useful life of three years, it will be depreciated by £300 a year. This means that it will be written down to £600 after one year, £300 after two years, and £0 after three years. Depreciation simply spreads the cost of a fixed asset over its lifetime; it does not write the asset down to secondhand value, nor does it provide a fund of money for replacement.

> **34** See that an asset's life and depreciation rate seem fair.

▼ CALCULATING DEPRECIATION

With the "straight line" method, a computer would be written off by an equal annual amount throughout its depreciable life. Using the "reducing balance" method, the depreciation of a car would be recalculated every year based on the net book value (or written down value) reached to date.

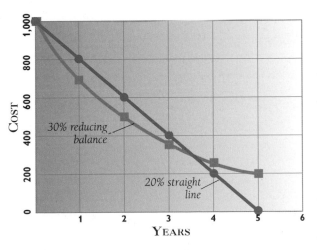

30% reducing balance

20% straight line

COST / YEARS

FLYING ON TIME ▼
The useful economic life of an asset is usually written off over a number of years. With an aircraft, however, the number of hours flown is considered to be a far better determinant of age.

SETTING A RATE

The depreciation life/rate of each asset is set by the business, so although different companies are making the same trading profit, because their fixed assets have different depreciation lives, each will show a different accounting profit. In addition to the straight line on cost and reducing balance methods of depreciating an asset, there are any number of other ways to depreciate assets, most of which are simply based on common sense and generally accepted practice.

DEFINING INTANGIBLES

Most fixed assets are real and tangible; in other words, they physically exist and can be touched. Yet balance sheets recognize that certain long-term assets may not be tangible. There are two main types of intangibles: traditional and modern. Traditional intangibles include items such as patents, intellectual property rights, and know-how, while modern intangibles (or those that have recently become popular) are goodwill and brands. Intangibles, by their very nature, are often difficult to value, but – like all fixed assets – once their worth has been calculated, they must be depreciated over their useful economic life.

35 See if intangibles make up a realistic proportion of the balance sheet.

EXPLAINING GOODWILL

Goodwill is generally taken to mean the value of a business's good name, reputation, and client base. Goodwill is shown as a fixed asset by an organization when it buys another business at a higher price than the value of its assets. Any decent business will be worth more than simply its assets, but the problem is how to get the accounts of the buyer to balance. When buying a business for £10 that has assets of only £6, the difference of £4 is called goodwill. Goodwill is shown as an intangible asset and is amortized (depreciated) over its useful economic life.

Purchase price is established by mutual agreement

NOTES TO ACCOUNTS

COMPANY	A	B	C
Amount paid for company	155	15	23
Fair value of acquired assets	95	2	-2
Goodwill	60	13	25

Amount of goodwill depends on the purchaser's perception of worth

Purchaser is so keen that it pays money to acquire liabilities

◀ **BALANCING THE BOOKS**
This extract from the notes to accounts shows an organization that has bought three companies during the year. The purchase price reflects the value of the acquired company as a whole, not just its assets. The amount of goodwill is simply the difference between the purchase price and the fair value of the assets acquired.

UNDERSTANDING BRANDS

A new development has seen the concept of goodwill taken even further, which is known as brand accounting. The idea is that because some organizations do not want to show a cost to the profit and loss account every year when depreciating goodwill (either because their profits will not stand it or because they do not believe that the asset in question should be written down), they categorize the asset as a "brand" rather than as goodwill. They argue that any spending on marketing and advertising means that the brand does not fall in value – and so is not being depreciated.

36 Check whether any brands should have been reduced in value.

EXPLORING INVESTMENTS

The final category of fixed assets is called investments, which covers any monies or shares held outside the company. These may be shares in another organization held for the long term, investments, or any other asset that will be sold, but not within the next 12 months. Again, the issue is that of cost. For example, should shares be valued at the price originally paid for them or according to the stock market price for that day? It is generally agreed that they should be shown at market value.

CASE STUDY

Peter, the sales manager of a confectionery company, was disappointed that profits were down in spite of increased sales. In the latest set of accounts, Peter discovered that large amortization (depreciation) charges had been made because his company had acquired two businesses. Since the assets of the new businesses had been bought for more than their book value, the shortfall had been categorized as goodwill, which had to be written off over its useful life. As a result, profits were being reduced by the amount of the annual write-off. Peter approached David, the finance manager, to suggest that since so much money was being spent on marketing and advertising (expenditure in support of the brands), the goodwill should be classified as a brand. David agreed, and profits increased again.

▲ AVOIDING DEPRECIATION CHARGES

Peter's understanding of the issues of goodwill and brands prompted him to approach the finance manager with a sound proposition. By classifying goodwill as a brand, David was able to amend the company's accounts so that there was no annual write-off. As a result, Peter was happy to see his team's improved sales performance clearly reflected in the increased profit shown on the next period's profit and loss account.

QUESTIONS TO ASK YOURSELF

Q Are all fixed assets fairly stated in cost and depreciation?

Q Do the figures demonstrate adequate investment for the future?

Q Should any intangibles be ignored when analyzing figures?

Q Have investments been valued and accounted for correctly?

WORKING WITH CURRENT ASSETS

Current assets are short-term assets that a business holds that will convert into cash within the next 12 months. Learn to recognize the four main types of current assets and why it is important to convert the first three into cash quickly.

> **37** Look at current assets with care; they represent a business's lifeblood.

> **38** Check that debtors change only in proportion to turnover.

UNDERSTANDING ▼ CURRENT ASSETS
Current assets, or items that will turn into cash in the next year, include stocks held for resale, debtors owing for credit sales made, sundry items paid for in advance, and cash itself.

LISTING CURRENT ASSETS
Included under current assets is cash, plus anything that will turn into cash in the next 12 months. The importance of current assets is that they show how much an organization has in the way of cash, or near cash, and therefore how viable the business is. There are three main categories of current assets: stock; debtors (people who have bought goods and owe payment); and other current assets, which include other monies owed and items known as prepayments. There is also cash (received when debtors pay their bills, and including petty cash or monies held in the business bank account or on short-term deposit).

TOTAL FIXED ASSETS	185	165
CURRENT ASSETS		
Stock	208	185
Debtors	337	254
Other	18	16
Cash	2	10
TOTAL CURRENT ASSETS	565	465
CURRENT LIABILITIES		
Creditors	80	109
Accrued expenses	20	18

Current assets in a business should be as "liquid" (close to cash) as possible

DEFINING STOCK

There are three components of stock: raw materials, work in progress, and finished goods. What is of interest is how much cash is tied up in each component, because the more raw materials there are, the further they must go to be converted into cash, incurring costs along the way. Finished goods are safer assets because they are more liquid. However, stock overall is the least liquid of all current assets.

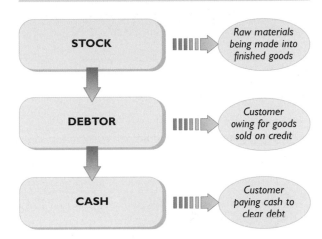

LOOKING AT ASSETS WITHIN THE OPERATING CYCLE

STOCK → Raw materials being made into finished goods

DEBTOR → Customer owing for goods sold on credit

CASH → Customer paying cash to clear debt

VALUING STOCK

Stock is usually valued either at cost or at net realizable value (whichever is lower), since stock should never be overstated. Cost is the price paid for the items when bought; realizable is what they could be sold for, net of expenses. An item bought for £5 with a selling price of £20 should be shown in stock at £5. If it could be sold for only £1, then that is how it should be shown, with a stock write-down of £4 (£5 minus £1) appearing as a cost of sales in that year's profit and loss account. The higher the stock at the end of the year (closing stock), the lower the cost of sales on the profit and loss account, hence the higher the reported profit.

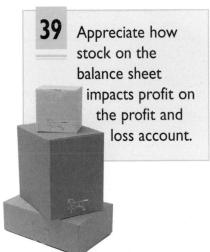

39 Appreciate how stock on the balance sheet impacts profit on the profit and loss account.

40 Realize that slow-moving and obsolete stock is a common problem.

DO'S AND DON'TS

☑ Do look for unexpected increases in stocks and debtors.

☑ Do be cynical about the valuation applied to stocks.

☒ Don't believe that more current assets are always good news.

☒ Don't overlook other current assets and what they tell you.

IDENTIFYING STOCK

Assuming that prices of stock are rising, then raw materials purchased earlier will cost less than those bought later. Accountants generally choose one of two methods of charging a material out of the stores and on to the job: FIFO (first in, first out) or LIFO (last in, first out). The method chosen will affect reported profits and assets, since under FIFO the profit and loss account profit and balance sheet closing stock figures will be higher. Under LIFO, both figures will be lower.

41 Check that your own stock has not been overvalued – reject amounts that do not seem right.

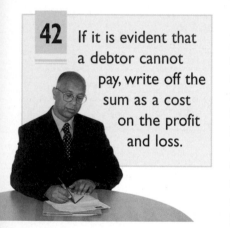

42 If it is evident that a debtor cannot pay, write off the sum as a cost on the profit and loss.

EXAMINING DEBTORS

Debtors, or amounts owed by customers for sales made on credit terms, is a more liquid asset than stock. The amount shown is the total of the invoices outstanding (issued but not yet paid) at the accounting period end, and it represents cash that is being held, albeit temporarily, by customers. Debtors will invariably be an organization's largest current asset – in which case it is vital that a business has them under control. This means making sure that customers pay, preferably on time and the full amount.

DEFINING DEDUCTIONS FROM DEBTORS

The problem with debtors is that not all of an organization's customers will end up paying – some may well default on the debt. Since accountants must follow the prudence principle and state all assets at a realistic figure, they must anticipate that a certain amount of debt will not be paid, and make a provision for it. This bad debt provision, which is estimated at the end of the year, is deducted from the debtors figure shown on the balance sheet. The difference between this year's and the previous year's provision then becomes a selling, general, and administration cost on the profit and loss account. Bad debts also impact on accounts during the year if, at any time, customers are unable to pay what they owe. Once this is apparent, their debt should be immediately cancelled. This is called a bad-debt charge or write-off, and is also an SG&A cost on the profit and loss account.

IDENTIFYING OTHER CURRENT ASSETS

CURRENT ASSET	POINTS TO NOTE
ASSETS HELD FOR RESALE Items about to be sold.	When a fixed asset such as land is about to be sold, it is shown on the balance sheet as a current asset, rather than as a fixed asset, because it will convert into cash within one year.
LOANS Advances to employees.	When an organization has lent or advanced money to its employees or directors, this is shown as a current asset of the business, since generally the monies will be fully repaid within the next year.
PREPAYMENTS Payments made in advance.	If bills are paid in advance, cash has been paid out – but the expense relates to a future accounting period. This means that a prepayment is, in effect, a current asset.
OTHERS Sundry items.	Insurance claims, tax refunds, deposits paid to secure goods, payments received by instalments, and stage payments represent sums owed that should be received within one year, hence they are current assets.

LISTING OTHER ITEMS

There are other items listed under current assets that can also be significant. Again the principle is that these will convert into cash within the next 12 months. Other assets typically include monies owed by people other than customers (such as a tax rebate that is due), and items that have been paid for in advance (such as rent or business rates), which could theoretically be reimbursed.

43 Think of your current assets as cash temporarily looked after by someone else.

44 Examine in detail the movement in cash for the period in question.

CLASSIFYING CASH

The most liquid of all current assets is cash – either at the bank or in hand. Cash includes everything that is a liquid asset, ranging from money in a bank account to cash in shop tills and petty cash tins throughout an organization. Money in a term deposit or with limited access rights is not strictly cash, so is listed under other current assets.

UNDERSTANDING LIABILITIES

Liabilities are debts payable in a future period because of events that have already happened. They are either current (due in the next 12 months) or long term. Learn to identify both types of liability and why the split between the two is important.

45 Check that an organization's liabilities do not exceed its assets.

46 Make sure that all possible liabilities have been included.

SPLITTING LIABILITIES ▼

Liabilities are split into immediate and future obligations. On some balance sheets, current liabilities are deducted from current assets to give a net current assets subtotal. Then long-term liabilities are shown.

EXAMINING CURRENT LIABILITIES

Typical current liabilities are large items such as creditors (people who are owed money for goods purchased) and bank overdrafts (always repayable on demand). A business does not want what it owes (current liabilities) to exceed what it has coming in (current assets), since this is a recipe for insolvency. However, an enterprise that uses its creditors as a source of funding from a position of strength is not a cause for concern; if it cannot afford to pay its creditors, that is a sign of trouble.

Cash		
TOTAL CURRENT ASSETS	565	465
CURRENT LIABILITIES	80	109
Creditors	20	18
Accrued expenses	12	10
Dividends payable	7	16
Taxation	60	0
Overdraft	179	153
TOTAL CURRENT LIABILITIES		
LONG-TERM LIABILITIES	15	30
Bank loan	25	30
Mortgage	40	60
TOTAL ASSETS LESS LIABILITIES	531	417

Current liabilities are typically listed in order of liquidity

Deducting current and long-term liabilities from total current assets gives the balance sheet total

IDENTIFYING OTHER CURRENT LIABILITIES

LIABILITY	POINTS TO NOTE
CREDITORS Sums owed to suppliers for purchases.	Some purchases of goods or services used during the year may not have been paid for; amounts owed to suppliers are shown as creditors, which are usually due within the next 12 months.
TAXATION Amounts owed to tax authorities.	Tax on profits, tax on capital gains, and other taxes may not have been paid in full – especially if not legally required to be paid until later. Outstanding amounts are shown as current liabilities.
DIVIDENDS Monies payable to shareholders.	Dividends are typically paid twice a year, with the second (or final) dividend declared but not yet paid. This is a current liability since it will inevitably be payable within the next 12 months.
LEASING Sums owed to leasing and hire-purchase companies.	Amounts shown in current liabilities are only those that must be paid to the leasing or hire-purchase company within 12 months. Instalments due after that year are long-term liabilities.
ACCRUALS Payments owed to providers of goods and services.	General bills (such as for telephones and electricity), accounting fees, auditing costs, and so on will have been incurred but not yet paid for. These are all shown under the general title of accruals.
SHORT-TERM DEBT Sums payable to a bank or providers of finance.	A bank overdraft is a current liability, since it is strictly repayable on demand. A repayment towards long-term debt that must be made in the next 12 months is also a current liability.

RECOGNIZING LONG-TERM LIABILITIES

Amounts payable by a business more than one year from the balance sheet date are long-term liabilities. These are items such as long-term debts and loans, mortgages, and formalized borrowing instruments such as debentures. They may be more technical, as in the case of provisions, which are taken out of this year's profits to pay for something in a future period. The point of splitting liabilities into current and long-term groups is to see how comfortably the business can repay its immediate debt.

POINTS TO REMEMBER

● Liabilities are amounts owed by an organization because of transactions that have already taken place.

● In time, all long-term liabilities will become short-term liabilities, which will, in turn, have to be paid off.

● Any increase in debt should be for a good reason, whether to increase trading volumes or to acquire fixed assets.

ANALYZING SHAREHOLDERS' FUNDS

This part of the balance sheet shows the funds put into or left in an organization by its shareholders. It must therefore equal the total net assets, or balance sheet total. It is here that you can learn where the money invested in the balance sheet has come from.

47 Remember that the funds of shareholders are always at risk.

48 Look at retained reserves to discover past profitability.

LOOKING AT SHARE CAPITAL

Share capital is essentially the money that shareholders have put into the business, for no guaranteed return or guaranteed payment. If a company raises, say, £1 million of share capital, the share capital account and the bank account both increase by £1 million – all nicely in balance.

UNDERSTANDING RETAINED PROFIT

The second major source of shareholders' funds is retained profit. Calculated from the profit and loss account, this is essentially the cumulative retained profit made each year since the company started. Retained profit is usually the most important source (in terms of size) of continued funding of a business.

▼ **CALCULATING SHAREHOLDERS' FUNDS**
This part of the balance sheet looks at where the money has come from in a business and will typically consist of share capital, retained profit, and technical reserves.

The total equity and reserves must equal the balance sheet total of assets less liabilities

Shareholders' funds		
Share capital	220	120
Retained profit	301	287
Technical reserves	10	10
TOTAL SHAREHOLDERS' FUNDS	531	417

DEFINING TECHNICAL RESERVES

There are other items shown in this part of the balance sheet that are known as technical reserves. Two types that appear most frequently are share premium and revaluation reserve. A share premium is the result of a company selling shares for a higher price than their nominal value. For example, if a £1 share is sold for £5, then it has been sold at a premium of £4. This share premium is not strictly retained profit, because it has not been made in the course of trading, so it has to be shown separately under technical reserves. A revaluation reserve occurs when an organization revalues an asset (such as a property) to show its current value rather than its original cost. Again, this is not strictly retained profit since it is merely a revaluation and no profit has yet been realized.

▲ REVALUING ASSETS

Sometimes an organization chooses to show an asset, such as a building, at a higher current value rather than at its original cost, and the difference is shown in a revaluation reserve. This informs the reader of accounts that the profit exists but cannot be distributed because it is, as yet, unrealized.

LOOKING AT LINKING STATEMENTS

Although the principle is that the retained profit must equal the increase in the balance sheet, often there is so much information that a linking statement is needed to clarify the situation. This statement sets out recognized gains and losses, and movement in shareholders' funds, and it reconciles the profit and loss account to the balance sheet. In addition to listing the retained profit for the year, this statement may detail gains and losses in currency fluctuations on foreign assets, issuance of additional share capital, and other technical items. In essence, shareholders' funds show how much money shareholders have chosen to leave behind in the business, which is all at risk should the business fail.

CHECKING FOR CLARITY ▶

Ask an accountant to guide you through a linking statement, showing why shareholders' funds have increased in the year.

USING CASH FLOW STATEMENTS

The cash flow statement is key to understanding how well cash, which is the lifeblood of a business, is being managed. Give this statement the attention it deserves, since the profit and loss account and balance sheet can provide only a part of the picture.

49 Remember the adage that profits are vanity and cash is sanity.

50 Bear in mind that profits do not repay loans – only cash can do that.

CASH FLOW STATEMENT

Operating profit	63
Depreciation	45
Increase in stocks	– 23
Increase in debtors	– 85
Increase in creditors	– 27
OPERATING CASH FLOW	– 27
Interest paid	– 20
Dividends paid	– 10
Exceptional costs	– 10
Taxation	– 16
Capital expenditure	– 85
CASH FLOW BEFORE FINANCING	– 148

FINANCING		
Increase in overdraft	60	
Decrease in bank loan	– 15	
Decrease in mortgage	– 5	
Issue of share capital	100	140
MOVEMENT IN CASH		– 8

FOCUSING ON CASH

The third of the key financial statements, the cash flow statement, is practically the most important yet is often underused. When cash stops circulating, a business will die. The profit and loss account shows the profits made in the accounting period, but profits are not cash – and it is crucial to know how much actual cash has been received or paid out. The balance sheet shows the often large flows of investing activities, such as the purchase of fixed assets or the acquisition of a business, but it does not reveal whether the business has an excess (or lack of) cash. The cash flow statement links the other two key statements using cash as an objective, no-nonsense measure that is verifiable against the bank balance.

◀ **REVIEWING A CASH FLOW STATEMENT**
Starting with operating profit, the statement shows how cash has been generated or consumed. It reveals aspects of a business that are difficult to gauge from the profit and loss account alone.

Understanding the Principles

Cash flow statements generally follow a standard format and, while variations on the theme exist, similar principles are used worldwide in order to make the statement more useful and easily understood. The document is sectioned into meaningful blocks and subtotals, providing clear information on the cash movements within an organization's key activities. These include normal trading activities, interest and dividends, tax, investing activities, and financing. To understand the statement, you must know what is counted as cash. The generally accepted definition is that cash items are those to which an organization has immediate or one-day access, which means actual cash, bank accounts, and short-term deposits.

Cultural Differences

Two attempts have been made by different countries to quantify just what a statement based on the flows of cash should contain. The first is the Source and Application of Funds Statement, but this was unclear about what a flow of cash was, and has generally fallen out of favour. The second is a Cash Flow Statement, which more closely defines cash and produces an overall more meaningful document.

51 Manage your own working capital and control your cash aggressively.

52 Think of working capital as a sponge: it absorbs cash if left alone and releases it if squeezed.

Calculating Operating Cash Flow

The first and most important subtotal on the cash flow statement is operating cash flow, which shows how much is generated from simply trading. To calculate this, the operating profit (from the profit and loss account) must be adjusted. First, non-cash items, such as depreciation, which had already been deducted on the profit and loss, must be added back in. (Remember that depreciation is not – and never will be – a pile of cash.) Next, the working capital, or net current assets, from this and last year's balance sheet are adjusted, with the increase in stocks, debtors, and creditors being the difference between the two. If there is more stock now than a year ago, then cash must have been paid out. If debtors owe more, then they temporarily hold cash, so there is less in the business. If suppliers are owed more (because they haven't been paid), then the business temporarily has more cash.

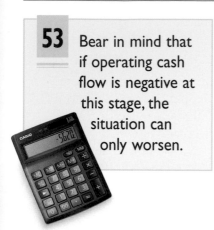

53 Bear in mind that if operating cash flow is negative at this stage, the situation can only worsen.

DETERMINING CASH FLOW BEFORE FINANCING

The subtotal of cash flow before financing shows how much the organization has either generated or will need to find to stay afloat. To calculate this, non-trading items such as interest, dividends, and tax must first be deducted or credited. Any interest paid or received in the year is shown, as are any dividends paid or received. The point is to reflect how much the organization is paying out simply to "service" its debt and share capital. Finally, taxation on business profits is deducted.

DETAILING CASH FOR CAPITAL EXPENDITURE

Once interest, dividends, and tax have been accounted for, then capital expenditure comes into the equation. Cash spent on purchasing, or received from the sale of, normal fixed assets is detailed here. If fixed assets are bought on hire purchase or leasing, then only the cash paid is shown. One-off items such as the purchase of a business are also shown. If an item is large compared to normal year-on-year cash flow and requires significant financing effort, this part of the statement reveals whether that item can be afforded or not.

54 Note that spending on fixed assets will often exceed profit.

Planning to open a new branch office, manager reviews cash flow statement and finds that cash is critically low

KEEPING UP ▶ WITH CASH FLOW
This illustration shows two possible outcomes to managing cash flow. A manager who looks only at profits may not even realize that there is virtually no cash in the business. A successful manager reviews the cash flow statement thoroughly before making any commitments and is able to prevent financial disaster.

Manager sees from profit and loss account that profits are up

MANAGING CASH FLOW

Controlling cash flow is management's prime financial task. It is critical that managers understand where cash flow comes from and how it is spent by an organization, since this can make the difference between financial success and disaster. When operating cash flow is negative, there are four levers that can be pulled to improve it: make more profit, decrease stock, decrease debtors, and increase creditors. These may not help, however, if an organization is expanding because growth inevitably means increasing sales, which results in larger debtors and stock, hence worse cash flow. This may be inescapable but must be recognized and planned for. Another key consideration is whether the annual dividend and interest bill is affordable. If not, does the funding of the organization need overhauling? Finally, buying certain assets may be entirely discretionary and should be carefully thought through before making commitments. Remember, cash is critical.

Prompt action to boost cash flow ensures that cash flow crisis is avoided

Manager postpones expansion and acts to collect cash from debtors

Manager fails to review cash flow statement

Manager goes ahead with expansion, runs out of cash, and the business fails

CALCULATING MOVEMENT

Two main sources of financing are debt (loans) and equity (share capital). Loans taken out or share capital issued are sources of cash; loans repaid or share capital repurchased are uses of cash. The difference between cash flow before financing and the subtotal of financing indicates the overall movement in cash for the year, which must agree with the difference between this and last year's cash in the balance sheet.

55 See that movement in cash and the bank account tally.

PRODUCING CASH FLOW FORECASTS

The forward-looking cash flow forecast is often forgotten because it is not required by law or regulations, yet it is an invaluable document. Use the forecast to help you predict cash flow in the future and keep an informed eye on your business.

56 Be aware that cash flow usually turns out to be worse than you plan for.

57 Remember to control capital spending properly.

58 Note that revenue and capital spending are often related.

ANTICIPATING PROBLEMS

Cash flow forecasting differs from cash flow statements in the perspective it adopts – it is forward- rather than backward-looking. Its purpose is to predict at what point the demands on an organization's cash resources become so great that cash is exhausted – whether from normal business demands or planned growth.

▼ **PRODUCING FORECASTS**
Involve colleagues regularly in forecasting cash flow. By planning in advance you can ensure you have the cash available for future commitments and solve problems before they arise.

Colleagues check timings of receipts are realistic, especially for new initiatives

Accountant ensures consistent assumptions about cash flow timings

Manager asks whether forecast capital spending plans are definite

USING A CASH FLOW FORECAST

Prepare a cash flow forecast from the profit and loss account and balance sheet. Working monthly, combine the anticipated amounts with cash flow timing predictions for each item of revenue and expenditure, remembering to include any likely one-off items. Then calculate the closing balance sheet, representing what is owed or owing from what you have not paid or received.

DO'S AND DON'TS

✔ **Do** be sensible about the timings of cash flows; they are often made more difficult by optimistic budgets.

✔ **Do** ask plenty of "What if?" questions about cash flows, should timings of significant amounts change.

✘ **Don't** assume that cash flow will not be a problem for you just because it has not been in the past.

✘ **Don't** presume that everyone will always keep to their terms about payments into or out of the organization.

▼ CREATING A CASH FLOW FORECAST

Extend the profit and loss account items and estimate the likely timings for each item. Add the predicted cash flow timings for each month to indicate cash surpluses or funding requirements.

Profit and loss account figures are divided into annual and monthly amounts

Timing of cash flow is estimated for the individual profit and loss account items

Actual cash receipts and payments are recorded for each month

PROFIT AND LOSS ACCOUNT			PREDICTION	CASH FLOW					
Item	Annual	Month	Payment	Jan	Feb	Mar	Apr	May	Jun
Sales	2,400	200	One month credit	0	200	200	200	200	200
Cost of goods sold	-1,800	-150	One month credit	0	-150	-150	-150	-150	-150
Office supplies	-48	-4	One month credit	0	-4	-4	-4	-4	-4
Rent	-24	-2	One month advance	-4	-2	-2	-2	-2	-2
Salaries and wages	-264	-22	Immediate	-22	-22	-22	-22	-22	-22
Selling and marketing	-36	-3	One month credit	0	-3	-3	-3	-3	-3
Delivery	-24	-2	One month credit	0	-2	-2	-2	-2	-2
Heat, light, and power	-12	-1	One month credit	0	-1	-1	-1	-1	-1
Interest payable	-24	-2	Immediate	-2	-2	-2	-2	-2	-2
			Monthly cash flow	-28	14	14	14	14	14
Profit	168	14	**Cumulative cash flow**	-28	-14	0	14	28	42

Annual profit is calculated by deducting expenditure from revenue

Monthly total for cash receipts and payments is calculated

Cumulative cash flow is calculated, showing actual money in the bank

MEASURING PERFORMANCE

Ratios are essential tools for interpreting the messages behind lines of figures. Learn how to use ratios and how to translate supplementary reports for a clear view of business performance.

UNDERSTANDING RATIOS

A ratio is calculated by dividing one figure by another. Used logically and consistently, performance ratios can provide important indicators and highlight trends. Understand where ratios are useful and what they can reveal about performance.

> **59** Analyze profitability first, closely followed by asset efficiency.

> **60** Always look at performance ratios in the context of the business as a whole.

USING RATIOS

Ratios are most useful when produced and analyzed regularly to help identify important trends in areas such as cash and profit management. They can also be used to help make comparisons year-on-year and between organizations. However, since no two businesses are alike, this is fraught with practical difficulties. There are many ways of calculating ratios and there is no one correct method. Avoid relying on ratios alone to provide a full answer as to why one organization is performing better than another – you must examine the business as a whole.

61 Obtain sets of comparative ratios for your business.

62 Show ratio results graphically to help you spot trends.

ANALYZING EFFECTIVELY

When interpreting accounts, most people are interested in four key areas: profitability, efficiency, financing, and liquidity. Profitability measures how much income is made from sales, and is assessed by analyzing the profit and loss account; efficiency measures the use to which assets are put; financing shows the degree and affordability of funding; and liquidity measures whether there is sufficient cash to continue operating. Efficiency, financing, and liquidity can be evaluated by analyzing the balance sheet.

MEASURING ROCE

The most important overall ratio for measuring performance is called Return on Capital Employed (ROCE). This reveals how much profit is being made on the money invested in the business and is a key measure of how well management is doing its job. ROCE is calculated by dividing the operating profit by the capital employed (shareholders' funds plus long-term liabilities on the balance sheet). The rate of return should be higher than a shareholder could make by depositing their funds elsewhere, such as in a bank or building society. The ROCE also needs to be higher than the cost of borrowings, or a business will be paying more in interest than it makes on the money borrowed.

DO'S AND DON'TS

✔ Do use ratios that are appropriate to the nature, type, and size of the organization under scrutiny.

✔ Do take a balanced and holistic view of ratio analysis.

✘ Don't be hidebound and inflexible in your choice of ratios for assessing performance.

✘ Don't be too accurate about the results you calculate from accounting figures.

USING ROCE TO ASSESS YOUR PERFORMANCE

Calculate your organization's ROCE

Assess whether your ROCE ratio is adequate for shareholders

Check whether this period's ROCE has improved on the last

Check your ROCE against that of your competitors

To boost ROCE, increase profit and reduce capital employed

ANALYZING A PROFIT AND LOSS ACCOUNT

*L*ine-by-line analysis of the profit and loss account provides a valuable insight into business performance. Find out what the figures really mean using a series of measures that show how profits are being utilized and determine whether they can be improved.

63 Always perform a quick top to bottom line review of profits.

64 Assess revenues and expenditures as a percentage of sales.

USING COMMON SIZING ▼
Express each line of the profit and loss account as a percentage of the top line – sales. Do this particularly for gross profit, total operating expenses, operating profit, and retained profit.

EXAMINING KEY LINES

Start by taking an overview. First, look at the top line of sales: are figures up or down on last year, and is any increase or decrease reflected in the retained profit on the bottom line? If not, examine the statement to ascertain where the profits have gone to. Use common sense, look for obvious trends, and watch for factors that may affect your analysis; has the accounting period been a long one, for example? Then, to make year-on-year or industry comparisons easier, calculate each of the key lines as a percentage of sales. Known as common sizing, this strips out the effects of both volume and size.

Salaries and wages as a percentage of sales has increased; find out why and take corrective action

65 Concentrate on operating profit, but also note what follows.

PROFIT AND LOSS ACCOUNT
(INCLUDING RATIOS)

	CURRENT PERIOD	%	PREVIOUS PERIOD	%
Sales	2,200	100.0	2,050	100.0
Cost of sales	1,700	77.3	1,600	78.0
GROSS PROFIT	500	22.7	450	22.0
OPERATING EXPENSES				
Office supplies	46	2.1	42	2.0
Bad debt charges	24	1.1	20	1.0
Rent	15	0.7	14	0.7
Salaries and wages	245	11.1	194	9.5
Selling and marketing	30	1.4	22	1.1
	20	0.9	18	0.9

ANALYZING FIGURES ▼

Calculate ratios for interest payable, taxation, and dividends. Compare the current accounting period figures with the previous period to ascertain whether a business's health has improved or deteriorated, and pinpoint reasons why.

ASSESSING AFFORDABILITY

Interest payable, taxation, and dividends are not directly related to trading performance, but how easily an organization can afford to pay them is a key measure of its health. Assess the affordability of these items using specific ratios. First, divide operating profit by interest payable to work out how many times an organization could afford to pay that amount of interest (interest cover). Use the same method (PAT divided by dividends) to assess the affordability of dividends. Finally, divide taxation by profit before tax to give the apparent tax charge as a percentage, which should approximate to the official tax rate on business profits. Investigate any glaring discrepancies.

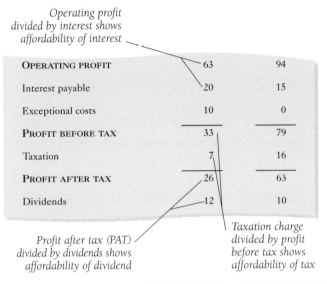

Operating profit divided by interest shows affordability of interest

OPERATING PROFIT	63	94
Interest payable	20	15
Exceptional costs	10	0
PROFIT BEFORE TAX	33	79
Taxation	7	16
PROFIT AFTER TAX	26	63
Dividends	12	10

Profit after tax (PAT) divided by dividends shows affordability of dividend

Taxation charge divided by profit before tax shows affordability of tax

---

EVALUATING PROFIT IMPROVEMENT METHODS

To boost profits, a well-run organization may use a profit improvement checklist. This is an accepted list of things to do in order of preference. Look at the following areas of the profit and loss account to gauge whether an organization has been putting this checklist into practice:

● Has it increased the selling price of products or services? (This could mean stopping any discounts, which would have the same effect.)

● Has it reduced the cost of sales (COS)?

(This could involve either buying in more effectively or introducing more efficient business processes.)

● Has gross profit improved? (This would be the effect of taking both steps above.)

● Has volume increased? (An efficient organization would take this step only after assessing the profitability of its products and services to decide which items make a real profit.)

● Have selling, general, and administration (SG&A) costs been reduced?

READING A BALANCE SHEET

*A*nother way of improving business
performance is to reduce the amount
of capital tied up in the balance sheet and
increase the uses to which it is being put.
Examine the balance sheet thoroughly to
gain some clear measures of efficiency.

66 Note that figures
in a balance sheet
may be seasonal or
unrepresentative.

67 Look at the
notes to accounts
to find the right
figures to use.

GAUGING EFFICIENCY

Assess the overall efficiency of a business by
measuring the number of times its assets (you can
use fixed, current, or total assets) divide into the
top line of sales. This is called asset turn and it
shows whether more sales are being made with
the same number of assets. On its own the ratio is
meaningless but, when compared to the asset turn
of previous years, it can indicate whether a
business is becoming more, or less, efficient.

EVALUATING CASH MANAGEMENT

The amount of time that stock is held before being
sold (stock days), how long customers take to pay
(debtor days), and how long a business takes to pay
its suppliers (creditor days) are classic efficiency
measures. Using the stock, debtor, and
creditor figures for the end of the
current accounting period, calculate
the number of working capital days.
Then look for period-on-period
trends and examine how the figures
compare against the industry average.
Too many working capital days can
cause a cash crisis; too few mean that
a business cannot operate properly.

*Stock divided
by COS x 365
gives stock days*

*Debtors divided
by sales x 365
gives debtor days*

*Creditors divided
by COS x 365
gives creditor
days*

▼CALCULATING WORKING CAPITAL RATIOS

*To calculate working capital days, use the
balance sheet figures and the two lines of
sales and cost of sales on the profit and loss.*

BALANCE SHEET

	CURRENT PERIOD	PREVIOUS PERIOD
FIXED ASSETS		
Tangible	170	150
Intangible	10	10
Investments	5	5
TOTAL FIXED ASSETS	185	165
CURRENT ASSETS		
Stock	208	185
Debtors	337	254
Other	18	16
Cash	2	10
TOTAL CURRENT ASSETS	565	465
CURRENT LIABILITIES		
Creditors	80	109
Accrue	20	18
Divide	12	10
Taxati		
Overd		

PROFIT AND LOSS ACCOUNT

	CURRENT PERIOD	PREVIOUS PERIOD
Sales	2,200	2,050
Cost of sales	1,700	1,600
GROSS PROFIT	500	450

68 Calculate the cost effect of one extra day of debtors.

▼ USING BALANCE SHEET RATIOS
The key balance sheet ratios of fixed asset turn, working capital days (stock, debtors, and creditors), and current and quick ratios are calculated to measure efficiency.

BALANCE SHEET RATIOS

	CURRENT PERIOD	PREVIOUS PERIOD
FIXED ASSET TURN	11.9	12.4
Stock days	44.7	42.2
Debtor days	55.9	45.2
Creditor days	(17.2)	(24.9)
TOTAL	83.4	62.5
CURRENT RATIO	3.16	3.04
QUICK RATIO	2.00	1.83

Deleting stock from current assets in the numerator will reduce the ratio, but it will still be comfortably more than 1

Dividing current assets by current liabilities gives a ratio comfortably more than the target of 1

ASSESSING FINANCING

Lenders and investors in particular like to assess how long-term financing is structured, since an organization that borrows heavily is riskier than one that has borrowed little. The key ratio used is known as debt to equity, or gearing. To calculate this, divide long-term liabilities by total shareholders' funds plus long-term liabilities, expressed as a percentage. For example, if long-term debt is £70 and shareholders' funds £30, gearing is 70 per cent. There is no target figure here; instead closely monitor trends.

EXAMINING SOLVENCY

To assess whether an organization has enough money to cover its debts, or is liquid, there are two commonly used measures: the current ratio and the quick ratio (or acid test). To calculate the current ratio, divide current assets by current liabilities. Most textbooks suggest that the target for this ratio should be at least 1 or, in other words, that current assets should be greater than current liabilities. To calculate the acid text, divide current assets less stock by current liabilities, on the grounds that stock will not convert to cash quickly. When using these ratios, remember that businesses showing a ratio of less than 1 are not always a cause for concern. For a cash retailer, for example, nil debtors, low stock, and high creditors equal efficiency, not inefficiency, as such ratios might suggest.

69 Remember that the popular current ratio has its limitations.

70 Assess whether a business is properly financed and structured.

UNDERSTANDING INVESTORS' RATIOS

The world of the stock exchange and external investors uses its own ratios to determine the viability of a business. These hard-nosed measures can be very revealing, so learn how to assess accounts from an outsider's point of view.

71 Note that investors focus on performance within industry sectors.

72 As with all financial analysis, always look at more than one ratio or measure.

DETERMINING WORTH

A stock exchange index is a list of the largest quoted companies on the stock market as measured by their overall worth, or market capitalization. Whether you work for a quoted company or want to know how competitors, customers, or suppliers are performing, market capitalization gives a crude estimate of a company's worth in the marketplace.

CALCULATING MARKET CAPITALIZATION

Market capitalization is calculated by multiplying the number of shares that the company has issued (a finite, known figure) by the share price (a fluctuating figure). Share prices are irrelevant on one level because the price at which they are traded will not affect a firm's daily production or selling routines. However, the market's perceived worth of a company may well affect its ability to borrow or raise more funds from the investment community.

◀ **LEADING THE MARKET**
Companies in stock markets are ranked according to their total worth, with the highest valued businesses forming that country's stock market index (such as the Dow, FTSE, DAX, and CAC).

LOOKING AT PROSPECTS

The price earnings (PE) ratio provides a good indication as to how the market views a business's prospects. To arrive at this ratio, first calculate earnings per share (the profit that each share has generated) by dividing profit after tax (from the profit and loss account) by the number of shares that have been issued. Then divide the market price per share by earnings per share to give the PE ratio, which reveals how a share is currently valued compared to the profits that it made last year. A high PE ratio is a sign of confidence in a company; a low PE ratio indicates the reverse.

73 Pay particular attention to what the price earnings ratio tells you.

▼ **WATCHING THE FIGURES**
Investors and interested parties use the financial press's figures of corporate performance to see how key organizations are performing and to make comparisons between similar business types.

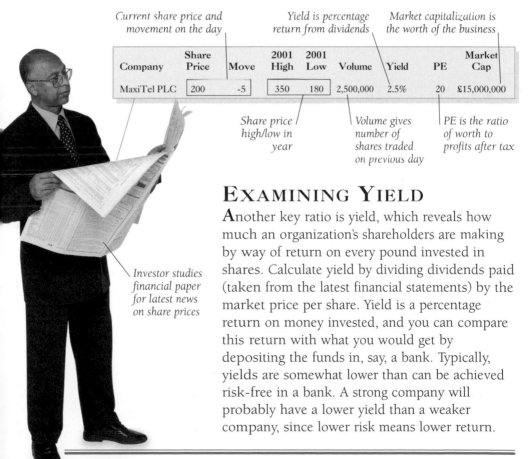

Current share price and movement on the day

Yield is percentage return from dividends

Market capitalization is the worth of the business

Company	Share Price	Move	2001 High	2001 Low	Volume	Yield	PE	Market Cap
MaxiTel PLC	200	-5	350	180	2,500,000	2.5%	20	£15,000,000

Share price high/low in year

Volume gives number of shares traded on previous day

PE is the ratio of worth to profits after tax

Investor studies financial paper for latest news on share prices

EXAMINING YIELD

Another key ratio is yield, which reveals how much an organization's shareholders are making by way of return on every pound invested in shares. Calculate yield by dividing dividends paid (taken from the latest financial statements) by the market price per share. Yield is a percentage return on money invested, and you can compare this return with what you would get by depositing the funds in, say, a bank. Typically, yields are somewhat lower than can be achieved risk-free in a bank. A strong company will probably have a lower yield than a weaker company, since lower risk means lower return.

GATHERING MORE INFORMATION

*I*n *addition to the key statements, large organizations disclose a wealth of extra information, either voluntarily or because they are legally obliged to do so. Know where to look for these details and what you can glean from them.*

74 Get to know what is contained in a published report and accounts.

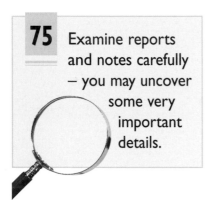

75 Examine reports and notes carefully – you may uncover some very important details.

INTERPRETING AUDITORS' CODE

The role of auditors is to report on whether financial statements have been properly prepared in accordance with company law and GAAP. Rather than stating that accounts are correct, however, they choose such phrases as "give a true and fair view" or "fairly represent", which mean that these accounts are said to be "unqualified", or clean. Watch out for "qualified" opinions, as these point to areas where there is either uncertainty or, more worryingly, disagreement.

UNDERSTANDING QUALIFIED PHRASES

PHRASE	EXAMPLE	MEANING
"SUBJECT TO"	"Subject to continuing support from its bankers…"	Without the bank's support, the business will fail.
"EXCEPT FOR"	"Except for the valuation of certain stock items…"	There has been a fundamental disagreement between the auditor and management about a matter.
"DO NOT"	"The accounts do not…"	The accounts have not been properly prepared.

READING THE DIRECTORS' REPORT

When annual accounts are published, a company's directors often comment on the results. Since there are strict laws on disclosure, whatever is said must be objective rather than propaganda-led. Pay attention to the section on salaries (companies today are sensitive about what they pay their directors, since salaries must be seen to be commensurate with overall corporate performance) and look at details on share options. Both sections provide clues as to how well the directors think that they and the company have done in the year.

76 The larger the organization, the greater the scope for information.

COMPARING REPORTS ▶

In their report, directors generally outline how they expect the organization to perform in the coming year. Most will be optimistic to reassure shareholders, but watch for cautious qualifications or predictions of a "tough year ahead".

77 Read the reviews by key directors for optimism about prospects.

78 Dig into the notes for interesting further details and information.

FOCUSING ON NOTES TO ACCOUNTS

Copious notes are attached to the main financial statements of balance sheet, profit and loss account, cash flow, recognized gains and losses, and movement in shareholders' funds. It is important to read these in conjunction with the actual statements. While the notes to accounts may appear daunting at first, persevere with them because they are an integral part of the message and must be understood. Domestic and housekeeping items, such as important dates for the diary and a timetable of the annual general meeting and immediate future events, are also to be found in the notes.

BROADENING YOUR KNOWLEDGE

The complexity of accounting means that "grey" areas abound. Learn where anomalies arise, how accountants deal with them, and how to improve the quality of your own internal accounts.

EXPLORING INTERNATIONAL ISSUES

Many organizations today operate on an international level, yet, despite increasing globalization, accounting practices and formats still differ significantly around the world. Understand the differences to help you pinpoint where problems can arise.

79 Always be clear about on which rules the accounts are based.

80 Accept that profits and assets can vary significantly between countries.

HIGHLIGHTING PROBLEMS

Accounting measurements are dependent on the rules of individual countries, and this is often a hindrance to international business transactions. Investors must negotiate cross-border obstacles, multinationals face differences in profits concepts and taxation, and governments creating trading blocks face unequal opportunities and economic distortions. As a result, efforts are being made to reduce differences through harmonization.

DEFINING DIFFERENCES

Because countries have different legal systems, taxation regimes, historical influences, and business practices, their accounting systems are also different. Continental Europe's strong legal framework of accounting plans and commercial codes contrasts with the UK and US combination of legal principles and a separate set of accounting rules. Some countries require the figures in financial accounts to be the same as for tax purposes, while in other countries no connection is needed. Political and historical factors also play their part, with much of the world influenced by the UK system. The need for open information for shareholders has ensured that appropriate financial statements have evolved.

81 Get to know the key international differences that affect you.

▼ EVALUATING SYSTEMS

Countries influenced by the UK and the US tend to have a more pragmatic approach to accounting, the onus being to inform shareholders. In other parts of Europe and in Japan, strict taxation and legislation rule out any subjectivity or deviation, so that accounts are less useful and informative to interested outsiders.

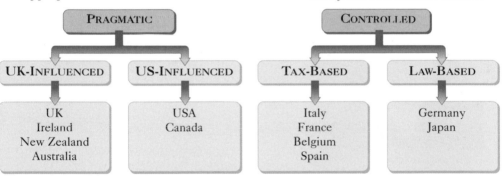

PRAGMATIC		CONTROLLED	
UK-INFLUENCED	US-INFLUENCED	TAX-BASED	LAW-BASED
UK Ireland New Zealand Australia	USA Canada	Italy France Belgium Spain	Germany Japan

HARMONIZING ACCOUNTS

Since accounting systems around the world measure items such as assets and profits differently, international comparison and analysis are difficult. As a result, there has been mounting pressure to harmonize accounting. For ten years, an international accounting body has been working to produce International Accounting Standards (IAS). These now provide the bench-mark worldwide and are used by many multi-nationals, some of which even prepare two versions of accounts. One version will comply with General Accepted Accounting Principles of the country in which the organization is based, and another will be in accordance with IAS. The EU is a useful example where law-based harmonization has taken place but no GAAP convergence has occurred.

LOOKING AT COMMON PROBLEMS

Accounting is technical by nature and there are many complex issues facing accountants. As a manager, there is little to gain from poring over technical details, but it is useful to know where problems can occur and how they can be dealt with.

82 Grasp the essentials, not the details, of technical accounting.

83 When dealing with unfamiliar technical issues, seek advice from an expert.

LISTING LEASED ASSETS

One type of fixed asset that causes controversy is a leased asset. This is an asset that a business uses for three years or more but that it does not legally own (unlike all other fixed assets). At some point in the future, annual lease costs may be substantial, but organizations prefer to omit this liability from their accounts to avoid giving the impression that they are borrowing more now. Accountants prefer to treat a leased asset as if it were owned in order to give a fairer picture. The debt can then be shown on the balance sheet for all to see.

CONTROVERSIAL INTANGIBLE ASSETS

Goodwill and brands can cause controversy (see pp.514–515), and other intangibles can do the same:

● Patent (an object or process patented by someone else and bought by a company). The amount paid for the patent is written off over the period of time for which it has been acquired.

● Know how (similar to a patent but the

object or process purchased may not have been formally registered).

● Copyright and intellectual property, typically on music and books.

● Research and development. Costs are taken out of the profit and loss account and shown as an asset in the balance sheet. If this is the case, current profits and assets may be overstated.

MAKING PROVISIONS

When the cost of a future event, such as a reorganization, will seriously hit profits, an appropriate figure must be deducted from the current year's profits. This is known as making a provision and is a way of alerting users of accounts to what lies ahead for the organization. If an impending event may potentially hit profits (perhaps there is a threat of legal action, for example), it is often not included on the financial statements but should be noted in the accounts as a contingent liability. Finally, if an event with significant financial impact should occur between the balance sheet date and the date of signing off accounts, this must also be noted.

ACCOUNTING FOR GROUPS

Gleaning useful information from the accounts of a group of companies, where some businesses are controlled by others, can be a difficult exercise. Accounts should give a picture of the whole business entity, but that picture may be blurred if, for example, the holding company has been juggling with the figures of one of its subsidiaries. As a manager, you will probably be interested in the performance of other companies in your group, as well as in the group's performance as a whole. Accounts of groups of companies are sometimes called "consolidated" accounts.

POINTS TO REMEMBER

- You should try to form an opinion on the financial health of an organization.
- Provisions have traditionally been devices for "smoothing out" the fluctuations in profits.
- It helps to appreciate the principal accounting logic behind each technical treatment.

▼ UNDERSTANDING GROUP ACCOUNTS

Subsidiary companies produce their own accounts, which are incorporated into those of the parent company to give more meaningful results for the group as a whole.

Parent company prepares the accounts for the entire group

GROUP HEAD OFFICE

Company directors pass individual sets of accounts to the parent company

Individual company prepares its own accounts separately

COMPANY A   **COMPANY B**   **COMPANY C**

RECOGNIZING CREATIVE ACCOUNTING

An accountant is expected to present a company's figures in the best possible light, while being accurate and truthful at all times. Learn to recognize when the figures are being manipulated, since this is a sure sign of creative accounting at work.

84 Recognize that one person's smoothing is another's creative accounting.

85 Check if creative accounting is increasing or suppressing profits.

WHY HIDE THE TRUTH?

Every organization has its own agenda for creative accounting: the larger company wants to report bigger profits, the smaller to pay less tax. Being creative need not involve adjusting figures: merely choosing an accounting date to paint a rosy picture, extending an accounting period to bolster profits or confuse the picture, or failing to file accounts at all are popular ways of hiding the truth.

REVIEWING PROFITS

On the profit and loss account, watch for a high number of invoices at the year-end, which is a method of boosting profits. Similarly, postponing invoicing until the start of the new accounting period ensures that tax is payable later. Depending upon whether a business has had a good or bad year, it may lower income by recognizing too many costs, or raise it by not recognizing enough. To determine disproportionate activity, look at the first month of the next accounting period: discrepancies will usually be compensated for here.

▼ SMOOTHING THE RIDE
Making profits is unlikely to be a smooth process, so a creative accountant will smooth out peaks and troughs to show a steady, well-managed line of profitability.

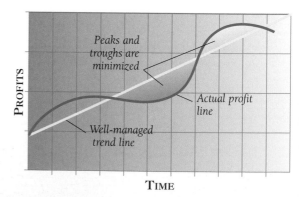

Peaks and troughs are minimized

Actual profit line

Well-managed trend line

PROFITS

TIME

COOKING BOOKS ▶

Accounts can be based on books and records that might range from being lightly cooked to completely burned. But the task of the reader to distinguish between what is acceptable and what is simply going a little too far will always be difficult, since creatively produced accounts will always look normal on the surface to the untrained eye. Always seek technical advice if you suspect that anything is not right with the figures.

CASE STUDY

Happy Nappies wanted to increase its profits, and decided to use some typical creative accounting techniques. First, it recognized revenue on sales earlier: on confirmation of order rather than on delivery of goods, thereby increasing sales revenue. Second, it reduced costs by taking out of the profit and loss account expenses relating to a new factory and adding them to the factory's costs – again

increasing profits and the balance sheet. Third, it extended the depreciation lives on certain high-value assets, again increasing profits and the balance sheet. Finally, it changed the method for translating the value of foreign-located assets into domestic currency, again manipulating the value of its balance sheet. Not all of these treatments are within the spirit of accounting law and practice, but they are commonplace nevertheless.

TAKING STOCK

On the balance sheet, the first item to watch is stock. If its value is too high, stock on the balance sheet (and profits) will be too high. Look at creditors as well: managing working capital efficiently involves stretching creditors (suppliers), but within reason. Payment of bills may be postponed before the year-end, increasing creditors and giving an impression of a good relationship with suppliers who are willing to extend credit. Check the first day of the next accounting period to see whether large cheques are subsequently despatched to suppliers.

> **86** Remember that the balance sheet and profit and loss move together.

▼ CHECKING THE BALANCE

Remember the principle that when profits increase, so does the balance sheet. Think of two ends of a dumb-bell moving in tandem, so that what affects one statement will also affect the other.

| PROFIT AND LOSS | BALANCE SHEET |

Undervaluing closing stock results in higher cost of sales and lower profits

Undervaluing closing stock gives a lower balance sheet stock amount

Benefiting from Management Accounts

T he fact that management accounts need not follow any rules makes them usefully flexible but more open to error. Recognize the uses and drawbacks of internal accounts and how you, as a manager, can improve the information they contain.

87 Remember that management accounts lack standardized rules.

88 Understand the purpose and use of management accounts.

Understanding Management Accounts
Prepared and distributed internally within an organization, management accounts are governed by the needs of managers. They are used to help keep control of, and make decisions regarding, the everyday running of a business. As a result, they often contain more than mere financial information. They generally focus on four main areas: past score-keeping, present problem-solving, present controlling, and future planning.

Comparing External and Internal Accounts

External Accounts	Internal Accounts
Are published externally and available for the public.	Are distributed internally within an organization and kept confidential.
Must conform to legal requirements and GAAP principles.	Are not bound by any rules or regulations, and may follow any format.
Are generally published once or twice a year and look backwards at the past year's results.	Are produced on a regular basis and focus both on previous and future periods' results.
Reflect the financial reality of what has happened in an organization.	Provide a means of controlling the financial side of an organization now and into the future.

DRAWING CONCLUSIONS

A striking feature of management accounting is that, having been liberated from the usual accounting format strait-jacket, endless different layouts and formats can be used. Unfortunately, because there is no one correct way of producing these accounts, there is considerable room for error. But how can you gauge the accuracy of your management accounts? A useful exercise is to attempt to reconcile the internal figures to the external financial statements, since the external ones will inevitably be more accurate. If internal accounts differ seriously from the external statements, there is cause for concern.

89 Try to reconcile internal to external accounts.

90 Examine your company's internal accounts package.

▼ **INFORMING MANAGERS**
The content of management accounts should reflect what managers want them to show, namely how well the business has performed according to plan, and what corrective action, if any, should be taken.

The current month's actual figures are compared to the budget

The year to date is perhaps a better indicator of long-term trends

MANAGEMENT ACCOUNTS FOR AUGUST

ITEM	MONTH				YEAR TO DATE				FULL YEAR
	ACTUAL £	BUDGET £	VARIANCE £	%	ACTUAL £	BUDGET £	VARIANCE £	%	FORECAST
Sales	195	200	-5	-3	1,520	1,600	-80	-5	2,300
Cost of sales	-150	-150	0	0	1,190	-1,200	10	1	-1,770
Office supplies	-5	-4	-1	-15	-35	-32	-3	-9	-53
Rent	-2	-2	0	0	-16	-16	0	0	-24
Salaries and wages	-21	-22	1	5	-166	-176	10	6	-250
Selling and marketing	-4	-3	-1	-33	-30	-24	-6	-25	-40
Delivery	-2	-2	0	0	-18	-16	-2	-13	-27
Heat, light, and power	-1	-1	0	0	-8	-8	0	0	-12
Interest payable	-2	-2	0	0	-16	-16	0	0	-24
PROFIT	8	14	-6	-43	41	112	-71	-63	100

Actual results are compared to budget and expressed as a variance

Variance is also expressed as a percentage

A forecast is made for the full year's results

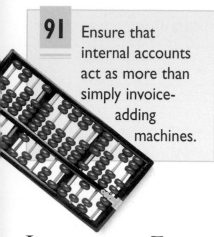

91
Ensure that internal accounts act as more than simply invoice-adding machines.

ASSESSING QUALITY

The quality of management accounting varies considerably. Even large, successful organizations can produce poor management accounts. Yet it is vital for managers to have financial documents in excellent user-friendly shape. Your accountant is bound to feel happier giving you a traditional profit and loss account – it is, after all, what he is used to. But this will not always contain the information you need to help you to manage your business into the future. If your management accounts are sub-standard, take steps to improve them.

IMPROVING EFFECTIVENESS

As a manager, it is important to take a more enlightened view as to how well your company is performing. This involves moving away from accountant-dominated management accounts towards those that are tailored specifically for you. Think of the quality of management accounts as a spectrum. At one end of the spectrum are traditional accounting statements, midway along are accounts containing targeted management information, and at the opposite end are manager-led accounts containing indicators tailored specifically to your particular needs. Make sure that your organization is evolving in the right direction.

92
Take responsibility to improve management information.

Manager looks for practical measures that will help him in the future

Accountant suggests showing information graphically for greater clarity

ASKING FOR ▶ INFORMATION
Ask your accountant what information is available internally that will help you in your role as manager, and discuss ways of presenting that information to make it easy for you to use.

USING PERFORMANCE INDICATORS

To ensure that the information you receive from accountants is valuable, consider using a set of measures known as key performance indicators (KPIs). These can be whatever you want them to be, provided that they are important to you and your organization. Generally, KPIs will include a financial component in their calculation, but this may not always be the case. Typical KPIs could be made up of the following: sales per employee, cost of sales per customer, marketing costs per new customer, labour cost per pound of sales revenue, and percentage of leads converted into sales. Often KPIs can lead on to league tables of performance internally.

▼ BRAINSTORMING MEASURES

Sit down with your fellow managers and decide which indicators would be most valuable in helping you to monitor and improve your performance.

Manager invites group to make suggestions for appropriate performance indicators

POINTS TO REMEMBER

- Your traditional financial accounting information should be up to date and bullet-proof.
- The measures you take should be meaningful to you in your role.
- Developing a package of easy-to-obtain management information with your accountant will help you manage your department.

93 Consider using scorecard-type performance measures.

TAKING A HOLISTIC APPROACH

Just as some say that a business should be measured on more than its financial results, it is also necessary to use more than one performance indicator. A popular management information tool, the balanced business score-card sets out the following four cornerstones for measuring performance holistically:

- Customers: Are we pleasing them? Are they coming back? What is our market share?
- Internal business processes: How can we improve processes to serve customers better?
- Learning and growth: Are we equipped to deal with customer and business-process demands?
- Financials: How is the organization faring financially? The score-card suggests that if the first three aspects are right, this will be, too.

MAKING FUTURE FINANCIAL DECISIONS

For a business to succeed, it must focus on using accounting concepts and techniques that look to the future. Set an example by basing your calculations on the right costs and using simple but effective tools for sound financial decision-making.

94 Remember that future-looking decisions require new financial skills.

95 Accept that future-looking decisions of most companies are flawed.

ADOPTING A NEW MINDSET

To make the right accounting decisions for the future, you need to rethink the way that you look at figures. Rather than rely on the backwards-looking perspective of the past, accountants, organizations, and managers must learn to adopt a new, forward-looking mindset. Traditional accounting uses historic costs and bases all analysis on those figures. However, when looking at decisions into the future, simply adding up the figures will not give the right answer.

COMPARING PAST AND FUTURE ACCOUNTING NEEDS

PAST	FUTURE
Traditional accounting uses historic costs and what has happened in the past.	Future decisions ignore sunk costs and what has already happened.
Traditional decision-making uses the concepts of profit and return on assets.	Future decisions use the concepts of incremental cost and opportunity cost.
Traditional measurement treats all money as being of the same value – whenever it arises.	Future decision-making looks at discounted cash flows rather than simple profits.
Historic accounting arrives at a simple result of pounds profit.	Future-looking decision-making compares projects and the option of doing nothing.

IGNORING SUNK COSTS

Getting the costs right is paramount to correct decision-making. A golden rule is to always ignore "sunk" costs, or those that have already been paid and cannot be recovered – hence sunk. Although someone will try to allocate blame for what has been spent, you should reject it as a cost when assessing whether to go ahead with spending in future. How often do you hear, "We have to go ahead because of all the money spent so far"? This is a common yet potentially calamitous approach.

96 Compare the cost of doing a project with the cost of doing nothing.

FOCUSING ON INCREMENTAL COSTS

Costs that are incremental are those that increase or decrease – the point is that they do in fact change – as a direct result of something taking place, hence the term incremental. If a project uses two people for a month and there are none available internally, then you will have to buy in people from outside; this is a true incremental cost. If, however, people are available internally and you use them, there is no incremental cost to the business as a whole, so these are not relevant costs. The rule is to ignore irrelevant costs and count only incremental costs.

97 Only costs that are incremental to a company as a whole are relevant.

▼ COUNTING COSTS
There are three golden rules to follow when considering which costs should be taken into account to help you make a decision on future spending: ignore sunk costs, disregard irrelevant costs, and count only incremental costs.

Money spent on hiring Tom to conduct market research could not be recovered

Alice was asked to take over the project as well as continue with her own projects

Peter was recruited from outside the organization to finish the project

PROJECT

SUNK COST　　　　**IRRELEVANT COST**　　　　**INCREMENTAL COST**

98
Ask your accountant what the cost of money is to your company.

99
Be aware that future cash flow predictions need not be accurate.

USING SIMPLE MEASURES

Once the costs are right, consider whether the outlay will be worthwhile using measures known as accounting rate of return and the pay-back period. To calculate the rate of return, simply add up all the figures and express them as a percentage. For example, an outlay of £1,000 with returns of £400 for the next three years gives a profit of £200, or a return of 20 per cent (about 6 per cent per annum) on the initial investment. Then assess the amount of time taken to recover the initial outlay – the pay-back period – which in this case is two-and-a-half years. Acceptable pay-back periods vary from six months to several years, depending on your organization and its view of the future.

APPLYING DISCOUNTING

When making decisions about the future, it is essential to recognize the time value of money. The example of a £1,000 outlay providing returns of £400 per year over the next three years is misleading, since the £400 will be worth a different amount in the first, second, and third year. To add together future sums of money fairly, you must first discount a future sum back to its value today, or "present value". Assuming a 10 per cent interest rate, £1 in one year's time is worth only 91p today (91p plus 10 per cent equals £1). The value today of 91p in one year's time is about 83p. Multiplying cash flow by the discount factor gives the discounted cash flow, or DCF, and the sum of them is called the net present value, or NPV.

▼ CALCULATING DISCOUNTED CASH FLOW
Multiply the amount of the cash flow by the discount factor to give discounted cash flow. Add down to give the sum of all the discounted cash flows, or net present value (NPV). Normally, a project will be undertaken if its NPV is positive.

Cash outflows typically happen at time 0; inflows occur annually thereafter

Total anticipated future cash flows are estimated

Discount factor will typically be around 10 per cent

TIME	CASH FLOW	9% DISCOUNT FACTOR	DISCOUNTED CASH FLOW
0	£–1,000	1.00	£–1,000
1	400	0.92	368
2	400	0.84	336
3	400	0.77	308
TOTAL	£200		£12

Sum of all the discounted cash flows gives the NPV

AVOIDING PITFALLS

There are some drawbacks to be aware of when using discounted cash flow:

- Timescale: for how many years should a project run? (The longer it runs, the better it will look.)
- Accuracy: predicting future events will always be difficult and subjective,

especially when projected several years.

- Significant figures: keep it simple and do not try to get too much unrealistic accuracy into predictions.
- Cost of money: use actual cost, average cost to the organization, or even a "hurdle" rate in order to sleep at night.

USING A HIGHER FACTOR

Applying a higher discount factor will make future cash flows more attractive and a project appear more viable. There will be a point (or discount factor) for a project where the NPV is £0. The discount factor that gives a NPV of £0 is called the "internal rate of return", or IRR, and is approximately the project's inherent profitability. NPV and IRR both point to the same conclusion, but many people prefer the easily compared IRR because it is expressed as a percentage.

▼ USING INTERNAL RATE OF RETURN

A 9 per cent discount factor gives an overall project NPV that is just positive. A higher discount factor will give lesser weighting to future cash flows, so the figures are reworked using a discount factor of 9.7 per cent. This factor gives a NPV of £0, which is the IRR of the project, or its inherent profitability.

100 Use spreadsheets to check your calculations when discounting.

101 Remember your decision is only as good as your estimated figures.

Timescale same as for previous example

Individual undiscounted cash flow amounts are unchanged

Since the NPV was positive at 9 per cent, a higher factor is used

TIME	CASH FLOW	9.7% DISCOUNT FACTOR	DISCOUNTED CASH FLOW
0	£–1,000	1.00	£–1,000
1	400	0.91	364
2	400	0.83	332
3	400	0.76	304
TOTAL	£200		£0

Revised NPV is 0 per cent, so 9.7 per cent is the project's IRR

ASSESSING YOUR ACCOUNTING SKILLS

A knowledge of accounting practices and the three key financial statements will ensure that you can interpret and use the information supplied in any set of accounts. Use this questionnaire to test your understanding. Answer the questions as honestly as you can. If your answer is "never", mark Option 1, and so on. Add your scores together, and refer to the Analysis at the end of the questionnaire.

OPTIONS

1 Never

2 Occasionally

3 Frequently

4 Always

1 I am aware of the financial statements that my organization produces.

1   2   3   4

2 I know accounts serve different purposes and adjust my conclusions accordingly.

1   2   3   4

3 I explore regulations and practice to see how they affect my company's accounts.

1   2   3   4

4 I follow fundamental accounting principles when preparing my own figures.

1   2   3   4

5 I use my profit and loss account to keep abreast of income and expenditure.

1   2   3   4

6 I plan my department's activities with reference to its overall gross profit.

1   2   3   4

7 I understand what operating profit contains and how to interpret it.

1   2   3   4

8 I refer to retained profits as the key measure of growth potential for a business.

1   2   3   4

9 I explore my balance sheet to investigate how to become more efficient.

1   2   3   4

10 I closely assess my capital expenditure amounts by analyzing fixed assets.

1   2   3   4

11 I am aware of the meaning and impact of intangible assets.

1   2   3   4

12 I refer to the type and amount of current assets to manage working capital.

1   2   3   4

13 I pay attention to whether stock and debtors are long-standing.

1   2   3   4

14 I consider the impact of the amount of debt and its repayment date.

1   2   3   4

15 I examine shareholders' funds to see how a business has grown.

1   2   3   4

16 I understand the difference between profits and cash.

1   2   3   4

17 I analyze the cash flows that my organization generates.

| 1 | 2 | 3 | 4 |

18 I plan my department's future with reference to a cash flow forecast.

| 1 | 2 | 3 | 4 |

19 I use only accounting ratios that are specific to what I want to understand.

| 1 | 2 | 3 | 4 |

20 I express all lines in a profit and loss account as a percentage of sales.

| 1 | 2 | 3 | 4 |

21 I have certain preferred balance sheet ratios that I use and fully understand.

| 1 | 2 | 3 | 4 |

22 I understand the external investor ratios commonly used in stock exchanges.

| 1 | 2 | 3 | 4 |

23 I read the supplementary disclosure statements in my company's annual accounts.

| 1 | 2 | 3 | 4 |

24 I am aware of how key international differences in accounting affect me.

| 1 | 2 | 3 | 4 |

25 I accept that I will need to seek help with some technical accounting issues.

| 1 | 2 | 3 | 4 |

26 I consider how creative accounting may have influenced the figures.

| 1 | 2 | 3 | 4 |

27 I refer to management accounts to help me control my department's finances.

1 2 3 4

28 I seek to improve the content and quality of internal financial information.

1 2 3 4

29 I realize that I must use different financial criteria in making future decisions.

1 2 3 4

30 I use discounted cash flow to appraise the financial viability of a project.

1 2 3 4

31 I recognize that accounts contain certain subjective and flexible elements.

1 2 3 4

32 I learn from and continually improve upon my accounting analyses.

1 2 3 4

ANALYSIS

Now that you have completed the self-assessment, add up your total score and check your performance. Whatever level of success you have achieved, there is always room for improvement. Identify your weakest areas, then refer to the relevant sections of this book, where you will find practical advice and tips to help you establish and hone your accounting skills. **32–64:** Your understanding is not as thorough as it should be at manager level.

65–95: You are reasonably proficient in your understanding of accounting. Make renewed efforts to improve areas of weakness to ensure better results from your accounting skills. **96–128:** You are a highly competent user of accounts. However, do not become complacent: keep using your accounting skills by practising them regularly.

INDEX

C

E

e-business, 330
  customer-relationship management
    (CRM), 331
  marketing, 331
  publicity, 315, 328–31
  and real world presence, 331
  security, 331
e-mail, 139
  communicating by, 400
  marketing by, 331
  see also Internet
effectiveness, improving leadership,
  112–27
electrical equipment:
  abroad, 243
  support network, 224
electronic mail, *see* e-mail
emotional intelligence,
understanding needs of others, 14–15,
  25
emotional outbursts, 180–1, 188, 200
employees, *see* staff; staff development
energy, *see* drive and energy
enthusiasm, 108, 229
equality, 110, 111
equity, 427
Europe:
  accounting, 467
  gestures in, 268
  knowledge co-ordinators, 399
  negotiation in, 152

exasperation, 185
excellence:
  inspiring, 36, 132–43
  rewarding, 27
exercises:
  breathing, 252–3, 259
  to reduce tension, 254–5, 259
  voice, 252–3
expenditure:
  capital budgets, 438, 452, 454
  estimating, 454
  see also costs
experience, 45, 84–5
expertise, 88–9, 110, 287, 361
eye contact:
  with audiences, 274
  in negotiation, 182–3
  in presentations, 262

F

face-saving, 190, 198
facial expressions, 185, 268
failure, 64, 65
fair-mindedness, 36, 61
families, negotiation, 151
fears:
  of negotiation, 151
  in presentation, 217
  see also nervousness
finance, *see* costs
financial statements, 421

J

Japan:
  accounting, 467
  action learning, 37
  managers, 85
  negotiation in, 152
  office design, 121
  personal difficulties, 57
  project management, 391, 394
  see also Asia
job interest, 15
journalism, 139, 277

K

Kami, Michael J., 39
Kennedy, John F., 151
know-how, 440, 468
knowledge, *see* information;
  self-development
knowledge co-ordinators, 399
KPIs (key performance indicators), 475

L

laptops, 169
  see also computers
lateness, 65, 405

leadership, 80–143
  administration, 86, 89
  assessing your potential, 92–3, 385
  assessing your skills, 128–31, 133
  authority, 100–1
  boosting achievement, 15, 140–1
  change agents, 88, 89
  collegiate leadership, 24, 110–11
  communicating, 95, 106–7, 138–9
  competitiveness, 142–3
  consistency, 101
  credibility, 133
  crises, 101
  decision-making, 112–13
  delegation, 102–5
  discussions, 120–1
  duties, 87
  dynamizing groups, 108–9
  expertise, 89, 110
  framework, 95
  gaining experience, 84–5
  goals, 90, 91, 95, 114–15
  ideas, 136–7
  improving your effectiveness, 112–27
  information gathering, 94
  inspiring excellence, 36, 132–43
  leading others, 94–111
  learning from others, 82–3, 99
  learning to lead, 79–93
  and managers, 87, 106
  managing by exception, 100
  mastering figures, 90
  meetings, 122–3
  monitoring progress, 101, 140

M

O

office design, 20, 121
office politics, 49
  rumours, 23
offices, *see* working conditions
open-mindedness, 268
operating cycles, 433
opportunities, 124
organizations, types of, 21
organizing:
  presentations, 222–3
  venues, 224–7
outlines, using, 234
output, 141
outsourcing, 47
overhead projectors, 241, 243
ownership, 24, 29

P

PA (public address) systems, 227
participation, 19
partnerships, with employees, 70–1
PAT (profit after tax), 429, 434, 435
patents, 440, 468
pay, *see* remuneration; salaries
pay-back periods, 478
PBR (paying by results), 67
PBT (profit before tax), 429, 435
PE (price earnings ratio), 463

people management, 12–75
  assessing and rewarding, 60–71
  assessing your ability, 72–5
  basic skills, 12–29
  behaviour, 12–13, 56, 86
  building confidence, 18–19, 51, 127
  consulting, 29
  developing people, 30–47
  encouraging initiative, 49
  ensuring cohesion, 48
  finding solutions, 48–59
  gaining commitment, 25–7, 356
  gaining trust, 24, 126
  improving performance, 44–5, 65
  management styles, 28–9, 106
  nurturing talent, 38–9
  office politics, 49
  opening closed minds, 50–1
  supporting people, 56–7, 126–7
  understanding needs, 14–15, 25, 56
  see also coaching; communication;
    conflict resolution; emotional
    intelligence; motivation
performance:
  business score-cards, 475
  evaluating, 60–1
  improving, 44–5, 65
  investors' ratios, 462–3
  maintaining momentum, 45
  measuring, 456–65
  performance indicators (KPIs), 475
  ratios, 456–7
  Return on Capital Employed (ROCE),
    457

ACKNOWLEDGMENTS

Dorling Kindersley would like to thank the following for
their help and participation in producing this book:

Index Hilary Bird

Models Tracey Allanson, Roger André, Phil Argent, Clare Borg,
Marian Broderick, Angela Cameron, Anne Chapman, Kuo Kang Chen,
Brent Clark, Jane Cooke, Russell Cosh, Roberto Costa, Felicity Crowe,
Sander deGroot, Patrick Dobbs, Miles Elliot, Carole Evans, Vosjava Fahkro,
Jeanie Fraser, Mark Fraser, John Gillard, Ben Glickman, Lucy Kelly,
Emma Harris, Kate Hayward, Sasha Heseltine, Nigel Hill, Richard Hill,
Gill Hooton, Cornell John, Aziz Khan, Janey Madlani, Zahid Malik,
Maggie Mant, Frankie Mayers, Sotiris Meliomis, Ian Midson, Sophie Millett,
Roger Mundy, Karen Murray, Chantal Newall, Mutsumi Niwa, Ted Nixon,
Pippa Oakes, Mary-Jane Robinson, Kiran Shah, Lois Sharland, Lynne Staff,
Daniel Stevens, Kaz Takabatake, Suki Tan, Peter Taylor, Fiona Terry,
Anastasia Vengeroua, Dominica Warburton, Michael Weinkove,
Ann Winterborn, Roberta Woodhouse, Tessa Woodward,
Gilbert Wu, Wendy Yun.

Make-up Elizabeth Burrage, Nicky Clarke, Evelynne, Debbie Finlow,
Jane Hope-Kavanagh, Lynne Maningley, Janice Tee.

Special thanks to the following for their help:
Ron and Chris at Clark Davis & Co. Ltd for stationery and furniture supplies;
Pam Bennett and the staff at Jones Bootmakers, Covent Garden, for the loan
of footwear; Alan Pfaff and the staff at Moss Bros, Covent Garden, for the loan
of the men's suits; David Bailey for his help and time; Graham Preston and
the staff at Staverton for their time and space, Tony Ash at Geiger Brickel
(Office Furniture) and Carron Williams at Bally (Shoes).

Suppliers Apple Computer UK Ltd, Austin Reed, Bally, Cadogan and James,
Church & Co., Clark Davis & Co. Ltd, Compaq, David Clulow Opticians,
Elonex, Escada, Filofax, Gateway 2000, Geiger Brickel, Gieves and Hawkes,
Marc Holman, Jones Bootmakers, Moss Bros, Mucci Bags,
Positive (Computing), Staverton, Viper Microsystems.

PICTURE CREDITS

Key: b bottom, c centre, l left, r right, t top

About the Authors

Moi Ali has worked in marketing for over 15 years and runs her own public relations and marketing company, specializing in clients with limited budgets – in particular small businesses and charities. She is a regular contributor to marketing and PR journals and is the author of a number of books.

Stephen Brookson qualified as a chartered accountant with KPMG and went on to work for Ernst & Young before setting up his own management and training consultancy. He has presented seminars and training events in many countries, and is the author of *Mastering Financial Management*.

Andy Bruce is the founder of SofTools Limited – a specialist business research and consulting company. Following completion of a largely academic MBA programme, he has spent the past eight years helping a variety of organizations manage major projects and cope with change in the real world – more information on tools and techniques can be found at www.SofTools.net.

Robert Heller is a leading authority in the world of management consultancy and was the founding editor of Britain's top management magazine, *Management Today*. He is much in demand as a conference speaker in Europe, North and South America, and the Far East. As editorial director of Haymarket Publishing Group, Robert Heller supervised the launch of several highly successful magazines such as *Campaign*, *Computing*, and *Accountancy Age*. His many acclaimed – and worldwide best-selling – books include *The Naked Manager*, *Culture Shock*, *The Age of the Common Millionaire*, *The Way to Win* (with Will Carling), *The Complete Guide to Modern Management*, and *In Search of European Excellence*.

Tim Hindle is the founder of the London-based business language consultancy, Working Words, which helps international companies to compose material in English and communicate their messages clearly to their intended audiences. He has been a contributor to *The Economist* since 1979 and is now their Business Editor, as well as being editor of *EuroBusiness* from 1994 to 1996. As editorial consultant and author, Tim Hindle has produced a number of titles including *Pocket Manager*, *Pocket MBA*, and *Pocket Finance*, and a biography of Asil Nadir, *The Sultan of Berkeley Square*.

Ken Langdon has a background in sales and marketing in the computer industry. As an independent consultant he has lectured on strategic thinking and planning in the USA, Europe and Australasia. He has helped companies, big and small, to review their strategies at board level and widely at team level. Companies for whom he has provided strategic guidance include computer majors such as Hewlett Packard, and utilities companies such as a European electricity supplier.